Kenelm Henry Digby

The chapel of St. John

Or, a life of faith in the nineteenth century

Kenelm Henry Digby

The chapel of St. John
Or, a life of faith in the nineteenth century

ISBN/EAN: 9783742836670

Manufactured in Europe, USA, Canada, Australia, Japa

Cover: Foto ©Lupo / pixelio.de

Manufactured and distributed by brebook publishing software (www.brebook.com)

Kenelm Henry Digby

The chapel of St. John

The Chapel of St. John;

OR, A

LIFE OF FAITH

IN THE NINETEENTH CENTURY.

BY

KENELM HENRY DIGBY.

Κἀγὼ τοιοῦτός εἰμ', ἐπεὶ δυσμηχανῶ
Λόγοισι τὸν θανόντ' ἀνιστάναι πάλιν.
                ÆSCH. *Agamemnon.*

LONDON:
THOMAS RICHARDSON AND SON,
26, PATERNOSTER ROW,
9, CAPEL STREET, DUBLIN, AND DERBY.
1861.

TABLE OF CONTENTS.

CHAPTER I.

Introduction	PAGE 1

CHAPTER II.

A Life of Faith slightly sketched—The value of such an example . 24

CHAPTER III.

Its Catholicity 49

CHAPTER IV.

Its piety 58

CHAPTER V.

Its wisdom 88

CHAPTER VI.

Its character in relation to society and the world . . . 121

CHAPTER VII.

Its character in relation to art and literature 159

CHAPTER VIII.

Its character in regard to the family 185

CHAPTER IX.

Its justice, humility, and charity . . .

CHAPTER X.

Its kind and amiable manners . . . .

CHAPTER XI.

Its cheerfulness . . . . . .

CHAPTER XII.

Its affectionate character . . . . .

CHAPTER XIII.

Its courage in affliction . . . . .

CHAPTER XIV.

Its resignation . . . . . .

CHAPTER XV.

The narrative of its last hours . . . .

CHAPTER XVI.

The conclusion . . . . . .

THE CHAPEL OF ST. JOHN,
&c.

CHAPTER I.

T is well, and by no means, even in this age, unusual, when pleasant sites frequented for their beauty, or places through which many have to pass in the pursuit of their accustomed occupations, present objects that are suggestive of some elevated thought or inspiring and tender remembrance, which may conduce to the intellectual and moral education of those who visit them. The ancients, in their municipal arrangements, seem to have expressly provided for this result. The high roads, for instance, leading out of Rome, and stretching on across the sunny plains of the Campagna, were, as every one knows, marked at intervals for many a mile by the solitary tombs of heroes; and allusion to the same provision may be found in the fragments of the old Greek poets, as where Philemon desires us, when going out into the country, and passing by the tombs and sepulchres, to remember that each of those for whom they were constructed, used to the last to exclaim, "I will sail, I will plant, I will build;" and, as where Menander says, "when you are on the high road, and wish to know yourself, turn your eye towards

the monuments in which are the bones and light dust of the great, and rich, and beautiful." Nor were such associations lost in the wreck of the ancient society, for after Christianity had moulded the forms of things throughout the whole civilized world, there were few cities that had not in their immediate suburbs or extramural vicinity some pillar, shrine, chapel, or religious house, to which persons desirous of spiritual impressions were wont to repair. The modern civilization, so far as it affects a visible contrast with antiquity, cannot, of course, be expected to entertain such views as led to this monumental result; but yet in some favoured nations, as in our own, it is found to be incapable of not permitting, or even of not ordaining through different motives some things of a corresponding tendency, which can be made to answer the ancient and eternal purpose of training men by the right method. Thus London has not only in its neighbourhood, in every direction, fields and solemn gardens consecrated to the dead, but even at a distance within those very places to which her citizens are in the habit of resorting for innocent amusement and healthful occupation during their summer holidays, there exist, thanks to the freedom we now enjoy, and to the links which bind us to the ancient generations, spots set apart, as of old, where the religious instinct bids us find "sermons in stones," or where tombs have a certain voice which can yield very high and profitable instruction to those who can find time to listen to it.

I propose in the following pages that we should proceed to visit one of these spots in order to profit by such vocal stones, and to catch the harmonies of the voice which may be said to issue from them; for which purpose we shall not have to strike into any solitary, tortuous, and labyrinthine path, as it were, of our own discovery, but merely to follow with the multitude one of the great frequented lines pursued by summer travellers leading to the sea, and to a town where, in point of fact, they have from time immemorial been most inclined and accustomed to congregate.

Passing down the Thames, or crossing the land in a more southerly direction, we come to that region of England—εἰς τηλουρὸν πέδον, as Æschylus perhaps would call it,—and which Tacitus describes as being in its climate, and even in the manners of its inhabitants, more similar than any other of its districts to those of France. One breathes, certainly, along its white cliffs, which in the shades of evening assume a dusky hue, a more elastic air; the sky is generally clearer, and you perceive as much of that magic splendour of the sun as our northern latitudes can ever enjoy. It is not, indeed, for all the haste evinced by some to get there, that we can hope to be presented with such a spectacle as is offered by the enchanted coast of Chiaja, or by the shores of the island of Capri, or even by those of our own Devonshire; but that in reality there is no part of the British Islands where the climate so nearly resembles that of the Continent. No where is there more effulgence of that

——————— πάντων
Αἰθὴρ κοινὸν φάος εἱλίσσων—

and, as after all the deficiencies in the general scenery, there is ever before your eyes the blue sea and an unobstructed horizon, with a sky that is most frequently clear and cloudless, there is enough to refresh and satisfy those, who from time to time experience a want to soliloquize a little while gazing, as we say, on the face of nature. Besides, there are certain indentures of the coast which present the appearance of bays, that are by no means without picturesque beauty. Then you have also, intersected by long dykes and almost blending with the sands, vast marshy tracts, over which herds of cattle wander, forming a landscape full of attraction for those who have a taste for Cuyp scenery; and not less for those who in a boyish way are enamoured of the brooks and rushes and the green lowlands, and who are fond of spending hours thus with a dog or two and some choice companion amidst the calm of rural solitude, while hearing, as they saunter along, what the old poet calls

——————— ποντίων τε κυμάτων
'Ανήριθμον γέλασμα.———————

Then from plains that gently rise above these salt-marshes the amplest range of prospect may be enjoyed—low brown or purple tracts, where a winding river stagnates, are stretched out westward; beneath, right at the cliff's southern base, you have the ocean breaking audibly, not far distant from the Goodwins, as I think they call the place,—a very dangerous flat and fatal, where the carcases of many a tall ship lie buried, as they say; and south of them, far away in pale-tinted regions, forming a long ridge, that some might take for a perishable cloud, you behold the coast of France, the cultivated fields that streak its tawny summits, its churches, and even its golden image of the Virgin shining from a dome, being all at times discernible, while the revolving lights, after sunset, cast a fitful gleam upon the dark waters from its desert capes. Again, looking northward, you have the open champaign country, which has also a certain beauty of its own, constituting what a great author distinguishes as that of "field lands," which, though capable only of an inferior and material art, and apt to lose its spirituality, present however the advantage of having sight of the whole sky, and of the continual play and change of sun and cloud, and also of greater liberty, being like the moss-lands, at least at certain seasons, the freest ground in all the world, while commanding all the horizon's space of changeful light[*]. On a spring morning the voice of waters must here be softened down into a vernal tone; a spirit of desire and enjoyment, with hopes and wishes from all living things, must seem to pervade the entire region. Beast and bird, the lamb, the shepherd's dog, the linnet and the lark, must appear to be all complying with their Creator's invitation to rejoice and be happy. It would be the moment, methinks, for some Autolycus to sing:—

> "When daffodils begin to peer—
> With, hey! the laddy over the dale,—
> Why then comes in the sweet o' the year;
> For the red blood reigns in the winter's pale.
> The white sheet bleaching on the hedge,—
> With, hey! the sweet birds, O how they sing,
> The lark, that tirra-lirrah chants—
> With, hey! with hey! the thrush and the jay—
> Are summer songs for me and my mates,
> While we lie tumbling in the hay."

Some, who in later months of the fine season chance to walk

[*] Ruskin.

alone beneath those cliffs at sunrise, or above them with this sauntering crowd, that like one family is listening to music under the rising moon, are not left without memories of affections old and true. At all hours, inland for many a mile the elm-grove murmurs with a sea-like sound, though still the habitual sight of fields with rural works is cheerful. Far towards the north-western limits of your view, lies an ascending country, dappled over with shadows flung from many a summer cloud; those many spots lie in long streaks determined and unmoved, with steady beams of sunshine interposed, pleasant to him who on the soft cool moss extends his careless limbs.

Now is the day declining, and the faint evening breeze plays on the meadow. Why is there not a Claude here to see and paint these groves and these long undulating tracts which mount up to purple elevations, with the zig-zag road that breaks the uniformity of tone, and leads to these mills that stand like towers for a sea-mark? How would an artist have delighted in this foreground, too, of rich entangled weeds, with its goats and sheep and the rough dogs that watch them! Then, sufficient in itself to form a picture, you come ever and anon to some old broken bridge across a rivulet, seeming to be half rock, half brick, here covered with plaster, there lined with weeds and beautifully interwoven plants; beyond it are the fields, now undistinguishable, as they are fast darkening in the twilight, while the horizon is coloured with the lovely hues of sunset, diffused higher up amidst some rosy clouds, fringed with gold, thinly floating motionless in an azure so calm and profound, that you can hardly imagine its being any thing else but heaven.

So, without any thing that an untrained eye would deem in the least remarkable, our travellers find themselves, they know not how, soothed and satisfied,—a few tufts of pine or elm, the blue or warm radiance of a lake-like bay, a meadow or a corn-field, the edge of a cliff, and the distant shores that mingle with the clouds—such is the nature that contents them.

Disdained by some, as being thronged in summer with a motley crew of Shakspeare's "Sunday citizens,"—though Charles Lamb does not shrink from telling us, most innocently, that he read Burns there,—the whole scenery of the district recommends itself to those who hold with a great authority in matters of art, that "all true landscape, whether simple or exalted, depends primarily for its interest on connexion with humanity, or with spiritual power*;" and that even "fragrant tissues of flowers, and golden circlets of clouds, are only fair when they meet the fondness of human thoughts, and glorify human visions of heaven†."

Nor is the interest attached to historical recollections wanting to this region; for on one of these upper solitary plains the Anglo-Saxons had their place of solemn burial. Here first Cæsar saw Britain, and here Augustine landed to bring light and immortality.

But where is the voice that we have come to listen to? You must wait a moment until we describe a distinct locality. In the sequel, after pausing to take this general view of a whole neighbourhood, it will be heard.

On the last line, then, of cliffs,

> "Where Ocean mid his uproar wild
> Speaks safety to his island-child;"

on the grassy summit, where the chalk, emerging from the yellow clay for the last time, grows proudly ramparted, there stands a dark solemn pile, made up of church and tower, of cloistered cells, and halls that announce themselves, as in the ancient style, monastical. Here these stones become already audible, at least you must say so if you will believe Chateaubriand, who tells us that the Gothic chapel of St. Malo had a great part in his own conversion. But this echo of general truths is not all or precisely what we have come to listen to. Pass within the portal. There is at the north entry, and at the intersection of the two sides of an arched cloister, a chapel, under the invocation of St. John, being a chantry over the bones of the dead. There is a monumental slab and solemn imagery representing some who sleep below. Of late that vault has been thrice opened, when was seen each time verified how man by living longer has often to experience that variety of what the ancients called Fortune, of which the philosopher of Flo-

---

* Ruskin, Mod. P. 199.   † Ib.

rence treated*, and how, in most cases at least, he has to lay aside, one by one, his garlands and his crown.

"Omnia paulatim consumit longior ætas,
 Vivendoque simul morimur, rapimurque manendo."

This sepulchre then beautiful! as the chorus in Æschylus exclaims,—for it covers manners that were beautiful and dear,—

ἢ φίλος ὄχθος·
φίλα γὰρ κίκευθεν ἤθη †—

constitutes the school in which during the following pages we are, as it were, to listen and to study.

Of course, every where in such places there are general impressions produced of which one knows by instinct alone the tendency. Many, not content with such passing emotions, carry away from them tracings of the monumental stone which preserves the name, and unambitiously relates the death of those in whose virtues they feel an interest. During the middle ages the events of a domestic circle would be represented in painting, or on stained glass, or on plates of enamel, or on brass, or carved on trunks of iron, as on that specimen of the thirteenth century which is preserved in the Hôtel de Cluny, representing the chivalrous history of a wedded pair. Indeed that collection abounds with similar tracings, of which one at least, fraught with antique simplicity, might be supposed taken, with a substitution of names, from this very chapel; for such is the epitaph by Pierre de Ronsard on the death of Charles de Boudeville, enfant de Vaulx, mort le mardy xiiie de mars mvlxxi. :—

"Icy gist d'ung enfant la despouille mortelle
Au ciel pour n'en bouger volla son ame belle
Qui parmy les espritz bien heureux jouissant
Du plaisir immortel, loue Dieu tout puissant
Qui l'a ravy de Vaulx (tant délicat pour pris,
Jeune enfant de huict ans), pour mettre en paradis
Ou s'esbatant là sus d'une certaine vie
Au vivre d'icy bas ne porte point d'envie.

---

* Poggius, de Varietate Fortunæ, lib. iv.   † Persæ.

Au vivre que vivons douteux du lendemain
Soubz les iniques loix ou naist le genre humain.
O belle ame! tu es én ce temps de mjsère
Gayement revolée au sein de Dieu ton père ;
Laissant ton père icy : là tu plains son malheur,
Qui de regret de toy, porte griève douleur
Qu'il témoigne de pleurs, arrosant l'escriture
Dont il a fait graver ta triste sépulture."

These, though rude, are affecting lines ; but in general it is too true that legendary or monumental lore of this kind tends to no very ennobling consciousness of a departed grace, whose light was in any particular way worth preserving. The poet even says that—

" If the mute earth
Of what it holds could speak, and every grave
Were as a volume, shut, yet capable
Of yielding its contents to eye and ear,
We should recoil, stricken with sorrow and shame,
To see disclosed, by such dread proofs, how ill
That which is done accords with what is known
To reason, and by conscience is enjoin'd ;
How idly, how perversely, life's whole course,
To this conclusion deviates from the line,
Or of the end stops short, proposed to all
At its aspiring outset."

This is, no doubt, to present the dark and discouraging side of human life ; but it will, at all events, serve to show in a stronger light the beauty of the unmistakeable contrast that is about to be presented here, and to impress us still more with a sense of the value of the facts that are to be submitted throughout the pages that follow.

It is an ancient custom to transmit to posterity a knowledge of the actions and manners that are deemed remarkable at the period in which they appear; nor is the usage unfollowed in our own age, though little curious respecting things that want great external lustre, and even perhaps somewhat indifferent as to every detail that concerns the more private, and what the old philosophy would have considered the more noble virtues. But formerly there was much zeal to celebrate great examples of this order, without being influenced by favour or ambition, and actuated only by the reward of a good conscience. By means of such memorials there was kept alive a certain tradition of manners, which we are told is as dear to the Christian Church as that which has preserved the integrity of its doctrines and the purity of its faith *. This chain has never been broken even with regard to what it transmits relative to persons living in the society of the world. There have always been attempts made to hand down a knowledge of such graces as may have particularly distinguished them, as in the instances of those pious and charitable French ladies of the seventeenth century— the Duchesse d'Aiguillon, the Princess of Mantua, the Marchioness de Magnelais, Mme. d'Aligre wife of the chancellor, Mme. Fouquet mother of the sur-intendant, Mmes. De Brienne, De Traversoi, De Villesavin, De Sénecey, De Bailleul, De Sainctot, and of many others †. The Catholic literature of England is not without specimens of the same kind of writing, which, independent of the môral purposes to which it may be made at least indirectly instrumental, seems the natural result of ordinary love and friendship; as when Georges de Scudéry, after defending his friend Théophile when arrested, composed in his memory after his death the book entitled " Le Tombeau de Théophile." It is true we still are presented each year with biographical notices of persons in one way or another remarkable; of some of whom the words are deemed oracles for mankind, whose science is known to all countries, and whose discoveries are destined to sound through all ages; but however interesting such records may be in a general manner according to the ideas of the day, it is well, and even in the interest of the world itself, it is important to keep up the ancient custom also of leaving to posterity a memory of persons living in the midst of it, practising what a noble French writer lately calls the monotonous life of the Gospel,—lest, in fine, what is by no means a groundless hypothesis, persons like ourselves should begin to suppose that what used to be called a life of

---

* Vie de Madlle. de Louvencourt, 1778.
† Vie des Dames Françaises dans le xviie Siècle.

faith, with the manners consequent upon it, ought to be regarded as merely an ancient theory, or at the most as a vestige of the past; for, in fact, such a life spent and practised in the world, has for the last two hundred years been so seldom a theme in England for literary composition, that we might truly say in the style of Tacitus, that within such domains we should have lost the memory of it, if it had been as much in our power to forget as to be silent.

But now that the sweet voice of a gentle Christian woman has just ceased, for one about to speak of her retiring goodness, there is no doubt great need of indulgence, which he would not have asked if he had not been confronted with an age not perhaps hostile, but indifferent to merit of this high order. And yet to those who would object that details of this kind were not befitting any but a private audience, he would reply that such a life is either rare or common. If rare, it ought to be written for its singularity; if really, what seems so incredible, common, still more ought it to be made known to the literary public, since certainly there are many who do not seem aware that it is with goodness of this kind they, living in the nineteenth century, are every day surrounded, as such an hypothesis requires them to believe. In either case this chapel of St. John shall not be made the grave of her deserving. Nor is it a boastful extravagance to add, that England should know the value of her own; but it is a most natural conclusion to say with the poet, that to suffer it to pass into oblivion

"———————— were a concealment
Worse than theft, no less than a traducement."

To hide the light inherent in such a life, and in an instance of so grave a kind, would be to furnish fresh ground to the complaint of the Florentine philosopher, who, speaking of such examples, laments, "ut notiora sint nobis quæ prisca tempora tulerunt, quam quæ nostra ætate acta sunt *."

When Fontenelle pronounced his eulogium on the celebrated Du Hamel, he felt it necessary to apologize for having presumed to touch upon that part of his life which ought to have

* Hist. de Varietate Fortunæ, lib. i.

been spoken of in front of the altar, and not before an academy [*]. Perhaps, with regard to this book, what would have furnished ground formerly for bespeaking pardon, might now on the contrary be advanced as substantiating a claim for favour; since contrary to the ancient usage, as in the instance of a Marcella and a Paula, an Eloi and a Francis, whose lives were written by a Jerome, an Ouen, and a Bonaventura, the portrait here presented will be sketched by one who has no pretensions to a similarity with what he delineates. The world has often heard of the lives of holy persons written by the holy; but though it is enough to make one pause to think of the ancient saying,

μισῶ πονηρὸν, χρηστὸν ὅταν εἴπῃ λόγον [†],

it will excite perhaps its attention as a novelty, and even conciliate in some degree its regard as an instance of unbiassed and unsuspected testimony, when it hears of such a portrait being drawn by one who cannot by the pattern of his own thoughts cut out the purity of hers whom he portrays,—

"Car en moy n'est entendemens ne sens
D'escrire, fors ainsi comme je sens [‡],"—

and who in consequence of that dissimilarity of character cannot be suspected of any partiality or predilection in favour of a subject which what some call the destiny of life, rather than any meritorious inclination on his part, has cast in his way. It is even a very religious contemplatist who says, "Books written in a devout way often weary me. I yawn at the first page. A theologian who speaks of such grave subjects moves me much less than a man of the world who seems to think about them [§]." And Fontenelle, speaking of M. de Ressous, remarks, that if religion can be said to receive honour from what some men have done for her, perhaps may she take some little credit to herself for the weak efforts in her favour extorted as it were from men whose condition was the most different from that of her natural and professed advocates. Possibly, too, the

[*] Œuvres, tom. v. [†] Menand. frag.
[‡] Alain Chartier. [§] Mme. Swetchine.

very manner in which such a person taking up a pen is likely to treat a subject of this nature, may present certain advantages that are not to be wholly disdained; for

"The world which neweth every day,"

as old Gower expresses it, will not be content with writings composed to suit the taste of the thirteenth or even of the seventeenth century. It may be well to present it with goodness and faith as seen with modern eyes, with eyes that are accustomed to the perspectives of the present civilization; and, after all, gratitude, admiration, reverence,—not gratuitously offered or supposed, but extorted, will be of all ages. One may reasonably hope, therefore, that this book, devoted to the memory of one who was accessary to such violence, will be not alone pardoned, but praised,—"professione pietatis aut laudatus erit aut excusatus."

"Neither," as Pliny said, "ought it to operate to his disadvantage that the person to be commemorated was our own contemporary;" for, as that Roman writer observes, "it is malignant not to admire one most worthy of admiration, for the sole reason that it is one who has been seen by ourselves, and also loved." Moreover, not to remark, as yet, that the life and death of such a person are full of tender mysteries, unutterably profound and capable of yielding food for poetry and philosophy, it is not in the present state of literature as it was with painting in the school of David, which had disdained as beneath it the representation of the ordinary scenes of life in which only private persons take part, and which, like tragedy, required heroes or demi-gods. A disposition has arisen, at least among a certain number, to think with the philosopher of Florence, that "plura suppetunt vulgaria humanorum casuum exempla, quæ efferri in lucem merentur*." These critics not only admit but proclaim, when eminent goodness in any one, however otherwise removed from the sphere of public notice, leaves this earth, that it is both natural and expedient for those who feel irresistibly impelled in that direction to attempt to recall its image.

* Poggius, de Varietate Fortunæ, i.

"I regard it as a right thing in itself," says Ballanche, writing to an accomplished friend, "that you should be loved and appreciated when you are no longer here on earth *." The same opinion is expressed by many. "If I could venture to suggest to you any thing, I would pray you," wrote Madame Swetchine to M. de Falloux, on the death of the Princess Alexis Galitzen, "to put down on paper some dates, some words, to preserve the memory of this holy woman. I know she needs it not, and all that concerns her is, that her name be inscribed in the book of life; but for us, for those who will follow, it is a great consolation to know somewhat of such a person †." Be that as it may, there is a moment, as Saint-Beuve remarks, in the life of most men when they feel bound to render what they owe to the memory of some one, the most regretted, and whose absence is most sensibly felt; when some loss so cruel and unforeseen carried at first such astonishment with it along with grief, as to leave no liberty of judgment; but when, after the first shock and confusion have subsided, when one can behold the vacancy that has been left, one naturally attempts, without drawing up any thing like an exact account, to give a rude general estimate of the extent and nature of the desolation. Perhaps for some it is now one of those moments, as Ballanche told M. Récamier. Perhaps some one else might say that his future destiny consists in contriving that some traces should be left on this earth of a noble existence that has lately passed from it. Certainly it would be more than a private misfortune, if so excellent a creature should vanish from our eyes as if it had been only a vision, making it momentary as a sound, swift as a shadow, short as any dream. And, in fact, of what use is memory or the art that helps to hand it down, if it be not to select for the object that it seeks to perpetuate what may be termed religion in action, faith in actual life, or in mind and manners the beautiful and the good?

You would transmit only the memory of the learned, and those who have erected for themselves a statue in the temple of Fame. Unwise and injurious limitation! when even the coryphee of

---

* Souvenirs de Mme. Récamier.
† Mme. Swetchine, Préface.

modern sophists, and the most voluminous of literary celebrities, felt himself constrained in a moment of awakened conscience to exclaim—

"J'ai fait un peu de bien, c'est mon meilleur ouvrage."

There are, however, two reflections that might indeed arrest one in this enterprise; for, in the first place, as M. Berlioz said in the "Journal des Débats," on occasion of the death of the poet Brizeux:—" When one sees so many villainies attract the crowd, one ought to wish that noble things should not resemble them even in this respect. Things fine and delicate are for the fine and delicate; one may lead the multitude to make pretence of liking them, but at the bottom it detests them." And with regard to the latter consideration, which is graver still, could she whose innocent character we are about to notice, have anticipated a consequence of her departure hence, so little consonant with the humility of her whole existence, the words would certainly have been heard—" Sir, make me not your story." Alas! it may be doubted sometimes whether one ought to proceed; but then all the while who knows not that

"——— Our doubts are traitors,
And make us lose the good we oft might win,
By fearing to attempt ——— ?"

Besides, there should be no fear in the present instance, since, as our Shakspeare saith,—

"A heavy heart bears not an humble tongue."

It is not for the transmitter of such memories to speak of the general interest of an intellectual kind which the subject is capable of eliciting; for an object connected with the purposes of literature was but very remotely and indirectly, and that too only towards its completion, aimed at; and yet, even on this ground, he may be permitted to remark that there is no want of encouragement for such a task as has devolved upon him, did it only answer the conditions, from the most devoted friends, and even kings, of literature itself. For what is it after all, even in regard to men, the most eminent for science, art, and literature,—what is it that their biographers seem most to trust to for exciting the interest of their readers? In the instances of the great celebrities, of whom Fontenelle pronounced his eulogiums before the Academy, it is to some trait of goodness or of simple piety that they trust; as, for example, when speaking of the disciple of Newton—M. de Montmort, the geometrician and algebraist—it is to the fact of his " having possessed qualities infinitely more estimable than intellect and scientific knowledge *," that our author appeals. Again, in the case of the mathematician and great Captain Marsigli, whose adventures in the wars were so striking and even heroic,—it is to his piety, as furnishing " the most remarkable ground for his panegyric," that the academician has recourse; for that great man having been captured by the Turks on the festival of the Visitation, the 2nd of July, and being ransomed on the day of the Annunciation, he was led to the reflection that, on these two festivals, the august protectress of the faithful had obtained for him two favours from heaven,—the one consisting in his salutary punishment for his past faults, the other in the cessation of punishment. This is what Fontenelle terms "la plus remarquable partie de son éloge puisqu'elle decouvre en lui un grand fonds de piété †." Then coming down even to our own times, in an Ary Scheffer, for instance, it is merely simple goodness that is wept for. "Scheffer," we are told, "had himself in his character something attractive, not easily defined, which caused him to be loved. He exercised," it is added, "on all who approached him a sympathetic attraction. Of a tender and devoted nature, he in his turn easily inspired a tender devotedness, which his death has changed into inconsolable sorrow. He was of boundless generosity, and the young who came to him never failed to find with him encouragement and counsel ‡." Such is the nature of the details that are evidently dwelt on with most interest; and it is the same trait that we find expressed in other books which relate the lives of the most eminent and illustrious characters. Their authors seem obliged to leave great things, revolutions and destinies, missions and glory, dynasties and

---

* Tome vi. 62.   † Ibid. 402.
‡ Louis Ratisbonne.

battles, even too, like Fontenelle himself, what will surprise some more perhaps, discoveries and science; and then sinking down all of a sudden, in order to inspire real interest, and to verify the grave remark of Bossuet, that "le plaisir de l'homme c'est l'homme," they are obliged by their mere literary tact to give some lowly familiar details, which might be thought suitable only in the life of such a character as we are now engaged with. They have to come down at last, after all their altitudes, to this level of humanity, and to record some humble matter relating to a domestic existence, such as can indicate that their hero or philosopher is, like another, dear to some one, that he has a heart and qualities in the possession of which he only resembles a woman or a child. And rightly do they descend thus in appearance, in order to rise to true majesty; for, as Sir Philip Sidney says, "the ending of all earthly learning being virtuous action, those arts that most serve to bring forth that have a most just title to be princes over all the rest." The subject before us, therefore, involves no ground for any just discouragement, since the very theme itself almost inevitably furnishes, in spite of all demerits on the part of him who treats upon it, a pledge of success. "However agitated," says Saint-Beuve, "may be the times we live in—however withered or corrupt you may imagine them—there are always certain books exquisite and rare, merely in consequence of the materials of which they are composed, which manage to appear. There are always hearts to produce them in the shade, and other hearts to gather them. They are books which are not like books, and which sometimes even are really not books. They are simple and discreet destinies thrown upon cross-roads off the great dusty highway of life, and which, when wandering yourself off it, when you come up to them, arrest you by their sweet odours and purely natural flowers, of which you thought the race extinct. The form of these books varies—sometimes it is a collection of letters from the drawer of a person lately dead; sometimes it is a surviving lover, who consecrates himself to a faithful remembrance, seeking to transmit and perpetuate it. So under an exterior more or less veiled, he gives to his reader a true history. There are examples of more forms among those productions of hearts, and the form is a thing indifferent provided there is still a simple naked record of the circumstances experienced, with as little view as possible to the creation of a novel; for those sort of treasures should never be turned into romance, according to the notions of those times when the Astrée was in vogue, with all their fancies about idealization and ennobling, and giving the quintessence of real things *." One might apply the epigram of Martial to the kind of compositions which Saint-Beuve admires, and say of them,

> " Qui legis Œdipodem calligantemque Thyesten. . . .
> Hoc lege quod possit dicere vita : *Meum est.*
> Non hic Centauros, non Gorgonas Harpyiasque
> Invenies ; hominem pagina nostra sapit."

It is, however, perhaps such productions which most strictly verify the remark of Madame Swetchine, that no two persons have ever read the same book, as no two have ever seen the same picture; and moreover, in addition, that the interest of many books depends upon their being read when they can be interpreted by a great sorrow.

We live not in times like the sixteenth century, when Boccacio, in his Latin work on illustrious women, and Cornelius Agrippa, in his treatise on the superior excellence of women, raised and agitated the question respecting the comparative merits of the sexes. Whether Montaigne decided against women, or the Monk Hilarion de Costa, and the celebrated Paul de Ribera, in their favour, troubles or pleases no one very much at present. But no doubt, even still there may be an interest from which men of letters themselves need not be excluded in presenting a portrait from the life, a simple but strictly faithful picture of one woman who existed in the midst of us but yesterday, a study perhaps not so much for those who would revive that often disputed question about comparative merits, as for every one who would seek to purify his imagination and to amend his heart.

This leads us to another view of the subject; for if such things can prove interesting even in a literary point of view, what may we not justly advance concerning their importance with respect to matters of infinitely greater value? The philanthropists, as

---

* Portraits de Femmes, 20.

Philarete Chasles remarks, have made " wholesome the material life, but without touching the interior life," while all that is of real lasting worth depends upon the latter; for, as Sir Philip Sidney says, "to be moved to do that which we know, or to be moved with desire to know, hoc opus, hic labor est." How useful then must it be to introduce, by means of studying examples of great success in that secret world, reforms there! One such picture as we intend to propose is of far greater efficacy in convincing the judgment and determining the will, than any philosophic or general propositions can ever be. This portrait, like poesy, as an old writer would say, " yieldeth to the powers of the mind an image of that whereof the philosopher bestoweth but a wordish description, which doth neither strike, pierce, nor possess the sight of the soul, so much as that other doth." This which teacheth by no abstract considerations, but by only bidding you follow the footing of one that has gone before you, will be found also to appeal, not to our understanding alone, but to our passions likewise, setting them on the side of judgment, and making in him who studies in this school of example the whole man of a piece, which, as Lord Bolingbroke himself admits, is more than the strongest reasoning and the clearest demonstration can do; a fact which was so well known in ancient times, that the Romans used to place the images of their ancestors in the vestibules of their houses, in order that whenever they went in or out those busts should meet their eyes and recall the dead to fire the living, " whereby the virtue of one generation might be transfused by the magic of example into several." " It is at the present day more important than ever," says the Père Ventura, " in the interests of religion. and goodness, that examples of their power should be made known to the public, even at the expense of private virtue and humility."

Never, perhaps, was this need more sensibly experienced than for a twofold reason at present in the European states. It becomes of an importance which affects collective nations, that such lives should be known; for, as Madame Swetchine says " the governments that are the most free, and those that give the least liberty, present the two conditions under which religion, and consequently a study of such examples down to the minutest details, is most necessary for men. In the first, there is an excess of life, and of development of the will, which might be a cause of disorder or danger, if a repressing and interior law did not regulate its exercise. As for the second, involving all the evils of social existence, the hopes of heaven, which the same study is calculated to inspire, are needed to support men under humiliation and woe *."

No doubt there must be differences of minds and merits to suit the different mansions prepared elsewhere for mankind. There ought to be indulgence and affection for those who are the least distinguished for merit of this kind in the race of life; but whatever be the dangers and weaknesses of society, it is not useless to be aware of "the advantages that may be gained by living with the firm and the good †."

The epoch of the middle ages, as Cousin remarks, "had its powerful philosophy comprising the contempt of perishable things, disdain of matter, and the worship of mind." As a countercheck to the modern views of education and civilization it would be difficult to estimate too highly the results of an influence which may operate in that old direction.

But now to speak briefly of the manner in which we propose that the subject should be treated. It is a saying of a classical English writer that "an author's harp must be tuned in the hearing of those who are to understand its after harmonies." There is need, then, here, in the first place, of bespeaking liberty, which he would satisfy by repeating the words of Charles d'Orleans :—

"Laissez-moi penser à mon aise !
Hélas ! donnez-m'en le loisir."

When one's last years have been sufficiently troubled, one desires to be left, here and there, some untouched corner of remembrance where one can find one's self alone, or nearly alone, with one's thoughts of former times. True, as Alain Chartier says,

"De cueur dolent ne pourrait joye yssir."

But still let such a one be excused, if his pen treat of the subject at times lightly—as haply it will wander—and even so as

* P. xi. 35.   † Souvenirs de Mme. Récamier, avant-propos.

to contravene the notions of Sir Philip Sidney when he deprecated the tragic poesy of his own times as admitting of such interruptions instead of maintaining what he considered "its dignity in a well-raised admiration."

Nevertheless he has equally felt the responsibility which he incurs by undertaking to delineate such a character as is to be presented here, which can only be represented by giving an exact transcript of things as they occur to memory. In fact, the likeness that is to be presented can only be caught by snatches, as it were, just as the fresh recollections of certain looks and words and actions cross the mind in the course of the day. We must try to put life in our composition by seizing them as they pass, these birds of Paradise, that show themselves and are gone! and it is always with expressions taken from the poet, with the quill dropped from the swan, that one should write of her who passes now across our path as but the perfume of a minute—no more. Permit your author even occasionally to give way to that cheerfulness, or even gaiety, which does not offend sorrow; for, as Charles Lamb remarks, "there is a kind of levity which will not unfrequently spring up in the mind in the midst of deep melancholy." Besides, for the sake of his audience as well as for his own relief, others, as well as himself, will have leave to speak, to whom accordingly he has gone from time to time to borrow scraps just as a nephew will have recourse to the purse of his uncle; and it is no less judicious a critic than Coleridge who encourages him to do so, saying in the Friend, after accusing our elder writers of having quoted to excess, that it seems to him "as if we now avoid quotations with an anxiety that offends in the contrary extreme." Wherever I found that the character and manners to be spoken of in this book had been already delineated in a most graphic manner, and with the most exact precision in detached traits, by such pens as Bishop Fisher, Joinville, and others still more ancient, besides by French writers of the seventeenth century, I thought it better to give the words of those authors rather than my own; for while by transcribing them the resemblance was still kept as perfect as if the phrases had been originally composed with an exclusive view to my particular model, there would be the additional interest attached to such instances of the wonderful, and, indeed, often startling identity and perpetuity of graces with regard even to those forms in different persons in all ages in the Catholic Church. Of course all this might offend those who dislike quotations, but the advantage of not consulting their taste in this respect seemed to exceed that which would arise from conforming to it.

Again, "there are two ways of thinking," says a great master of art,—"the one diligent, methodic, resolved to fulfil an imposed task—the other capricious, not in a hurry, and less anxious to prove than to know; the one determined to arrive at a fixed hour by a road previously traced out at a proposed term;—the other disposed to seek adventures in the country, at the risk of not arriving either this evening or to-morrow, so passing the night under the stars*." It is well, in accordance with his conclusion, to try to unite these two methods—to know by faith where is truth; but not content to have found that magnificent sheltering-place, before resting there to follow for a while the adventurous way of others, and enjoy the advantages which it offers.

It has been said, by a man of great literary taste, that "to compose a work of art and genius is at some epoch of one's life to receive from God a look within the soul, to seize and comprehend it, and to be so happy from it that one seeks to perpetuate for one's self, and for others, the knowledge and the happiness of an instant." Intensity of feeling partakes of a similar privilege, even when one writes as one talks and as one thinks; and it is the same incomparable judge of literature who says, "I have always had a great weakness for authors who are such without being aware of it. One lives by their side, plays in their presence, and is at a hundred leagues' distance from thinking of a man of letters; and, in fact, nothing less resembles it. But somehow at one time or another such a person takes up a pen and carelessly traces some lines on paper; and it is this lively language fresh from the heart that years afterwards people love to read, when men of letters by profession are read no more." Independent of such considerations, the events of life, as Mme. Swetchine says, are like a sacred text for our mind to study

* Topffer.

and to comment on. How can one not follow with interest, attention, and respect, often with gratitude and admiration, the chain of circumstances which have accomplished a thought of God? Coleridge promised among the subjects of the Friend to "give characters met with in real life." To present one such portrait, with "thoughts and remembrance fitted," is the object of our ambition; and in this attempt, though we shall be unavoidably restrained by many considerations, there will be no disguise, as in the allegorical narrative once so celebrated under the title of "Le grand Cyrus," in which Mlle. de Scudéry described Mme. de Longueville under the name of Mandane[*]. It will not be a psychological romance, as they now say. It will be a strictly true delineation of a real character. This some one feels it his duty to attempt, and this is the end and the scope of his design—no more. It is to comply with the desire of the poet saying,

> "Give us, for our abstractions, solid facts;
> For our disputes, plain pictures;—
> Or rather, as we stand on holy earth,
> And have the dead around us, take from them
> Your instances;—
> Epitomize their life; pronounce, if you can,
> Authentic epitaphs."

There is, moreover, every guarantee for the fidelity, at least, with which the work will be executed, since it is one who for many years was never absent for a single day from the original that will hold the pencil. It is a copy made as it were on the spot, and then submitted to the correction of those who were best qualified to judge of the likeness; so that nothing was wanting to ensure success in the attempt to revive what the poet speaks of as having been once

> "a conspicuous flower
> Admired for beauty, for her sweetness praised,
> Whom he had sensibility to love,
> Ambition to attempt, and grace to win."

---

[*] Cousin, La Société Française au xviie Siècle.

It will not be a continuous narrative of facts, as if we were justified in considering as trifles all that might appear so to those who recognize no virtue in the mind, and can conceive no dignity in any incident which does not act on their senses by its external accompaniments. Indeed, to-coutinue using the words of a great author, "the spirit of genuine biography is in nothing more conspicuous than in the firmness with which it withstands the cravings of worthless curiosity, as distinguished from the thirst after useful knowledge. The great end of biography," he continues, "is to fix the attention and to interest the feelings of men on those qualities and actions which have made a particular life worthy of being recorded." What shall be mentioned here will not seem frivolous to those "who know," as this author says, "how great a thing the possession of any one simple truth is, and how mean a thing a mere fact is, except as seen in the light of some comprehensive truth *."

Antiquity has known instances of grave and thoughtful men, who sought an escape to the beautiful forms of a noble conversation, intermixed with piety, during intervals of active life, and in the most sorrowful hours of their country, or of the world, though it were but to breathe for an instant the fragrance of an embalmed air. They took their way unblamed through flowers—

"Sutilibus sertis omne rubebat iter."

Why should not the same permission be extended to others in our own times, however little disposed to what is calm and profound in the moral phenomena of human life?

"Communities are lost, and empires die,
And things of holy use unhallow'd lie;
They perish; but the intellect can raise,
From airy words alone, a pile that ne'er decays."

To awaken such an intellect, under the most adverse conditions, and enable it to achieve its purpose, is one of the consequences of studying an exquisite model. Such is the power of dispensing blessings which Providence has attached to the truly good, that they cannot even die without advantage to their

* Coleridge.

fellow-creatures: for death consecrates their example, and the wisdom which might have been slighted at the hearth, becomes oracular from the tomb.

If the writer might, in conclusion, just touch one chord, attending to what concerns no one, he would repeat the poet's lines, and say,

> "Stripp'd as I am of all the golden fruit
> Of self-esteem, and by the cutting blasts
> Of self-reproach familiarly assail'd,
> I would not yet be of such wintry barrenness,
> But that some leaf of her regard should hang
> Upon my naked branches."

Or he might seek to console his fancy by repeating what the Italian said of his own condition amidst the solitude of his latter years:—

> "non omnia terræ
> Obruta! vivit amor, vivit dolor! ora negatur
> Dulcia conspicere: flere et meminisse relictum est."

CHAPTER II.

JANE MARY was the youngest daughter of Thomas Dillon, of Mount Dillon, and of Edestown, in the county Kildare, in Ireland. Some of her nearest relations had long been naturalized in France, where the celebrated Count Edward Dillon was amongst her earliest friends; the gallant general who fell at the head of his own troops, a victim to the revolution, having fulfilled his destiny long before her birth. Married at the age when one espouses not a fortune, but a heart; possessing, too, what St. Chrysostom calls the bond of marriage, σύνδεσμος τοῦ γάμου, namely, that beauty which God, as he says, "having compassion on our laborious and miserable life, gave to us, as an adornment and a consolation*;" led to the altar, to use the common phrase, in a kind of granary, which served the Catholics of Dover at that time for Chapel,—the children of the place might have sung before her with Jasmin, while throwing a few flowers or green leaves upon the pavement,

> "Les chemins devraient fleurir,
> Tant belle épousée va sortir ;
> Devraient fleurir, devraient grener,
> Tant belle épousée va passer."

Those were days, when many being smitten with a taste even for the oldest French literature, she might have been thought a living instance to suggest the lines of Alain Chartier, written in his own excuse.

> "Cuides tu faire basilisques
> Qui occient les gens des yeulx,
> Les doulx visaiges angeliques
> Qui semblent estre fais és cieulx,
> Dieu ne les a pas formé tieulx
> Pour desdaigner et non chaloir,
> Mais pour croistre de bien en mieulx
> Ceulx qui ont desir de valoir."

Allied thus at an early age, through a younger branch, to the Digbys of Laundenstown, whose lands those of her father nearly joined, she became a happy mother, and while uniting the employments of Martha and Mary, may be truly said to have passed doing good. From her first entrance upon the world, with few and short intervals, she lived either abroad, or in domestic retirement, comprising but a small external circle. As daughter, sister, wife, mother, mistress of a family, and friend, wanting nothing that is praisable in a woman, she moved with firm yet light steps, alike unostentatious and alike exemplary. She attained in years but to half the duration usually allotted to human life, departing rather than dying, as we shall observe fully later, at the age of forty-two. This is a short biography;

---

* St. Chrysost. in Dan. cap. 1, Interp.

and as stated thus there certainly seems to be nothing whatever in its circumstances to justify any one for seeking to construct out of it a public monument. But the drama of such a life is in general what German philosophers call subjective; and, with regard to this particular instance, if one has leave to speak one's conscience, it would be difficult to find an existence in any sphere more capable of serving one of the highest and most important purposes to which the loftiest of human minds could in another form devote its faculties, for it might be made to show what is a life of faith, even in the times we live in,—the value not being diminished in consideration of its having been seen in the person, not of a hero or philosopher, but of a simple woman; for in every human being the results of the faith which animated her are analogous, and if well considered heroic, consonant with the highest wisdom, grand and beautiful; and with regard to the circumstance of those having been witnessed under such conditions, it must not be forgotten that the experience of each successive age of the world, not to say of each generation, and even year that passes, will only prove with what accurate judgment, and with what practical knowledge of all that contributes to the safety and happiness of human life, that mind was formed which prompted the oft-repeated exclamation, "Fallax gratia, et vana est pulcritudo; mulier timens Dominum ipsa laudabitur,"—well-known words indeed, but which are only one form of expression for a life of faith; since fear supposes belief in the existence of the power contemplated.

Let us in the first instance, therefore, consider the subject of our notice in relation to faith, which gift constitutes in truth the basis, and, one might add, the whole superstructure of the character which is now to pass before us; though here we are to consider it only in relation to that gift, and without any reference to what will follow later.

A genuine thing when once found can never be too deeply and attentively considered. Now the faith which animated this one mind, and governed this entire life, this collective energy, this total act of the whole moral being, of which the living sensorium was in the heart, presents a spectacle which the greatest and loftiest intellects, as well as the most weak of the human family, should study and ponder on, if they have any regard for what more than all things else in the universe concerns them. It is in regard to the possession of this attribute especially that the mere remembrance of her whose remains lie here, with the image in our mind's eye of what she was when in joyful innocence she walked amongst us, makes, to use the expression of our great dramatist,

> "This vault a feasting presence full of light."

For of every thing great and good of which humanity is capable this faith is the source and principle, rendering each person who is animated by it "a theme of honour and renown, a spur to valiant and magnanimous deeds;" and without it, where malice is not called into operation, there is nothing but inaction, depths calling upon depths, and darkness at the end of all. "Faith," says a French writer, "when existing in great men, great writers and poets, as viewed at a certain point of their career, renders them like rivers wide beyond all visible bounds at their mouths. All know them and they know all. Their glory is a thing like common-place. Oh! I do love," he continues, "faith higher up its channel, nearer its source, almost unknown, unvisited; when its course is mysterious, and so confined that two old willows leaning across from the opposite banks can mingle together their branches and serve it for a cradle." It is in this obscure and tranquil form so far removed from public haunts that we are now to view it. When studying the woman of faith, of the Credo, of the love of God and of His Church, eke out our performance with your mind, and methinks you are about to see the living person. But start not, my spell is lawful: do not shun her; she is soft as infancy and grace.

The subject, as already observed, may be said to abound with curious instructive meaning now, even in an historical and literary point of view; for here, by merely beholding one woman's faith, you might have been taught how to read the ancient Christian annals which record the results of that of whole generations. Here you had old history in a young heart; instead of ages, only years of faith in one existence. What more curious study, what more useful even to a student of history? "Would you know," asks the poet, dropping a hint that ought not to be lost on the historian, "the manners of an age? study with care one family,—'sufficit una domus.'" Here the *domestica facta* furnished a mirror and a clue to history.

Nay, you might find light thrown by means of her example upon even the municipal customs of London in former times, as where you read in the Liber Albus how the mayor and aldermen on certain days, and at a particular spot in St. Paul's church, used to pray for the soul of Bishop William, "who, by his entreaties, obtained from William the Conqueror great liberties for the City of London, the priest repeating the De profundis; and how careful the mayor and aldermen showed themselves on a certain occasion at the sale of houses to provide for divine service to be celebrated for the souls of certain testators of the remaining monies over and above only, after founding the chantry, to be paid towards the repairs of London bridge." In her you behold that solicitude for all the faithful departed which so profoundly characterized those ages.

In her, not to anticipate what must be stated later, you behold at least a certain adumbration of the character of those holy women and generous patricians, the Marcellas, Paulas, Fabiolas, and Melanies, described in the immortal pages of St. Jerome ; or rather, fearing to contemplate the details of that antique grandeur, and descending to ages in which the details of life have necessarily a greater resemblance to those of our own times, here we can observe in what was but yesterday daily done and spoken, the domestic manners of which the tradition is transmitted to us by the Bollandists. In her you witnessed the very spirit which animated the municipal corporations of the thirteenth century, when, as we find from Stephen Boileau's Livre des Métiers, and from the Liber Albus of the City of London, the motive for many enactments was declared officially to be "the pleasing of God, and the salvation of souls." As Montaigne says of L'Hopital, you will often be induced to exclaim, while fixing your regard on some fresh distinctive trait, "Belle âme, riche de vertus et marquée à l'antique marque." In fact, she seemed to expect to live surrounded as if born in ages of faith with manly virtue at the side of holiness ; or, as Montalembert expresses it, amidst heroes elbowing saints*. Calmly and dispassionately judging, you will be convinced that she was the living expression of the ancient Christian society as represented by St. Cyprian, and as distinguished from the pagan. With her all was complete and fixed,—what one must believe—what one must say and do. No fables, nothing equivocal, no myths; serious and sweet, the unity of her character answering to the unity of her thoughts—the whole moral theory simply exposed, precepts for all situations, encouragement for every one,—instead of amusing sophisms sparkling like nocturnal lights upon a tomb, luminous instructions shining like an aureole upon a cradle †.

It is but the plain unvarnished statement of a fact, to say that she comprised in herself the most noble traces of former ages, and of ideas that in the sphere of her ordinary life have nearly disappeared. In her you witnessed what reigned with such vitality in past ages, that sole force which is truly worthy of respect—force of soul excluding weakness and baseness, which constituted precisely, as a great writer says, " what was most unknown to those times." No, no, she must not be forgotten; a whole world sleeps with her.

But look only at the literary interest. The Ménagier de Paris, for instance, written in the time of St. Louis, seems drawn up expressly to paint her individual mind and manners. When the great poet Luis de Leon, too, composed his book on the perfect wife, it is her that you might fancy he must have had constantly in view. Of many other old curious books of portraits it might be truly said, O sweet holy picture! and thee, Jane Mary, which of the two has imitated the other? But how can one describe the beautiful varied imagery, the antique, exquisite miniatures presented here? In her you found what is written by M. Monteil in his history of ancient manners; all that he collected in parchment scrolls, and in the dust of forty thousand houses with towers and battlements, you saw not in separate fragments, but living and united in her. How often does it happen now that old monuments, vestiges of

---

* Moines d'occident, i. 27.

† Philarète Chasles, Études sur les premiers Temps des Christianisme.

ancient times of Christianity, seem to want an interpreter! Well, if you visited them in her company you did not experience that need. Montalembert mentions his having found over the gate of one of the dependencies of the abbey of Morimondo, near Milan, near a farm-house called Casina Cantaluco di Ozero, on the side of the wood from Abbiate Grasso to Pavia, these words: "Entra, o passaggiere! e prega Maria Madre di grazia." How one seems to have before one's eyes, when reading these lines, Jane Mary, not to explain them herself, but to enable you to explain them by beholding her heart kindled by the invitation contained in those sweet words! "In our contemporaries," says Saint-Beuve, "we like sometimes to search for certain traits of character that seem to belong to preceding ages; and we would wish to see them in their true light as referable to certain social epochs. This kind of supposition, when not overstrained, has its advantages. It is like a picture that one sees better by looking at it from different points, nearer or more distant." If we found that she whom we are about to delineate was of the seventeenth century by her solid qualities of mind and disposition, we might discover that by her faith her place would be found rather in more remote antiquity. It is like a saint of the middle ages, that appears to us, a saint of the thirteenth century, or even of the primitive Church, and of the holy women that entombed our Lord. In her instincts, in her tastes, in her inclinations, in her appreciations, in her judgments, in her language, you might have read the spirit and manners of Christian history, the part of cruelty and intolerance alone left out; for she seemed to know of what spirit we are; yet she was eminently of her own times, by her charity and her admirable good sense hostile to whatever is paradoxical and absurd. In point of fact, asking indulgence for the allusion, which I fear may be hardly pardonable, if there be any thing of life in certain works professing to contain monuments of the ages of faith, and to show the Meeting of the Ways at the central focus of the Catholic Church, their author owes the advantage almost entirely to her. Not alone did a rude sketch of her character, inserted in the fourth chapter of the first book of the latter work, constitute its purest page; but, all through both these compilations and compositions, without premeditation, the whole was conceived and moulded so as to exemplify what was actually seen and heard in her; for each passage was unconsciously selected with a view to its striking conformity with what she admired, and prescribed, and practised, and enforced by the lustre of her sweet example.

It would detain us too long were we to give here a detailed account of the varied manner in which this lively genuine faith operated, as its development in action will constitute the theme of this entire book. Let it suffice, for the present, to observe a few general instances, and to express them without reference to details. As we read of Mme. de Montmorency, " prosperity did not puff her up, nor misfortunes discourage her; for, to use the old language of Alain Chartier, le mespris de Dieu rend l'homme subjet et serf à toutes choses: so, for a contrary reason, her moral courage was great; and her heart, always firm and equable in its movements, was ever fixed on God as the true glory and happiness for ever*." Like the Countess of Richmond, as described by Bishop Fisher, "to God and to the chirche full obedient and tractable serchynge his honour and pleasure full besyly. Fryvelous thynges that were lytell to be regarded she wold let pass by, but the other that were of weyght and substance wherein she myght proufyte, she wolde not let for any payne or labour to take upon hande." This courage and activity in one who, in other respects, was nervous and diffident to an extreme, were assuredly remarkable; for, no question, she verified the remark that virtue is bold and goodness never fearful; but God was her retreat and her strength. That is why she would not fear though the mountains were thrown into the sea, or the heavens troubled. Her mind was ever at rest. She had no curiosity to hear about the wonders of philosophers—respecting magnetism and mediums, like those who consult such Humes as Shakspeare speaks of. She avoided all discourse about them, and seemed unwilling to think that such things even needed explanation. Her heart was ever set upon the salvation of all, who from any errors of opinion came within the sphere of her influence. Too well acquainted with their general answers, as ready as your borrower's caps, she was

* Vie de Mme. de Montmorency.

ever seeking by prayers, acts of kindness, and letting fall in season solemn words, and lending books, and offering suggestions in conversation, as if in play, to effect the conversion of hearts to truth; and in fact her plainness moved them more than eloquence. She looked like truth; as we read of that wife of Claude Aynard Romanet, she wished every one to be sanctified and blest; and she never omitted an occasion of rendering persons of all conditions service with that intention *. All her projects for those she did a kindness to were based on the wish to facilitate their arrival at the summum bonum, namely, the knowledge and worship of God. She ever thought of their souls; and when obliged to have recourse to physicians she thought more of things of eternal interest, than of what she wanted for herself. When speaking to infidels, her words seemed like music to their souls; and when she would apologize for speaking to them on such a subject, they would pray her to continue; and she used to get them to promise that they would say the Memorare and the Paternoster. Neither was she indifferent to the fate of those who lived in distant regions. The first notice in the English language of the work of the Propagation de la Foi was given and published at her instigation. Whatever had reference to faith commanded her whole heart. On setting out on her last journey, a few days before her death, she said, " Take that book with you," alluding to the work of Cardinal Wiseman on the connexion between science and revealed religion. And when some one said it is only a work for Protestants, " Take it," she replied, "it is a fine work for all." It was sent with the rest, and taken up after her death by one who knew not how it came on the table, but who, in the agonies of the days that ensued, could read no other book—thus, even after her departure, proving herself "the anchor of his purest thought, the nurse, the guide, the would-be guardian of his heart and soul—of all his moral being." People did not praise her, or talk of her, or write about her, or call her a confirmation of Plato's theory that beauty is in the mind, or indulge in metaphysical subtleties to account for their opinion of her character, writing

* Idée de la véritable Piété en la Vie de Demlle. Marguérite Pignier, femme de Claude Aynard Romanet.

as philosophers to more celebrated women—for the truth was, every one seemed to feel instinctively that already she belonged to a region of more lofty serenity, to which the clouds of such eulogies could not ascend, or which, if they were to reach her, would be dissipated as so much smoke and vapour. In truth, she often had the air of an angel that had somewhat lost its way in coming on our earth of agitation and lies. I will not of course dare to say that in her you had one to whom, in regard to faith, you could never find an equal, either among the Scythians or in the places of Pelops—

οὔτ' ἐν Σκύθῃσιν οὔτε Πέλοπος ἐν τόποις.

But she shall be dignified with this high honour, to declare that from observing what was evident and almost visible, one cannot conceive her thoughts and ways when in the presence of God in heaven as being different from what they were when on earth every hour in the bosom of her family. If one may be permitted to speak on such a theme poetically, one might say with truth that her presence exercised the sort of influence which is ascribed to the daisy in the familiar lines,

> " A hundred times, by rock or bower,
> Ere thus I have lain couch'd an hour,
> Have I derived from thy sweet power
>   Some apprehension;
> Some study rare, some brief delight,
> Some memory that had taken flight,
> Some chime of fancy, wrong or right,
>   Or stray invention.
>
> " If stately passions in me burn,
> And one chance look to thee should turn,
> I drink, out of an humbler urn,
>   A lowlier pleasure;
> The homely sympathy that heeds
> The common life our nature breeds;
> A wisdom fitted to the needs
>   Of hearts at leisure.
>
> " When, smitten by the morning ray,
> I see thee rise alert and gay,
> Then, cheerful ' bride,' my spirits play
>   With kindred gladness:

And when, at dusk, by dews oppress'd,
Thou sink'st, the image of thy rest
Hath often eased my pensive breast
  Of careful sadness.

"And all day long I number yet,
All seasons through, another debt,
Which I, wherever thou art met,
  To thee am owing;
An instinct call it, a blind sense,
A happy, genial influence,
Coming one knows not how, nor whence,
  To heaven calling."

Well, such are, as it were, the first tracings that we make in the Chapel of St. John. The figure of an individual stands out prominently, but so as to convince those who have seen the original that they convey an exact copy, a fac-simile. Let us proceed to observe the lesson which such an example imparts for the instruction, not alone of a few saunterers under Gothic arches, but of mankind.

I love science, I love intelligence, but, adds a deep contemplatist, "I love still more faith—simple faith[*]." Who shall estimate, viewing the subject on which side he will, from domestic peace and joy to the happiness and stability of empires,—who shall estimate the value of that singleness of eye with which the whole body is full of light; of that faith which is a total act of the soul, the whole state of the mind, following, as Sir Thomas Brown says, "the great wheel of the Church, by which the person moves, not reserving any proper poles or motion from the epicycle of his own brain?" The first lessons in the divine school of the youthful world, were assigned to the cultivation of the reason and of the will, or, as Coleridge says, rather of both as united in faith. "What is commonly called," says a member of the French Academy, "the faith of the charcoal-burner (la foi du charbonnier) imparts to the earth more consolations, virtues, and even understanding, than result from many voluminous treatises and their commentaries. I am far from concluding that it may not be sometimes necessary or useful to aspire at becoming learned in matters of religion; I

[*] Mme. Swetchine.

only infer that when once penetrated with fundamental truths, and the duties which they impose, it is better not to consume in long researches a time which would be better employed in prayer and good works. Our imperfect studies might conduct us to certain half-acquirements, sources of error and pride. There are studies which heat the head and cool the heart. It is not well to have a taste for contentious discussions, transforming the Gospel into a book of metaphysics. When we say, 'Deliver our minds from doubts,' we should add, 'and from subtleties.' Christianity," he continues, "explains all the events of life. If the Christian succeeds in a project, he thinks that the supreme goodness encourages his intentions and favours his efforts. If he fails, he receives as a trial, or as a chastisement, the reverse which he experiences. These explanations can only shock the pretended philosophers. They distrust, say they, a system which has an answer for every thing; they would be right, if it were only a system imagined by themselves; but this comes from on high, and we confide in it as the word of its Divine Author[*]."

"Yea," saith an enlightened physician, quoted by Coleridge, "there is but one principle which alone reconciles the man with himself, with others, and with the world; which regulates all relations, tempers all passions, and gives power to overcome or support all sufferings, and which is not to be shaken by aught earthly, for it belongs not to the earth, namely, the principle of religion. This elevation of the spirit above the semblances of custom and the senses to a world of spirit, this life in the idea, this it is which affords the sole sure anchorage in the storm, and at the same time the substantiating principle of all true wisdom; the satisfactory solution of all the contradictions of human nature, of the whole riddle of the world. This alone belongs to and speaks intelligibly to all alike, the learned and the ignorant, if but the heart listens . . . for it is an immutable truth that what comes from the heart, that alone goes to the heart; what proceeds from a Divine impulse, that the godlike alone can awaken."

"En vain vous trouvez Dieu dans un froid argument,
Toute raison n'est pas dans le raisonnement.

---

[*] Droz, Pensées sur le Christianisme, 12.

> Il est une clarté plus prompte et non moins sûre
> Qu'allume à notre insu l'infaillible nature,
> Et qui, de notre esprit enfermant l'horizon,
> Est pour nous la première et dernière raison."

We shall observe later, in very minute and interesting details, how all this was verified in Jane Mary. De Maistre says, "there is nothing so difficult as to be only one." This unity formed one of her most remarkable characteristics. Her whole life was like one act, such consistency reigned in all her actions and words; and yet with what an exquisite sense of humanity were these high principles exercised! With a mind antipodal to the pagan, you would have thought her the most natural person you ever conversed with, and withal the most tender. As an instance of what Saint-Beuve calls the Christian euphonism, Saint-Beuve cites the phrase of the Abbé de Rancé when, while wishing to give advice to his somewhat weak, old, and sick friend, the Abbé Nicaise, he avoids pronouncing in his ears the word death, and only says to him one should have these sentiments, particularly "when we are nearer feeling the happiness which results from having loved them," meaning when we are nearer the tomb. The ancients, when alluding to death, used to say, "si quid minus feliciter contigerit;" to persons of faith alone it belongs to improve the delicacy of this expression, and say, "si quid felicius contigerit." Horace said of death, "in æternum exilium," while the Christian says, "return to our eternal country;" there lies all the difference. Of the value which she attached to faith, it would be difficult to speak so as not to appear exaggerated. It was not from having formed a philosophic estimate of its nature, and as if from knowing with the metaphysicians, that "the understanding in its utmost power and opulence culminates in faith, as in its crown of glory, at once its light and its remuneration." It was not that she had arrived at this conviction by the scientific process, which led Ozanam, the corrector of the tables of logarithms in 1670, to declare that he would not understand religion otherwise than as the people understand it, adding that "it belonged to doctors of the Sorbonne to dispute, to the Pope to pronounce, and to a mathematician to go to Paradise by a perpendicular line—the straight line *." But it was, that from a living and practical possession of this treasure, she would have been ready at any moment to die rather than relinquish it. To love and suffer seemed to be her maxim. She was ever ready for the heroism of devotedness and of immolation, with the resolution of Abraham and the heart of David. This is not coining phrases with a view to honour her memory. It is simply stating facts. Of course in this respect she presented only one instance, one of the millions of examples that exist in every age, attesting a conviction equally profound, and a fidelity as constant. But still, examples of this kind, simple, spontaneous, and vital, when met with in the ordinary walks of the world, impress one always with a sense of a supernatural and divine novelty. . Jules Janin stumbles upon them in his poetic perambulations through modern literature. The parents of Madame Desbordes Valmore for instance, he tells us, being reduced to extreme poverty, were invited by their great uncle, exiled in Holland at the revocation of the edict of Nantes, to accept the reversion of his immense property, on condition of adopting the reformed religion. The destitute family held a council; there were many tears shed; but they came to a unanimous decision to refuse the inheritance; and so fearing, as he adds, to sell their souls, emigrated to America †. In the instance with which we are concerned, there would not have been even a deliberation, still less, for all her humanity, tears.

All this may seem very common-place matter to such readers as only fly like butterflies from one light flower of our railway literature to another, finding perhaps not much sustenance in any; but I would ask men of thought and experience whether it is possible to conceive an instruction more important than what is involved in it? For in fine you can see how the world proceeds around us. Not to speak of the contrast between the faith of this noble woman and the unmanly disposition of those poor diseased minds, which, with all their acuteness existing in a weak and imperfect organization, can never decide or take a resolute part in any thing, unless in a perverse and pretentious attempt to undermine the religious belief of others—not to

---

* Fontenelle, tome v. 516.　　† Variétés Littéraires.

speak of the deistic publications verging upon atheism, which have been sent forth from time to time by men who were still eating the bread of the Anglican establishment—one cannot but perceive how inclined the world is at the present day to set aside and ignore the supernatural, that is, the real, and to look on all the wonders that are involved in it with the eyes of animals incapable of a thought beyond what the senses suggest. Yet how clearly is this state of mind generating contempt for such an example as is now before us, the result of mere slavish habit, both utterly baseless and unworthy of regard; for, say what they like, common sense, though they want it in this instance, proclaims loudly that their own existence is a most supernatural fact, even according to their notions of what is natural. Let us offer a trifling fancy of our own to explain my meaning. The moon is, to speak their language, a natural object; and without any great effort of imagination you can for a moment suppose yourself living on it. You know we can suppose any thing. A brother of Escobar supposes "infinite ants on infinite hillocks;" and you need not tell me that it has no atmosphere. For an instant you can fancy yourself as able to breathe without air and living on it, and that is all we demand. Suppose, then, that when so situated it were made known to you that there was such a scene as human life presents, being acted on the luminous globe revolving in space, which the world would seem to you to be; that there were churches on it, and that prayers, and processions, and mass, and vespers, were being celebrated night and day in honour of the Creator of the universe, while there were many Bolingbrokes and Voltaires going about to scoff, and denying that there was any such Being, or affirming that if there were He heeded them not, how supernatural would it all appear to you then! How you would escape from the low grovelling impression produced by habit making you fancy that the natural side of things, as you call it, was the only one philosophically true! How readily would you admit what faith now demands of you; namely, that the fact of human life on this earth being supernatural, it must also have a supernatural object and corresponding end! One grows weary of hearing solid proofs; let this fanciful one then serve its turn.

Meanwhile, the fact, look you, is that the present generations are disposed practically to deny all that is supernatural. We are concerned here therefore with an example that is curious, if it were only in consideration of the contrast which it presents to what is witnessed on all sides of us. Socrates of old used only to put questions; but the Christian, who is seen in this portrait, adheres to unquestionable truths, as Sarasin said to Balzac, "truths conveyed in maxims for the defence of which it is glorious to die. The latter does not amuse herself with refuting Gorgias and Prodicus, or reducing to the absurd Polus and Hippias; her object is to inspire love and veneration for divine things." What things are now deemed divine and what beyond ourselves is now the object of affection or reverence? Even when we find doubt and opinion, "which," asks a French author, "of the two dominates in men? which is uppermost if you let down your plummet? Is it the solid foundation or the undulating? You think it is the undulating; but is there not a solid bottom farther on? You think it is the solid; but is there not a shifting failing bottom still more evanescent? There is the knot of the problem. Who can explain the secret of others? Can one," he adds, rhetorically alone I hope, "be sure of one's own? Frequently, if I dare say it, there is no true real bottom or foundation within us—there are only surfaces multiplied ad infinitum*." Yet, if you have ever thought at all, you must come to the conclusion of the French author, who says, that "without a philosophy and a poetry, both of which require faith to have any true foundation, an individual and a nation can have only weariness and despair." "Long indeed will man strive to satisfy the inward querist with the phrase, laws of nature. But though the individual may rest content with the seemly metaphor, the race cannot†." And then, too, looking to the effects on noblest and purest minds, how ugly sound such explanations which are only another term for doubts from the mouth of a woman or a child! Accordingly sheer disgust and the force of truth extort from many, and from very opposite characters too, strange complaints and avowals respecting the present condition of society. "Formerly," says Saint-Beuve, "even dissipated people be-

---

* Saint-Beuve of M. de Rémusat.   † Coleridge, The Friend.

lieved. Whatever might be the storms at the surface, in the depths was faith—there was a return to it; and great minds soared aloft. But to-day, even when the appearance is of faith, honourably and philosophically avowable, below is doubt; and even great minds have no return, they do not believe that they need have one, and they dissipate themselves." Nay, we are told by grave authors on the side of order, that even "the beauty of old age, which is to have confidence in truth and virtue, is not, at present, without a certain mixture of a general irony and a slight scepticism *."

But perhaps you do not like pulpitry; and all this seems to smack of it. Well, then, take courage, for this is rather the echo of your polished Academies judging from their own chairs, from which they would have us believe that there is no appeal. For observe how even the guardians of literature trace with regret the progress of infidelity in authors whom they admire. Hear, for example, Saint-Beuve speaking of a contemporary. "The invasion of scepticism in the heart of this poet from the time of his first hymns produces," saith he, "a slow impression of fear, and makes one attach to the results of human experience a painful morality. Vainly does this poet cry repeatedly, Lord, Lord! as if to be reassured in darkness, and fortified against himself. Vainly does he speak of the immortal soul and the eternity of God. Neither his prayer for all men, so sublime, nor his alms so Christian can conceal the bitter reality—the poet no longer believes. God eternal—humanity astray and suffering—nothing between the two. The luminous ladder of which the son of the Patriarch once dreamed, and which the Christ-Mediator has realized by his cross, exists no more for this poet. I know not what funereal blast has thrown him back. He has only to wander over the earth, to interrogate all the winds, all the stars, to lean over the precipices, to seek the secret of the creation from the murmuring of rivers, or of blighted forests. . . . . It is no longer to believe in Redemption to speak like him. It is to behold the universe and humanity as before the Coming, as before Job; as in those days before the

* Paul Janet, La Famille.

sun, or that the Spirit moved upon the waters. That, if you will have it so, may be fine, and grand, and poetical—but it is sad—that causes the mind to return, as he himself says,

'———— avec un cri terrible,
Ebloui, haletant, stupide, épouvanté!'

There is then in this book of our great poet," he continues, "a progress in art, a progress in lyric genius, a progress in profound emotions; but as to a progress in religious faith, in philosophic altitude, in moral results—shall I say it? there is nothing of the kind. That is a memorable example of the dissolving energy of the age, and of its triumph at last over individual convictions. One thought them indestructible; one suffered them to fall asleep as sufficiently secure, and some fine morning one wakes up and searches for them in one's soul in vain. They have sunk down like a volcanic island under the ocean. So this poet," who certainly by a singular good fortune retains a will, as his indefatigable life can prove, "either through practical indifference, or consciousness of human weakness in these matters, can no longer make use of this will to the study or defence of certain religious solutions—he lets his soul be borne away, and receives as a benefit for the Muse all storms, and all shades of darkness in fearful combination."

For such intelligences, for such Tritons of the minnows as I would make bold to call them, what is the portrait of a Jane Mary? We can feel sure beforehand that even such an example will be lost upon those who, as St. Augustine says, "quærunt non ut fidem sed ut infidelitatem inveniant." The poet Loyson said to a French philosopher travelling in Germany,

"———— ———— Tu cours les grandes routes
Cherchant la vérité pour rapporter des doutes;"

for "there are a set of heads," as Sir Thomas Brown says, "that can credit the relations of mariners, yet question the testimonies of St. Paul." And it is droll enough that they will not learn to doubt with uncertainty, and that incredulity should be dogmatic; while the fact is, as Coleridge observes, that as materialism has been generally taught it is utterly unintelligible, and owes all its proselytes to the propensity so common among men to mistake distinct images for clear conceptions, and, vice versa, to reject as inconceivable whatever from its own nature is unimaginable. How wanting in penetration and logic are narrow minds! This is what Mme. Swetchine used to remark. Of some, indeed, Coleridge says, that the sense of understanding them must be given, not acquired; but to demand that is asking rather too much from any one; for, in fact, as he concludes, a revelation unconfirmed by miracles, and a faith not commanded by the conscience, a philosopher may venture to pass by, without suspecting himself of any irreligious tendency. Education, he remarks, consists in educing the faculties, and forming the habits; but who can wonder at the scarcity of such examples as the instance we are considering, when it is supposed to be the mere imparting of knowledge with a tacit understanding that there is no exclusive truth in any particular form of Christianity? Such a writer can be cited the more willingly as being at all events no partial or prejudiced witness; and he goes on to say, "I do not hesitate to declare, that whether I consider the nature of the discipline adopted, or the plan of poisoning young minds with a sort of potential infidelity under the 'liberal idea' of teaching those points only of religious faith in which all denominations agree, I cannot but denounce those schools as pernicious beyond all power of compensation by the acquirement of reading and writing *." Evidently then he would have halted in the Chapel of St. John rather than have taken his seat among the scorners.

However, be our opinion on modern systems of education what it may, there is but too much reason to credit the testimony of those unsuspected writers who represent the present age, abounding with men perilously over-civilized, and most pitiably uncultivated, as standing in singular need of that faith which produced the character that it is our object in these pages to portray. "Somehow or other," says Charles Lamb, "there is a want of strong virtue in mankind at present. We have plenty of the softer instincts, but the heroic character is

---

* Statesman's Manual.

gone." It is Topffer, in his last admirable work on art*, who speaks of his own times as forming "an epoch without moral life, without faith, without enthusiasm, without grandeur, when on the ruins of what is past nothing rises up but the worship of riches, of industry, and of matter; when productions, fabrication, and consumption, are the only things that are thought of, the end and the term of all efforts, the present and the future of society, the only wonders of the age."

But waiving such general views, let us observe from other standing-ground the need which exists in society at present for profiting by the great lesson which is yielded by such a life as we are considering under these vaults,—namely, a life of faith.

Now it is difficult not to be struck with the contrast presented by the energy of this character as witnessed in Jane Mary, and the weakness or nullity of wills where the faith that animated her is wanting. How ready for action and resolved on it in every emergency was this simple woman! As if well read in Alain Chartier's Bréviaire des Nobles, and knowing

> "Poure et riche meurt en corruption,
> Noble et commun doivent à Dieu service :
> Mais les nobles ont exaltation,
> Pour foy garder et pour vivre en justice."

How morally strong, and how intellectually and practically heroic was this physically weak and singularly nervous creature! Her place evidently, to adopt the classification proposed by a great author, was among "persons who do, as distinguished from those who talk and think,—the former being now called," as he says, "practical persons, anciently believers." There is the secret: she trusted, she obeyed, according to a persuaded submission—$\pi\iota\sigma\tau\iota\varsigma$, the root and essence of all human deeds, being called by the Latins "fides," which has passed into the French "foi," and the English "faith †." Now look around you whenever this is wanting, and where are human deeds rightly so called? "Qu'est devenue," as Alain

---

* Réflexions et menus Propos.
† Ruskin.

Chartier might say with more justice than when he wrote, "la louable ordonnance de vivre, la constance de courage, et de meurs, et la haultesse de cuer et d'entreprise que tes devanciers laissèrent aux successeurs*." "What is soonest worn out in us is the will," said a celebrated writer. "Assuredly," adds Saint-Beuve, "this is most true in our times, when the rarest of all spectacles is to see the moral energy of the will. Our age seems to have exhausted all its force in that respect. The intelligence is extended, science has increased; it has studied and learned many things and in many ways, but it no longer dares, or is able, or wishes to will any thing. Amongst men devoted to the labour of thought, and who have the moral and philosophical sciences at their fingers' ends, there is nothing now more difficult to find than a will, a conviction, a faith. There are infinite combinations, impartialities without limits, vague and inconstant assemblages, but excepting for the dispute of the moment, a radical indifference. Looking on them the most favourably, they are great minds unfolded to all winds, but without an anchor when they stop, and without a compass when they proceed. . . . . We wish to comprehend without believing, and to receive ideas after the manner of a limpid mirror, without being determined by that as to, I do not say acts, but even to conclusions. The most impassioned derive from this moving succession a kind of passing and intoxicating pleasure, which reduces on them, the impression of each new idea to the charm of a sensation. . . . . . Yet one does not adopt this epicurism of the intelligence at once, and with a deliberate intention. One says that every thing must be known, and then there will be time to choose; but as time passes the energy of will fades away, till at last it wholly passes from the mind as well as the heart. The will then only serves the meanest passions, the wildest caprices or vicious habits; then the love of place, of gold, of the table, becomes the ruling passion. These secret and habitual objects can no longer be acknowledged without shame. With the noblest it is the love of their reputation which dominates, and they are seen with grey hair contending eagerly for this puerile garland.

* Les Trois Vertus.

Great men in some respects, they are no longer men in the intimate sense of the ancient wisdom; they no longer present intelligences served by organs, but intelligences which deceive organs and betray them. How few are there who in the order of thought fix themselves in time, and adhere without reserve to what is recognized by them as truth perpetual, universal, and holy; who, not content with recognizing it, devote themselves to it—their faculties, their natural gifts; rich their riches, poor their farthing, passionate their passions, indolent their ease, proud their illusions; who become here below an humble and strong will, believing and active,—animating with its sovereign unity doctrine, affections, and manners; true men in regard to mind, sublime and encouraging models! I am aware," he concludes, furnishing, by the way, a useful lesson for ourselves, "that in speaking of those who in our time present the noblest example of this consubstantial and sacred union of the will with the intelligence under the seal of faith,—of those whose mind and practice, all whose thought and all whose life are sumissive with such docility, and employed with such ardour in following out the consequences of doctrines, I know that we have to be on our guard against that fruitless study, that curious admiration without results, (Oh, what a smart lash for some consciences!) of which we have been indicating the mischief! The best way to profit by these moral activities is not to interpret or describe them, but it is to acquiesce in the general totality of the truths which they restore, and to render one's own personal testimony to the fundamental principle of which they are the simple organs *."

"Amidst all this wild adulation of humanity," says another great author, "I remain sadly impressed by the spectacle of the sinking lower and lower, of the growing weakness and powerlessness of each man, taken in himself, in the modern society. This apotheosis of the wisdom and power of the masses seems to threaten to extinguish all personal initiative agency, and all strength of character in which virtue and nobleness consist †."

* Saint-Beuve.
† Montalembert, Les Moines d'Occident, i.

Another reflection that is calculated to impart a high sense of the importance of the lesson emanating from this tomb, is the misery of those who follow a different standard, and who, without faith, excepting in themselves, live and die. "What we fail in," says a distinguished author, in one of his purely literary works, "is the study of supreme perfection, and the sentiment of our own imperfection. We have neither the ideal nor the real, neither humility nor energy in regard to moral greatness*." There can be no joy in such a condition; yet nature has done her part most generously with many, nor is that great corrective ever withheld which should give it strength and vitality. But still, after all, in these times, the infallible support of faith comes to be found wanting, and consequently we hear it lamented of each of those proposed for objects of our hero-worship, that,

> "——————— In despite
> Of all this outside bravery, within
> He neither felt encouragement nor hope;
> For moral dignity and strength of mind
> Were wanting, and simplicity of life,
> And reverence for himself, and, last and best,
> Confiding thoughts, through love and fear of Him,
> Before whose sight the troubles of this world
> Are vain as billows in a tossing sea."

Without faith no life is happy, and no death serene. Again I say, it is men the farthest removed from the sanctuary who acknowledge it. "This alternation of doubt and faith caused me," says Chateaubriand, "for a long period of my life, a mixture of despair and of ineffable delight. Who could paint that bitter disenchantment, that grief of not believing—or the ecstasy that accompanied a revival of faith?" Alas, to how few in our own country does the return appear to be granted! The form which the infidelity of England especially has taken, seems to a great author of our times, as one hitherto unheard of in human history. "The undisturbed imbecility," he says, "with which I found persons engaged in the study of economical and political questions declare that the laws of the Devil are

* Philarete Chasles.

the only practicable ones, and that the laws of God are merely a form of poetical language, passed all that I had ever before heard or read of mortal infidelity. So far as in it lay, this century has caused every one of its great men whose hearts were kindest, and whose spirits most perceptive of the work of God, to die without hope,—Scott, Keats, Byron, Shelley, Turner! Great England has not yet read often enough that old story of the Samaritan's mercy. He whom he saved was going down from Jerusalem to Jericho—to the accursed city (so the old Church used to understand it). He should not have left Jerusalem; it was his own fault that he went into the desert and fell among the thieves, and was left for dead. Every one of those English children, in their day, took the desert by-path, as he did, and fell among fiends—took to making bread out of stones at their bidding, and then died, torn and famished; careful England, in her pure dress, passing by on the other side *." Now hear the voice from these vocal stones. Look at the sweet noble image that seems to hover over and look down upon them. They who would be happy, therefore, are directed to listen to the harmonies that sound within the Chapel of St. John; for what can facilitate the acquisition of faith more than the remembrance of such a life? "O mon ami," says an accomplished French writer, "quel argument contre l'incrédule que la vie du vrai Chrétien!" "I invite you," writes Madame Swetchine, "to hold to that foi du charbonnier, to which I have returned after all my religious oscillations. I read much, and the more I read the more I wish to return to those first elements which are so simple that childhood learns them. I confine myself to them, only hoping that the vessel which receives them may be purified. In this neighbourhood," she adds, "are many schismatics, and yesterday, having asked a poor peasant woman if she belonged to them, 'No, little mother,' she said; 'I walk on the old road and take what God gives me.' When one is born in the bosom of Christianity, is not that the dictate of supreme reason? and ought not the wisest and best to follow the teaching of my poor woman?" If you will hear men most conversant with the world, so it is with many others in regard to their late,

* Ruskin, Mod. Painters, v. 253.

but ultimate convictions. "At the present day," says Droz, who had fathomed for himself all the depths of philosophy, "souls are fatigued with the vacancy which they feel. Fathers of families, sensible men, young people the most distinuigished by their intellectual faculties—all have a thirst for religion [*]." As many, at least, as are in the position of those who have had such a model before their eyes as we are contemplating, and who are inspired by such a memory as haunts this cloister, will desire to profit by the lesson. "For indeed, look you," as an English philosopher said, in allusion to some friend whom he had recently lost, "were it but for the remembrance of her alone, and of her lot here below,

'—————— One fading moment's mirth,
With twenty watchful, weary, fearful nights,'

the disbelief of a future state would sadden the earth around me, and blight the very grass in the field." "Yes, truly," as the Duc Mathieu de Montmorency said to a friend, "you may easily conceive that their thoughts now pass beyond this world, which must for every one so quickly finish." We represent here the problem of living in one world with the instincts of another; and the question to solve, adds Madame Swetchine, is this: How can the creature of eternity find the road to its royal dwelling? This sweet tomb, that in its circuit doth contain the perfect student of the eternal years, emits an audible voice to guide us thither; for she whose whole life appears like a beacon over a tempestuous sea, has shown by her example how one can arrive at this great and all-important solution, since every thing else, be it what it may, is secondary, or rather to speak more truly, nothing. Be it ours, therefore, in allusion to her, to say with the poet,

"The monarch may forget his crown,
 That on his head an hour hath been;
The bridegroom may forget his bride
 Was made his wedded wife yestreen;
The mother may forget her child,
 That smiles so sweetly on her knee;
But I'll remember thee, my Jane,
 And all that thou hast done for me."

---

[*] Pensées sur le Christianisme.

CHAPTER III.

ANOTHER "sermon" in these vocal stones, is that which teaches Catholicity. "To every thing," as a great thinker observes, "God has attached a form. If the Catholic form had not existed, Christianity would have become only a system of morality, like that of the Porch. It would have had no duration as a religion, but simply it would have taken its place as a system of ethics." It is with religion, as Loyson says it is with true poesy, "the vague ought to be its soul, but not its body." In the contemplation of the infinite in which the former consists, we are necessarily lost and overwhelmed; and whatever relates to it must, to some extent, be included under the term of what is undetermined; but in regard to the forms, through which it has pleased Omniscience to hold communion with us, which constitute what may be termed the body of religion, there must be nothing vague; indeed these it was a main object of revelation to determine for us. "The Bible, in regard to them," as a great author remarks, without observing this inference, "being a book as much for shallow and simple persons as for the profound, this main and leading idea is found on its surface, written in plainest possible Greek, Hebrew, or English, needing no penetration nor amplification, needing nothing but what we all might give, attention [*]." In regard then to this outward and, as it were, incarnate form of religion, obviously precision and definite shapes, amounting to a tangible and living reality, are requisite. Accordingly there was no uncertainty or distrust with regard to them in the mind of this true Catholic. As M. de Pontchâteau said of Madame de Longueville, "she loved greatly the Church and the poor." What could be more exactly determined? For, with regard to the former, merely in consequence of her simple docility as a believer and a disciple of our Lord, there was no danger of her

[*] Ruskin.

being mystified like that poor Poinsinet, who wanting to learn the English language was taught the Bas-Breton; and, besides, she had never been subjected to such influences. "There are many, without going far back into historical events—many like Josephus, who seek to accommodate their religion to the ideas and manners of those who think to subdue it—who try to assimilate it to national ways of thinking of recent growth, substituting for ancient doctrines ideas and objects familiar to the new civilization, being themselves neither of the past nor of the present, and all whose finesse and capacity terminate in an untruth *." There are many who, in consequence, find their road beset with difficulties; while others, by wanting her singleness of eye, find themselves distracted and unable to pursue it with the calm of a solid conviction. All such persons would do well to meditate over this tomb; for never did there exist a mind more Catholic in a genuine and healthy state, or an example more calculated to inspire Catholicity in others. It was not that she had an imagination which, taking pleasure in the beautiful forms and æsthetic consequences of the genius of Christianity, controlled her judgment and determined her acquiescence. It was not that she had the imagination Catholic, independently of the foundation of faith, like those who admire the pomps of worship, the solemnity of fêtes, the harmony of chants, and the order of ceremonies,—because though all these things moved and affected her, the foundation was still simple piety,—but she had what Saint-Beuve calls the Christian sensibility,—the morality of the Gospel affected her most. Certainly not insensible to the charm of those other associations, still they did not influence her. A religion of poetry, or of archæology, or of whims and fancies, and "matters which are not stuff of the conscience," though under a devotional form, as being merely such, she could not endure. What she regarded as paramount, was a solid devotion in which entered nothing of her own humour. She did not "give any unproportioned thought his act;" she did not carry her particular fancies into her religion, as so many do, following the habit of some who study philosophy: she simply received and was thankful.

* Philarete Chasles, Etudes sur les premiers temps du Christianisme.

"The natural man," says Madame Swetchine, "is not exactly impious, but he is essentially an idolater. He worships whatever suits his own taste or his own predilection. He wants every thing to bend to his indomitable will. He deifies what he likes, and wishes to be himself the end and terminus of all that he loves." No contrast, therefore, can be conceived greater than that which Jane Mary presented to this type. Moreover, she never seemed to think that her approval or acceptance of Catholicism had any thing to do with the question of its merits; whereas how many are there who resemble La Harpe replying to a young man, who showed him a certain tragedy: "The subject is not fitting; if it had been a proper one, Voltaire and I would have chosen it long ago." Just in this way do they say secretly to themselves, when pressed with the truths of Catholicity, "Neither such and such men, nor myself have followed this way. We should have adopted it if it had been the right one." There is no use in arguing further.

But to return to what concerns the imagination. She saw things then, I repeat it, from the point of view of practical Christianity; and the custom of using religion for a poetical and sentimental end, seemed to her as a danger, or as a weakening of a thing august and severe. Her Catholicity was simply belief, acquiescence, fidelity; she had that high moral education, which consists in having on all occasions a side taken, un parti pris. She had that profound consciousness of belonging to the household of faith, which often expresses itself in a kind of harmless irony, as when some one, in alluding to a hostile banner, cries, "But it was a strong composure a fool could disunite;" she was, therefore, immoveable and heroic. A wonderful quickness, too, in combination with an infantine innocence, belonged to her in detecting sophisms against the doctrines of faith. It was impossible to deceive her with regard to truth of this order. In worldly matters you could cheat her any day; but in religion, in regard to which she was all humility and deference, there was no imposing on her judgment, which she felt was backed by the whole Catholic Church. There you met with the exact logician and the clear-sighted judge, who could detect the fallacy as soon as uttered. In an instant she used to point out where the error lay, and expose it in warm but simple language. It was not indeed, you would say, precisely as if a father of the Church spoke to you, for she was a person whom no one had the heart to flout; but it sounded like the rebuke of a child or the voice of your own conscience. However learned and philosophical you might have thought yourself a minute before, you had only to blush and be silent.

No question she possessed an intimate sense of the need of that harmonious and ordinate exercise of all our faculties, which Catholicity supposes and requires; for, as an eminent philosopher remarks, "every heresy has originated in and supported itself by arguments rendered plausible only by the confusion of our faculties, and their demanding for the objects of one a sort of evidence appropriated to those of another faculty." No doubt, also, the delicacy of her conscience served her greatly in regard to her perception of truth; for, as Saint-Beuve says of Madame de la Fayette, "to a fund of tenderness of soul and of romantic imagination she joined a great natural exactitude," and as Madame de Sevigné said of her, "a certain divine reason," which never failed her. She had an instinct, too, of Catholicity, a certain tact of faith which made her shrink from the touch of whatever wore the semblance of novelty, or of compromise with error. She had the air of one who always carried about with her, though concealed through humility, and only to be produced when called for, the passport of a Catholic Christian, like that used in the primitive ages and down to the fifth century, at the head of which were the letters P. U. A. P., or, Pater, Uios, Agion Pneuma. "How proud one ought to be," she used to say, "to be a Catholic when one is in a country not Catholic!" She wore her faith as a piece of defensive armour, and no insult could reach her through it. Decus et solamen. And in point of fact, when she talked of being proud, interpreting her words in the sense in which she used them, the sentiment was only a fresh proof of the precision of her judgment. The least appearance of fawning upon power when it was a question of faith and its integrity, for on other matters she had no predisposition to think ill of governments, would draw from her a mild but irrevocable sentence, saying,

"He doth affect the courtier's life too much;
——————— making his fancy giddy

With images of state, preferment, place,
Tainting his generous spirit with ambition."

She never forgot, quamvis inter togatos, the greatness even in a temporal point of view that belongs to Catholicity. Though she might have just left only the cell of some poor "friar Patrick," you would have thought that she had come from visiting one who, now a priest, had lately been amongst the illustrious of the earth,—one, perhaps, of the most powerful in the Roman Empire,—a senator whose father had been Prefect of the Gauls. Oh, with what withering contempt would she hear such lines as,

"Des prêtres fortunés foulent d'un pied tranquille
Les tombeaux des Catons et la cendre d'Emile."

Judging from her high disdain, you would say she must have known well, as Saint-Beuve remarks, that if the priest has at first trod with a tranquil foot these great floors, and we must add, with a majestic step; if still at the present day, to see his high demeanour in the Ara Cœli, he has the air of the hereditary master, and of the patrician of old (gentemque togatam), it is, that in point of fact he has from the beginning been the legitimate descendant, the relation in right line of these Catos, and of these Emiliuses. She must have felt as if this continuity of the old Rome in the midst of the new had been stamped even on the forms and attitude of the latter in the thought and movement of the Vatican. Where afflicting contrasts were presented to her, and from the very nature of human things she knew that no where on earth could miseries and abuses be wholly avoided, the Catholicity of her mind found only a fresh field for its operation, as she would reply to the same purport as the Count de Maistre when the Emperor Alexander spoke to him of being scandalized at the vices of Vienna, "You think, sire, that you behold Catholicism; you behold only its absence." She too seemed fully impressed with the conviction expressed by Madame Swetchine when she said, "I have always thought that no cause here below can be upheld long if one has the misfortune to see always men where one ought only to see principles."

In general, she verified the observation that Catholicity imparts some of the qualities of genius, enabling those under its influence to change their point of view, and even to find fresh objects for their tastes while retaining, whole and entire, their consistency. Thus she would have praised alike the cathedral of Amiens or the past, the architecture of St. Peter's or the present; the devotion of Paris, or the supernatural side of life, and the honesty of the English face, as representing what is consonant with it in the natural view of humanity. You could not confine her within narrow limits, or to one point of view; and "it is thus," as Saint-Beuve says, "great minds too act. They are already at the other pole when you think them still at its opposite. Like rapid and indefatigable generals, they light up fires on certain heights, and you think them camped behind them when they are already many leagues' march distant, and they take you on the flank." It was the same with her in regard to matters more of thought, in regard to which such universality of mind is but a necessary consequence, when we once admit the truly Catholic doctrine, as Saint-Beuve calls it, and which he says is now established, that Christianity is "the rectification of all universal credences—the central axe which fixes the sense of deviations." "In point of fact," as Sarasin remarks, "almost all the sects of the ancient philosophers, and consequently all shades of opinion, even in modern times, for there is nothing new in the world, met each other in the Church." One can only except of course those of Epicurus and Pyrrhon. The first fathers followed the old Academy. Our last doctors, in many things, side with Aristotle. Zeno had his disciples in cloisters, where could be found the silence and frugality of Pythagoras. All precipitous ways, however winding or at first seeming to lead in a direction opposite, tend to the centre constituted by Catholicity. Much more do the ordinary walks of our approved humanity lead to the same goal; and the poet seems to ascribe the same tendency to all that he has himself been uttering; for when reverting to the Scottish Puritans he asks himself, saying,

> "How, think you, would they tolerate this scheme
> Of fine propensities, that tends, if urged

> Far as it might be urged, to sow afresh
> The weeds of Romish phantasy, in vain
> Uprooted?"

As with her views, so was it with her virtues, though this is not perhaps exactly the place for us to remark it. If we were to lay down on tracing paper here, and mark upon this tomb what might have been taken from it, as in the instance of that Louise de Savoye, who is represented in the Hôtel de Cluny, how many diversified graces should we behold emblazoned, while the vice opposed to each would be seen trampled upon!

> "Humilité contre orgueil,
> Libéralité contre avarice,
> Charité contre envie,
> Patience contre ire,
> Diligence contre paresse."

However, as I said, this is not the time for such observations; but the remembrance of what indicated the Catholicity of her mind necessarily recalls some moral prerogatives of an immense attraction, at which I would not pass by even here without a glance; for if ever to a human creature was given nobleness and latitude of heart, it was to her.

> "——— Low desires,
> Low thoughts had there no place; yet was her heart
> Lowly."

Though she had a country that she never forgot, it was not one nation only that she loved. And truly I think one cannot wonder at her contempt for the kind of narrow patriotism that would place such limit to affections; for, recurring to an hypothesis somewhat like that proposed on a different occasion, what would any one think of an inhabitant of some distant star confining all his regard to those who occupied one atom of its surface as constituting his own country, forgetful of the kindred spirits that inhabited the rest of its globe having been fashioned by their common Maker? She loved God too, as if He were alone in the universe, while she had pity on the human race as if there were no God,—two terms, as Madame Swetchine said, which are separated by an abyss, but which is bridged over by our Lord Jesus Christ, God and man. See, then, as Alain Chartier says, "comme saincte Catholique religion honnore souveraine divinité, et pourvoit au régime de povre humanité*."

Above all, this sweet voice calls upon us to consider the blessedness of receiving the kingdom of heaven as a little child, —that is, with submission to the authority of the Church,—of being ever ready to say like her, in the words of that brave young knight, Olivier de la Marche, "Heaven defend me from any disobedience à l'encontre des commandements et ordonnances de nostre sainte et salutaire mère et ressource, l'Eglise; et supplie à celuy qui est garde de tous bons et catholiques courages, qu'il me deffende et garde en ceste partie de toucher ou mettre chose qui soit contre l'estat de ma conscience†." Of course such docility involves the condition of an unchanging belief, and a deliverance from the need of continual researches with respect to it; but is that a great misfortune for any one excepting for a dreamer, and one who wishes to dream on for ever? Sarasin, who could think a little for himself I suppose, and whom no one can set down as being priest-ridden, considered it in his own praise when he could say, writing to Balzac, "Le temps ni l'étude ne m'ont point fait changer de sentiments; ils les ont fortifiés encore." So it was with Jane Mary. That which was good and venerable to her when a child, retained its authority over her mind still. She never, as Elia says of his cousin, "juggled or played tricks with her understanding." She had nothing to change or modify. Incapable from the first, like Rome itself, of yielding to the dictates of exaggeration—("for here," says Chateaubriand, speaking of Rome, "they exaggerate nothing, here they detest noise. I have found every where here a moderation of sentiments which our devout politicians might take example from")—she had at no later period to recede from any former positions. She had not to provide for any progress in regard to doctrinal religion— there was no such stuff in her thoughts. In regard to her theology, perhaps she might have incurred the contempt of those fine writers who speak of persons being incompetent "to

---

* Les Trois Vertus. † Chap. vi.

produce thought," as if thought in itself were any such inestimable production. She would not have been classed by them among the "persons who think." "But theirs is a dangerous profession," says a great author; "and from the time of the Aristophanes thought-shop to the great German establishment or thought-manufactory, whose productions have, unhappily, taken in part the place of the older and more serviceable commodities of Nuremberg toys and Berlin wool, it has been often harmful enough to mankind *." She did not give up, for as a Christian she never undertook, what they call the difficult and painful duty of inquiring and thinking for herself; being rewarded, not by what they term authoritative anodynes, but by the peace announced for men of good will; for, in brief, she was resolved with the Church, let who would philosophize, to light her candle at the old lamp; and she left behind her to be associated and united for ever in the minds of those who knew her, the worship of the ancient and true faith, its rites and ceremonies, as well as its spirit and its doctrine, with a devotion, if one may so speak, unalterable and undying to her own memory. The old Catholicism, with its old ways, that is what she respected, while esteeming at just their true value new ways of thinking in matters of religion. Her Catholicity, you might say, consisted in following our Lord and His blessed mother. She sat at the well of the Samaritan, mounted Calvary, rested on Tabor, or adored at the foot of the cross. To her the same hours brought back the same thoughts, and labours, and cares. Her life was the same continued succession as witnessed in others belonging to the olden time, of prayer, reading, work, interrupted by the necessities of life, and the indispensable claims of her own position in society. What Fleury says of the early Christians was strictly true of her. "She regarded every thing as subordinate to religion. Her profession was to be a Christian purely and simply. Had there been occasion for such an interrogatory, her reply would have been, like theirs, 'I am a Christian †.'" She knew, and every one intimate with her knew, that she wished for others quite as

---

* Ruskin, Mod. Paint. v. 104.
† Mœurs des Chrétiens.

much as for herself only one thing—the one thing necessary. Her race, short as it proved, was run "non quasi in incertum." She had no doubts in her own mind, no uncertainty, no misgivings, no discouragement. She had in her possession, and she felt that she had, the priceless pearl. She seemed to live in the atmosphere of the beatitudes of the Gospel. She strictly verified, in fine, the remark of a deep observer, that the Christian is the only person who can, without inconsistency, love life and desire death, which seems the solution of the problem of the sovereign good that Plato sought for. Her life, in its ordinary routine of social and domestic duties, was, through her pure intention, the service of the Redeemer—and she could love it; her death the union with Him for ever, and we at least may reasonably believe that she received from it her crown.

You have as yet heard nothing of the mere woman, and yet we can hardly conclude this walk with more appropriate words than those of Proteus,—

"How will you dote on her with more advice,
That thus without advice begin to love her!"

CHAPTER IV.

N entering St. John's Chapel for our fourth visit, one feels, as one's thoughts take a direction less simple than when we first conceived the idea of recording them, that it is an occasion for defending what at the commencement one little thought of,—namely, the literary character of our enterprise, which might now seem exposed to that charge of monotony which one of the most brilliant and profound of modern French writers believes to have himself incurred, though in a work which has excited an immense, and indeed a European interest, which one may affirm without hesitation is destined to immortality. When one

has to speak of the piety of a Christian in any age of the world, it is difficult to feel perfectly assured that one has succeeded in avoiding this inconvenience, for such a life must of course be in all cases pretty similar. It is still the same old principle, the same old motives, the same old struggle; always prayer and thoughtfulness, and generous actions to befriend others, and donations to the churches, and self-sacrifice, and amidst all great patience. In this instance, as Léon Aubineau observes in his Life of the Marchioness Le Bouteiller, " c'était la commune vie Chrétienne, simple, exacte, et heureuse." Nevertheless, as the former writer observes, all these graces, of which there must be made such frequent mention during the course of these visits, are at some epochs sufficiently rare in the common walks of the world, while certainly they appear less often than one might wish before the ordinary tribunal of biography. Moreover, while with regard to the essentials of piety a person so disposed must resemble in a general way every one else who is devout, there will be always certain characteristic marks, and delicate shades of feature, which belong peculiarly to an individual, so as to render each true portrait distinguishable from every other; for, as Sir Thomas Brown says, "there was never any thing so like another as in all points to concur; there will ever some reserved difference slip in to prevent the identity, without which two several things would not be alike, but the same, which is impossible." And sooth to say, though you appear inclined to doubt it, all nature is in part our birthright. Your Southern happening besides, perhaps, to have been not overgiven to the study of analogies, may wish naturally enough through his own national impressions to subject all souls and bodies to one unvarying type; but we of the North, as some one says, even without having made such studies, prefer that primitive element, which Christianity, at least in the North, substituted in the human individuality.

We are all more or less familiar with pictures like those of Raphael or Fra Angelico of fair and holy women; but how shall my rude art be ever able to transmit an idea of the model as representing piety that has to be copied now? The pencil of Saint-Simon in a few gracious lines could have drawn her entire. As Elia says, "I must limp after in my poor borrowed manner as the fates have given me power."

Perhaps, then, it would be well to say in the beginning that the first foundation or ground tone, as it were, of this character, consisted in a kind of childlike disposition of innocence, which, as Fontenelle, speaking of the botanist Blondin, says, "comprises already a part of what religion requires," and she, like him, "had the happiness to join to it the rest." It was a disposition which argued the nearest conformity to the image of God to which quoad nature our mortality can ever attain under the ordinary circumstances and conditions of common life, showing that the human soul is still a mirror, wherein, however broken, may be seen darkly the image of the mind of God. Indeed, as Sir Thomas Brown says, generally, "he that understands not thus much hath not his introduction or first lesson, and is yet to begin the alphabet of man." But a great contemporary remarks besides, "that it is only by studying the soul that men can discern even the meaning of the attributes ascribed to God, as when, for example, being told that God is love, we desire to know what is love. Out of one such heart you may learn that which revelation does not and cannot tell you; for all the sounds and words ever uttered, all the revelations of cloud or flame or crystal, are utterly powerless; they cannot tell you in the smallest point what love means, or what justice means—only the broken mirror can. The revelation proclaiming Him to be just cannot teach you what justice is. You have still to study the human heart and conscience to see what is the image of God. No other book than that to learn it in will you ever find; for without it there is nothing that can be understood, no frankincensed manuscript, nothing sacred, nothing hieroglyphic, nor cuneiform; papyrus and pyramid are alike silent on this matter; nothing in the clouds above, nor in the earth beneath. That flesh-bound volume is the only revelation for such a purpose, that is, that was, or that can be; and in that is the image of God painted. The not knowing which fact," he adds, "and the consequent caring for the universe only, and for man not at all, is the error of modern science*."

* Ruskin, M. P. v. 202.

Her piety then, which was a thing of thoughts and deeds rather than words, a thing of love and justice and hope, may be said to have consisted mainly in the keeping of this broken mirror as clean as since the fall it is possible to be kept; and in preserving it by supernatural means from the defilement which renders faint or illegible the original writing. It consisted also in a filial love for God, and for all that immediately related to Him,—a sort of angelic reverence, and affection, and wonder, and admiration for the heavenly, as well as for what is generous and heroic amongst men.

> "It was the innocence of a child,
> And an entire simplicity of mind,
> A thing most sacred in the eye of heaven."

"There was nothing," as Elia would say, "to stagger you, nothing to make you mistrust, no suspicion of alloy, no dross or dreg of the worldly or ambitious spirit." As we read of some one else, "what above all moved her was to think of the adorable perfections of God *." With all her transports as a mother, it was still her primal joy to speak of the divine perfections, and to hear of them. The tone of her conversation with intimate friends, in respect to such topics, had a striking resemblance to that of Saint-Louis, and was calculated, on rare occasions, to elicit pretty much the same kind of saucy replies as those of the young Sire de Joinville, which she used always to meet with a similar sweetness and tender expostulation. But every day she seemed to have said to herself, like the holy king, "Ad te levavi animam meam," which words, as Joinville relates, being those with which the mass commenced on the day of his coronation, he used them frequently as expressive of his own condition; and one may truly apply to her the words of his biographer, "eut en Dieu moult grant fiance dès son enfance, et jusques à la mort." Like him too she used to invoke the prayers of certain saints in an especial manner, for all which devotion, one may truly add, was she protected by God, quant à son âme. With all her thoroughly human and affectionate, instinctive, though at the same time strictly logical, deductions from the doctrine of

---

* Vie de Demlle. Pignior, &c.

the Incarnation, of which we shall have the details presently presented, no one could have ever had a more profound or exalted sense of the awful power and overwhelming majesty of God. As we read of Madame Romanet, " the majesty of the Creator was for her an object of fear and of love *." Her wisdom, indeed, as we shall remark on a future occasion, began with fearing Him as the Creator, but she rejoiced while awe-struck to think of his power. She never, it is true, spoke of God under the denomination of the Almighty; but when she observed instances of his omnipotence, when she heard thunder, or beheld any great manifestation of his sovereignty, her eyes would glisten, and breaking out into ejaculatory expressions of admiration, she used to exult as if it were her own triumph. Her predominant desire was to please God: she had a taste for justice and for truth; she never sought herself under pretence of serving God; she never wanted people to be occupied about herself. You could trace in her piety nothing selfish, no morbid brooding over the state of her own mind, no reference to her own spiritual progress. What you detected was a generous abandonment of all that belonged to her own individual being—it was a notion of religion in accordance with that maxim of St. John Chrysostom, " that alms are more efficacious to efface sins than virginity and fasts and vigils and all mortifications, for the reason that while the latter are only useful to those who practise them, alms conduce to the welfare of others †." When she applied therefore to the ministry of those to whom authority was given, it was not, judging from her conduct elsewhere, to weary them with a detail of personal scruples and narratives about herself, but simply through obedience and humility, emanating from a faith and a charity exalted to a degree of perfection such as they had not probably been every day in the habit of witnessing in those who had recourse to their hallowed ministry.

Whenever you heard sung, or read any of the Psalms, the verses that struck you most seemed to have been written for the very purpose of furnishing a kind of exposition of her individual mind. Most remarkable, most singular, most phenomenal was

* Vie de Demlle. Pignior, femme de Claude Romanet.
† Hom. 62 in Ep. ad Titum.

this conformity. All her thoughts seemed based on the ruling motive to do the will of God, and that, too, more from the thought of its being His will, than from being impressed each hour, as if with hearing for the first time, " Qui facit voluntatem Patris mei qui in cœlis est, ipse intrabit in regnum cœlorum." As Agnes de Harcourt describes Isabella the sister of St. Louis, "mirouer d'innocence tous ses désirs et toute l'intention et tous ses labeurs si furent de planter vertus en soy et en autruy." The strict truth is, that for every act she ever performed, and it may be believed for every word she ever uttered, there was at the bottom in operation the delicate spring of a pious and holy and almost seraphic motive. Now this is no page of a romance, remember. What use would it be to draw a faultless picture merely with the intention of doing so? But naturally one feels anxious, however unworthy, to transmit a knowledge of facts which strike one, and which always did strike one as being, however common, something that surpassed all one's conceptions, something for which there is not a name. She never seemed to be so thoroughly content as when she was in the act of adoring Jesus Christ—there is the naked truth— and even at sitting down to table with a sweet smile for every one present, one used to remark latterly that she always audibly pronounced his sacred name in signing herself, with a look that no artist could ever catch, though peerless in his power. Employing the language of a great French author, I would say that "in her heart she kept the individual God—the God made man—the God invoked by children without rejecting the universal God who regenerates humanity in mass by necessary trials. There is no want of men in this age," he continues, "with great hearts, who seem to admit for use only this latter aspect of God; this inexorable universalism which assimilates Providence to a fatal law of nature, to a vast system of wheels, intelligent if you will, but before which individuals are annihilated under an incomprehensible chariot which mows and crushes for a distant and the living generation, without there springing up for each any immortal destiny." She was more happy than these men, though even these belong to those who hope. She was more religious: she believed as firmly in the general ends of humanity, but she believed also in the particular destiny of each soul. She did not immolate to the vast presentiments which she nourished either the continuous order of tradition, or the moral belief of ages, the intimate and permanent relation of the creature to the Creator, or the humility, the grace, and prayer which constitute those antique elements from which rationalism seeks to wean the adult humanity. Her supreme reason was no other but the eternal Logos, the Word of John, once incarnate and dwelling perpetually amongst men. She did not conceive any transformations of humanity however adult, unless within the domain of the heritage of Christ, in the boundless fields that have been purchased and named by his blood, always in view of the Cross, and at the foot of that unfathomable mystery.

Thus solid, philosophical even we might say if it were in keeping to use a term that never escaped her unpretending lips, was the piety of this woman of faith. Inclined to all the exact and minute observances of devotion, she was able, without any apparent exercise of theological skill, to avoid all the rocks and shallows on which an uninformed piety is apt to suffer wreck, and to keep ever in the deep pure waters that waft straight to heaven. She never veered, never oscillated, never deviated, but kept in the direct course of aiming at conformity in life with our divine model, submitting her will to justice and her heart to charity. If she was ever drawn out by some necessity to allude to morals as the fruit of faith, it was easy to discern that she was capable of teaching them by her discourse as well as by her example. But in general, in regard to piety and its consequences, there was in her a great reserve of language. Hers was what the poet speaks of,

> "—————————— The instinct of repose,—
> The longing for confirm'd tranquillity
> Inward and outward—humble yet sublime;
> The life where hope and memory are as one,
> Earth quiet and unchanged; the human soul
> Consistent in self-rule, and heaven reveal'd
> To meditation in that quietness!"

Some months after her death a holy priest gave this testimony, saying in his letter, " I never came near her without being made happier and better, and never left her without being more and more convinced of her wonderful virtue, and her simple, childlike, yet intimate union with God."

It is true, her prayers to be delivered from ever seeing the evil one were sometimes offered with an ejaculatory fervour that might be qualified as Dantesque, or, as some in their wisdom would now say, fit for the nursery; but, as Elia remarks, however such terrors may under different forms reproduce themselves in the brain of superstition, they were there before. The forms are transcripts, types,—the archetypes are in us, and eternal. These fears are of old standing; they date beyond body,—or, without the body, they would have been the same. Hers was a fear purely spiritual, and, as the same author adds, that this fear should be strong in proportion as it is objectless upon earth, and that it should predominate in the period of sinless infancy, are difficulties, the solution of which might afford some insight into a very mysterious land. If, however, in her mind there was, as Bossuet said of Rancé, " a great fear of the awful judgments of God," (and·one is obliged in conscience to acknowledge that there was; it would be rash indeed to misrepresent any trait that entered into such a character; I am told that she frequently shed tears when she thought of the just judgments of God, and of the place,—

ὅπου τὸ χαίρειν μηδαμοῦ νομίζεται [*],—

and that she feared for herself while she endeavoured to conceal this fear from others,) yet it was evident also that love and confidence survived it, or rather, that these constituted the foundation of that mental state which had been granted to her. Excepting from a remembrance of what she occasionally let fall from her lips, you might have thought that the fear of punishment never passed through her mind, and that, like the woman of whom Joinville tells us, she did not even contemplate any personal advantage from her piety. Neither fear nor hope seemed to constitute its ruling power; she never, at least, seemed to think that she was heaping up a stock of precious works and personal merits for the exclusive advantage of her-

[*] Æsch. Eumen.

self to send before her to the other world, according to the unguarded and rather disagreeable phraseology, (for it is, perhaps, in application to an individual, more a fault of language that one alludes to than of general notions,) of certain grave people not overburdened with thought, or gifted with a sense of the decorum of style; but all she did was obviously the result of faith and affection and piety wholly spontaneous and perfectly disinterested. She seemed to be actuated irresistibly, though unconsciously, by the intense tenderness of a perfect love. To speak with a rigorous regard to truth, her love for God was something wonderful to contemplate, most beautiful to witness; it was exactly like that of an affectionate child for its human parent; while her love for the blessed Virgin, as we shall presently remark, was what one might call passionate. If any thing occurred in the course of the day to cause her pleasure or to console other people, she used always to say, and often, I think, with tears in her eyes, "How good is God!" It was exactly the same when visited with afflictions. She had so profound a love and reverence for Him, that whatever came from His hand, though it were death itself, and she repeatedly received that gift in the persons of others whom she loved more than herself, seemed to her as something gracious though adorable,—something that, however terrible to nature, inspired her with a kind of mystic and even sensible contentment. In trials and difficulties she had always the same confidence, saying, "God will support us." When the government of her household devolved upon her after her mother's death,—and to a person so inexperienced and so framed that was no light burden,—it was the same cry, "God will direct us. Pray to the blessed Virgin to pray for us." Her words were often literally those of Menander,—" No one has care of us but God alone,"—

——————— οὐκ ἄρα
Ἡμῶν ἐφρόντισέν τις, ἢ μόνος θεός.

In a word, she had fixed her choice with Mary on the better part. "There is but one thing necessary," says Lacordaire, "and Mary had chosen that better part which was never to be taken from her. What was that better part? It was a greater love of our Lord, merited by a greater return of love. Martha served, Mary listened and contemplated; Martha stood, Mary sat at the feet of the Saviour; Martha complained, Mary was silent."

Allusion has already been made to her love of the blessed Virgin as the mother of Christ. We must not be content with an indirect notice of what constituted a very salient feature in the character we are recalling.

To speak of her piety in this respect, allied as it was to her intimate familiarity with all that related to our Lord,—with the history of His life and passion,—and associated as it ever was with a deep and solid knowledge of the whole scheme of the Christian religion, would almost require a volume by itself; or rather, I should say, a different pen from mine. Her bosom passion was a love for the blessed Virgin. She seemed to dwell in Galilee, where our Lord after His resurrection was to be found. You can easily understand, therefore, how each recurring festival of Mary must be associated, in the minds of those who knew her, with the memory of one who seemed to be her companion rather than the lowly handmaiden who daily and hourly besought her prayers. As long as life below is granted to them, those who knew her can never hear that name of blessed Mary, or see that image which represents her, without this other remembrance and this other image being recalled and placed before it, and lost, as it were, in one effulgence of love and glory. There was something so genuine, yet so thoroughly human in her love for the blessed Virgin, as indeed in all her high spiritual devotions, not the less supernatural for containing such an element,—that one could not avoid experiencing, whenever one thought of it, a sensation of amazement which sought to remain hidden in the silent depths of one's heart. It was not a pious part learned by rote from a book, and practised in a spirit of thoughtless routine; it was not a personal and logical and theological deduction from the fact to which Christianity owes its origin, backed by patristic and scholastic and infallible authority; it was not a scientific development of a dogmatic decision respecting a divine fiat, still less a mere traditional inheritance, of which the origin and meaning and use are nearly unknown. It was a spontaneous sentiment; it was, as it were, the natural result of a connexion by blood, just as if she had really been her relation, had known her personally, and had been in habits of living with her, and of following her about every where, which, in a certain way, by means of the annual festivals, she actually did. Others might perform it with more pretension, but she did it, as an old writer says, "more natural." The beads in commemoration of the fifteen mysteries of the Mother of God were her daily pastime. She was admitted into many confraternities erected in her honour, and she induced others to belong to them. She repeated continually the Memorare, and other prayers of such sodalities, and by every event recorded of that blessed life, she seemed as much personally affected as if each time she had been herself present, with a consciousness of the mystery that was involved in it. The reasonableness of this affection, too, was always present to her mind, and an instance has been given elsewhere without naming her, where it is related how some one, more officious than wise, on one occasion expressed fears lest this devotion of hers should interfere with her confidence in the atonement, and she replied to him, with a smile too sweet to be interpreted as a reproach, "As if I did not know that it is to Christ we owe all!" With the same kind of natural affection, too, she used to invoke the prayers of all God's friends. She never lay down to rest without her lips uttering the names of Matthew, Mark, Luke, and John; and to many saints, as to her patron St. Jane, to the Apostle of Ireland, and to St. Thomas of Canterbury, to whose prayers she ascribed the recovery of a son still left to her, after he had received the last sacraments, did she ever show herself grateful and devout.

But we must hasten on, though I would crave of you your leave, first to give a reply here, in haste, to an objection which has been urged against what has been said elsewhere, with her approval, respecting the consequences of this devotion, as especially directed to the mother of our Lord. For now, methinks, already I hear some critic who is resolved on putting us in a desperate assurance that we cannot stand before him, expressing himself, to use the words of Andrew Marvel, as a synodical individuum speaking of himself, plurali majestatico, as Coleridge says; and saying, "We must profess our inability to understand how the worship of the Virgin can specially conduce to the blissful state of mind that our author has the project of describing." This remark was made in reference to what was said to be requisite for the attainment of serenity, and here one may anticipate a similiar criticism on another score. Well, we must stand to both our propositions; but as I would decline the indignity of having to meet a charge in such a place as this on religious grounds, which would seem a kind of insult offered to her gentle memory, let me say with regard to the former, in which she was not concerned more than by yielding an example to prove the truth of the proposition, that there was nothing strained or psychologically erroneous in proceeding on the principle, that devotion to the blessed Virgin constitutes an element of, what she ever loved and possessed, serenity. Yes, no question, for who does not perceive that to enjoy the sort of happy turn of mind that was there advocated, and which the mere remembrance of Jane Mary can reproduce, one must respect as well as love women? not reverencing them through a vague sentiment, like our German forefathers, but venerating them on a sure foundation of absolute truth. To enjoy this blessed state of mind, you must have within you, as a vital element, the loftiest as well as the most tender and human sentiment of womanly excellence. For that sole reason then, you must, if you please to express it so, worship the Virgin as being the second Eve who, through God's mercy, has done more than reinstate woman in her original character, since she already presents her as gloriously transfigured.

But to return from this digression, if it can be called so. It is one thing to read in books a description of graces, or a recommendation to acquire them; it is another to see them possessed and exercised. The life of which we are attempting to give an account might be qualified as having been a life of prayer. Prayer was her daily bread—her joy and her serenity. On journeys, at home in the house, walking in the fields, or sitting in the garden in front of the fountain, even to within the last three minutes of her life on earth, her thoughts were expressed in prayer. In this occupation, which never interfered with other duties, she seemed to place her chief delight, though, to use the words of Bishop Fisher, speaking of the mother of

King Henry VII., "as for meditation, she had divers bokes in Frensbe wherewith she wolde occupye herself, when she was weary of prayer." "Whenever she had any time for herself," writes some one dear to her, "it was always spent in prayer; even when she was out, whether alone or with her children, she would take out her prayer book or her rosary. When first starting on a journey, she used always to say a De Profundis for the repose of the souls of the dead." The greatest part of the journey was beguiled by prayer, intermingled with propitiatory smiles to gain the indulgence of those wishing her to talk nonsense; and whenever any thing occurred to make her feel uneasy or anxious, she would spend the interval on her knees. A recent and most eloquent author in casting a look of sublime regret over the ruins of the monasteries in modern times, and nobly disdaining even to allude to the sophistry that now seeks to deny the value of what he prizes, seems to have had his attention particularly excited by the fact that, in their removal, a certain organized power of prayer and supplication to God, in behalf of all of us, had been taken away from the world. Spontaneously, a similar impression was produced on the mind of those who knew Jane Mary, when they heard of her being no longer in the midst of them. It was as if the laus perennis had been abolished, as if an institution had perished, as if there was to be no more choir kept under the common domestic roof; nay, it would have been pardonable if their first impression almost had been, that there was to be no longer a struggle between moral liberty and the servitude of the flesh, no more continued effort of a will, consecrated under a female form, to the pursuit and conquest of Christian virtue. The Prie-Dieu is vacant—the books that you hardly venture now to touch are closed. The chaplet, which it is impossible now not to venerate as a holy relic, is laid aside. Go where you will to find the same service, I'll make no provision to satisfy the self-love of any one, who is there left to pray just like her—to meditate just like her—to recall, just like her, the mysteries of Jesus and of Mary? It is as if a power, constituted for the express purpose of offering most innocent and pure and holy prayer on behalf of the whole world, had been suddenly overthrown. Now, be it declared solemnly, that this thought is not the premeditated exaggeration of rhetoric, but the first and natural suggestion of those who are wholly determined in their judgment, and as to their very language, by what they have with their own senses seen and heard.

But it is the churches that recall her image, intently and quietly at prayer. Pass the portal. In England, or on the Continent, you knew the very spot where she would have knelt. It was there, in some retired corner near the blessed Virgin's altar. The Duc de Laval Montmorency, writing to Mme. Récamier, says, in allusion to the late pious Duc Mathieu, " We enter on the holy week, which naturally brings to our recollection that angelic friend whose example we should always do so well to follow;" so it is with her memory associated with all the festivals in the ecclesiastical year. At mass, at vespers, at the procession, at the sermon, impossible for those who knew her to assist, without having her now before their eyes. The holy rites of our religion seem, if one may be allowed to say so without offence, to be now a part of her bequest to her survivors—a dying legacy, and no one can think her absent while they are being celebrated. In church, always grave and imperturbable, of late years her tears used to fall continually. In hearing sermons, it was not a literary pleasure that she sought, though after hearing Father Faber she used to return speaking rapturously about the beauty of his thoughts, and the noble character of mind which his language indicated. But what she expected and obtained from every preacher, was simply and purely instruction and edification, both of which she had the secret of extracting from the rudest discourse, which had left others indifferent, if not contemptuous. Whenever, too, in a sermon, any allusion was made to the sufferings of our Lord, or of our blessed Lady, or of the poor, or of the faithful departed, she used to cry so much that she even affected those strangers who were near her. During her last years she used to say, that at the Benediction she always felt as if her two departed sons were close to her in presence of the blessed sacrament; their gentle souls seemed to hover about her with their airy wings, and to hear their mother's lamentation. Does not this remind one of that charming legend of the abbey of St. Maurice, which tells of the mother weeping for her son, and of her being informed in a vision that she should ever afterwards, as long as she lived, hear his voice in the choir at matins; and of her finding it realized, during the rest of her life assisting at the office, and hearing his beloved voice mingling with the sweet and holy harmony of the liturgical chant, which vocem infantuli seemed to the historian who has last related the anecdote as being, of all the melodies that the human ear can catch, the purest and dearest and most near to heaven*? But to continue. As we read of Mme. de Louvencourt, from her earliest years Jane Mary was never known to omit assisting at vespers and the Benediction. After mass she would always remain about half an hour, being, in fact, the last person to leave; and before mass she would never open any letters, lest the contents might distract her attention. During her last summer, when she resided close to this church, every evening she used to remain in it for hours praying before the blessed sacrament; and she used to light tapers constantly as offerings, before the image of our Lady, in testimony of love for her. Many lamps elsewhere she kept burning, and furnished what was needful for their perpetual maintenance. Whenever there was a procession of the blessed sacrament she used to be greatly affected; and after her boy's death, she used to say that on those occasions also little John seemed to be at her side, either following it or seeing it pass round. But in her happiest, gayest years there was the same overflowing of the heart. Who could describe her rapturous devotion when assisting at the night office in the church of Notre Dame des Victoires at Paris? While residing in that capital she never once missed the evening office there, giving up for it every thing else, meekly submitting to a little raillery from age at her late return, and assisting at it with a joy and effusion of soul indescribable; and even afterwards in England, when any of her friends, even though many were Protestants, went to Paris, she used slily to extort a promise from them to go to that church to pray for her, she would say, and for themselves; thinking it a great triumph when she had succeeded in suspending a medal of the blessed Virgin round their necks, which many thus invested did engage to wear, and even pledging themselves to say an "Our Father," and even a "Hail, Mary!"

* Montalembert, Les Moines d'Occident, ii. 305.

every day for their own spiritual good. In later years there were days at Kensington, when, like St. Elizabeth, she used to steal out from her house and secretly repair to some church or oratory, in order to adore God in the blessed sacrament; taking occasion by the way to speak to the poor women who were working for the market in suburban gardens, and to relieve their distress. She felt, alas! obliged at times to recur to secrecy, in order to visit churches and to pray. She feared to appear too devout by doing so! With all her active attention to other duties, as we shall observe later, she found time to pass hours every day in prayer, and each morning her reverence at mass was as great as on the days she went to communion. At the elevation she used to be all in tears; and latterly her different domestic anniversaries used to be announced by her weeping in the church more than after her accustomed wont. Similarly, though we have already noticed it, she listened to sermons as to the voice of God. In short, as the Père Ventura says of another Christian woman, "in public or in private, in church or at home, in foreign lands or in her own country, without affectation and in perfect simplicity, she accomplished in all liberty her duties of religion at the proper times *." Nor was it only in celebrated sanctuaries that she felt the influence of this fervent devotion. A few evenings before her death, on visiting Dover, she came out of the chapel there in a sort of devout ecstasy, so as even to excite the silent attention of those who knew her best. "Did you ever hear," she asked, "the rosary so well said as by those brave soldiers of the 47th? How I wish that a French regiment were to witness it! No puny infidels, these gallant Irishmen. I like to see manly devotion;" and then she asked, "Did you mark their reverence? They held themselves like so many monks; they never raised their eyes!" But witness all this in its highest strain. 'Tis evening coming. Whither hastens she? It is, like Silvia of Verona, to the cell where she "intends holy confession,"—for the morrow is a Sunday, or some festival. On ordinary days she would only go to communion by stealth, lest the servants should know it — through humility she sought to conceal it

* La Femme Chrétienne, ou la Vie de Bruni.

from them. In general breakfasting, though in the simplest manner, late, she used to have brought to her a small piece of toast, after she was risen, at an early hour. The grave difficulty then on those days was to get rid of this morsel without her sly maid knowing how. So a certain little one used to be called in, who often wondered why she was asked to eat it; nor was it till after her death that the secret of this truly childlike policy of her humble mind was disclosed. But nothing could surpass her reverence for the great mystery. She wished even that the fleshly organ that received it might be sanctified. When any one in conversation spoke of the blessed sacrament, she used to close her eyes and bow down her head. You may judge of her feelings when she approached the altar. These could be wholly concealed from no one; and I knew one marble-breasted person who for some years latterly used to shrink back from contact with her gown as she advanced for communion. I merely mention the fact, to show how those who knew her best held her as a thing enskied and sainted. The motive for the act, such poor creatures are we, being a base fear of imbibing the contagion of her sweet, unoffending, heavenly sanctity, which had no tongue to vex you, nor even a look to throw a strange regard upon you; for some men fear vilely what they should wisely and generously wish for most.

But the Sunday, or festival, is arrived, and "far off its coming shows." Let us mark her in these bright visitations. Wordsworth speaks of that heavenly lustre,—

> "Which makes the Sunday lovely in the sight
> Of blessed angels, pitying human cares."

With that light she seemed then encompassed. Her Sunday morn with rosy steps in the eastern clime advancing was indeed joyful. Her steps, her haste, her countenance, the sound of her voice seemed to make every one around her happy; and from the first dawn till night, for the whole house, it was a day of jubilation. After communion at an early hour, she never, as we already said, missed high mass; nor would any interruption detain her from vespers unless it was absolutely impossible for her to leave the house. Throughout the entire day it used to be observed that she was full of joyfulness. The church offices were antedated too by another ingenious artifice of her child-like piety; for on these days, as well as on all great festivals, she used to be caught slily putting on the different clocks in the rooms so that they should be five or six minutes in advance of the true time, lest any one of the household should arrive in the church after the mass or other office had commenced. She used often to return from church in a kind of ecstasy, and this was the case on the last Sunday she spent on earth, when the simple music of a country church, and the singing of some children, and the piety of the same soldiers just before spoken of, who formed a large part of the congregation, affected her to tears. Her Sundays were, in external things, like those of other people. She would have no one give evidence of his pride by seeking to be unlike those who are well dressed and smart for the occasion; while, as I said, from the first streak of day there was a supernatural joy about her that was almost irresistibly communicated to every one who approached her: but all festivals she sanctified, never being content on any holy day with merely hearing one mass, or without assisting at "evening song," and Benediction. Her very language too, respecting such things, was somewhat remarkable; it was popular in regard to the kind of practical importance affecting her domestic arrangements, which she attached to them; for she would distinguish days of the week, not as at some modern courts, where even Christmas day is chronicled as the 25th of December; but as distinguished in the old calendar, and under the title of the day or eve of some saint, as the artisan poet Jasmin commemorates the Veille de St. Joseph. She was as good as an almanack for those red-letter days, and could tell you what saint's day falls on next week, and what the week after. But indeed, in this respect also, her mind was singularly mediæval; for she would have liked to hear of no markets being opened on any day in London, "before the hour of Prime rung at St. Paul's," as is related in the White Book, and of no traffic "in another part" before mass has been celebrated at the chapel on the bridge, or at the church of St. Martin; and of the rate of wages being regulated by the epochs of the year designated as the days between the Feasts of St. Michael and St. Martin, the Purification and Easter. Great was her ambition, at each recurrence of a festival, to have chapels and altars decorated in its honour, for which purpose she used to send tapers and costly flowers; and when her own garden did not yield the latter in sufficient abundance she would hire them from nursery grounds in the neighbourhood, to which she would repair in person, causing pleasure to others who were glad to see her make even this kind of excursion, which was more in accordance with their own idea of amusement. Oh! who could describe her sweet mystic, and yet most human and communicative joy, on the festivals of our Lord, or blessed Lady, or of the Apostles and Saints? Truly it was she, above most persons on this earth, who seemed as the poet says,

"Content upon each holy annual feast,
Remember'd half the year and hoped the rest."

The fête days of her children too were great days for her; and even after their death, without having ever heard of the German poet who was caught decorating with flowers the bust of Shakspeare on St. William's day, she used to celebrate the festivals of St. Thomas the Apostle, and of St. John the Evangelist, with an effusion of resigned piety which may be conceived rather than expressed; but, in fact, all these days used to form epochs in her life, to each of which she would sometimes recur many years after, recalling all the particular circumstances under which each was passed. Her Easter days, and her Christmas nights, are things to be passed over in silence as quite surpassing our power of description. With regard to the latter it will be sufficient to cite a few words from the life of a French lady, the daughter of the Viscomte de Galard, as they simply relate what was the case with respect to herself. "She would have felt it," says her biographer, "as a great privation, during her tour in Italy, if she could not have gone to communion at the midnight mass, according to the privation required by the discipline of the Italian churches. Being accustomed to the French and more ancient usage, in this respect, she was permitted to follow it every where in her private oratory [*]."

It seems hardly necessary to add in concluding these humble details, for which I am aware many apologies should be offered,

---

[*] Vie de Victorine de Galard Terranbe.

that her devotion to the churches was characterized by the liberality of her offerings, and by her veneration for the priesthood, which disposition led her to furnish supplies to some who had a wish, but wanted means to enter into that state, and to provide for their scholastic course; but yet as indicative of her individual character there are a few things connected with these points that might be related; for "the sweet ornaments that once had decked her person" she used to give to adorn the images of our Lady. The churches of Paris and of Boulogne, to be silent as to those of our own country, have still to show within their treasures for production upon great occasions, some objects of no little value that were her gift. She used to present sacred vessels, candlesticks, lamps, crowns, lustres, and curtains, wherever she observed a deficiency; and there are still living in distant regions of the world, prelates and archbishops, whose mitres and whose emerald rings might serve to bring back her memory. But it will be more agreeable to dwell for a moment upon the affection and respect with which she always treated priests. "Show him kindness," she used to say of many. "He is a good Priest:" she could conceive no eulogy which exceeded that. In fact, she used to venerate such men, and would in secret pour a little water on her hands, after she had shaken hands with them, because, she whispered afterwards to others, it was not respectful to handle any thing, after having touched those hands which daily touch our blessed Lord himself. On one occasion, falling on her knees to have the blessing of a holy missionary priest of great simplicity, the old man insisted on going on his own knees to ask hers in return, and so there they were both kneeling opposite to each other, as she used to relate afterwards, in arch moments, laughing very heartily at this droll kind of leave-taking.

Moreover her piety, grounded as we have seen on the most solid principles, was not above taking the form of attention to the minor and ordinary resources, of which the holy ever seek to avail themselves. She practised in this respect the manners of the early Christians; for Fleury shows, as Gibbon discovered too, that like her, "on the least occasion they used to make the sign of the cross as an abridged blessing, when going out, or returning, or rising, or lying down to rest, or dressing, or drinking, or eating, or bathing, and, in brief, whenever they commenced any thing *." Jane Mary would always, when at home, say the Angelus on her knees. She would have every one sit down at table and rise from it as a Christian, remembering the giver and pronouncing distinctly the sacred name of Jesus. But then what would have pleased Elia, when he was desiring to be "a friend to graces, both theoretically and practically,", the object of her thanks in general was "sustenance, not relishes; daily bread, not delicacies; the means of life, and not the means of pampering the carcass. Her grace, therefore, never seemed to involve any thing awkward and unseasonable;" for graces, as he says, are "the sweet preluding strains to the banquets of angels and children;" like Margaret, Countess of Richmond, "her sober temperance in metes and drynkes was known to all them that were conversant with her." Days of abstinence she kept inviolably, though when the health or strength of others required it, she was as firm to insist upon indulgence, not enduring to hear of their refusal. It would be the strict truth to affirm, that no one could have ever caught her forgetting the Friday, as when the bourgeois de Paris surprised even Joinville in the act, when on being reminded of it by the young man, he threw both meat and plate on the ground behind him, saying that he had not thought of it, and that it was not his custom to neglect fasts, that the Pope's legate used even to remonstrate with him sometimes, saying that he was not strong enough, but, nevertheless, that even though in prison he would not refrain from fasting on Fridays. Then, again, in every room of the house she would place some object of devotion, and the Protestant guest has been known to declare, with youthful earnestness, that he felt quite pleased at seeing what surrounded him as he lay in bed. Béranger, at twelve years of age, was struck down in a thunderstorm at the threshold of his aunt's house; on recovering speech, his first words to his aunt were, "Eh bien! à quoi sert donc ton eau bénite?" for he had seen the house as usual sprinkled with it at the beginning of the storm; and apparently the preservation of his life on that occasion did not seem to him a motive either for

* Mœurs des Chrétiens.

confidence in the future, or for gratitude for the past. Be that as it may, I fear our moral philosophers,—who are never easy unless when seeking to remove those wise prejudices, if they are to be so called to do them pleasure, with which nature has guarded our innocence, as with impassable barriers, against the commission of crimes,—would take great scandal were I to relate instances of such pious usages as are brought back to memory in presence of this tomb; though I am aware that, if it were worth while, one might discover on Jane Mary's side even some men of science, like M. Ozanam for instance, of whom Fontenelle said in presence of the Academy, that "his piety was not only solid, it was tender, and did not disdain certain little things which are less usually practised by men than by women, and still less for the uses of mathematicians who might regard ordinary men as so many women*." But let us observe the particular model which we are copying. Every night she would sprinkle the rooms with holy water; and whenever she removed to a different house, she observed this usage in regard to each chamber and corner. Her pious practices too, in general, were for all times; for, as Agnes de Harcourt says of Isabella, the sister of St. Louis, " Elle estoit de moult tendre conscience et de moult bonne. Moult volontiers se confessoit, et souvent aussi et moult devotement." What Fontenelle notices in his eulogium on Boerhaave was observable in her. She always bowed when she heard pronounced the sacred name. Having permission to have mass celebrated in her private oratory, she paid the strictest attention to ward off the possibility of any inconvenience or neglect, bordering on what she would have considered profanation. Thus, if the person who had charge of the vestments, or other matters relative to the altar, ever came into her room while holding them, though it were only the little bell, she would not allow them to remain an instant, saying that she was unworthy of such things being left there. When travelling she always carried with her a reliquary containing a particle of the wood of the cross; for relics were wound up with her belief in the credibility of tradition, which she would express in words like those of the young

* Œuvres, tom. v. 516.

Prince to Buckingham, who, when a popular tradition was in question, answered,—

> "But say, my Lord, it were not register'd :
> Methinks, the truth should live from age to age,
> As 'twere retail'd to all posterity,
> Even to the general all-ending day."

A thought which seemed so little unphilosophic to the acute, wily, and circumspect Gloucester, that it drew from him the exclamation,

> "So wise so young !"

On leaving the house, before she started, she would always, as we before observed, repeat the De Profundis and the Memorare, which latter was one of her favourite prayers. Every morning before going into the chapel, she would salute on one knee, with smiling reverence, a picture of our blessed Lady, that had long been in her family ; and in her choicest treasury she preserved the relics that had been given to herself or to her ancestors. It was a strange way for Sir Thomas Brown to justify his own "little devotion unto reliques," and to account for it by saying, that he had only a slender and doubtful respect unto antiquities, and that too for the reason that what he admired is far before antiquity, being eternity and God himself. In urging such a reason, in which there is so little reason, the good doctor seems to have enjoyed a nap, in which one may leave him with great complacency. At all events, Catholic of an ancient race, Jane Mary never thought it necessary to philosophize on this devotion, or seek to make out its apology ; but while she thus was nature and the thing itself, it may be left to philosophers following the poet, like Wordsworth, to find a very sufficient explanation and a perfect justification for it in the common sentiments of the human heart ; for, alluding to the latter usage, what more in accordance with them, since, as he says,

> " ———— The lover doom'd
> To love when hope hath fail'd him, whom no depth
> Of privacy is deep enough to hide,
> Hath yet his bracelet or his lock of hair,
> And that is joy to him. When change of times

> Hath summon'd kings to scaffolds, do but give
> The faithful servant, who must hide his head
> Henceforth in whatsoever nook he may,
> A kerchief sprinkled with his master's blood,
> And he too hath his comforter."

The cross entered thoroughly into all her routine of manners. She would always recommend people to begin their picture, or whatever they were writing, with tracing its sign upon the canvas or the paper. She abhorred superstition and all tampering in an inordinate way with spiritual things; but living as she did at the foot of the cross, she would never associate any thing agreeable, either in the way of recreation or of utility, with the Friday, and when laughed at on these occasions, as she was sure to be,—being, in fact, at all times one of those persons who are so loveable, that people try to detect weak points in their character, for the express purpose of loving them more,—she used to reply very gravely, that Friday being the day of our Lord's Crucifixion, there was nothing superstitious in devoting it to greater recollection than might be at other times required. Her apology was deemed very unsatisfactory by wise people; but others seemed to be of Elia's opinion, who says, "I love the safety which a palpable hallucination warrants, the security which a word out of season ratifies." No doubt it entered into her character to be affectionate in the minutest points that in any way bore upon Christianity; but, as a member of the French Academy observes, whose words may in consequence be cited with more exact propriety, when it is a case of meeting "well-informed men," "If we are to have indulgence for those who seem not to make sufficient exterior acts of piety," and she was the first to say so, and to show it, "why should we not equally make allowance for those who appear to exceed in multiplying them*?"

In general, we may say, that she was all habits,—customs based on piety and goodness. She did nothing by fits and starts. Her attendance at the church offices, for instance, was regulated every year by as exact a following of precedent, as used to be in the case of the usages and observances of the Mayor of

* Droz, Pensées sur le Christianisme.

London, which were chronicled in the Liber Albus of the City in the time of Whittington, where we read, for example, on what festivals he was accustomed to remain in St. Paul's until complines are finished, and on what days immediately after vespers it was the rule for him to withdraw[*]. Such was her exact routine throughout the course of each year; and, consequently, all seemed natural and easy in regard to the manner of her life. She had, no doubt, her " stoopings and reposes; but her proper element was the sky, and in the suburbs of the empyrean." It was the same in regard to her language. She possessed, I am ready to admit, a great tact for turning discourse to holy things in rather a childlike manner, that could not but please through its earnestness; and she would let fall the most edifying words, never omitting an opportunity for giving useful hints in a way singularly gracious, or for reminding people who openly contradicted them of the Christian principles. Disposed thus to give to conversation a holy tone, or when occasion was presented to recall things of religious moment, she was notwithstanding greatly averse, but merely through instinct, to any thing that wore the garb of sanctimonious pedantry. She would never suspect that such a thing was or had been before her; but she had no liking for your

> " Choice word and measured phrase; above the reach
> Of ordinary men, a stately speech,
> Such as grave livers do in Scotland use."

While others would never employ any but great and grave words, which they pronounced with an imperious and solemn tone, though they said only what was very insignificant, she, on the contrary, made use of only common words to say things profound and admirable.

We have made some delay upon this commonly trite theme grown so insipid in an age of words; but it was difficult to be less diffuse when reminded of her piety, which, besides being divine, was so charming, so natural, so womanly a thing, that humanity could not but adore it. We have seen many of its features; to all these must now be added a great fund of good

---

[*] P. 25.

sense. She had "a native disrelish of any thing that sounded odd or bizarre." Nothing went down with her that was quaint, irregular, or out of the road of common sympathy. She held nature not alone more clever, as Elia adds, but more Christian. Probably, if a discussion had ever occurred on the subject, she would have had the wisest doctors on her side; for they agree, I believe, with that great modern author who says, "that while the basest thought possible concerning man is that he has no spiritual nature,—the foolishest misunderstanding of him possible is, that he has, or should have, no animal nature; the fact being, that our nature is nobly, coherently, and irrevocably two-fold, neither part of it being able, but at its peril, to expel, despise, or deny the other*." "It is interdicted to the faithful," says a French author, "to seek an imaginary perfection; and as for what is prescribed, it ought to vary according to the state, occupations, age, and even character of persons, who ought not to be subjected to a uniform rule." Such, at all events as far as one may venture to suggest, were her views in this respect. I yield to you that they would not suit all complexions, at least that they would not agree with all sentences that have been uttered or written. "I assure you, sir," wrote De Rancé to a friend, "that when one wishes to be wholly given to God, and in separation from men, life is only good for being destroyed, and we ought to consider ourselves tanquam oves occisionis." Generally I would refrain from a touch that seemed uncalled for by my original,—there is danger in the least tint not found in it. But here, for all that needful circumspection, I am free to confess, that it was difficult to see any full development of such sentiments in the character we are attempting to delineate. Patient, resigned, if need were, heroic in regard to danger and self-sacrifice, she did not, however, at any moment of her life, wear the semblance of some whose givings out are at an infinite distance from their practice, or perhaps even from their true-meant design. I know she would not have approved our saying what one is about to utter; since of falling short she was ever ready to plead guilty, rather than willing to take credit to herself for not exceeding. She would

* Ruskin.

have held such talk blaspheming of the good and mocking her.
I know all that; and I feel too that I am wading out of my
depth. But still there are the facts. Marry, she was by no
means, in any respect, "a kind of puritan," the description of
whom would be somewhat tedious. Of St. Jerome's writings
she knew nothing, though her mother's and a daughter's
name recalled them. Nor will I dare to say that she would
have disrelished any words let fallen by a father of the Church;
she that for their names alone, and for the aspect of their
tomes, was always in the most practical as well as profound
sense reverential. Never consciously would she think to be
herself wiser than another by taking a lower aim. But such
was her gift, such her high grace,—or if you would rather,
such the determinative force of the circumstances of the age
and country in which she was placed, that she did not in all
respects respond to the ideal which that reverend doctor had
during the latter years of his life in view. She did not, as if
living in the fourth century, represent moral exaltation at its
apogee,—what seems to some as having been the excess of the
Christian movement in the times of persecution and barbarism,
seeming to have overpassed all the bounds of practical
morality, beyond which the world could not last for three days,
—appearing to have pushed all ideas to an extreme, acqui-
escing in no rules that were fit for a living society, admitting
in direct terms of no virtue but that of abnegation, of no social
existence but that of asceticism, of no knowledge but theology,
of no purity but virginity, having no marriages, no relations of
interest or of family, adopting that incomprehensible austerity
which would be incompatible with the continuance of any
social condition, leaving the world to die and wishing it to
die*. No; you who dislike the fair sex (I say fair sex,
imitating a French author's parenthesis, expressly to make you
a little angry) would not reap much satisfaction from con-
sorting with spirits of this mark; though, indeed, no one, however great a traveller he might be, having scaled the Alps and
Pyrenees, who had seen storms of all kinds, and had ventured

---

* Philarete Chasles, Études sur les Premiers Temps des Christianisme.

on the steepest summits, need have expected, on approaching such a presence, to find himself on Mount Rhodope. As far as she was concerned, he risked nothing there; but love with all its sanctity, marriage with all its hopes and joys, the tenderness of children, the domestic affections and the innocent pleasures of a quiet home, were not excluded from her views of duty and religion; for hers was not a theory of spiritualist felicity and an ideal happiness. She thought that piety, and all that was implied within the wedding-ring, could well exist together. Perhaps if one might use such classical allusions when speaking of one so divinely simple, there seemed to be in her character what Saint-Beuve ascribes to a certain philosopher,—"a mind which appeared to temper Pascal by Fenelon and by Virgil." Her virtue had nothing rude in it—nothing, excepting indeed secretly, and that with good sense, for herself austere;—but being attached solidly to good, she had no reason to mistrust her own judgment, or seek to satisfy it by false and deceitful appearances. When some one in her presence would mutter, saying, "Do not send us so quickly to the Prytanée—we do not relish black soup, and we are too far from the Eurotas," she would confess that violent or harsh sermons by men of great genius, above all, expressions which seemed to trample on parental rights and on maternal tenderness, did not please her either. True, I can but recollect one instance of such displeasure, but on that occasion she said audibly, on her return, "I own I did not like it." Void of all human respect, never concealing or blushing when it was a question of her faith, she dreaded to give the slightest shadow of pretext for thinking her a bigot, which is a trait that I find approved of by no less grave a writer than the Père Ventura, who expresses himself to that effect in his biographical notice of a person of approved sanctity[*]. She would not have felt drawn towards that Jean des Cauves, who in the same book published an ode in honour of the Saint Bartholomew, and a sermon against the fashion of dressing their hair adopted by the women of that time. She would have been less scandalized had she accompanied Mlle. de Seudéry at Avignon, when, going to see the tomb

---

[*] La Femme Chrét., ou Vie de Virg. Bruni.

of Laura which is with the Observantins, a friar of the house, a friend of her brother, actually pressed her to accept a chamber from which, with the superior's permission, she could walk in their garden full of orange trees, and this in a house a few steps from the Inquisition; and where this good Father even showed her some verses written by the hand of Petrarch, which are kept in the convent with religious respect. You may hold forth as you will upon incongruity and the renaissance movement; but at all events practically as a pious mother, such was her disposition, and such her practice. "To prepare the young for a solid and active life, without spoiling their imagination or compressing their vivacity and grace, to cultivate their mind without encouraging a fastidious pedantry or a fatal exaltation, to bring them up in the family, and for the family, without keeping them strangers to what is elegant and becoming," such were the difficult conditions which she sought to fulfil. In a word, full of humility and full of love, she laboured, to use the expression of Mme. Swetchine, "as if desiring to render her piety reasonable, and her reason pious," while all the time her tongue

> "Made this as sweet as ditties highly penn'd,
> Sung by a fair queen in a summer's bower,
> With ravishing division, to her lute."

But we must conclude this visit; and we cannot perhaps better bring it to an end than by citing the opinion which those who knew her entertained of her piety. The first testimony is from a layman, but a founder of three churches, to whom England also owes an abbey: he had seen her when a girl, before her marriage, and what is remarkable enough, in this place he is remembered to have then expressed his admiring surprise to witness her assiduous assistance at holy mass. Now, after so long an interval, hearing of her death, his words were these,— few but significant,—" How holy a person she was! What would not thousands give if they could say the same of friends who are taken from them! This was indeed to have the lamp trimmed, and the oil brightly burning in the socket." The clergy follow. First a Parisian priest, whose sister was the friend and governess of her youngest boy. "Oui," he writes, "sa 'mémoire est en bénédiction. On est mieux où elle est avec Dieu qu'elle a servi si constamment, qu'au milieu de notre triste monde. Sa vie était surabondamment remplie, voilà pourquoi Dieu l'a pris." Then follows the attestation of her near relative, once her playmate, now, after relinquishing riches and a title, a priest and a Jesuit. "I have not the least doubt," he wrote, "but that she is now in heaven, interceding for us all. She was one of the purest and most holy women I have ever known, and she left the impress of her mind on the children who went before her." In fine, as it were, to close our little procession in a manner suitable, a bishop of England, who had known her for many years, concluded a letter with these words, "I will only add that I have offered the adorable sacrifice for the soul of her whom I am more disposed to believe is praying before the throne of God for us."

> " 'Tis by comparison, an easy task
> Earth to despise; but, to converse with Heaven—
> This is not easy."

We have seen, however, how this latter and greatest object was achieved by one who laid claim to no proficiency of any kind, by one untutored in the schools, by one like a child to the last, by one in the midst of the world a simple unpretending woman.

And are we to pass out now through the portal without being impressed with a sense of the value of such a lesson? Piety thus practised, is this a mere common-place theme? a subject on which words are wasted? a matter of tedious details which are of no direct personal practical importance to any one? "All nature," says a philosopher who would not be of that opinion, "obeys God. Each reign, each species, each individual of either remains within the bounds prescribed to it without confusion or arrogation of the part of others. No where is there a tendency to escape from its conditions. Star, ocean, flower, bird, all wish to be what they are, and proclaim their universal acquiescence. True, it is only by a fiction that one attributes a will to them; but the order and measure that they keep reveal the plan which governs them. And does not this plan give the idea of God? Does not the creation proclaiming a universal submission to his laws assert also that in the moral order there is a similar route traced out for nations and individuals, the limits of which should not be transgressed? and man, to whom alone freedom is given, is he to interrupt this sublime concert by his revolts and his impatience?" Oh, no! let the voice of a woman from this tomb be listened to. Beneath these arches all of us may learn more than he may care to talk about. It has been a most majestic vision and charmingly harmonious.

CHAPTER V.

T is the remark of a witty and elegant French writer that you can draw nothing from poets unless you are very lavish in praise of their genius. Homer, he says, was perfectly aware of this fact, when he makes Ulysses say to one of them from whom he desired a song, Demodocus, "I esteem you without doubt far above all other mortals together; for it is the Muse herself who has taught you—the Muse, daughter of Jove, or rather it is Apollo who has inspired you." "This compliment," adds our sly painter of contemporary portraits, "from the beginning is indispensable, ever since the time of Homer down to—down to all those of our age *." Nor is it only disciples of the Muse who are so exacting. Of how many philosophers and great guides of the reading public might one say with a poet of a better school, that

"——— He is sincere
As vanity and fondness for applause,
And new and strifeless wishes would allow."

Where can you escape besides from being confronted with what he complains of,—namely, personal under the mask of national or universal vanity,—with

* Saint-Beuve, Portraits Contemp.

> "A proud and most presumptuous confidence
> In the transcendent wisdom of the age
> And its discernment: not alone in rights,
> And in the origin and bounds of power,
> Social and temporal; but in laws divine,
> Deduced by reason, or to faith reveal'd?"

I am much mistaken if we are not liable to meet instances even near the precincts where we stand, in some cool boasters contemptuously withdrawing, and inviting each other " to whisper o'er a couplet or two of most sage saws." It would be difficult, with much prospect of success, to speak before such proficients, or even perhaps before any of your practical men that are pushing their way in the world with the reputation of being eminently qualified in all respects, of listening to a voice that speaks wisdom from a woman's grave,—from the ashes of one too who was as simple as the maid whom Martial d'Auvergne speaks of in his vigils of Charles VII.—

> "Cette pauvre bergère
> Qui gardait les brebis aux champs,
> D'une douce et humble manière,
> A l'âge de dix-huit ans."

Nevertheless, as Sir Walter Raleigh says in his famous ballad,—

> "Tell wit how much it wrangles
> In tickle points of nicenesse;
> Tell wisdome, she entangles
> Herselfe in over-wisenesse;
> Tell schooles, they want profoundnesse,
> And stand too much on seeming.
> If wit and schooles reply,
> Give wit and schooles the lye."

Besides that, as Sir Thomas Brown says, " there are a bundle of curiosities not only in philosophy but in divinity, proposed and discussed by men of most supposed abilities, which indeed are not worthy our vacant hours, much less our serious studies," the truth is, that wisdom is ofttimes nearer when we stoop than when we soar; and it is a grave and profound writer who exclaims, not without viewing what we praise in the light of conformity with the highest wisdom, "Oh, what a charming thing is the ignorance of children and of the humble!" Nothing in their countenance indicates "the cloudy coldness of knowledge," and what a great observer calls "its venomous character." No, certainly; it looks as if they could not even give you a scientific explanation of any thing when they want you to understand them. Perhaps, like Elia, guessing at the star Venus only by her brightness, or, like Madame de Sevigné, saying of the comet that she had just seen "sa queue est d'une belle longueur," and of poor Fouquet in the Bastille, having received the news of his sentence "par l'air," that is, by signals, they have nothing to offer but what the French call "explication de cuisinière;" but that involves pleasurable. observation and personal experience which are not without their office even in the schools. They have their own way of saying what the Spaniards utter as a proverb, that it is wiser to stay at home than run over the world in search of better bread than wheaten. They don't seem eager to know historically and authentically things that do not much concern them; they have but a slight acquaintance with geography, and cannot form, perhaps, a conjecture of the position of countries in which they hold a correspondence with humble people whom they still befriend in a distant portion of the globe. Of history and chronology they possess some vague points, such as every one picks up; but they have most dim apprehensions of the four great monarchies,—and, like Elia still, there is nothing, perhaps, which they dread so much as the being left alone for a quarter of an hour with a sensible, well-informed man that does not know them. In short, they know nothing of science; but so much the better for them, says my Spanish author,—because nature with all her magnificence belongs to them. They cannot analyze the mysterious relations of the family; still, he cries, so much the better for them,—because the family has for them, and for them alone, treasures of tenderness and love. They do not scan God; to the last he has only exclamations; "So much the better for them," a thousand times he cries, for God reveals Himself to their heart[*]. Here, in the particular

---

[*] Donoso Cortes.

instance to which our attention is now directed, was no doubt a simple woman much too weak to oppose men's cunning. Yes; while she lived, often twitted for her want of what some were pleased to qualify as "useful knowledge," while others secretly applied to her, as she bore all with such calm cheerfulness, the lines,—

> " Thou art not daunted,
> Nor canst if thou be set at nought;
> And oft alone in nooks remote
> We meet thee, like a pleasant thought
> When such are wanted."

So far, then, when proceeding to speak of wisdom, some might at first think us singularly unfortunate in our selection of an example to illustrate the theme; yet was she wise, but for one choice. " Wise, or I'll none," says Benedick, when summing up the qualities that must enter into the character of her who is to convert him. Let us proceed, then, to observe in what way she over whose paved grave we now tread responded to his ideal.

It is not to be questioned, that the wisdom to which she attained was greatly facilitated, to speak in a human way, by her possession of remarkable good sense. This natural gift will not fully explain it, as we shall observe presently; but no doubt it conduced to its acquisition, for it formed her to that state of mind in which Pascal makes Christianity consist, namely, " en doutant où il faut, en assurant où il faut, en se soumettant où il faut." Her good sense was, in fact, synonymous with wisdom, though in regard to the latter she practised the precept,—

> " Qui sapit, in tacito gaudeat ille sinu."

If you would hear her, she had no pretensions but to know, as the Spaniards say, the number of her own fingers ; but, in fine, before long you discovered that she was one of those " quorum usque ad extremum spiritum est provecta sapientia."

> " The reason firm, the temperate will,
> Endurance, foresight, strength, and skill ;

> A perfect woman, nobly plann'd,
> To work, to comfort, and command;
> And yet a spirit still, and bright,
> With something of an angel light."

There never was an instance in which one saw more curiously verified the common-place propositions of the celebrated Gilles de Rome,—" Qu'il n'est riens plus utile à prononcer conseil que sapience, qu'il n'est riens plus utile à soubstenir moleste que sapience *." This is the poetical side, perhaps you will say; but what was the strict truth? It is that she was wise from being enlightened by her submission to the law of God. After every sermon that she heard, after every mass at which she assisted, she seemed to act precisely like her in whose footsteps she always sought to follow, and of whom we read at Christmas, " Maria autem conservabat omnia verba hæc, conferens in corde suo." Truly this humble follower must have been known familiarly to the court which she was fondest of, as one who thought day and night upon what belonged to it, according to the assurance, " Novit Dominus viam justorum, qui in lege ejus meditantur die ac nocte!" In these words, sung at the festival of all the saints, you have the secret of her whole life, and the principle of all her wisdom. The testimony, the promise of salvation! " bright as the sun beyond all the earth-cloud, it makes wise the simple; all wisdom being assured in perceiving it and trusting it; all wisdom brought to nothing which does not perceive it †." She sought not to solve the infinite in God by scrutinizing His majesty. She mounted to Him, as we observed on our last visit, up the old worn track by prayer. And, as Mme. Swetchine says, we can proceed towards perfection, as far as our nature admits of it, much more by action than by speculation, of which the lofty summits will never teach us more than the precepts contained in the Pater noster. Like the Lady Anne, Countess of Arundel, "she used

---

* Le Mirouer exemplaire et tres-fructueuse instruction selon compilation de Gilles de Rome, Du regime et gouvernement des Roys, Seigneurs, &c.
† Ruskin.

continually to beg of God not to leave her to herself; and on all occasions she had humble recourse to Him for help and assistance, which yet was accompanied with so great a confidence in His infinite goodness and mercy, that she remained as it were with a kind of assurance that He would never forsake her, having the eyes of her soul after a hopeful manner ever lifted up to Him." It is to be granted, therefore, that her wisdom was thoroughly Christian, having no flavour of any other source. But philosophers themselves, who are deserving of the name—for every one is not so innocent as to be imposed upon by a few medical students or pompous sophists from a university, giving themselves out for philosophers—will admit with the Prince de Conty that one ought to believe the rules of the Gospel and of the Church to be more sure than all the policy of men; and that, while following these rules, one stands on ground that is intellectually impregnable. In fact, as an illustrious contemporary said, "true wisdom and true simplicity consist in following, step by step, the maxims of the Gospel, without losing one's self in interior speculations reserved for a small number,—in estimating our actions by the standard of the sanctuary, and in submitting ourselves humbly to life instead of proudly attempting to rise above it." At all events, hers was the wisdom of the first Christians, which I suppose is not to be considered quite obsolete. "For, to refer to earliest times, I see," continues this author, "only one road approved of, and every kind of deviation from it severely condemned. I see the brilliant dreams of imagination discountenanced as the source of illusion,—a boundless submission to what is established by common consent,—a respect for tradition almost equal to that inspired by the Holy Scriptures, and a perfect conformity of opinion with all true Christians, by the bonds of a fraternity full of charity without weakness." Now with such views did she advance day by day, having for sole consolation the sentiment of a firm resolution to love more and more the law of that God of mercy in whom we all have need to hope. Accordingly one may affirm with truth, that such was the excellent judgment of this truly wise but humble woman, that there could be no greater security on all occasions than in following her counsels. She resembled that cousin of whom Elia says, " Where we have differed upon something proper to be done or let alone, whatever heat of opposition or steadiness of conviction I set out with, I was sure always, in the long run, to be brought over to her way of thinking." With a hand tender and firm, at once directed by a good sense that nothing troubled, and by a heart that was full of charity, she would lead you through paths full of thorns, trenches, deceptions, and perils. As Fontenelle said of some one whose panegyric he pronounced before the Academy, " her understanding attached itself to truth by a kind of sympathy, and perceived what was false without discussing it; which faculty enabled her to dispense with the long and circuitous process which others are obliged to adopt,—it being in her a certain happy instinct which anticipated her reason*." One might apply to her what Mme. Swetchine said of the Count de Maistre; she was "like a sporting-dog: she could detect at a prodigious distance whatever was directly or indirectly associated with the ideas of the world;" which, in general, however they may be new clothed, savour very much, I rather think, of what the fool of old said in his heart. Nothing found favour with her from the moment when there was the least deviation from fundamental principles. Wherever there was this tendency, neither eloquence nor elevation of thoughts and sentiments in other respects, nor the public voice, however loudly pronounced in its favour, could make amends for it. The meteor, she might have said, is often more brilliant than the star.

At the same time, she never thought herself competent to decide a question merely on her own judgment, as being her own; for, as we read of the Lady Anne, Countess of Arundel and Surrey, "she ever gave proof of her interior humility of mind by asking and taking counsel in all kind of affairs, and by her willingness to be directed therein. In matters of moment she would always ask the advice of others, whose judgment she would commonly rather follow than her own, being ever willing to be directed in spiritual affairs, and ready to put good advice in execution." She followed the advice given by the Prince de Conty to all persons belonging to the upper ranks, in loving

---

* Œuvres, tom. v.

"all her life those who told the truth, and in fearing and avoiding as she would death those who would strengthen her faults by flattery*." But, on the other hand, possessing such a character, which was formed as it were by the daily practice of meditating on the law of God, and by being docile to the teaching of his Church, it stands to reason that she could not, for all her humility, but feel her strength when confronted with the sophistry of the passions and the maxims of the profane world. There was, however, no rigidity or formality in her censure at any time; for, in relation to all matters, she had regard more to the obvious intention than to the imperfect execution. Analysis is of man: synthesis of God. Unconsciously she followed the latter method. She judged, too, while employing all her faculties. Her imagination went with her faith; and she made wisdom consist, not in the separate employment of either the reason or the fancy, but in the harmonious enjoyment of both while believing practically, as her conduct every day demonstrated, that happiness consisted, not in rank or fortune, or pleasures of this world, but in following God. As Saint-Beuve says of Madame de Longueville, "she was one of those esprits fins whom Pascal opposes to the geometric character; one of those minds which are chiefly fine, as we might say of an instrument, accustomed to judge of things by a single rapid glance, easily rebutted by a detail of definitions, in appearance sterile, and incapable of patience to descend to the first principles of speculative and imaginative things." But the fact is, she took her flight far above them, and while you were busy and engrossed with your abstractions, savouring of the fogs of earth, and beholding things in a dark and doubtful perspective, from that pure elevation did she judge even of the things of earth, with all the serenity and certainty that result from a consciousness of viewing them in relation to their Creator, and, consequently, in truth. Who can appreciate the value attached to the great practical wisdom of such a character? Galen counts one hundred and fifteen maladies incident to the bodily eye; but could he determine, think you, the number of those to which the eye of the mind is liable? As Jules Janin

* Le Prince de Conty, Les Devoirs des Grands, 9.

observes of some one else, substituting our capital for his own, one might say, "that she was the Cour de Cassation for the judgments of London. She judged with her mind and with her instinct, whereas London judges with its mind alone. She had time to give for the consideration of a question eleven hours and a half a day more than London. She had smiles of approval which were very tender, and regards that were very sweet. To obtain them was an object of wise ambition, as also to live known to her and unknown to the world, for her approval was health of mind and soundness of judgment." In fact, as we shall observe later, even in regard to literature her praises without art would have pleased men of genius like Sarasin, perhaps nearly as much as those of the Academy; for there was nothing more just than her sentiments, nothing more sound than her opinions, nothing more correct than her simple glance, nothing more instructive, consequently, than her conversation, in which nothing escaped from her that a perfect judgment would not approve of. And so it was felt, if not acknowledged. Quite unconsciously it turned out, that some persons had been in habits of referring all their views of life, and even pleasures, to the test of her approval. Perhaps, if some were mystically turned, they might now be accusing her of having been the innocent cause of their excess in this regard; for it certainly used to be thought by some a sufficient sanction if her consent could be obtained, and one was accustomed to regard it as an unshunned consequence that all must be solidly right in the sight of heaven if she were only pleased; whereas now, there is left in her absence the dread consciousness of only a higher tribunal. Nevertheless, it is but doing her justice to add, that the practical result was precisely the same as if the latter, all the while, had been solely in your view. In regard to this world, if you consulted her before acting, whatever might be the matter in debate, and acted as she wished, you were always sure of not having to be sorry afterwards for a foolish step; nor had you ever to repent having omitted or committed any thing in accordance with her judgment. There were some who never would undertake the thing wherein her counsel and consent were wanting; and, in point of fact, it was impossible in the long run not to like what she liked, and to dislike what she disliked. As Mdlle. de Scudéry said of the Countess de Maure, "there was nothing so elevated that she did not speak of it in a proper manner, which was often to say but very little, nor any thing so low and familiar, though it were the et cætera of notaries, and the qui pro quo of apothecaries, that she could not speak of with nobleness and advantage to those who asked her opinion." She was, in brief, a friend from whom, as Coleridge says of another, one never received an advice that was not wise, or a remonstrance that was not gentle and affectionate.

> "Mine eye's clear eye, my dear heart's dearer heart;
> My food, my fortune, and my sweet hope's aim,
> My sole earth's heaven, and my heaven's claim."

Nor was it alone in the ordinary sphere of social and domestic relations that this clearness and soundness of judgment was seen in operation. It was difficult not to be struck with the traces of its action, in regard to questions that are now forced on every one, of a more speculative, but, withal, no less important kind, since they bear upon the former, namely, with reference to philosophical opinions, as also to political principles and to the estimate of the facts and deeds which followed from them.

With regard to the former it is evident, from all we have already observed, that she yielded the example of one who remained stedfast to the ancient fundamental notions of wisdom diffused throughout all ages and nations, though there may be now a few to ask us contemptuously what they are. She did not relish the air of men of great influence, commanding any number of votes they want, with whom all old opinions, such as are found in Plato and Homer, to say nothing of the Bible, and not to say virtues essential to the happiness of mankind, pass for being erroneous in principle, and, at least in practice, mere anachronisms—things arriérées, as the French say. While a stranger held up some article in a public journal as a triumphant explanation, she seemed to know instinctively, such was the clear-sightedness of her natural intelligence, that, with whatever ability it might be written, the general sentiments of the good in all ages ought not to be laughed down. Tradition and innovation are said to be the two legs of humanity; and she never seemed to look forward with pleasure as indicative of its progress in a good sense to an epoch when only the latter were to be left, and we should consequently, according to this ancient view of the matter, have but one leg to stand upon. No question, for this very reason, the views which she entertained would not by many be deemed deserving of much consideration; for instead of "the town," which was the old phrase for a tribunal to which, after all, however corrupted, every thing genuine, as the gravest articles of Addison, might have appealed with a certainty of favour, " we have now that reading public, which Coleridge so despised, being as strange a phrase, he thought, as ever forced a splenetic smile on the staid countenance of meditation; and yet no fiction! But what, he asks, is the result? Does the inward man thrive on this regimen? From a philosophic populace, good sense deliver us*!" "But, alas!" as he says elsewhere, "the halls of old philosophy have been so long deserted, that we circle them at shy distance as the haunt of phantoms and chimeras; and whoever should have the hardihood to reproclaim its solemn truths must commence with a glossary;" though all the while perhaps, even in our estimate of its inferior attraction, we are mistaken; since, as Mme. de Sévigné thought, " there is no experiment in physics more amusing than an examination of the diversity of human sentiment†." Be that as it may, as we read of Mme. de Montmorency, "she avoided the conversation of those who wished to favour or propagate new opinions in regard to wisdom, and who took a pride in subtilizing with regard to matters of that class."

It will probably seem to some that such an instance of adherence to what has always had the sanction of the wise and good, ought not to be lost upon thoughtful minds in the modern society, with its accelerated course, its thousand deafening shouts of triumph, and, as one who loves it is constrained to add, "its perpetual sounds of successive shipwreck ‡." Much that is talked of with such pretensions is not even new in the world. It is always the same froth.

---

* The Statesman's Manual, or Lay Sermon.
† Lett. 676.   ‡ Saint-Beuve.

But then it will be urged that it is both natural and just to desire to have praise from our contemporaries. Well, of course, as Jules Janin says, "to be applauded you have only to wish for it. You will see all of a sudden what a great man you become in twenty-four hours. You will be Luther, Mirabeau, the future itself! Yes; but in reality perhaps you will be a great criminal; you will have abused the turbulent innocence of young minds; you will have set fire to those warm bloods that desired no better than to follow you through good paths. But this comes of wanting to be applauded, not sometimes, but often and always! and then when all the bad passions of these children, who fancy themselves men, are excited by the culpable imprudence of your eloquence, and by the deceiving treachery of paradoxes, what master will be bold enough to show them the danger of the fables that flatter them, and the vanity of their pride?" Ah! let the sweet voice from this tomb gently awaken them to a happier consciousness of life, of its duties and of its end. Let them observe the example of this one, so distinguished by seeking to avoid what is uncommon, so little learned in the study of new theories, so little noisy in defence of her own, so calm and simply good, and collecting flowers of such exquisite beauty even at the very mouth of the volcano.

Nor would I be understood as implying that she was unaware of the danger around her, and ignorant of the true spirit of her own age. She knew both perfectly. Taught to feel assured by her Christian instinct that, as St. Chrysostom says, God does not pursue with so much hatred him who sins as him who acts impudently, and that what he punishes most, for the instruction of future ages, to whom the penalty may serve as a mother of philosophy, is the impudence that does not blush[*], she wished that to many whose literary fame had reached her might yet be given what the Prophet Daniel calls the "heart of a man," which, as St. Chrysostom observes, would render them humble, mild, and gentle[†]. She could not but know how little many corresponded with such a type. Alas! who is ignorant of the crowd of lettered sciolists who have—

[*] Hom. in Psal. vi.
[†] In Dan. cap. vii., interp.

"no better stay
Than the dull product of a scoffer's pen,
Impure conceits discharging from a heart
Harden'd by impious pride?"

Who is not aware that he lives in the midst of men retaining a kind of Sardonic bitterness against Christianity, as ages have seen it constituted and transmitted? The old philosopher used to speak of a certain impression or opinion armed with a great nail strong and very sharply pointed, to transfix the body and soul of a man together, in order that the soul may have the same opinion as the body. This is the sort of fabricated article for which the demand and production seem greatest now; and when its consumption has attained the maximum, there is not much likelihood of pleading with any success in behalf of those who prefer the example that is thought of in the Chapel of St. John. As Daunon said of one of his fellow-countrymen, "people are then too much occupied with hating to have time to think;" though their tongues are never tired in celebrating this religion of humanity that has been set up by convinced sceptics; but after they have finished, when all representatives of the ancient wisdom are thought to be for ever settled with, some, in their turn, attached to the memory of these last will say, like an ingenious French writer, that they too must take up their spy-glass in order to scan those whose souls have been thus transfixed and welded; for our eyes can look as swift as theirs, and we won't permit any one of these philosophers to make game of our friends. They are children, he says, and might be better employed on serious things, such as politics, which might be sometimes called Satanics, on statistics and the funds, or on philosophy and science in general. "I own," adds our author, "I have a grudge against these philosophers. Just look at them passing their life in tapping on abstractions to extract morality from them. From the beginning of the world what have they done to make us happier? Nothing; to oscillate, that's all!"

Some, however, who as philosophers even are certainly entitled to a hearing, are of opinion that this is not all. You might discover, says one of them, not suspected of being a scrupulous Christian, "twelve thousand new acids, and find out a way to kill 60,000 men in a second; and the moral European world would not be in a different condition from what it is; and by that," saith he, " I mean dying—for L'Europe s'en va!"

> "—— Here Nature is their guide,
> The nature of the dissolute; but thee,
> O fostering nature! they reject."

Let us turn from them to contemplate with rather different impressions her who ever showed herself as one

> " That from truth's central point serenely views
> The compass of the argument."

For, take the instance of a question now so often agitated that even our drawing-rooms are familiar with the theme. What were her views respecting the education of the people, and the nature of that instruction, grounded on the alleged fear of fanaticism, in the success of which the state itself is said to be interested? They were simply those expressed by Mme. de Sévigné, where she says, " La morale chrétienne est excellente à tous les maux; mais je la veux chrétienne; elle est trop creuse et trop inutile autrement*." Too hollow, and too useless are the very words she would have used in reference to this kind of governmental training, when unaided by other elements. It would be impossible to state her opinion, on this point, more exactly than it is already expressed in the following passage from the work of Droz, entitled, Thoughts on Christianity. "The office of the ministers of the Saviour," he says, "is to teach doctrine and morals, let what scandals may follow. When the pretended philosophers wish to reduce the priest to the part of a moralist, they evince an equal ignorance of the truths of heaven and of the interests of earth. Of what use would be moral instruction separated from the courage to practise it? Does not every one know that if we violate our duty it is seldom from a want of knowing it? The great service to render us is to correct our weakness, to deliver us from our cowardice.

* Lett. 135.

Strength to practise the precepts emanates above all from faith. Suffer the priest then to fulfil his mission. Do not, through a dread of fanaticism, ask him to abjure it for another which he would hold from you, and which may lead to results quite as injurious to the civil society. Do not seek insanely to substitute yourself for Christ."

Or, again, would you ask in what light she regarded this materialization of the intelligence, and this vulgarization of ideas and facts, which constitute, in some places, the very atmosphere that men breathe? With the woman's instinct she would reply, "that as a madman's epistles are no gospels, it skills not much considering them;" and in point of fact, as a philosophic writer truly says, "you overthrow all false systems by an adherence to what used to be called common sense and an exposition of the Christian doctrine. For example, these suffice to overthrow your theory of morals, according to the utilitarian point of view. The interest of all and of each religiously cultivated by the individual without religion, without self-sacrifice, without suffering accepted, cannot conduce, says a distinguished French writer, to the happiness of the world. But suffering so accepted, they tell us, to uphold their theory, is good for the individual. Nothing," he replies, "more puerile than this moral of utility. It is not useful personally for a man to die for another. It is not true that we attend to our material interest by acts of devotion and sacrifice; in every age we see men 'qui fruuntur diis iratis,' as the ancients used to say."

But even leaving such philosophy, were you to listen to the voice from this grave, you would feel in a still more invulnerable way armed against all these sophists who oppose Christianity; for, as the same writer says, "you overthrow false systems, by showing from the catechism and the common experience of life, that materialism is, from the beginning, a mistake, an entirely erroneous view, as by showing that man is a soul and a body, that in him all is naturally imperfect, that the most complete welfare of his physical and material state is not sufficient for him; that the most developed industry cannot correct the imperfections of his moral nature; that it is by this last your reform ought to begin; and that instead of delivering him over to the impulse of his nature, you ought to restrain egotism to encourage the charitable, loving, devoted, and generous element, what Christianity has already done with no small success*."

This leads us to a consideration of the lessons respecting political principles, and the acts and deeds resulting from them, which is imparted by a remembrance of the example with which are confronted those who visit the Chapel of St. John. She had nothing to do with the politics of the world; and that sad pre-occupation which consists in meddling with them in an inordinate way, seems at the present day to enjoy the exclusive privilege of impassioning opinion, and of popularizing a name. She was simply an amiable Christian; neither whig nor tory, legitimist nor revolutionary, economist nor socialist. Too indifferent even to what is ironically called l'humani tairerie, she played no part in the changing drama of our destinies. Her conversations were calculated to undermine no throne, to overthrow no ministry, to defeat no ancient law. She was neither red, nor white, nor blue. She led no one to speak much about her, excepting it were some one belonging to the number of the poor and the holy. But her lot was fallen on extraordinary times, when political conversations would occur to her, without on her part any slips of prolixity, or crossing the plain highway of talk. She was often confronted with what our great poet sums up as constituting, in a word,

> "The seeming truth, which cunning times put on
> To entrap the wisest."

Therefore, it is necessary to observe how she had learned to avoid its influence, and to impart a lesson that still is yielded by her memory, momentous to us all in whatever privacy we pass our days; for, as another poet says,—

> "Alas! when evil men are strong,
> No life is good, no pleasure long."

In the first place, let it be remarked, that she did not belong to the floating world, guided by the choice and master-spirits of this age who leave it to revolve undecided amidst the unre-

* Philarete Chasles, Etudes sur les Hommes au xix⁰ Siècle.

strained play of all the passions, and in the medley of all principles, or rather in the presence of none. She, on the contrary, belonged to the world of ancient virtues, of ancient belief,—to the world which reveres the Church, the family, and the throne. Her side was on that of the old royalty, the old faith, the old manners; it was with the poetic and Christian party, if you will call it so, and with the convictions of all whom the spirit and convictions of royalty inspired, that she took her stand. While resident in France, possibly she had a predilection for the journal of M. Michaud, which united the knightly spirit of true gentlemen and, what seemed to some to be, the deceptions of a local opinion. " Antiquity, tradition, ancestors, the majesty of ages, all that, in her eyes, was great and venerable." She wept when she heard of the overthrow of monarchy. " It seemed to her as a shipwreck, in which had disappeared, as it were, something holy, some ruin in which she had read the fragility of man and of his works; for the idea of destruction weighed upon her, and she never saw perish any thing glorious of antiquity, without yielding the tribute of an eloquent lamentation*." But for all that, there was nothing in her views opposed to the spirit of the noble freedom, which, as a Briton, she enjoyed at home. She had an instinctive sense of the good and necessity of conciliating modern freedom and royal legitimacy. As Saint-Beuve says of Chateaubriand, " when listening to her, you heard those praises of freedom and of youth from the same mouth, which expressed admiration for the chivalrous splendours of the middle ages and the antique ritual of kings." Without having read Tacitus, she desired "res olim dissociabiles—principatum ac libertatem." She hated the harshness of the old administrative organization,—the politics of power; the evils which really constitute oppression and tyranny, which render those who employ them the most guilty and responsible for all consequences that may ensue; the cruelty of subalterns, who come in personal contact with the people; the "instrumenta regni," as they are erroneously denominated, since they are rather the weapons of its enemies to cause its overthrow. These would not have existed, if the influence of her

---

* Lacordaire, Discours.

views had reached the elevated regions of sovereign or governmental power. Distrust she knew, and would often say aloud, has also its dupes. As for the excesses of what is distinguished as legitimacy, I believe what would be nearest the truth, would be to say, simply, that she could never comprehend them; and, in fact, these things are not necessarily associated with any epoch in the world's history that she felt interested in. Charlemagne, St. Louis, Henry IV. were for her household words; but she had not to defend their memory by invoking despotism. Louis XII. encouraged liberty, convinced that in the free development of mind there was no danger for good princes. He wished, said a contemporary, that truth should reach him:—
" Et que sur les théâtres libres on joue tous les abus de sa cour et de son royaume espérant apprendre ainsi beaucoup de choses qui autrement lui seraient cachées." The truth is, as Saint-Beuve observes, "the doctrine of legitimacy in its excess, as unaffected by the abuse of power, took body from the birth of Protestantism; Anglican with Henry VIII. and James I.; Gallican with Louis XIV., while engendering collaterally the dogma of the sovereignty of the people." She was always a lover of freedom; but she might have expressed her mind in the concluding lines of the same Greek passage, quoted by Mr. Coleridge, saying that, "in those who would appropriate the title, she found too many points destructive of liberty and hateful to its genuine advocates[*]." With poor King Henry she would exclaim,

> " O God, what mischiefs work the wicked ones;
> Heaping confusion on their own heads thereby!"

Nor would she shrink from expressing an opinion like that of Mme. Sévigné, that as for the revolutionary troops and other soldiers, sent to keep down the refractory, " on gagnerait beaucoup si c'étaient des cordeliers." Her notion of liberty was not that of modern liberals.

> " Smooth words they have to wheedle simple souls;
> But, for disciples of the inner school,

---

[*] In the " Friend."

> Old freedom was old servitude, and they
> The wisest whose opinions stoop'd the least
> To known restraints, and who most boldly drew
> Hopeful prognostications from a creed,
> Which in the light of false philosophy
> Spread like a halo round a misty moon,
> Widening its circle as the storms advance."

She felt no admiration when she heard of a repetition of the miserable French scenes which Gibbon beheld with such sorrowful amazement, when in his letter from Lausanne, of December, 1789, to Lord Sheffield, he spoke of "the clergy being plundered in a way which strikes at the root of all property." Yet, what she loved was, after all, nothing but the old and even the Italian notion of liberty, as expressed by the philosopher of Florence and by Petrarch in his "Horta;" for here, saith the latter, "in this one good of liberty the religious will find the permission of their rites and forms of worship; the students their learned leisure; the aged their repose; boys the rudiments of the several branches of their education; and fathers of families the dues of natural affection, and the sacred privileges of their ancient home. 'Spem atque gaudium omnes invenient.'" While the Florentine so far agrees with such views, that as the fruits of a good government, without noticing the checks and guarantees which we wisely hold to be needful, he is content with celebrating "peace, leisure, quiet, tranquillity, and personal security, such as they never before remember to have enjoyed [*]." She loved our own constitution, while certainly admiring and desiring to gather these fruits from it. There was nothing therefore immoderate, or as we should now say, un-English in her political views as to what constitutes the good of nations; but this fact leaves us greater freedom to pronounce with vehemence that she dreaded and hated revolution. She had no fanaticism for "peoples," a term that never escaped her lips. If, in an old monarchy, you must have her willing to admit the virtue of a new republic, it will only be perhaps on the condition laid down by Fauriel, when speaking of it to his intimate friend, namely, "that there be no re-

---

[*] Poggius, Hist. de Varietate Fortunæ, lib. iii.

publicans." One may feel quite sure, though she did not live to hear the words uttered, that a minister of the British crown could never have persuaded her to regard Oliver Cromwell as furnishing "an illustrious example, and one of the highest authorities that can be cited or appealed to by an Englishman;" and as for foreign governments, with whom every one now has to do, she felt no enthusiasm for such a deliverer from superstition as Æschylus describes,

'Εξ ὀμμάτων δ' ἤστραπτε γοργωπὸν σέλας,
'Ὃς τὴν Διὸς τυραννίδ' ἐκπέρσων βίᾳ *.

She had no weakness for the assassins of kings, all of whom, as Jules Janin says, are ever great readers, heart-sick with thought,—a pamphlet being always in their cupboard, under their pillow, within the prie-dieu †, when they find one in their room. Of the young emperor of Austria she used to speak with passionate admiration, for the reason that he represented what was antipodal to such an atmosphere. It would be with regret that she could not join you in praises of the scholar and the statesman; though grave and thoroughly calm,

"—————————— Never did I know
A creature that did bear the shape of man
So keen and greedy to confound a man."

But she could not avoid being, in general, of the opinion expressed in "Measure for Measure," that "slandering a prince deserves a whipping." She would have approved of the law in our statute-book "against slanderous reports or tales to cause discord betwixt king and people." "Tout cela," she would say, "est d'une canaillerie abominable." And as for the success that might attend such calumnies amidst the intoxication of victorious iniquity, she would be content with saying, with Corneille,—

"Je serai du parti qui affligera le sort!"

Why should a sovereign be less protected than a mayor? And in the White Book of the City of London we read, that on one

* Prometh.   † Variétés littéraires.

occasion there was "judgment of pillory for a lie told of the mayor*." But this was in the dark ages, and you tell me I am confounding things. Well, for all that, to speak in general,

> "———————— what king so strong
> Can tie the gall up in the slanderous tongue?
> O place and greatness, millions of false eyes
> Are stuck upon thee! volumes of report
> Run with these false and most contrarious quests
> Upon thy doings! Thousand 'scapes of wit
> Make thee the father of their idle dream,
> And rack thee in their fancies!"

As for " our own correspondent," Heaven help the man, she would not reply, in Latin, to your eulogies of him; but the drift of her meaning might have been expressed in the old lines,—

> " Parisios stolidum si quis transmittat asellum
> Qui fuit hîc asinus, non fiet ibi equus."

She used to treat the fearful roar of the leading article as if she had been previously let into the secret by him who played there the lion's part, telling her that she ought to think him not a lion; adding, " No, I am no such thing—I am a man, as other men are; and, indeed, if you would have me name my name, I must tell you plainly I am Snug, the joiner." At the best their word is but the vain breath of a common man; and truly, alluding in general to the public press, she would have wished to see that fourth power in the state not merely a power of calumny and of darkness,—she would have wished to see it use a sword rather than a poïgnard, employ truth as well as lies, and justice as well as defamation. I know a race disposed to turn vagabond with profit,—when boys, disagreeable, tyrannical, and odious at school; when adolescent, arrogant, and pedantic at college; thence, after an interval that need not be inquired into, launching forth upon Catholic countries to send home the result of their hateful wanderings in letters that are

---

* P. 522.

framed at so much a line perhaps, to gull the votaries of what has certainly no resemblance to good will. Chateaubriand said in his day that "intelligences on all sides seemed almost all to be in the service of lies." And we may even go back farther to find proof in this respect, that there is no novelty in one of the salient features of our present civilization; for Poggius speaks of a place called "le Bugiale"—the "mensongerie," or lie-shop, for which formal establishment something nearly equivalent may possibly be familiar to our Londoners, though now deriving its title from some court or square, of which the name, as serving to designate its precise locality, is ever on their tongue as one of their pet household words.

It will disgust, no doubt, many modern politicians, to be told of the advantage of learning such a lesson as that which prescribes as a general duty the wisdom of contentment with what exists above and around one in the government and institutions of one's country. Short-armed ignorance, itself knows, is so wanting in any patience, that it will not in circumvention deliver a fly from a spider without drawing its massy irons and cutting the web. As Mme. de Stahl said, speaking of a pamphlet of Lally-Tolendal, "men of this kind flatter the passions of the discontented, seduce frivolous people, and shake the foundations of weak minds. If you take all these beings, and then reckon the class of the ignorant whom they influence after their manner, you will see how few remain to resist the torrent, abide by truth, and acquiesce in the providential order of the world's government." Jane Mary, in this respect, would, under such circumstances, be found among the minority; for this mind that could still remain firm and unmoved was hers. It is a deep thinker, though another of her sex, who says, as if approving of her disposition, "Confide in what is. What is has force of law. What is has the sanction, or at least the permission, of God. And what would you put in its place? Our own ideas, which have so often deceived us, of which we know neither the tendency nor the consequences. When by chance we can decide, we hesitate, we search, and the least arrangement escapes us. And after that we pretend that our views are exact and certain, when it is a question of these myriads of combinations by which the crowd of beings that move in a similar orbit accomplish unconsciously the providential designs. We soon, however, arrive at a demonstration, that the object of our repugnance is always what is the most indispensable for us, and the most infallibly necessary [*]." It cannot be denied, but that many features of the mind of the seventeenth century, in regard to a disinclination for political discussions, entered into this character that we are attempting to delineate. Assuredly she had never read "Le Grand Cyrus," and yet whole pages from that work might be taken for a report of her habits of thinking and conversing. For example, while yielding to no one in an appreciation of the need of proper safeguards for the popular interests, her decision no doubt would have been in conformity with that expressed in the amusing chapter, where politics one day becoming the subject of conversation between two lovers, of whom the Comte Fiesque represents the grumbler, the lady very sensibly reproves him for it. "How is it possible," she says to him, "that you do not comprehend the folly of such talk? for since there must be distinctions between men, there have always been some who commanded badly, and others who obeyed badly; so that it is a useless waste of time to amuse one's self with these endless complaints which serve no purpose." "What!" he replies indignantly, "you would have me not complain when I see things done against all reason; when I see people thinking themselves free because they have not a king, while they are slaves to a hundred tyrants! What! you can endure in silence to see the noblest state in the world ill governed!" "I assure you," she calmly answered, "there is nothing I would not try, rather than see you torment yourself as you do; for, in fine, if you can govern, govern better, and you will do well; but if fortune is not pleased to give you the conduct of affairs, believe me, let them proceed as they can, and be persuaded that, as you are not pleased with what others do, what you would do would not please others if you were in their place." "If it did not please them, it ought to please them," he retorted, "for I should do nothing unjust." "Even though you did nothing unjust," she rejoined, "people would complain of you; for, in fine, be it royalty or be it re-

---

[*] Mme. Swetchine.

public, people will complain; and I own, such is my turn of mind, that I would be for complaining as little as possible. But there are people of a certain feather who have acquired such a habit of eternally speaking about the public good and affairs of state, that they are become insupportable. You will see young slips, not yet free from their tutors, who have not yet learned how to dance, and who pretend forsooth to be reformers of the republic; and you will see women, who have not even sufficient tact to dress their hair, who will boldly pronounce their opinion on state matters as if they had the wisdom and experience of Solon. Yet it would be less strange to see all the seven sages of Greece occupied in choosing ribbons, than to see so many young people of both sexes meddling with the government of the state." "I admit," says another of the party, laughing, "that politics are odious when made the topic of conversation for a whole afternoon." "Notwithstanding all that you say," adds the count, "I am resolved to speak of them as often as I choose, for I am the declared enemy of injustice, and zealous for the public good." "But supposing them to be ever so just," rejoins the lady, "what use in all these multiplied words and complaints, since, after speaking for a whole day, nothing that you desire will be the result? But this is putting the best face on it; for the truth will be, that you will have most frequently been reasoning all the while on false foundations, from having known the things without knowing their motives. On the whole then," she concludes, "let us pray Heaven to put able men in the government of affairs; but when it will be pleased for a time not to do so, let us see their faults without committing them ourselves. Keep yourself quiet then for a while, I beseech you, and do not throw us all into trouble and confusion; and, if you will be advised by me, rather than give way to these incessant murmurs, speak about balls and music, and verses and painting *."

It is true, indeed, leaving what seems only matter of history, and descending to the modern times, that the rise of a new civilization, and the fall of another, operate always in a vague and moving twilight, the last rays of an expiring day being

* Cousin, tom. i.

confused with the aurora of a morning that begins. But what appears to some to be the point that ought to be distinguished and learned here, is the wisdom that cannot be imposed on by the meteoric light while mistaking its delusive gleams for the harbingers of a new day, as " when the great Revolution broke out, and a fever of enthusiasm seized young heads. People said they were about to be delivered at last, and, consequently, imagined that till the eve of this event they had been greatly oppressed. But the fact is," says Saint-Beuve, " they had been very little oppressed; and it did not take a long time to convince M. Daunon of that fact. Those years spent in the oratory at Montmorency, which seemed to him a little under restraint while their course was prolonged, offered to him subsequently from a distance, and when seen out of tempests, a kind of ideal perspective of sheltered peace and felicity. How often, when speaking of the conditions of a happy life, has he expressed to me, without hesitation, his preference of the former period to that which succeeded it*!" In such times it would have been difficult to persuade one who " meditated," like Jane Mary, " on the law of God," and the consequences of abandoning it, that at each lull of the storm the Revolution was at an end, and that the world had arrived at the definitive. She knew how to suffer but not how to be deceived by such assurances; and yet, though for a noble course she was subject to all the exaltation of first impressions, she would nevertheless quickly return to the tone of ordinary life, and through love of her own become all patience and abnegation; for the truth was, she distrusted every voice but that of the clear and obligatory duty of each day. She dreaded political enthusiasm, and what wise person does not? " I distrust enthusiasm," says Daunon, " when it is allied with the sweetest virtues, and when it leads to generous actions; but the enthusiasm which condemns is always ferocity. Il ne faut pas ensauvager the manners of a people, which hitherto have been gentle, just, humane, and sensible. The severity of a politician is not the barbarism of a cannibal; one must not call hauteur de la révolution, what would be the region of vultures. Let us remain in the atmo-

---

* Saint-Beuve, Portraits contemporains, tom. iii.

sphere of humanity and justice." The fact is, as Saint-Beuve observes elsewhere, " that we are in general too credulous in believing society and civilization to be things inherent in man, imperishable, and as it were, eternal." " Reflect a little," he says; "at each revolution, at each social calamity of any duration, what a notable interruption to both does one perceive all of a sudden! and what a little thing alone is required to intercept and to extinguish this civilization, on which one counts with such certainty, even in the localities where it seems most brilliant! Society, they say, is an invention of Orpheus; but it won't be amiss to watch over it, and to surround it with a perpetual tending, on pain of having again to invent it."

Such used to be her spontaneous reflections whenever a great political and social crisis seemed impending. "Tremble," she would say, "at the results which may follow from a liberty without morality." It was that, as Mme. Swetchine said of herself, "she had the fault of believing only in actions;" it was very vulgar to doubt, but so it was with her. The result of her influence was to produce that general tone of mind which would suggest a further warning, couched in such terms as these: dread still more that banner, on which might be inscribed the imprecations and blasphemies of Prometheus; dread that calm irony, bidding men " worship, invoke, and flatter" the eternal ruler, whose reign nevertheless it announces is soon to finish, for long he shall not reign, and which is changed for serious assurances to proclaim that already he is less than nothing in the mind of the new deliverer—

'Εμοὶ δ' ἔλασσον Ζηνὸς ἢ μηδὲν μέλει.

The cohort of philosophers, whatever might be their denomination, produced no impression on her mind. Though in her childhood the French had overthrown a monarchy to prove the holiness of human nature, as Philarete Chasles humorously says, "she utterly despised and rejected this new deification of man, this strange fanaticism, of which she could not avoid hearing some of the echoes, having for idol humanity, as if that aggregate constituted perfection itself. She distrusted the new civilization that was to be inaugurated on barricades, free, happy, industrious, rich, powerful, sensual; constituting the definitive apotheosis of human nature—abstraction made of God*."

"One has seen men," say Droz, "who came, they said, to ensure the happiness of the majority, begin by destroying the treasures of hope, courage, and resignation, which faith supplies. What legislators! Certes, they carried presumption far, who without fearing the dreadful responsibility which they incurred, promised to find in their genius the means of substituting something better for that source of happiness which they cut off from society. Let us not condemn them—they were insane †." Saint-Beuve relates an anecdote which shows that at times they even felt themselves that they had been in somewhat that condition. "One must not judge us too strictly, said to me one day," he tells us, "an old man with an accent that I still hear,— Monsieur, nous avons été trompés par les mœurs de notre temps ‡."

It may reasonably be concluded that the example of a person fearing such results, constitutes a study that need not be without its importance for statesmen themselves; since experience proves that the savage Cyclops, of which John Paul speaks, and which always dwells at the bottom of the heart of man, will suddenly at times start forth from its den and ravage all things; then, indeed, desires are wolfish, bloody, starved, and ravenous; "but all utopias," as Mme. Swetchine observes, "in their attempts at application, have been ever works of destruction. The ardent desire of happiness in contempt of duty ever becomes a source of calamity. It is a displacement of forces, an ignorance of measure and proportion, a trespassing of our present on our future lot." "Truly surprising and deplorable is it," says M. de Falloux, "that the men who have inscribed on their banner progress of intelligence, solicitude for humanity, and the universal amelioration of public manners, should be always the first, from one end of Europe to the other, to appeal to force, and to plunge the world back into bloody insurrection." They treat the nations that are to be "delivered" after the manner

* Etudes sur les Hommes au xixe Siècle.
† Pensées sur le Christianisme.
‡ Saint-Beuve, Portraits divers.

described by Tacitus, "Si locuples, avari; si pauper, ambitiosi; quos non oriens, non occidens satiaverit; soli omnium opes atque inopiam pari affectu concupiscunt; auferre, trucidare, rapere, falsis nominibus, imperium; atque ubi solitudinem faciunt, pacem appellant." And what is the result in the sense of liberty?

> "The sensual and the dark rebel in vain,
> Slaves by their own compulsion! In mad game
> They burst their manacles, and wear the name
> Of Freedom graven on a heavier chain!"

Mme. Tastu divides men into three classes; "the one, living from day to day in the present; the others wholly given up to the future, with all the ambition of hopes; in fine, the last, all in love with the past, and the melancholy of remembrance." It is well from time to time to be reminded of a fourth class to which belonged the simple but wise and consistent Christian, whose voice may be said to be still audible within the Chapel of St. John. Can it ever be more important to meditate on such an example than at an epoch like the present, when every one justifies by his personal will his manner of thinking, judging, and speaking; "when there is an equalization of all caprices, and the tumult produced by a multitude of equivalent fractions, which refuse to submit themselves to a common denominator; when each one places his will in the centre of a Pantheon, and multiplies it to make his gods. Even this will deified by each becomes uncertain, and this is the strangest phenomenon of the present time. Each man's mind contains two or three opposite theories; one desires liberty, and at the same time despotism; another war, while wishing peace; another professes religious opinions, while destroying the last vestiges of faith; and all the while many are living in a profound ignorance of this illogical and perpetual contradiction." Hesiod says that kings are created in order to administer justice to the oppressed, and to take away unjust deeds. Such were her notions of government. Consequently she could not understand those philosophers who taught them the legitimacy of success, the holiness of force, the grandeur of doing whatever they chose, and whose system consisted in believing that whatever each one's will suggests is lawful. The occasional inconsistency of nations in this nineteenth century, long civilized, seemed to her as truly barbarous. At those times, no doubt, she was devoted to the kind of things which, in the language of the Moniteur, not to cite the words of its apes elsewhere, were " likely to act on scrupulous minds!' But such considerations can only serve to enhance in the minds of at least some thoughtful men the value of such reminiscences as we wish to perpetuate. What in fact more admirable than to observe such unity of views in an epoch so confused as our own, —when the habits of the Christian civilization are so often interrupted,—when courage is combined with perfidy,—when the most contradictory ideas are propagated,—when every thing that used to be thought fundamental seems mined, threatened, shaken,— when the notions of just and beautiful shine and are effaced in one and the same day,—when the true and the false are combined, —when belief seems to fade away, and the soil to tremble under the footsteps of men?

But this day's visit must not be too long protracted. Let us, returning to consider the more general features of her intellectual character, finish with a short summary.

It is the remark of an acute writer that Cicero persuades less than Virgil. "The orator," says he, "establishes truth rather than searches for it. Therefore every orator is somewhat suspected. The poet, on the contrary, neither establishes nor seeks truth, but he sings it. It resounds in him, and he is its echo. Thence it is that, independent of the music of his language, from age to age and every where, without trying to do it, he persuades." We are commemorating here the wisdom of one who in this respect seemed to be a participant of the poet's privilege. Jane Mary persuaded more than the philosophers. Secure, beyond the influence of "that weakness of the human mind at the period of greatest talent in great men," she, it must be confessed, seemed more susceptible of movement by the sentiment of the heart than by the logical deduction of the head. But check thy contempt; for how well would it be for many if they were like her in this way, impregnable! for by their sentiment many are on the true road, while by the intellect, and by the mind of the encyclopedist they are on that of falsehood. No question hers were often reasons of sentiment; that is to say, reasons which are in one sense, philosophically speaking, pitiable. True; but that is not a motive for us to reject them. We seem, in fact, to recognize in them that voice of the inward sense, which is for the intelligence of man what conscience is for his reason—a guide given him by God, not indeed precisely to conduct him to the heights of knowledge, but only to retain him in the confines of truth. If he discards them, he may mount quicker and higher, but it will be at the risk of losing his way*. The intimate sense is like an instinctive revelation of which doctrine is the clear formula. The two are of such simplicity that one can hardly call them methods; but this simplicity, which deprives them of all claim to confidence with subtle minds that pretend to be free-thinkers, seems to others the sign and pledge of their superiority; in fact they understand well enough that notions, of which the importance is the same for all, should not be reserved only for a few. Associated with this general direction of the intelligence there was in her whom we commemorate a disposition to believe or to wonder rather than on every point to seek an explanation; and here too we have to learn much that would often prove of vital utility. After all, it was but another instance of the wisdom of following the oldest worn tracks consecrated by the experience of ages; for, as even Topffer observes, "the ancients in thought embraced much and explained little. They were ignorant. Yes; but they had not the rage of false knowledge, that need of the positive which narrows the mind, ruins feeling, eloquence, and," he adds, " I believe, history as well; whereas the moderns are always seeking to explain what is by human powers of intellect inexplicable." She on the contrary would say, as if she had read Philemon, " Believe that God is and worship Him, but seek not to penetrate Him, for you will reap nothing but the seeking. Don't inquire as to whether He exists or not, but as existing and as ever present adore Him." "In wonder, τῷ θαυμάζειν," says Aristotle, "does philosophy begin: and in astonishment, τῷ θαμβεῖν," says Plato, "does all true philosophy finish †."

* Topffer, Réflexions et Menus Propos.
† Coleridge.

Again, who will not be struck at the attitude of calm assurance in this noble and antique figure? "In these strange times we live in," says an illustrious author, "how few seem certain respecting their ground, or resolved to stand by any thing! How easily are the masses led to adopt any new cry, or follow any standard—some through sheer ignorance, others bewildered by their metaphysical and personal views." She, on the contrary, had the tact of discerning what was the side for true men, and with unerring simplicity what she clung to was the cause of justice and of honour. Certainty! who will give us that? Let the persons who ask this question turn in here and think awhile. This was the way to it; here was the secret; no trifle either, in good faith, if the learned should speak truth of it: and what has philosophy to offer in comparison with her intrepid security and her deathless reliance? Consider the metaphysician; "Which of them," says Topffer, "is serious in regard to their own system? I mean, which of them regards his system as the real shelter and safeguard of their destiny? Of course they are sticklers for it, and grow warm in its defence; but what does that signify? Children also build castles of cards and defend them, and cry if they are knocked over; but do they lodge in them? The evil of this method consists in its making men disdainful of the more simple and natural way of intimate sense and sentiment. Skill in this sort of complicated fencing causes them to have no taste for the common employment of their own strength; accordingly, in general, their situation is singular, even in regard to questions that they solve. They have neither the faith of believers, nor the negation of infidels, nor the certainty of physicians, nor the balancing of thinkers, and they offer the spectacle of people who have demonstrations in quantity and not one conviction."

I will add to these characteristics of the intelligence of Jane Mary another singular attribute, which in her latter years belonged to it, that of being able to discern characters—almost to read souls. Bossuet, speaking of the dream of the Princess Palatine, says "Je me plais à répéter toutes ces paroles, malgré les oreilles délicates; elles effacent les discours les plus magnifiques, et je voudrois ne parler plus que ce langage." Somewhat of the same impression might be experienced here. It was not that she was skilled in physiognomy, according to the curious observations laid down by Gilles de Rome in the long chapter, where he treats de la physionomie des hommes, which he calls a science noble et merveilleuse, though that treasury of curious deductions might be read by any one with profit. Nor was it alone that in a general way she judged well of characters, which, in most cases, turns out to be the right way. She seemed gifted with a sort of intuitive knowledge—a peculiar penetration like that which was ascribed to Tiburtius, who observing the words and manners of a certain Torquatus, when pretending to be a Christian, maintained before the Prefect Fabius that he was not one, when so it turned out. She had an insight into souls, and could tell your thoughts. What Mlle. de Scudéry says of the Countess de Maure was applicable to her—" Her imagination was so prompt and lively that it could detect the hearts of those who spoke to her, and one might qualify as divination the manner in which she understood thoughts, while it was nevertheless certain that she never suffered her imagination to get the start of her judgment, but that she judged always of every thing with equity!" Still, to some consciences her artless speech would give a smart lash at times. It seemed in her, however, rather a supernatural perception, a certain sense of taint where there was an inward spot of shame; for, as just remarked, it was not by physiognomy that she judged: and the poet would have been of this opinion, for he says—

> "Ah! surer than suspicion's hundred eyes
> Is that fine sense, which to the pure in heart
> By mere oppugnancy of their own goodness
> Reveals the approach of evil!"

But darkness has overtaken us over the bones of the dead. We must, for this time, leave the sanctuary in which the wisdom of a great example is enshrined.

We may sum up its general character in few words; for, indeed, while she lived one might have spared one's praises; knowing her was enough. Her soul was as the ideal accomplished of those whom irony has not withered, whom novelty has not intoxicated, whom worldly agitations leave still delicate and free. Truth breathed by cheerfulness characterized her whole life. Her head was not disjoined from her heart; and as an old French writer says, "those who have the heart right have the head and understanding right also, whereas those whose hearts are double and complicated, have never a sound judgment, there being always some false light which gives them distorted and unproportioned views*." The sensibility and elevation of her mind were evinced on the least occasion; passionate for truth and honour—in regard to anger sinless. Indifference for good is truly said to be the most dangerous of immoralities, while, as the Spaniards say, "irresolution is worse than bad execution." She, in the cause of justice, was impassioned; but it was not a sterile satisfaction of the fancy—it was drawn into action by her deeds. She presented an example to justify the words of Mme. Swetchine, saying, "I have a taste for metaphysics, and even for mysticism, but a single good action performed at first thoughts seems to me to have more value than the sublimest conceptions, and the ravishments of the third heaven." By day and night invoking the prayers of her whom she loved to qualify in the language of the Litany as being the seat of wisdom—sedes sapientiæ, in whom it rested and fructified, she was ever in regard to the highest and the lowest things discreet. Entrusted with many a secret, when you had spoken it 'twas dead, and she was the grave of it. Yet on other occasions no one was less reserved, her prudence being any thing rather than finesse, for a frank nature was her great prerogative. To end with the lines so truly applicable to her—hers were

"———— three treasures, love and light,
And calm thoughts regular as infant's breath;
And three firm friends, more sure than day and night—
Herself, her Maker, and the angel Death."

---

* Le Chevalier de Méré.

CHAPTER VI.

THERE is no spot so sweet and sacred, no voice so musical and impressive, as not to be seen and heard at times in immediate contrast with the impatient pride of frivolous minds, and the despotism of inattention. How shall we hope to escape from being confronted with such dispositions now, when we have to speak of one who belonged not to what is called by holy tongues the world, and who kept aloof from what it exclusively admires? Yet will there be some to hear with observant souls this recurrence of the voice that comes now from the chapel within which we stand, to publish the example of one who soared above the world, and fed on thoughts that were not of it.

I would not exaggerate or depart in aught from strictest truth. In this character there were at times impressions which oft affect the wisest; there were such allowed infirmities that honesty is never free of. But "she had always the air of one who, as St. Augustin recommends, tolerated rather than loved the presence of the world*;" and after all, as he says elsewhere, "in omnibus talibus, non usus rerum, sed libido mentis, in culpa est †." Moreover, as some one else is described, "her temper had that sweet and noble frankness in it, which bespake her yet a virgin from the world." Besides, she had seen with an awakened intelligence what the world is,—"the world in its nature," as Mme. de Sévigné distinguishes; and, as a gallant writer of the seventeenth century has truly said, "one is no longer of the world as soon as one begins to know it; at least," he adds, "the journey is then far advanced; I do not know a better road ‡." That road she followed early. Of the world, to which she never really belonged, she understood in smiling at it what she had learned too from judging with her mother's eyes, its cowardice, its egotism, its ambition, its bad

---

* Serm. 105, and Conc. 3 in Ps. 30.
† Lib. 3, de Doct. Christ. cap. 11.
‡ Le Chevalier de Méré.

faith, its sanguinary resentments, its secret treasons. "Alas! that poor child," said her cousin, the Countess de Rochefort, one day on perceiving her guileless nature, "why if it were not for her mother she would let herself be trampled on like the dirt under foot." "Nay, is it true?" she replied many years afterwards, when hearing of this remark having been made. "Did she say that though?" But she felt herself unarmed for the external struggles of life; and so some years after when she lost the guardian of her youth, she said to one who alone remained to her, "They're a pretty pair to be left alone together with the world to bustle in." She saw besides the ridiculous side of all worldly proceedings, and had no desire to join them, or make one in them. As a mere woman, who was content to be a woman, and to play that adorable part well, she disliked the worldly character: as a Christian, she dreaded and detested it. Indulgent to frivolity when it could possibly be excused, she had a horror for lies and egotism, for all that narrows the mind and dries up the heart; yet she judged not of the world from being unqualified to understand its meaning, and to grace with the charm of a foreign flower its most exalted circles. As we have been lately told of Mme. Swetchine, her example might have taught people of the world how the duties of this life are more reconcileable than they suppose with those of fervent piety; and could demonstrate to persons naturally inclined to consider a life of faith as a sterile contemplation, how it can be made compatible with all the devotion to a family, all the solicitudes of friendship, and all the activities of a cultivated mind. The aristocratic feeling respecting blood and fortune is not confined, as a literary Frenchman observes, to any one class. No where is it found to exist with more force than amongst the people[*]; and certainly it would not be very philosophical to found an accusation against any one on the ground of being susceptible of the same impressions. It is not to be denied that in the instance we are confronted with, there was no studied or pedantic rejection or disavowal of a sentiment which is of all ages, and of all races. "Like your true nobility," as Henry VIII. said of Queen Catharine, always bearing herself towards high and low alike, her least words and all her movements were

[*] Louis Ratisbonne.

characterized by delicacy and distinction. As Bishop Fisher said of Margaret, Countess of Richmond, "in favours, in words, in gestures, in every demeanour of herself, so grete nobleness did appear that what she spoke or dyde it mervayllously became her." It was impossible for an utter stranger not to recognize in her at the first glance the sort of grandeur which belongs to the deep practical humility of a true lady. There was something even in her face, sweet as it was, that spoke of dignity. On one occasion, being at her devotions in the church of St. Roch at Paris, on leaving the chapel of the blessed sacrament, she was greatly surprised to find that she had to walk through a lane of persons, who were in fact waiting to see her pass to her carriage, having mistaken her for a foreign queen who happened to be at that time in Paris; but though the mistake caused her and those who heard of it a hearty fit of laughing, it would have been only the truth to say with the poet, that

"——— Each her doing
So singular in each particular,
Crown'd what she was doing in the present dee ,
That all her acts were queens."

Leon Aubineau, in his memoirs of the Marchioness Le Bouteiller, condescends to notice the attention of that admirable lady to her dress, which was conformable to her condition, and characterized by an incomparable decorum and simplicity. She whom we delineate loved also, it is true, the elegant propriety of the world. "We who do not much mix with it," she used to say, "ought not to offend it, at least, by our appearance." Her dress was ever in accordance with its notions of what is fitting, while far removed from what was showy and expensive; and this conformity with the world we may hear praised by gravest authors, as by the Père Ventura for instance, in his "Portrait of the Christian Woman." In fact, her acts of acquiescence in this respect, seemed only to furnish another example of the compatibility between the accessories to her condition and the most profound piety; as when Isabella, the sister of St. Louis, told Agnes de Harcourt, "that in the time when she lived in the world, and used, by the desire of her mother Queen Blanche, to wear very rich and costly apparel,—qu'elle avoit aussi bon cœur et aussi devot à nostre Seigneur quand elle avoit ces riches ornemens, comme elle eust habit plus religieux." On the person of Jane Mary, however, you remarked no rich jewel with which she played while conversing with you. She had, it is true, her diamonds and other costly gems, all gifts,—gifts on her marriage, gifts on the fête days of her children,—but it took her a week to find them when she was to assist at the marriage of her niece. The ugliness of costume, which is sometimes affected by aristocratic pride, ought not to please in either sex a genial and cultivated eye, even though to avoid it, one had recourse to a compliance with a little fancy savouring of lower walks; but she used to admire how the Parisian women "avec un rien d'étoffe," as Saint-Beuve says, arranged themselves so as to appear, even when not naturally handsome, always charming. But she possessed an exquisite tact with regard to all the social exigencies of life, and while soaring so far above them in her homely thoughts, no one understood with more subtlety the ordinary things of what is called society in the world. She had that simplicity of taste and of manners, which belongs to those influenced by the refined centre which the noble society of Paris presents. "The profound study of the world," as the Count Xavier de Maistre remarks, "almost always brings back those who have made it to the disposition of being simple and without pretensions, so that it is sometimes only after a long labour of initiation that one arrives at the point from which one ought to commence." She was at ease and simple every where; and in this respect it is curious enough to remark, how things most widely separated present in some points an analogy; for this careless, negligent way of hers when speaking of greatness in the world, was, after all, the manner at all times of what is greatest, even in a worldly sense, and most socially eminent upon earth. Cæsar himself, for instance, has been remarked for this very disposition to express himself, never pompously, methodically, and gravely, but always in a careless, simple, light, unaffected way. "These masters of the world," says the Chevalier de Méré, "who are placed, as it were, above fortune, regard only with a kind of indifference the things that we admire, and from being but little moved by them they speak of them in an off-hand way, and with a certain negligence." It must be acknowledged, in fine, that if people of the world showed a certain diffidence and distrust in her regard, as if fearing the contagion of an elevation of thoughts that they felt to be far above their own, there was no direct intention discernible to withhold respect; for the fact is, as a French novelist remarks, if the world almost always penetrates and exposes false and culpable sentiments, it never secretly, whatever it may pretend, doubts an instant those that are natural, generous, and true.

Though it is not within the scope of our enterprise to revert to the fact and circumstances of the existence which was characterized by the interior features that we have to delineate, it will serve to throw light upon our present subject, and to facilitate our better comprehension of what is to follow later, if we briefly recall some few external matters which belong to the history of its early position; for, in fact, many things would not be sufficiently appreciated, if one were ignorant of the society in which she had passed her youth.

Resident in Paris at an early age, closely allied to the Dillons of France, to the Rocheforts of the Landes, and to the Carolis of Hungary, she may be said to have seen when a girl the salons of the ancient régime, and even to have lived in her childhood with some of the most eminent personages of the former court. And here is an occasion presented where I would allow my pen that liberty of wandering, to the enjoyment of which I began by laying claim. Some narratives, in which all concerned are now departed from this life, will not come in awkwardly, I hope, in a talk of salons and friendly circles, but appear appropriate as showing what was a type of faith in the midst of the society of the nineteenth century. Let me then relate a pleasant anecdote connected with the Beau Dillon,—that Count Edward in whose society her parents spent their first years of residence in Paris. The narrative was told the present writer by M. Chevalier of the Bibliothèque of St. Geneviève. It was on his return from Asia, when he had visited the Troad, that being at Vienna he went to a masquerade at the opera. Seated alone on the front bench of a box, he suddenly heard many steps in the lobby behind him, and the door being thrown open some masks entered, and one to whom the rest showed deference, begged him with rather a stately air of patronage not to leave or disturb himself, and then took his seat by his side. "Truly," thought the other, "I was not going to do so; but who can you be, I wonder, to suppose that I was about to give up my seat for you?" The strange mask then asked him if he was of Vienna. "Not so, fine mask." "Of Germany?" "No." "Of France?" "Precisely so; and I return from Constantinople." "Indeed! What a pleasure to have met you! Pray, then, tell me what say the Turks about our line of defence, and our detached forts?" "They say, fine mask, that they mean to surprise you; and when you least think of it, to penetrate your lines between your forts and carry off your women and children." "You make me tremble," replied the stranger; "but say, to change the subject, do you know Paris well? Have you known there Count Edward Dillon?" "Yes, mask. I know him a little." "Proud—eh?" "Nay—all amiability and kindness." "Indeed!—well, perhaps you are right. I had thought differently. Gallant Frenchman, good night." Then rising hastily, all those in the two adjacent boxes who had entered with him rose, and the party left with some noise and manifestations of respect to him who seemed to be the chief of the party. Next day, going to the embassy, he was asked, "Were you not at the opera last night?" "Yes;— what of that?" "And you spoke to a strange mask?" "Yes." "Do you know who it was?" "Not so." "It was the Emperor Joseph; and he is so pleased with you that he says whatever you ask he will grant it." "Two days after I received orders from C——l to retrograde to Belgrade, where the plague was raging. M. de C——l, without having been ever there, had just published his journey to the Troad, and being, I believe, angry at my book's appearance, had a deep grudge against its author. This, I was convinced, had led to the new order. 'Well then, said I, now is my time. Let the Emperor grant me a passport, and at Paris will I justify myself.' I obtained it; I set off; and as I entered Paris, the head of Mme. de Lamballe was borne on a pike by my carriage. 'This is not then exactly the moment,' I said, 'to justify myself to the King's minister;' and so collecting some trinkets I fled to England. Landing at Southampton, I was asked about these watches and trinkets. 'What do you want with so many?' 'It is to eat,' I replied. The officer smiled; took me to his house, where I spent the next day, and there I made my first acquaintance with the hospitable English." Such was the narrative of this interesting old man, and, as nearly as possible, the words that he related it in. Count Edward did not survive many years after the arrival of his relatives in France; but the Countess, who lived to a very advanced age, after being well known at the court of George IV., who possessed, as she maintained, many excellent qualities, continued her friendship for them till the last. Soon after their first arrival, being resident at Bellevue, the attention of the royal family was elicited by the beauty and demeanour of two English children, who were among the assistants at mass in the royal chapel at St. Cloud. The King, Charles X., having expressed himself graciously on hearing of their names —for it was Jane Mary and her sister, whom the mother had conducted there,—they take advantage of such favour in a very innocent way, obtaining permission to have the bath-chair of their father, who was then an invalid, rolled into chapel every Sunday, as it was nearer their house than the parish church. Adventures, too, of an analogous kind used to be a source of diversion to her on her journeys, which wanting the aid of later inventions, that serve nearly to realize Mme. de Sévigné's wish of her daughter's being mounted on a "Hippogryphe," and able to breakfast with her at Paris, and to dine the same day in Provence with M. de Grignan*, somewhat resembled those of former times, when the court of France, as Benvenuto Cellini said, used to travel like a funeral.

At no period had Jane Mary the air of one who tried to unite the form of religion and the spirit of the world. Her devotion was not in alliance with that spirit; but, in general, when circumstances enabled her, she made of her worldly position not an end, but a mean,—all her thoughts in regard to it being aimed at the object of pleasing and serving God. That trait related of the Lady Anne, Countess of Arundel and Surrey, of sending her coach when she heard that certain resolute Catholics were intending to take up the body of Mrs. Line,

* Lett. 1 6.

after her execution at Tyburn, for having given entertainment to a priest; and of her having the body conveyed in it to her own house, where it was kept with reverence till it could be disposed of; that trait, I say, of pious heroism was quite after the style of Jane Mary, had there been an occasion. One can fancy seeing her give the orders from the resolution of a moment, the sparkle in her eye that denoted the great heart—impulsive, fiercely disdainful of human opinion and human power in a question of justice and of the soul; indicating a mind that was ever proud to offer its worldly position, as well as every thing also that it possessed, at the feet of Jesus; triumphant if it could but draw upon itself opprobrium for his sake. Nothing still that savours of the world, you perceive, in this character; while invested outwardly even with what the world esteems and worships.

Cousin, in his book on Mme. de Sablé *, has noted the different and rare qualities which are necessary to assemble and retain round a person a company of choice minds; the subject of our notice would be found perhaps to have presented many of these qualities in their harmony and perfection. To use the words of a great author, " she used no phrases of friendship," but it became pretty generally known that she " would not fail you at your need." As we read in Joinville of St. Louis, she "aymoit moult toutes manieres de gens qui se mectoient au service de Dieu." But it seemed to be in her destiny, moreover, to attract round her interesting as well as truly religious persons. It was impossible not to love and respect those whom she loved and respected, the fact invariably proving that she was right in her judgment. Even in regard to public characters, as, for instance, to the Queen of the French, one could not avoid contracting a kind of affection for those whom she constantly praised. Much more did one feel one's self drawn within the circle of her sympathy when it was a question of personal and familiar friends. It is true that she preferred occupations of charity to what are called friendships of sentiment; and it is Charles Lamb who says, " I know not whether they be not a spring of purer and nobler delight, as well as of a more disinterested virtue, than that which arises from the latter." But, for all that, she had her

* Chap. xi.

especial friends, who agreed pretty well with her in their tastes and habits, but, as Elia would say, "with a difference,"—their sympathies in general being rather understood than expressed. What she liked more than all the philosophers, more than all the men of letters, more than all distinguished people, was what Count Molé regarded as the greatest originality among the orators of the chamber, namely, "un honnête homme venant dire simplement et clairement des choses sensées." In her early life God sent her for direction and friendship three such men in the Father Scot, the Abbé Brady, and Father Lythgoe.

I shall not attempt to enumerate all her friends. Her memory might be associated now with many remarkable names that were at one time in vogue; but so quickly do we all pass from this life, which, as St. Colomban himself truly said, "non sit dicenda vita sed via," that there will be no obstacle to my giving the portraits of a few whom she most esteemed, and a knowledge of whom is not irrelevant or void of utility towards the better comprehension of her own character; for what Mlle. de Scudéry said of Angèlique Paulet was strictly true of her,— that no one has ever loved their friends with more warmth than she did. She has ever tried to render them service with joy, even at the expense of her health. She has loved them absent and in misfortune, and has carried her friendship for them beyond the tomb [*].

Amongst those whom she greatly prized, one ought to mention undoubtedly certain very obscure but very holy men from Ireland, of quite an antique, and, if one may use the expression of a great author, Colombanic type, who used at times to visit her on their different passages to and from Rome or Jerusalem; for, as in the days of the Merovingians, there were still men emigrating to the Continent on the track of St. Colomban, who, while desiring to offer the homage of their ardent devotion at the threshold of the holy Apostles, or our Saviour's blessed tomb, used gladly to stop for a night where they could reckon upon meeting a soul as dovelike innocent, and as fervent as their own. Besides these pilgrims of roving propensities, or palmer-friends of such a mediæval character—friends, one may call

---

[*] Le Grand Cyrus.

them,—for, after years of absence, they were as cordially received as if they had only departed yesterday, there were also many venerable priests always near her of stationary habits, the simple and manly character of whose minds endeared them to her judgment. Loving religion, and of exquisite, overflowing humanity, they were men not mercenary even when it was a religious object—perfect gentlemen; nothing of the "esprit de corps" could be traced in them; men always religiously moved, but not to be caught by the profane laity chuckling or waymenting when conferring professionally with one another on their money, gains, or losses; nevertheless, wholly unpolished and untaught according to some schools, presenting a very striking contrast to "that class of modest divines," described by Elia, "who affect to mix in equal proportion the gentleman, the scholar, and the Christian, though," he adds, and with what truth need not be questioned, "I know not how, the first ingredient is generally found to be the predominating dose in the composition." They were in general men of great holiness, who had rather an antique respect for people of birth, but by no means much consideration for what is called "the better classes;" partly, perhaps, because they observed that these latter were inclined to press hard upon the poor, and treat themselves too, if the truth must out, rather from top to toe, as the French say, and not in the least after the respectful fashion for which the terrible Merovingians were, for all their crimes, so remarkable. They were men of very warm hearts and very primitive ways of thinking, who, without being unknown to great personages, loved and respected poor industrious people,—being themselves, in fact, like that Ermenfroy, the monk of Luxeuil, who had such a regard for work and workmen, that on the Sunday, while distributing the pain benit at mass, when he perceived the hard rough hands of the labourers, used to stoop down to kiss them, with a tender respect for those noble marks of the work of the week*. With regard to the mention of her other friends belonging to the society of the world, one must of course be discreet, even though they are gone; but one may say in general of them all, that none of them had an austere de-

---

* Montalembert, Moines d'Occident, ii. 516.

meanour or a proud learning to make them despise the conversation of women. She would have preferred to such personages "a fishing, hawking, hunting, country gentleman." On the contrary, they were such as naturally liked to speak and listen, like others, on common, and even sometimes merely amusing topics. They were persons honest and sensible, who, when genius was added, no less defended with passion moderated ideas. But to begin with what wore a lighter character. Thrown, as already noticed, in her early life into the society of the old French noblesse, it is natural that we should find amongst them some of her most esteemed friends. Her cousin, the once beautiful and ever accomplished Countess of Rochefort, may be first noticed. This lady, whose husband was the personal friend of Louis XVI., having received from him the gift of a watch made with his own royal hands, which used to be always suspended in the bedchamber of his widow, used to spend every second winter in Paris, the previous one having been passed in her lonely castle of Bellade in the landes of Bourdeaux, where for company she had only her curé to dine with her on Sundays, and for music every evening the wolves howling round the fosse of the castle. This venerable lady used to make the journey to the capital with her own horses, being in the carriage at the first dawn, and stopping each day at one o'clock, through a dread of encountering thunder-storms, which, as if she had been studying Ruskin's chapter on the cloud-chariots, while fearing rather than admiring their "noblest conditions," she thought were more likely to be met with in the afternoon than at an earlier hour. In Paris she was the delight of a numerous and brilliant circle; and, in fact, nothing could surpass the exquisite suavity of her manners, the constancy of her faith, or the romantic charm of her exhaustless narratives, solemn and half-ludicrous themes—all were alike to her. She used to describe, for instance, the indignation of the country gentlemen, when, by order from Paris, the weathercocks were taken down from their chateaus; then the flight of the emigrés across the Jura, escorted by peasants, who used to meet their carriages on the road, and communicate with them by signs; then the imprisonments and escapes of her husband, who on one occasion attempted to pass through the bars of his prison while she was waiting for him below. Let me again give a narrative which this time used to be related by Mme. de Rochefort. "I was dining," she said, "at the house of a friend. A servant brought a letter to one of the guests. He handed it to his wife, saying audibly enough to be heard by herself, 'Le monstre est mort.' Who was this monster? The marquis, for such was his rank, had inhabited his chateau in the south of France, having only one son, a dissipated and desperate young man, generally absent from home. One day a strange carriage drove to the door. The marquis saw it from a distance in his own park. Servants came to him breathless to announce the arrival of a visitor, whom they had never before seen, long as they had lived there. The marquis returned to his house. It was, true enough, a total stranger to him, who said, however, that he was come about an affair of grave importance, which was to be heard in secret. He then told him that there was a plot to assassinate himself, the marquis, in his own house that very night; but that he must remain at home as usual and follow exactly his usual habits, only adding, that he must order his carriage for the next morning, as he would have to leave for Paris. The stranger said that he had himself come from the capital expressly to warn him, and that his life depended on fulfilling punctually all the conditions. So he departed as he came, and the servants were told nothing. When the night arrived, the marquis, obedient to his lesson, retired, through a long suite of rooms, to his bedchamber, and there he sat, read, knelt, said his prayers, undressed, and went to bed. Sleep was out of the question. So after a few hours that were not over agreeable, a step was heard advancing nearer and nearer, till at length a figure approached; and just as it was about rushing on him with a poignard, some men issued from under the bed, where they had been in ambush unknown to the marquis, seized and overthrew him. It was the marquis's own son. The father had been told to depart next morning for Paris. The object of the journey was now disclosed; it was to obtain a letter of cachet. So he proceeded thither. The king, Louis XV., who was aware of all that had happened, held in his hand the letter open when he received him. 'Malheureux père,' he said to him, 'Le voici.' Thrown into the Bastile the wretched son lived many years; and it was to announce his death that the present grim letter was now delivered to the marquis as he sat at table."

It seemed to be in the destiny of Jane Mary to have great and tragic events brought before her, both actually and by means of her intimate friends, in a striking and dramatic manner. In 1830 Mme. de Rochefort, who used to relate to her each incident of her own life in such a graphic way as to make her cousin feel the same impressions as if she had been present at each, going to the waters of Vichy, when changing horses met the Duchess d'Angouleme, whose horses were also being changed. The duchess, recognizing her, let down the glass, and said abruptly and eagerly, "How did you leave things at Paris?" "All well there, madam; but I have been stopping for a while with a friend at a day's distance on the road hither, before I set out on this journey." "Au contraire, tout est perdu," said the duchess, and pulling up the window, she was driven off towards the capital. The Bishop of Nancy, Monseigneur Forben Janson, who united the tone and manners of the "grand seigneur" with those of the fervent Christian, was another of her most intimate friends,—insomuch that the reliquary with the particle of St. Chârles, which he was in habit of wearing round his neck, was transmitted to her after his death by the marquis, his brother. From his lips too used to be treasured up unnumbered narratives of high and affecting interest concerning the Revolution and its horrors. Belonging to a different category was Olivier, curé of St. Roch, who afterwards became bishop of Evreux. He also had conversation, interesting and instructive, for all auditors. One of his personal reminiscences was singular. He said that he had been lately called to a sick lady in the Fauxbourg du Roule. He asked why she applied to him at such a distance? It was replied that she would send for no one else. He went immediately, and was presented by a young person to an elderly lady seated in an arm-chair, who received him politely, and began to converse on various topics. But in fine, "Madam," he at length said, seizing a pause, "as you sent for me, I presume it was to fulfil my sacred ministry." "Not in the least," replied the old Voltarian dame; "people said you were active and devoted, and I told them, I'll try him; so being in another parish I wanted to ascertain whether you really would come to an utter stranger at such an hour and living so far away. Adieu." On going out the young lady fell on her knees, and implored him to return after a few days, as the old lady was impenitent, and she could have no influence on her. The Abbé Migeon, who was at the time attached to the church of St. Germain en Laye, was another of her intimates, who had also many singular and suggestive narratives respecting his ecclesiastical career; and in general people knew that what most interested her was some trait or circumstance that had relation to the soul. For instance, he related one evening with great joy the success that had just crowned his efforts to convert an aged and long impenitent infidel of the French army. His manner of proceeding throws light upon his own character, and indirectly upon hers who so well appreciated its merits. Being told by a sister of the hospice of St. Louis that there was in one of the sick wards an old colonel day after day blaspheming terribly, and always refusing to see a priest, he paid him his first visit as if through mistake, having entered his room hastily instead of another's; but during the instants he stayed, and while slily apologizing for the error—God will have pardoned him for calling it so—he let fall in an off-hand way a pleasant word or two to encourage the old man as to his own prospect of recovery; expressing surprise that he should be in a sick room with such looks, and making himself for the moment so agreeable, that being pressed to return by the old soldier, who seemed mightily taken with him at first sight, he promised to do so if he could find time. Needless to add, that the rogue was careful enough to keep his word. During his succeeding and often repeated visits—for by this time the good man would hear of no other companion—he spoke frankly and bluntly, as if he had all his life been a soldier himself. What was it to him, he demanded roughly, who chose to accept his ministry? He had to do his own duty; it was for others to think of theirs. Brief, it was, in fine, the priest who had the air of needing to be persuaded to hear the gallant old officer's confession, which led afterwards to a total change of his interior dispositions, and to a holy, and happy, and supremely peaceful death. This good vicar, who afterwards "came all the way to England," as he would have said, to visit her, devoted his means and his time to the support of orphan boys, of whom he had about thirty lodged and fed, to the marvellous discomfort, as most people would think, of a domestic interior, in the house he lived in. Another frequent guest during her residence in St. Germain, who in fact became her intimate friend, was Monseigneur Affre, the archbishop of Paris, subsequently martyred. Frequently of an evening this simple-minded, fervent prelate, used to drop in, and refresh his wearied spirits with, what he was pleased to call, the sweet charm of a purely domestic conversation, not without his giving occasional hints as to his embarrassments and struggles with the government of that day. Mme. de Lézeau, the noble and venerable superioress of the sisterhood of the Loges in the forest, was also among the number of her confidential friends, to whom that lady's private chaplain, the excellent Abbé Brady, had introduced her long before in the Rue Barbette. An honester and truer-hearted man never breathed than this good priest—a saint after the fashion of St. Francis de Sales—who seemed to look on Jane Mary as his own daughter, and whose intervals of leisure in the capital were always passed in her society,—who at his death left to her his ivory image of our Lady, to her infant son his watch, and to her mother his sacerdotal vestments for the use of whoever might be her chaplain. Among her circle too one ought not to omit mention of Garibaldi the internonce, nor of the celebrated and illustrious Lacordaire, nor of Prince Theodore Gallitzin,—between whom and herself the bond of amity was formed by their conformity of tastes in regard to the poor, and by their zeal to promote the religious interest of the military. One might mention also the Duc and Duchesse de Laval Montmorency, whose affection for the holy offices of the Church resembled her own; also the Abbé Eleuthère de Girardin, grandson of the Marquis de Girardin d'Ermonville, whose deep and unaffected piety rendered him the object of her esteem. Count Schouvaloff ought not to be omitted, who afterwards became a priest and a Barnabite, and whose early and sudden death supplied another instance of the mysteries of Providence, in shortening, by a sweet and gentle process, the career of His elect. But above all, one must make mention of the cordial and venerated friend who so often came to England for the sole purpose of conversing with her for a few days, seeming to care for nothing else, and returning to the Continent when he had finished his visit. I mean the estimable, ever to be revered Count Peter Yermoloff, whose family will pardon, I am sure, this introduction of a name that she ever breathed before the altar in one or other of the two mementos, and whose memory is enshrined along with her own in the hearts of her survivors.

There were some who only crossed her path as birds of passage, while their regard for her passed with them to distant regions of the earth. Of this number were the Archbishop of New York, who became doubly endeared to her for the success with which he exerted his great humility in procuring the conversion to the Catholic faith of her nurse, for whose deliverance from error she had in vain laboured during many years; Pompallier, whose see was in New Zealand, and of whose holy narratives she was never weary; Gally, the confessor and missionary of China, where he had been for months encaged and unable to stand upright, from whom she obtained as a relic the autograph; and many others whose names I cannot recall. There were others also whose memory was dear to her: the Abbé Jammes, who departed from local usages for the baptism in the house of her infant in an alarming moment; Jourdan, who prepared its brother and sister for their first communions; the Curé of St. Severin, to whose predictions as to revolution that were later verified she listened with a trembling interest; and, above all, Desgenettes, the venerable curé of Nôtre Dame des Victoires, whom she made godfather of her youngest boy, ever revering him as a saint, looking up to him as a father, and loving him as a friend. I might have spoken of Blake, the patriarchal bishop of Dromore, whose memory is in benediction, great feeder of poor people; and of Father Kenny, the provincial of his order, a man of remarkable intelligence, who returned from America praising the citizens of that republic; but though successively the directors of her childhood, she saw them only at rare and long intervals in later life; and, of course, to most others, to whom death has not yet imparted its own sanctity, we are restrained from making even an allusion as we pass; but all whom I have mentioned possessed characters that evinced a close affinity with her own disposition, and, as such, they belong naturally to the background of a picture which is intended principally to represent herself.

It was not exactly in accordance with the general style of Jane Mary, for a thousand reasons, to think of having, at any period of her life, what the French call a salon; and yet, imperceptibly and undesignedly, she could not, while in Paris, prevent people from being attracted by goodness of heart and nobleness of soul. There was, then, the natural foundation of a true salon, which springs up of itself, and is the result of habit, and not of premeditation. Though she did not seek the pleasure of great receptions, no one, in an innocent way, enjoyed them more. Her mind and manners, though perfectly natural as belonged to her condition, had a certain vivacity which was ever restrained by an exquisite politeness, always negligent and always distinguished. Her drawing-room was neither a narrow conventicle, nor a literary coterie, nor a philosophical school, nor a political circle, nor a worldly assembly. Excepting as far as politeness required, she seemed anxious to be unregarded herself and to draw out others. It was her object, through kindness to her guests, always in her own house to have the conversation kept up, but never to engross it,—

φιλεῖ δὲ σιγᾷν, ἢ λέγειν τὰ καίρια.

She was the soul of the company, not their doctor or their patroness. Her house at other times, solely in consequence of her own influence, was leisure, recovery of health, freedom for all, gaiety for some, reverie and calm study for others. She had no ambition to have revived in her house the conversations of an hotel Rambouillet; and if you must have recited there certain pieces in place of old heroic ballads, you would have to manufacture them out of the prattle of her children; as when the young skater and his sister address each other thus,—

He. "Mary, I did not see you on the pond yesterday."
She. "No more you will to-day."

Arch and pleasant thus, and capable of being tuned to please your fancy, there was therefore nothing in the kind of talk that went on under her auspices to frighten any one. Her evening receptions did not differ much from those of a protracted visit of days; for every one felt quite at home, and at ease, and comfortable, and secure, where she presided. Induced for other reasons than those of Macbeth, she used to say, or at least she acted so as to enable her to say,

> "——————— To make society
> The sweeter welcome, we will keep ourself
> Till supper-time alone."

She would always have her table elegantly, but not expensively, maintained. She would never take any thing herself but what was of the plainest kind, and during Lent she denied herself secretly the most ordinary indulgence. In Paris, the scene of these reunions was successively, but with many intervals elapsing, in the apartment of the Princess de T——t, at 22 in the Rue de la Ville L'Evêque; at the Rond Point, in the Champs Elysées; in the Place Vendome; in the Hotel de Forben Janson, and in the Rue Tronchet, where the Revolution of February found, rather than surprised her, in confinement, her little John Gerald being just born. Subsequent to that event, Kensington became her residence, where these reunions were kept together by a link from old continental friendship; and here, with its removal to the Continent, three weeks before her own death, they finished.

Let me endeavour to retrace some of the characteristics in which they always and every where participated. Strictly applicable to them was every word in a passage which describes those of one assuredly far better known, and who exercised a much wider influence, to which, by the way, at one period, she had herself been no utter stranger, but which resembled hers, —through no premeditation on her part, or desire to imitate them, but merely as being invested unaffectedly with the same thoroughly Christian character. Though in her own apartment she had no desire to witness that luxury of inutilities of all kinds which surrounds so many in her position; though she took no delight in rare, singular, minute objects, things old and new, ugly and pretty, trivial and elegant, fragile and expensive, all jumbled together, as in a boutique de bric-à-brac; passing her time in rubbing and handling these little idols of worldly vanity, there was nothing in the aspect of her rooms that indicated a want of the sense of even artistic beauty. She retained from her habits of life in France a taste for well-lit rooms. Her salon was brilliant with lamps and tapers; so that the first impression on entering it was that of a worldly atmosphere, which might remind you of the anecdote that Mme. de Sévigné relates, of some one not over intelligent, who, on hearing of the canonization of St. Francis de Sales, exclaimed, "What he! a saint! why I have often dined with him!" But one soon perceived that if this exterior was studied to please people of the world, the interior appertained to God; and that she who possessed these advantages was not possessed by them. It was the same with regard to the commencement of her conversations. It would not have done to trot her out, if I may be allowed the expression, before any one who wanted something extraordinary in the way of devout or literary talk. Hers, it must be repeated, was neither the religious, nor the political, nor the literary, nor the artistic, nor the worldly salon; but, without ostentation, it was, as far as she could influence it, a Christian hearth. The Catholic spirit did not seek to impose itself there, but, emanating from her, it reigned naturally, as if there was no help for it, but that so it must be. Never could you detect in her a movement of impatience or weariness in regard to any one of her guests. When she could make nothing else of them, she would propose, what she herself detested, cards. Nothing could draw from her the least sign of dislike. Never with her was the humble sacrificed to the proud, the fastidious to the agreeable, the poor to the rich, the ignorant to the learned; rather, indeed, the balance was in favour of the other side. As already remarked, she seemed to possess a knowledge of the human heart like divination. A word, a gesture, a look, unperceived by others, became for her a revelation; and when later you came with an astonished face to tell her of something that had just occurred, you found that, whether it was a virtue or a fault, she had foreseen it all. The character of her mother, whom, as a guardian angel residing with her, she revered,—character, ardent, just, magnanimous,—her silence at times, her thoughtfulness, her knowledge of the world and long experience of its ways, without ever seeking to turn that knowledge to her own advantage, or to that of those whom she loved,— occasionally her profound sadness, perhaps only kept in check by her great sense, and her desire to oblige every one; the grandeur of her manner; her kind of seigneural politeness, never at a loss, never to be disconcerted; her remarkable self-command; her indifference to personal inconvenience, when it was a question of compliance with what she esteemed right and fitting; her never going out of doors, latterly, but twice in the year (to change her residence from town to country, and vice versa), redoubling the solitude round her in her solitude, and only appearing to the evening circle, whom she alternately instructed and amused; all these particularities are needful, perhaps, to explain the tone and physiognomy of these reunions, where, as is related of another circle, nullity in spite of kindness used to fall naturally into its place, and nobleness of heart to be exalted and magnified. The rich man and the titled person becoming there the generous rival of those who were without fortune, laid aside their titles, and the air of their riches, to contend on equal terms with gallantry, delicacy, amiability, and honour; for the mistress of this house was not like the lady of whom Mdlle. Scudéry speaks, as satisfied if only she could see within her circle "some blunt-witted lord, ignoble in demeanour, preferring to have in her drawing-rooms many fools than only a very few agreeable people." No question

" ———————— our feasts
In every mess have folly, and the feeders
Digest it with a custom."

But when she invited guests to her table, which never saw the lustre of ancestral plate that she left to be forgotten at a banker's,—and minute traits like this are not to be neglected in a portrait,—the affection of nobleness, which her nature showed, made the whole affair of what the ancients called the apparatus secondary; as when Mme. de Sévigné talks of three bishops being about to dine with her in her Castle of the Rocks, and of her having a piece of salt beef for them. Of habits, as we already observed, the most abstemious, she would always reserve for herself some dish that no one else regarded; but which the previous abstinence of the entire day had rendered more palatable than dainties were for others. Cordiality and simplicity constituted the tone of all her reunions. She saw, in general, but few of those persons who worshipped sumptuous fare, and that, too, at long intervals between; and still fewer of those who make their faces vizors to their hearts, disguising what they are. Mdlle. de Scudéry, writing pleasantly to Mdlle. Paulet, says of the society of Marseilles, "All disagreeable truths are related here without disguise; and frankness is so great, that if any thing whatever be concealed, it is only the good qualities which one remarks in one's dearest friends. Elsewhere, charity enjoins our keeping secret the faults of our neighbour; but in this place, for fear of causing vainglory, one is careful never to praise any one, however good he may be." This was not precisely the tone that reigned in her drawing-rooms. She measured every one with thoughts so qualified as her charity did best instruct her. Neither, in consequence of her never flattering any one's absurdities, did you meet with her, in general, those who bring beautiful and majestic things into contempt, by pretending to revere only what belongs irremediably to the past, resembling in this act of folly the giant Morgante, who, seeing his horse dead, cries, "Ah, you won't carry me any more? Well, then, I will carry you. Put this animal, whose only defect consists in being dead, on my back, Messire Roland, and lend me a hand." The giant departs carrying his steed. Symbol of dead things, which one tries to make walk; satire on the feudality of the middle ages, reduced to nothing excepting an appearance. But, in exchange, there might be often allusion heard to some new institution, vital with truth and charity, to act with beneficence on the present as well as on future ages. She would never take advantage of the position of her guests to solicit their alms for the poor, or for any other object; but she did not at any time, or in any place, forget their interests. It was in her drawing-room, in the Rue de Grenelle, that the Bishop of Nancy first announced his intention of founding a society for the ransom of Chinese children. She fell on her knees while the Bishop developed his plan, and her name was one of the first inscribed in it. Pedantry was seldom, if ever, represented in these unpretending reunions, where it would have been held as disagreeable as Mdlle. de Scudéry found it, in the company that she so humorously describes, into which she was thrown by chance upon a journey. "Travelling in a public carriage to Rouen," she tells us that "she met a very disagreeable company, amongst whom was a young lawyer, who could talk of nothing but Cujas. At first, I thought," she says, "that it was of the late M. Cujas he was speaking, but I found out that it was of an ancient jurisconsult doctor. If one spoke of the war, he said he preferred being a pupil of Cujas to being a soldier; if one spoke of travels, he assured us that Cujas was known every where; if one spoke of music, he said that Cujas was more just in his reasoning than music in its notes; if one spoke of eating, he swore that he would rather fast every day than never read Cujas; if one spoke of handsome persons, he said that Cujas had a fine daughter, and that although old she was not yet ugly. In fine, Cujas was every thing, and I was so bored with Cujas that, as this is the first, so is it the last time I shall ever pronounce his name."

Disputes in her society were left to die out of themselves, and that was quickly; for in regard to them she felt like Pontano, who makes Virgil exclaim after hearing a furious argument between pedants, "O grammarians, how inhuman are your humanities!" She would not have liked the company of that M. de Montansier of whom Mme. de Rambouillet said, "by dint of being very wise he is quite silly. Never man sacrifices so little to the graces. He cries, he scolds, he tilts with you. Never man has done so much to cure me of the humour for disputing." Hers was the tone of that kind of society in which there is nothing sharp or cutting; no collisions, no noise, or at least, only such as constituted a polite noise—un fracas de bonne compagnie. However, there were shades to come over even her innocent brightness: so true it is that to whatever shelter one flies no one here below can pass his life in absolute peace and repose. Political debates would creep in imperceptibly. Accustomed and willing to hear discussed the dearest interests of England along with those of Christianity, she recoiled from the vain turmoil of mere earthly complications; and in

Paris she was to be fatigued by the conflict, when her best
friends were defending, step by step, that alluvial soil regained
by the house of Bourbon from the revolution of 1789. At that
time, of French liberty people used to talk as if agreeing with
Jules Janin, who said of it "c'est un gros homme en tilbury."
She was condemned to hear oftener than she liked of chambers
and ministers, of journals and new pamphlets. Even in those quiet
salons people at that time used to feel uneasy about the emeute.
They used to ask, " What day will be the next revolution ? Will
there be scaffolds, or will pillage content them?" One Englishman assured her the latter was inevitable, and that he had concealed his valuables within mattresses. At last events arrived
to verify many fears; but of these disasters, which profoundly
affected her, for she shed tears when she heard the republic
proclaimed beneath her window, it is not necessary for me to
speak. But while all the divisions, all the struggles which
preceded the revolution of '48, had living echoes in her
drawing-room, where the graver events of 1830 had left a
poignant memory, her society presented an asylum of comparative peace and cheerfulness which was not easily found elsewhere. She could accommodate herself to the most opposite
characters, detect the good side in each and excuse what was
weak. People that would never have met elsewhere found a
point of union with her company; and she would never suffer
any one, however less agreeable to others, to leave her presence
slighted or discouraged. She was enthusiastic, and yet sensible;
she possessed a fund of reason as well as of imagination, while
always remaining in heart the pure woman, with a mind that
soared above the worldly mutability and referred all things to
the Sovereign Disposer. Perhaps on the very score of her
amiability there were some who might have required reflection
to be set right as to the consistency between her faith·and her
politeness. She needed not such an apology, for she was what
she was instinctively; and as the Vicomte de Ségur says of the
natural grace of Mme. Riccoboni, "she herself was not in the
secret of her own style and influence*:" but as for those who
might be disposed to censure, I would refer them to that pas-

---

* Les Femmes, tom. i. 312.

sage in the memoirs of Mme. Swetchine, where she is represented saying, " Politeness in the world is not a culpable dissimulation. It softens rather than dissembles, and besides, deceiving no one we cannot accuse it of falsehood. Incompatibility of characters, the profound and radical division which springs from opposite principles, the ardent pursuit of different objects—all these elements of discord put in motion by the irritability of self-love make it difficult to conceive how the reunion of people should not be often the occasion of contests and bitter provocations. The effects however are different. Without supposing elevated motives, urbanity comes to our aid; by the gentleness of its forms it supplies justice, and the moderation which should be internal. The most divergent opinions, by the measure of expression, while manifesting themselves, lose their dangerous character, and pass like clouds charged with electricity, near enough to be distinct, and never near enough to clash with each other. This consequence in a lower scale of civilization might be mistaken for indifference, or cowardice, or scepticism; but to those who can read in twilight, a word, a silence, a slight change of intonation, an allusion even, however distant, suffice; and the result is, that if no one expresses what he thinks precisely as he feels, no one is arrested by things exactly as they are said; their clear and positive meaning is discovered, and remains in the intelligence as the naked figure is distinguished under drapery. Politeness never conducts to lies, not even to the slightest concession on merely its own account, and to practised eyes the true thought is disengaged in all its integrity from the forms which envelope it."

But passing to other matters, let us proceed to consider this character in regard to its relations with the world in general, and to the light in which it was disposed to view its ordinary manners.

To a life of faith like hers nothing can render the atmosphere of what deserves, in an evil sense, the name of the world agreeable, or the routine of its conventionalism wholesome. That there are often elements which tend to neutralize its natural malignity must be yielded. Formerly, at least in France, as no doubt in other countries, where the spiritualism of Catholicity produced effects analogous to what is expected from the disinfecting properties of certain chemical combinations, there may have been much to impart a new and foreign character to what is of itself repulsive and antagonistic. In the life of Mlle. d'Esturville, for instance, we read of Mme. de Mercœur, one of the greatest princesses of her time, "having a great esteem for a certain family because it lived in innocence and piety, fearing God,"—a trait which recalls the manners of St. Louis, of whom Joinville says, "Il ama tant toutes gens qui craignoeint et aymoient Dieu parfaitement, que pour la grant renommée qu'il oyt dire de mon frère, sire Gilles de Bruyn, qui n'estoit pas de France, de craindre et amer Dieu, ainsi que si faisoit-il, il luy donna la connestablie de France." Of the high Parisian society in the seventeenth century Mlle. Scudéry says in the Grand Cyrus, that "the form of life there is, no doubt, very agreeable —parceque le mérite y donne plus de rang que la qualité." In this respect that high world is even contrasted with the disposition of a lower class; for, she adds, "Cléodore a bourgeoise, —has a fantasy which betrays her origin. It consists in making a difference between gentlemen of the court and others, as if she thought it impossible to be a thorough gentleman without frequenting the court *." In the high society of France at that period we find friendships renounced for the very reasons that in another country, in later times, they would perhaps be especially cultivated; for instance, "Do not name to me Mme. de Meckelbourg," writes Mme. de Sévigné to a friend, "I renounce her. How could she in times like these, when the poor are in such misery, keep by her so much gold and silver, such rich furniture, such jewels! My dear madam, I could speak to you for a year on this subject; and it is to offend me personally to act the miser like Mme. de Meckelbourg. We used to call each other sisters at one time,—je la renonce, qu'on ne m'en parle plus; but let us speak of the Duc and Duchesse de Chaulnes, who set such a different example, making so admirable a use of their property, giving with one hand what they receive in the other, and when they have not the lingots of St. Malo, taking care that the poor should come in for a share of their magnificence, being, in a word, people that one cannot too much love

* Grand Cyrus.

and honour and admire [*]." Where views were thus elevated and consistent with the aspirations of faith, it is clear that there was no invincible antagonism between close relations with the world and a life submissive to the latter influence. Besides, without taking such very spiritual ground, it is certain that society, at certain epochs, is less opposed to what is natural and simple and amiable, and consequently so far Christian, than at others. It is something, for instance, when, as in the mediæval period, high rank did not interfere with the discharge of any duties that could grace and sanctify a woman, and when under the same conditions of birth and fortune, manliness and labouring actively under what now passes for a servile form in the other sex, without reference to war, had more fair play. Olivier de la Marche, when a boy, was page in the court of the good Duke Philippe de Bourgogne, and he says, on one occasion, "I remember that when we pages had to take the duke's horses to water, there used to be in these troublesome times ten or twelve lances sent as an escort to guard us to the place where they were to be watered." It was rather a simple kind of dandyism, therefore, in an age, when in a normal state of things such duties devolved upon the young nobility; for this riding the horses to water would have gone on in peace just as well, only without the lances. A sweet careless frankness and humility too belonged to the same manners, of which I cannot think of an instance more fit to give an idea of it than the language of the same Olivier de la Marche, when after telling us how he asked some great man or other the meaning of a particularity that he remarked in a public ceremony, he adds, "et combien que je fusse Page, et du nombre de la petite extime, le bon homme s'arresta à moy et me dict que c'estoyent les blasons," &c., and then concludes with—"pour ce qu'à celle heure je ne voyoye plus rien qui fist à enquerir, je m'en allay avec autres de ma sorte, regardant partout." That humble phrase "autres de ma sorte," uttered by the scion of a noble house, seems to me charmingly significative of a worldliness that had been somewhat eliminated of its poison.

But whether we desire traits of manners in the upper circles,

[*] Lett. 1030.

which recall Fleury's Mœurs des Chrétiens, or only circumstances which conduce to the reign of what is natural and unaffected, as at a later epoch can be found in the company of Mme. de Sévigné, for obvious reasons, without calling in experience to give evidence, such a state of things cannot be expected to exist at all times, and in all countries.

It is true, there seems to be no reason à priori why of necessity any people, in regard to the upper and middle classes, should be a vulgar nation; or, at least, capable of being called such. We may think ourselves great nobles, almost, as it were, living under the ancient regime, and as Mme. de Sévigné says, "our servants may think us even far greater still"—and yet condescension in our social relations, politeness prescribed even to these same domestics towards strangers, would involve us in no inevitable domestic inconvenience or personal calamity. One might show a little of that heart which belongs to gentleness and true high breeding—a little of that sympathy so much more valuable than kindness, which only excludes a total devotion to politics, and affairs, and dissipation, even at times unfruitful, without forfeiting all claim to what are thought the more solid virtues of a national character. Neither does one perceive, from the first, why in any country it should be necessary to employ great personal efforts to avoid being left in solitude in a noble city with nearly every door and bosom locked against you, as being one of the unknown; or why, in order to escape from such a position, it should be indispensable, as Gibbon observed, to "graft one's private consequence on the importance of a great professional body to obtain connexions, which are cemented by hope and interest, by emulation and the mutual exchange of favours." Society, one might have thought, depended not so wholly upon selfish motives, and was more generally influenced by amiable feelings, or at least by a laudable taste for intercourse with persons whose merit did not consist in their rank or fortune. Such expectations are no doubt realized by experience in many places, as under certain conditions they would probably be in all. But the world, which, when left to itself, can seldom move exactly as young people, or those who court mental pleasures, would have it, is under the best circumstances but a tamed monster, that after all has been done to make it gentle will easily relapse to its true ferine nature.

> "Ces ames du commun font tout pour de l'argent,
> Et, sans prendre intérêt aux douleurs de personne,
> Leur service et leur foi sont à qui plus leur donne *."

So when favourable circumstances are presented, all the old phenomena return with astounding prodigality. Things over and over again denounced by poets, and historians, and even novel-writers, that you might have thought utterly discountenanced and buried under the weight of a universal opprobrium, spring up again into life just as fresh and luxuriant as the summer herbage. The Duchesse du Maine had amongst her ladies one who said, "The great by dint of stretching themselves become so thin that you can see through them. It is a fine study to contemplate, and I know nothing more likely to lead to philosophy." Occasion returns to verify the justice of such observations. Talk before such grandeur of some holy person having succeeded in the object of his life—conversion, and they, however elevated in rank, will reply like Launcelot the clown, "Truly the more to blame he: we were Christians enough before; e'en as many as could well live, one by another." You have spoken to her ears divinity, to these others profanation. Then what rules triumphant are state notions, governmental principles; and when you show them the altars of the God who created man, and of the Christ who has saved him, they exclaim, "These are only the gods of our country; but our gods are the gods of its rulers, fidelity and honour." "I tell you," adds the author, who observes this trait of the worldly character, "I tell you, in truth, since the seduction of the first woman by the serpent, there has been no seduction more fearful than that." Yet, as another and eloquent writer says, "This worship of honour, without any view to a celestial motive, and to a future palm, this vestige perverted and vilely parodied of an ancient chivalrous virtue, can it be really as M. de Vigny seems to imagine, a plank of safety for a whole

* Corneille.

society? is it any thing else, at the best, but a naked rock, precipitous, good possibly for a few, but sterile and offering small refuge in the universal submersion?" To a mind regulated by the principles of faith, and to a heart warmed and elevated by its lustre, the society of such a world presented no shadow of attraction. Though in her youth she excelled in the dance, and loved it—though every where graceful—smooth and still

> "As the mute swan that floats adown the stream,
> Or, on the waters of the unruffled lake,
> Anchors her placid beauty,"—

yet she used often to speak of remembering her chagrin as a girl, when, on leaving the ball-room in London on a June morning, the streaks of day and the singing of the birds over the squares in the pale lustre of the dawn,

> "———— when ev'ry glassy blade
> Droops with a diamond at his head,"—

used to seem reproaching her with a misuse of hours, and wound her young fancy. An aristocratic pretension natural to new democracies and to sudden fortunes, is never indeed pleasing; for then, as Alain Chartier said of certain courts in his time, "we are all like traders, who buy one another, and sometimes for what others give us,—nous leur vendons nostre humanité précieuse*:" but now, where she found herself, pretensions of this kind were seen combined with the defects of an ancient civilization. Mme. de Krudner need not have taken so much time to reflect on the causes which make most of those who, under such circumstances, live in the great world finish by detesting each other, and by calumniating life at their last hour. "Every thing contributes to their having sentiments, which are neither good for this world," as Mme. de Sévigné says, "nor for the next;" and, certainly, one has not to wait long to witness proof that "the labour of the foolish wearieth every one of them †." Mme. de Lambert endeavoured to impress this fact on the mind of her daughter ‡, and Mme. de Maintenon, another authority in such matters, at the height of her glory, wrote to Mme. de

* Le Curial.   † Eccles.   ‡ Œuvres, &c., tom. ii. 7

la Maisonfort, saying, "Do you not see that I am dying of melancholy? I have been young and handsome, I have tasted pleasures; and I protest to you that all conditions leave a fearful void." Even the Count de Bussy, naturally the gayest of the gay, was of the same opinion; for, writing to Mme. de Sévigné, and that, too, in praise of trifling amusements, he speaks of his conviction as the result of experience, during the last five or six years of his life, " que l'ouvrage du salut est seul capable de contenter le cœur*." There was no error, therefore, or oversight in Jane Mary's appreciation of the life which was thus inadequate to yield contentment; though even without taking its temporal results into consideration, she evidently understood with the Prince de Conty, that a practical carrying out of the idea, which supposes that to pass one's whole life in pleasure and amusement and idleness belongs to one's station, however disowned in theory, forms one of the four great obstacles to the exercise of Christianity in the higher circles †. Her feelings and views, in general, respecting the world were precisely those which we hear extolled in those learned and curious French works of former times, ever in the hands of the "old courtier," that treat upon the obligations of those that possessed its riches ‡. " Women, of course," as Topffer says, "give the tone to society. All is spoiled or brought to perfection by intercourse with them. Their standard determines either the charm of life, or its abuse and disfigurement. Sometimes their estimate is not what it ought to be. Hence that jargon without life or charm, which for being insipid is not without pretension and pedantry. What they look to is not talent, character, distinguished qualities, allied with agreeable and polished forms.—No; still less, the old chivalrous graces of fidelity, devotion, and honour. What gives the password is, simply, the advantage of rank and title, of some factitious claim, either of fortune or of party §." Under such

---

* Mme. de Sévigné, Lett. 1006.

† Le Prince de Conty, Les Devoirs des Grandes, 7.

‡ La vie des Riches et des Pauvres, ou, les Obligations de ceux qui possédent les biens de la terre. Paris, 1740.

§ Réflexions et Menus Propos.

circumstances there is no society, even in a capital; nothing but what Gibbon found in London, when he returned to it, "a noisy and extensive scene of crowds without company, and dissipation without pleasure*,"—great assemblies, which the Abbé Bautain qualifies as matrimonial bazaars, to which men are attracted by the kind of hunger for riches which tormented Grangousier,—reunions, as they are by a misnomer designated, of which the atmosphere is not exactly that breathed by the Cid, when he uttered the celebrated words,

> "L'infamie est pareille, et suit également
> Le guerrier sans courage et le perfide amant."

But, on the contrary, you only find there a meeting of traders, not one of whom would care to have a Chimène for his bride, unless the Count de Gormas, her father, would make it guineas instead of pounds; chance aggregations of individuals, without any tie to hold them together beyond what exists on the Exchange, where, to procure a human establishment, nobleness, with the simple manners that belong to it, and all other virtues, are to be unlearned and ignored, or stigmatized or laughed down. As for merit of an intellectual order, it holds there pretty much the same position as it did in the great assemblies of Berlin, when Chateaubriand observed them, and of which he says, in allusion to what was esteemed there, "though you were Racine and Bossuet, that would give no one the slightest concern." It is enough if you find there, as some one mentioned by Saint-Beuve says, "little merits walking and airing themselves in great vanities." In such society you may count upon never hearing a word of authentic history, or heroic poetry, or noble literature, or even any talk the while of objects common and accustomed, such as those from which all our Lord's parables are drawn. If ever any topic bordering on religion be introduced, it will very possibly be something that might remind one of Mme. de Coulanges on her sick bed, after hearing that those who had just assisted at the death of Beaujeu had cried out before her, repeatedly pronouncing the sacred names, replying to them with a voice, as if it came from the other world: "Pray,

---

* Mem. i. 116.

why did they not cry them out to me? I think I was as much
entitled to them as she was?" after relating which anecdote,
Mme. de Sévigné asks, " What do you think of that ambition*?"
It is only a fair specimen, however, of what is at the bottom of
the sack in such company. You will be fortunate if you do not
meet, amidst great external splendours, with something that is
very vulgar, very stupid, very insipid, perhaps even recalling,
as a French author says, " the cleverness of a portress, the
politeness of a cook, the rapacity of a sheriff's officer." Would
it not be better to meet people a little touched, like the Don
Quixote of Don Fernando Avellaneda, who is so far from belonging to the world as thus constituted, that if he only meets
two common lads on the road, he thinks they are illustrious
knights whom some giant has deprived of their horses and arms,
and left them to cover themselves with smock-frocks? " Valiant
knights," says he to the strange youths, " you whom a proud
giant, against all order of chivalry, has robbed of your horses,
taking away from you at the same time, no doubt, some beautiful
demoiselle whom you were escorting, daughter of some prince
or lord of these countries; speak, and relate to me your grief."
The two boys looked at each other: " My lord horseman," they
replied, " we had neither horses nor demoiselle for any one to
take from us, and the only fight we have had was against a
cloud of insects under these trees, that have been attacking our
skins, but we have come off victorious by the help of our ten
fingers."

Moreover, the world fashioned after this approved type of
men who never err on the side of thinking nobly of others, is a
tyrant, and as Danou said, " tyrants have always had recourse
to certain odious denominations, to vain names, which repeated
without ceasing, and never explained, seem to designate great
crimes, and are, in fact, but the passwords of assassins. The
fatal power of these magical expressions is," he adds, as if he
had been hearing of the thousands of " brigands " who have
come to trouble Garibaldi, " an old secret of oppression."
And they of the world must know and repeat such " slanders of
the age, or else they may be marvellous mistook." Besides,

* Lett. 463.

they must take up with the current maxims that, vulgar as they may sound, are not the less true exponents of the worldly mind in high places, which though in a politer form is, with regard to all observances of religion, moulded by the principle of the hostess: " What's a joint of mutton or two in a whole Lent?" It is true that Jane Mary was brave, and had no human respect to make her fear the world, or even " the dangerous classes," personally, as its politer circles might often be denominated; and, besides, with regard even to what the world itself is constrained to hold by the necessity of instinct, thus far I will boldly publish her, she bore a mind that envy could not but call fair. But, then, she knew also how little it esteemed the qualities that she loved best; she knew too, instinctively, the hideous wound, deep, and long incurable, which is left in the heart, and under the appearance of being cured, by following its manners, and the fearful knowledge which such a course imparts of all things, and the insatiable and depraved instincts with which it inoculates the victim. In addition to all this she feared, if not for herself at least for others, the seductions of the world. She did not speak about them; instinctively, again, she seemed to know how much evil can result from exaggerated or artificial pictures of that sort; but a look, a silence indicated sufficiently what she thought of the matter, and that look or silence was enough. From her mirthful lecture, I promise you, no innocent little page would want to escape; as when le petit Jehan de Saintré having obtained permission at last to leave the presence of the Dame des Belles Cousines and her bevy of fine court ladies, after she had been teaching him, so as to bring tears into his eyes through fright and modesty, how he was to act in the world, quitted the room with a quick step, and then took to running as if he had fifty wolves at his heels.

Upon the whole, therefore, one cannot be surprised if from the beginning to the close of her existence, she regarded with little favour the world, with which in faith, in manners, in spirit, and in ways of thinking on almost every theme, she felt herself of necessity at variance; and, accordingly, she did evince this feeling, or rather this conviction, in regard to it.

One great cause of the extraordinary beauty, and even where it might be least expected, attraction of her character, consisted in the fact, that she never suffered the spirit or the manners of the world to interfere with either her religious faith or with her natural womanly instincts; she never suffered them to cast an impenetrable veil over the charms of a fresh, frank, loving heart, much less over the impressions of grace on a soul that was thoroughly, and one might almost say passionately, Christian. Unlike the worldly, and in this instance resembling Mme. de Sévigné, who speaks of herself as possessing popular virtues —" avec toutes mes vertus populaires *"—she had, without in the least suspecting it, not only these virtues, but also popular ways of thinking on many subjects; and that, to the present hour, means old heroic ways of thinking. The ancient English ballads, songs, and other pieces of our earlier poets, as collected by Percy, which Addison remarked "form the delight of the common people," are in fact but the echoes of sentiments which live as fresh as ever within the hearts, at least of the female part, of the population of England at the present day. That they were but the echo also of her own, argued not alone the refinement of her taste, but also in one placed in her condition, the singular simplicity, the goodness, and, one might add, even the harmonious cultivation of her whole nature. This mounting of the popular spirit, in a good sense, into the higher classes, is of course no novelty, though it is always worth observing. There might be no end of citing instances. For example: when a person of great notoriety in the high world of Paris in the time of Louis XIV. accounts for her not keeping an engagement, by saying that a friend had sent to beg that she would come to her as she was sick, and adds, to justify herself, "What previous appointment could hold against such an invitation?" she did not certainly speak the language of salons, but rather that which belongs to many of the lower classes at the present day in England. When the same celebrity calls a young heartless marquis "un homme au-dessous de la definition," she evinces thoughts that have a different focus from those that centre in the maxims of the world. In fact, the affectionate, whatever be their rank, must always resemble each other, and show themselves to be poetical, so far at least as being able to

* Lett. 677.

feel the beauty of those popular songs like many of Burns', which, however homely, might be cited to indicate the frame of mind that belongs to them. Decked, therefore, with all the fair and simple attributes of woman, this life of faith that we are recalling was not alone thus unconsciously popular, but also free from all taint of the worldly disposition. In the very ground of the excuses that she would allege on common occasions, in her appreciation of character and in her estimate of the constituents of earthly happiness, she had a mind antipodal to that which dominates in the society of the world; and it was the same with her in regard to higher matters. "The poor always believe in God," says Menander*. She apprehended passing shrewdly that, at least for any practical purpose, the great world does not always resemble them in that particular. Accordingly, it was clear upon the whole, from an early period, that for infinite reasons she was disposed to take no very great pains to conciliate its favour. In fact, if the truth must be told, while never ceasing to fulfil the requisite enactments of politeness, for any thing beyond the strict mark, she showed herself at times shockingly negligent. Like Mme. Hélyot, of whom the Père Crasset wrote the life in 1684, "she had a dislike for making visits." Like Bruni, whom Father Ventura describes as "la femme chrétienne," she took no pleasure in paying court to worldly people, whatever might be their fortune; and, as Fontenelle said of Amontons on his reception at the Academy, "there was in consequence an almost total incapacity for pushing herself forward, and for what is called succeeding in life †." Like Bruni, too, "she had no ambition to be seen where every body goes;" that is, perhaps, as some understand it, in places where the chief element of amalgamation is something very like sheer vanity; or where the only result of repairing to them is a fresh verification of the truth, expressed by Menander, that nothing is so sweet to man as to prattle about things that don't concern him—"nihil tam dulce est hominibus quam garrire de rebus alienis." In this respect she resembled one of the characters in the Grand Cyrus; that is, you remember, one who figured among the most illustrious French

* Menand. fragment.   † Œuvres, tom. v., Éloges.

ladies of the seventeenth century; for, as we read in that curious work so completely forgotten until a brilliant French writer has again brought it into vogue, "she did not care to receive visits from persons who are only capable of a restless and vague enjoyment, which leads them constantly from visit to visit without knowing precisely what they seek any where, or what they wish to do; nor from women of that kind who seem to think that they ought to know nothing grave; who make their distinction consist in causing people to regale them sumptuously, and who would think themselves slighted if the entertainment provided for them was not sufficiently magnificent as to make it unlike that of all others. Nor, on the other hand, did she care to see those who would regard women as only fit for household drudgery, and who think that they should never read any thing but prayer-books, or sing any thing but a litany*." No doubt, as we have already seen, there was nothing of arrogance or of misanthropy in her wish not to be wholly submerged in the vast colouring mass that constitutes the element of worldliness. She had heard, indeed, of examples to show that there may be as much vanity in desiring retreat as when mixing in the crowd. It is Philarete Chasles, I believe, that speaks of some one who "shut himself up with his anger, a great dog, his Deistical library of more than one thousand volumes against Christ, and all for the purpose of educating his son,"—nothing very desirable in such retirement, I opine. She, at all events, was far more inclined to sympathize with those who were in danger of losing their way on a different road, and who exceeded in their participation of sentiments with the crowd. "Poor creatures!" she used to say, half laughing, of those hastening through the streets of London. "What a prodigious hurry they ever seem to be in, and all for what, I should like to know?" The sort of loving smile she wore when saying it, which even seemed to signify a kind of half approval, might have led one to believe that she had the same thoughts as Coleridge, when he said, "I have always considered the disproportion of human passions to their ordinary objects among the strongest internal evidences of our

---

* Grand Cyrus.

future destination, and the attempt to restore them to their rightful claimants the most imperious duty and the noblest task of genius." Elsewhere, describing the enthusiasm of a crowd on seeing the queen of Prussia arrive, " I involuntarily exclaimed," he says, " O man! ever nobler than thy circumstances! spread but the mist of obscure feeling over any form, and even a woman, incapable of blessing or of injuring them, shall be welcomed with an intensity of emotion adequate to the reception of the Redeemer of the world!"

Nevertheless, particularly in her latter years, it was evident that secretly she shunned the world each day with more and more intensity of desire, and with a still greater depth of tenderness for what she found out of it. It would have been difficult to induce her, as Shakspeare says,

> "——————— to haunt assemblies
> Where pomp, and cost, and witless bravery keep."

But who, I should like to know, in the silent hall of his conscience can blame her for indulging in this disposition? As Alain Chartier says after his quaint fashion,—

> " Curia dat curas, ergo si tu bene curas
> Vivere secure, non sit tibi curia Curæ.
> Curia, curarum genitrix, nutrixque malorum,
> Injustis justos, inhonestis æquat honestos *."

It was, indeed, one must admit even for the sake of one's literary reputation, the first poets who, as Sarasin remarks, assembled men together and civilized them, and, as it were, founded cities and courts. But for all that, Heaven forbid, will every wise man add with him, that I should blame retirement! " I love it," continues that frequenter of brilliant assemblies, "though I do not always enjoy it; I know that wisdom has no better friend, and that one might call it the life of the soul. I naturally seek repose; I need sleep. The crowd and tumult injure me, though I do not go to the length of Euripides when he makes Agamemnon esteem a man happy who is unknown."

* Le Curial.

Be all that as it may, and our sentence will, no doubt, be determined partly by our own circumstances at the time, the fact undoubtedly was that with all her qualifications to enhance the charm of society, she was disposed to comply with the old poet's invitation to confine within a small space our long hopes, and to accept as a necessity the strong impression on her mind, that quiet and retirement for her were best. She had not heard Chateaubriand saying, "believe me, who am an old traveller, there is nothing like repose, and in a corner some friends tried by time;" but she would have spoken like Ballanche writing to Mme. Récamier, and saying, "I have need of calm and repose; I have need of tranquil studies, of peaceful leisure." Perhaps these feelings entered into her profound attachment to that community of Ramsgate branching from Subiaco, and still so worthily representing that founder of placid quiet, St. Benedict, as he is qualified by a monk of Mount Casino,—"Ipse fundator placidæ quietis [*]." Certainly, it would be difficult to express with what calm desire she was drawn on to lead a life unostentatiously and, as it were, naturally separated from the crowd. To see her seated in her little garden, with her book in front of the fountain, with the birds singing round her, you might have been reminded of the lines of Menander, "How sweet to one who hates evil manners is a solitary place, and to one meditating the seeing no evil! A sufficient possession is a small field, for envy springs from a crowd of clients; and as for the things in the town, these delights, indeed, are splendid, but they last only a short time." Alas! some, perhaps, who used to blame her for such abstraction, to taunt her with neglecting what was necessary, though of that she was ever guiltless, to say unkind things, as if to try how much she could smilingly endure, and who little reflected on the cause of her inclination, which never affected to control that of others, will have learned, by this time, to esteem it an additional motive for now becoming enamoured on her grave.

[*] Ap. Montalembert, Les Moines d'Occident.

CHAPTER VII.

EFORE we proceed to recall virtues that address themselves more immediately to the heart, and all its sweet affections, let us during this day's visit to the chantry, indulge a curiosity that may be permitted by inquiring in what relation this pure character may have stood with those graces of the intellect inspired by faith and Catholicity, by piety and wisdom, and a spirit that soared above the world,—the graces, I mean, which consist in what may be termed a sense of art and literature; and this will be an inquiry that will form no digression or mere circling of the goal, for the result will be found to reflect much light upon the sweetness and depth of the whole picture, while adding no tint or contour that did not in strictest truth belong to the original.

It is related of Chateaubriand that he had a horror of meeting women who affected to pronounce their opinion on literary and learned questions, and that he could never forgive those who betrayed an affectation of superior knowledge. It was with a similar feeling that a poet of his nation attributes to a woman the lines—

> "Et que j'aimerois mieux être carpe ou merlan
> Que d'être bel esprit seulement pour un an."

Were I to continue in this strain, it would awaken, perhaps, suspicion that I was merely as a hired advocate pleading in the interest of a client, and bent on disparaging all who stood with her in honourable though decried opposition; for we must begin by admitting, that the first elements which enter into the composition of such a character as these literary men condemn, were wanting in her whose graces we are seeking to recall. All her conversation was simple and natural. She resembled that Mme. de Courbon, of whom Mlle. Scudéry says, "she speaks well on all subjects, and yet so admirably does she confine herself within the just limits which custom and good breeding prescribe to women, in order that they may not appear learned, that when you hear her converse on elevated topics you would think that it was merely by the means of simple good sense she came to have such knowledge*." Two classes of persons therefore were not to be pleased by her general tone of conversation; those who exclusively admired literary talk, and those who wished to hear of nothing but what was merely frivolous or relating to the prosaic drudgery of life in the world. Nevertheless, it is not every one who will be disposed to agree with either of these classes in their estimate of the worth of the picture which is offered for our inspection here; and yet truly, for entertaining an opposite opinion, these connoisseurs are not left without means of self-defence to justify it. Some one, indeed, has said, that the difficulty for women of having superior attainments in this respect with propriety, does not come so much from the fact of one woman's knowing it, as from others not knowing it. But most people, I rather believe, will be inclined to think that this is only a sophist's explanation; for the truth seems to be, that though by a general contravention of what nature intended, all women were to possess such cultivation, the disagreeable consequences for each would remain precisely what they were when witnessed only in a few. Mlle. de Scudéry represents herself as replying to a pedant who asked her at a concert what was her opinion respecting a verse of Hesiod, "I assure you it would be better to consult some one else; for as for me, who only consult my mirror to know when I am dressed least ill, I am not a proper person for being consulted on difficult questions †." Society has not gained so much in later times as to justify it in supposing that it can afford to discard, as of no importance, the opinion on this subject which prevailed during the seventeenth century; and it would be difficult to select a passage that would give a more true idea of this opinion than that in which Mlle. de Scudéry describes a conversation in which she was obliged to take part at a concert before the music began,—which shows how thoroughly she detested the reputation of a bas bleu, and the inconveniences which it exposed

* Le Grand Cyrus.
† Cousin, La Société Française au XVIIe Siècle.

her to. She desires that no one should treat her as a person who writes books or who judges of books, but as one who wishes to live the common life of all the world. "Since I must say it," she replies, " I am so weary of this literary reputation, that in the humour in which I at present am, I would place the supreme felicity in not knowing how to read, or write, or speak; and, if it were possible, to forget how to read, write, and speak, I protest to you that I would be silent from this moment, and never speak again as long as I lived,—I am so sick of the folly of this kind of world, and of the persecution inseparably attached to it, which every woman suffers who has the reputation of knowing more than to choose ribbons. How can one endure not to be talked to as other people are talked to,—one like me, too, who only wish to be as others are, and who cannot bear to be distinguished after such a fashion? But they never will speak to me as they speak to others; for if one of them apologizes for not having been to see me, he tells me that it is through fear of interrupting my occupations. If another accuses me of studying, it is to add that, without doubt, I am never less alone than when alone with myself. If I complain of a headache, there is sure to be some one to reply that it is the common malady of clever people. In short, I am driven to regard dulness and ignorance as the sovereign good. In fine, I beg to be left to my repose without any one either seeking or avoiding me; for I confess to you, that I do not like the idea of being either sought after or avoided as a singularly clever, talented, poetic, or literary lady*."

But perhaps, as already suggested, it will be thought by some that these preliminary remarks were hardly called for in the present instance, from supposing that where this feeling existed, and there was no pretension, there was not in reality any knowledge or attainments which rendered them meritorious. But to suppose this would be a great mistake; and the more we summon our recollection to aid our judgment on this point, the more shall we feel assured that it would be untrue. No; when brought back as it were to her presence, we can only say with our great dramatist,—

* Le Grand Cyrus.

"—— I cannot say 'tis pity
She lacks instructions; for she seems a mistress
To most that teach."

Let us begin with her judgment in relation to art, which might become a theme that would not be destitute of instruction for those who make it their especial study. And here, though it is rather an invidious task, one might be tempted to blame some of the biographical notices that were formerly composed with a view to perpetuate the memory of persons eminently good, for having wantonly depreciated faculties which were wanting in those whom they sought to magnify. One old writer, for instance, in his life of the Demoiselle Ranquet, among proofs of her piety says, "jamais elle ne prist plaisir uy dans l'éclat des pierreries ny dans la musique la plus agréable!" as if the good man thought a taste for expensive finery and a love of music to be things quite on a par. It is not over bold, perhaps, to express an opinion that such books ought to be rewritten. While waiting until they are so, one may observe, that in the example before us there was witnessed a very different appreciation of the worth and origin of art in general. Endowed with an exquisite ear, her love of music kept pace with the delicacy of her judgment in its regard. Her voice was sweet and melodious, and she played with great expression; but the shortness of her sight, which deprived her of many enjoyments, at an early age formed an obstacle to her pursuit of this art, which she thoroughly understood and always continued to love with an intense feeling of admiration and sympathy. For painting she had a most correct eye and a singularly exact judgment, so that you could always depend upon the truth of her first impressions, with regard to the drawing or colour of any picture that was submitted to her. She might be said to have possessed Topffer's sixth sense,—or the need of art,—if not of copying and of creating, that of admiring and enjoying. She had, also, a disposition to think very nobly of painting, as well as of music, regarding the former even as a source of high instruction. When you told her of that thought of the great English artist, Dyce, when he represented St. John leading back the blessed Mother, after assisting at the Crucifixion; or when you described the Visitation by Mr. Herbert, or spoke of any other noble or affecting idea, capable of being similarly expressed, those who knew her best were hardly prepared for the emotion and the enthusiasm to which she would give utterance. She had to restrain tears when she replied to you. To a true artist she would have served for muse; as we read of the sister of a celebrated poet, speaking to him with rapture of some scene or event, and adding, "Tu devrais peindre cela!" On the other hand, though she had never read M. Ruskin's fifth volume of "Modern Painters," she could hardly be brought to understand how any one might wish to imitate those Dutch artists, who aspired no higher than to give an exact copy of a boors' drinking-party, or of a dish of meat and a kettle. The lesson which might be suggested would be the advantage in regard to art of loving it with enthusiasm, and, also, of being imbued with true principles in its regard, while emancipated from the trammels that impede the progress or pervert the judgment of others.

A true love of art is not a thing very generally met with in some countries. We can hardly even any where, now-a-days, understand what we read in history attesting its extent and power. Indeed, even where this love still exists, we hear of things at present to excite wonder. "For instance, it is not without astonishment," as Jules Janin says, "that you see a pope in the midst of a civil war, surrounded by enemies, defeated on all sides, demanding to be given up to him his own property, his artist silversmith, before he can be sure of having sufficient gold to give him an order to remake his tiara, that had been melted down; or, that we hear of the emperor of the Spanish dominions, master of Rome, and of Francis I., who in the Vatican is able to remember the sculptured button of an engraver, which he once saw on the cloak of a pope, since dead*." One might have been tempted to feel somewhat of the same surprise, at witnessing the quiet rapture which inspired this unpretending observer, when presented with instances of painting

* Variétés littéraires.

employed, as I have just said, to convey, indirectly, rather than in a way forced upon you, some noble or some religious instruction. I say indirectly, for she liked that the mind of the beholder should be left to work a little by itself, and not to be dragged in to assist at a formal lecture, when perhaps it was not prepared for it. The true pleasure which she derived from music and painting, the childlike admiration which she expressed for them in most delicate language, might have appeared a sort of incense, which the greatest artist would love to breathe, as yielding the highest encouragement that it was possible for him to receive from any expression of human sympathy. But this was not all. We might draw great profit from her example, by reflecting on the consequences in regard to art, of being imbued like her with true principles, and emancipated from the narrow prejudices of any coterie or of any age. To any routine or conventionalism of art she was opposed, by the very fact of her remaining in her simplicity uninitiated in the maxims, or perhaps jargon, of any school. Now this is an advantage not to be underrated; for persons of such a character are not met with every day. "No," said Ary Scheffer, alluding to the progress of art in France, when what was termed the romantic taste superseded the more classical school of David, "persons of mature age, whose mind is sufficiently supple, sufficiently disengaged from the bonds of habit, to enable them to take pleasure in innovations, and in following the progress of the age, are always in minority." "But," say those who are unprovided with her simplicity and freedom, "schools of painting change. Do you advise us to be stable to nothing? Is there nothing absolutely beautiful and invariable?" "Yes, no doubt," replies a French critic; "but this absolute beauty God alone expresses in his sublime essence; it is not given to man to realize it wholly in his creations. He only draws from it, without being weary, contingent and diverse copies, which never express more than one side of it. Routine exclaims that he loses his way; it would have types always identical,—stereotyped from the first models. There would be less risk, no doubt; but man obeys an interior passion, which cries, Forward! So he pursues his journey, changes his works, and by the emotion which they inspire, one can recognize under their different forms if they are derived from the eternal type *."

We can learn again, from this example, the advantage in regard to art, of possessing the thoughts of genius, of which, after all, it is at the best of times but the feeble and inadequate expression. What great religious artists, for instance, would England now possess, if painting were guided in its most wanton manipulations by such thoughts as hers? Charles Lamb makes a free confession, saying, "Indeed, the race of Virgin Mary painters seems to have been cut up, root and branch, at the Reformation. Our artists are too good Protestants to give life to that admirable commixture of maternal tenderness with reverential awe and worship, with which the virgin mothers of Leonardo da Vinci and Raphael (themselves, by their divine countenances, inviting men to worship) contemplate the union of the two natures in the person of their heaven-born infant." Forms in nature are all in direct relation with their object or their end; it is this relation which constitutes their character; and this character is seized by man, not by the eye, but by thought, by means of the eye; as when we say those forms are gentle, rude, energetic, bold, or ignoble. Now to detect the object and end of all forms, the unconscious judge whom we are recalling, was enabled or assisted by the spirituality of her conceptions, and by the piety of her heart. Let us dwell a moment here, for there are others who will assist us to develope and explain our meaning.

The chemist who wants to know the nature of the diamond, gets a particle, submits it to his acids, and finds that the diamond is charcoal. All very well; but the charcoal is no longer diamond. Such was not her method in treating works either of art or literature. She viewed things synthetically, and judged not by her senses but her soul. "Is it not," asks Topffer, "with a sentiment of hope and of just pride that one recognizes this absolute incapacity of all physical laws—these which govern no less the universe and the stars, to produce the smallest of these effects, which in art the thought of man produces as if in play?" But here is an instance to show, that, in

* Louis Ratisbonne.

proportion as one rises step by step to the heights of a subject, the horizon extends, more objects appear, and one less knows what to choose. Unconsciously she held with Topffer, that the painter, in order to imitate, transforms; and observe, too, that the same law holds for the poet and for the musician. "What hinders," he continues, " the latter from imitating the common cries of grief? Nothing; but he knows better than to do so. He transforms. With him imitation is almost nothing—expression addressed to the soul is all. So with the painter and the poet, the sum of merit is the sum of expression; for the invisible labour of the human soul is superior to the visible work of means and method, as much so as this soul itself is superior to matter: it is nothing else but one of the most brilliant manifestations of that soul which the senses sometimes deny because they cannot see it, but which would be no longer what it is if it were visible; and which, being made in the image of God, like him reveals itself by its acts, and not by its substance *." She from the first arrived at the knowledge that the superior beauty resides in God, and without acquaintance with the philosophers, that the beautiful in its absolute essence is God. Remark, that they came to this conclusion after their own fashion; and how wonderful is this accordance with her knowledge! They arrived at this thought, which has at first the air of being only the respectable expression of a pious but not reasoned out acquiescence, by the sole labour of their philosophic meditations, independently of all religious consideration. And this accordance is found not alone between her and the great German thinkers of our time, but also between her and St. Augustine, and before him Plato. "The beautiful," says the celebrated Thierry, " in its absolute essence being God, it is impossible to find its characteristics without the divine sphere, as it is to find out of that sphere the absolute good or true. The beautiful belonging then not to the sensible, but to the spiritual order, important consequences result; for literature and art must approach to God when they are to possess a beauty which is not factitious. If in the expression of moral affections or in the scenes of physical life they have not an eye turned

* Réflexions et Menus Propos.

towards heaven, let them renounce the attainment of a durable glory. There is no ability which can give life to what does not repose on laws. Whatever be the talent in the employment of material means, there must be felt the invisible action of these general and absolute principles, as under the stone vaults of a church the fervent Christian feels the secret presence of his God *." In fine, here was what Topffer then proposed to treat of,—the beautiful conceived and the beautiful reduced to practice in action. The beautiful conceived, for she possessed the attribute of simultanity, the attribute of unity, and the attribute of freedom. She could discern at once the beauty of God's creation. From the least to the greatest of His works she took in at one view all the beautiful, past expression, but realized in the mind; she had the whole in view at once; an anticipated view of the beautiful before any of its parts were expressed before her. She was not arrested by details. She possessed also the attribute of unity; she looked to the design of God, to the object proposed, to the divine thought as manifested by nature and revelation. In fine, she possessed, as we said before, the attribute of freedom in her conception of the beautiful; for she was trammelled by no theories, by no conventional yoke or rules of art, by no limits prescribed, or conditions arbitrarily imposed on the conception of the beautiful. Her admiration at a poet or orator, or work of art, was not checked or troubled by the imposition of a model to which she felt herself bound to adhere. She was free to feel the spring of enthusiasm, the joyous courage of her heart; she was not subjected to the slavery of a philosophic or social system, or type, or by that of passions which did not clothe themselves in that form. In the bosom of that calm which she enjoyed of all occasional passions and of all temporary interests, in that intimate and profound freedom and retirement of the soul, all the rays of truth and beauty had undisturbed access. In fine, she possessed the beautiful in action. Her whole life seemed to realize the celebrated sentence of Plato, that the beautiful is the splendour of truth. She possessed, she followed truth, and all her actions in

* Thierry, de l'Esprit et de la Critique littéraire chez les Peuples anciens et modernes.

regard to beauty demonstrated the mysterious depth of what is beautiful.

Proceeding now to view the character of this mind in relation to literature, we shall find that the same causes led to an analogous advantage, and that the principles which unconsciously guided her in relation to art were no less successful when applied to her direction as to the latter. Possibly, I must repeat it, to some who knew her, this allusion to a literary judgment may seem misplaced in reference to one who was chiefly known for womanly graces, for cheerful humility, and the assiduity of her prayer in lonely hours; but a moment's reflection will dissipate the error into which, in this respect, they may have fallen.

With respect to positive attainments of this kind it is not necessary to dilate much. Speaking French with a precision and grace that but few English can attain to, that rich world of Christian literature was at her command. She knew a little Latin for the saying of her service, which she well understood, and would often laugh at herself for being able to seize the meaning of what was read or even spoken in conversation in that language. Like Mme. de Montmorency, a woman of the same type, "she had a sound instruction in theology," which is not altogether alien from the walks of philosophy, and poetry, and literature; and you could never detect her in error on such matters; as Bishop Fisher says of Margaret, Countess of Richmond, "right studious she was in bokes, which she had in grete number, both in Englysh and in Frenshe." Though she seldom spoke of what she read, her selection of authors, which she always travelled with, argued the excellent judgment of which I would now say something. There was seldom cause to set aside her opinion respecting books or any literary composition when once she delivered it; nor was its correctness often questioned; for, in fact, though she did not suspect herself of possessing any talents to warrant her being considered an authority in any but women's matters, and though her unfeigned humility prevented her from ever wishing to be regarded out of that sphere, the simplicity of her character, the grace of her disposition, the pure intensity of her convictions, and somewhat of French sprightliness, the gentle frankness that breathed in

all she uttered, exercised an influence which was the greater
from no one thinking it necessary to stand upon his guard
against it. Some one has said that "a writer in the interest of
his glory ought always to have women in view." It is certain
that no author, whether grave or lightsome, would have compromised his fame by attending to her suggestion. The delicacy
of her taste might have been studied, with advantage, by any
orator or poet. The 'decor,' the 'venustas,' the 'simplex mun-
ditiis' of the Latins, are recalled by this constant decorum which
reigned in her intelligence; the most exact likenesses, the most
living realities have still in her an antique perfume which
betrays an instinctive familiarity with the masters of the ages of
elegance. For all literary productions, as well as for works of
art, she had a naturally judicious and lively taste, and she received impressions from them as spontaneous as they were just.
She would never intentionally play the critic's part. We all
know how such a gentleman acquits himself. It would be well
for him if one could feel that there was a heart and a character
under his cuirass of a doctor, or sceptic, or other learned and
incomparably clever individual; but that is a conviction that
is often difficult to arrive at in his regard. "Do you know," he
asks, "what is a representation, a spectator, an actor? Yes, no
doubt. Well, all the same for that, this author will explain it
to you. You venture to laugh! What is a laugh? Here is
another examination which the professor obliges you to pass
through before taking a step farther. He will not allow you to
put one foot before the other without having, after his fashion,
tried the ground *." This, of course, is a proficiency to which
she never aspired to lay claim. Nevertheless, her judgment of
books was admirably sure. She had that tact of propriety and
fitness which the ancients ascribed to one who was "homo lima-
tissimi judicii." Of profane literature, it is true, she read but
little; yet did she not want any thoughts that are admirable
even in that regard. Read to her what you would; open your
Shakspeare, or your Goldsmith, or whatever you chose, it
looked as if you had been forestalled. It was as if she had her
books within her head, and found all that was sweet, and ten-

* Louis Ratisbonne.

der, and heroic, and even poetical there. When you had read the passage, there was the responsive echo; the thought was already there, the charm enshrined in the sweetness of that soul. It did not seem new to her—'twas only a recollection.

Her judgment, in this respect, as we said before, but it cannot be too often remarked, had the advantage of not being trammelled by any blind prejudice in favour of particular authors or schools. She would have liked the classic, minus its conventional restraints, and the romantic, minus the factitious, the affected, and the absurd. The best part of her intellectual funds was not embarked on board the renown of any contemporary, and she felt no danger of any thing that she cared much about perishing in their shipwreck whenever that might take place. Conscience came to her aid on all occasions, and while feeling herself independent, she could respect and admire what the public might condemn; for hers was the sure rule that literary merit, as well as art and morality, and all kinds of truth, exist independently of success; a maxim, indeed, which she had an interest in maintaining, for it is certain that many of her favourite books were in the condition of Sylvio Pellico's, of which Chateaubriand said, that "its holiness would be an obstacle to its success with our revolutionists, who are for freedom after the fashion of Fouché." People of genius, as it is termed, she knew were, as one who claimed to be of their number said, "as variable as barometers;" but she would not come to his conclusion that "genius alone is essentially good." Civilization in literature was with her a sine qua non.

And here there is no escape from our obligation to speak of the disgust and horror which she entertained for much that is qualified, though rather erroneously, as popular, since it is addressed much more to the reading public, in the light literature of the present day. In the presence of this unpretending and yet unbending little court constituted by her judgment, you would in vain appeal to the success of a publication; or, on the other hand, demand, with a recent critic, of what use to bring out a book against which the public voice has already pronounced? Her sentence would pass as if she agreed with Coleridge in his contempt for this kind of voice, in which disdain the best continental writers agree with him; as, for instance,

Topffer, who goes so far as to say, "that the public is but a pitiable judge, always wrong, in spite of its rage for the exact truth, and that in every thing 'the public' is at the tail of all the rest of the world *." Let me not be understood as implying that Jane Mary objected to light books of amusement gracefully written, or that the character of her mind evinced the slightest trace of that severity which caused La Motte and the Abbé Prévost, Pascal, and Malebranche, to be among the depreciators of rhyme and versification. Alas! a few days before her death, alluding to a particular instance, she expressed her sense of the vast importance of having such food provided for the young, and she did actually make such provision for them. Nor, while admitting that she had not much respect for that class of feelings which are qualified as sentimental, would I convey the idea that she set much value upon the pursuit of those graver follies under a stricter habit, to which so many are now directed, as entering into a course of philosophic education for the people, as when we are referred every moment to statistical tables; to that "abominable science," as a French writer humorously terms it, which reduces the human race to a machine, of which the products are held in fact double, the account being made out in this way: the city of Paris produces at the end of each day witty sayings so many, old rags so many, broken bottles so many, reputations reduced to pieces so many, new glories, gilt by the patent process, so many, talents wasted and abused so many. She would not have taken the side of Nisard, thundering against recreative reading, in his controversy with poor Jules Janin. No; she would have said with the latter, there is no such thing as an easy or a difficult literature—littérature facile or littérature difficile. There is a good and a bad literature, and that is all. There is, it is true, a literature of every day, a literature unstudied, which comes to every one laughing and at ease, without pretensions—little doctoral, little systematic, which seeks to please, and in order to please will sometimes throw its cap to the winds—quarrel with that?—fy!—that is shameful, that is of a pedant double lined with folly. For, as Fontenelle says, speaking of M. Homberg and the first barome-

* Réflexions et Menus Propos.

ters, which contained a little man in a tube, who stayed at home in it when rain threatened, and came out when it was going to be fine, it is not philosophy that excludes things of taste and pleasure; it is the injustice of philosophers, who, like the rest of men, esteem only what distinguishes themselves *. No doubt, under whatever grave and scientific, and even religious language, the thoughts might be expressed, our instructress here did not seem to like much that any one should keep on pawing, as it were, delicate themes, whether his object were to resist or to favour what Sir Thomas Brown calls "the rhetorick of Satan, which may pervert a loose or prejudicate belief." But, what she hated and recoiled from, with an instinct as if beholding the locked embrasures of toads, was that kind of author who, as even Voltaire said of Holbach, mistaking his five senses for good sense, would elicit that cry of conscience which we meet with in an old author,—" Marry, the immortal part needs a physician, but that moves not him."

"Trainant à ses talons tous les sots d'ici-bas,
Grand homme, si l'on veut, mais poëte non pas †."

When confronted with productions of this nature, there is a great deliverance that can be effected by a remembrance of what is learned in the Chapel of St. John; for

"———— still methinks
There is an air comes from her."

It is as if we heard the sweet harp that the wind plays upon, and that we could distinguish in the melodious sound, such lines as these of Wordsworth—

" He serves the muses erringly and ill,
Whose aim is pleasure, light and fugitive;
O, that my mind were equal to fulfil
The comprehensive mandate which they give!—
Vain aspiration of an earnest will!
Yet in this moral strain a power may live,
Beloved wife! such solace to impart,
As it hath yielded to thy tender heart."

No; when you take up such a book as that, for instance, of

* Tom. v. 376. † Alfred de Musset.

the modern Balzac, of which a French critic, alluding to its ignoble details, said that, after reading it, "il me semble toujours que j'ai besoin de me laver les mains et de brosser mon habit," or such a production as that which drew from La Bruyère the judgment passed upon the Mercure Galand, of which he said, "C'est un livre qui est un peu au-dessous de rien," a little less than nothing; or when, to feel more at ease, you have recourse to pale copies from the leaves of that author who might compare himself to Jupiter, the cloud-collector, and who even said of himself, "My talent consists in assembling doubts, and collecting nothing but doubts;" but still, above all, when you procure the books of men who resemble Sir Toby in the one point, that they object to "a song of good life," caring not for good life, but hating it "as an unfilled can," reckless of the disgust of the honourable, like "an ostler that, for the poorest piece, will bear to be called knave by the volume," who like certain French novelists descend so low that, to use the expression in reference to them of Saint-Beuve, "literature, strictly speaking, has nothing more to do here; there's an end of criticism,"—it might be well for you to cast one look back towards this sepulchral vaultage, and then give sentence like Louis XIV., when he found some vulgar and disgusting Dutch pictures in his apartment, and, as if he had just risen from the perusal of a page of Ruskin, who can no more lay hold of the temper of Teniers or Wouverman than he can enter into the feelings of one of the lower animals, said hastily to a servant, "Otez d'ici tous ces magots."

Certainly, whoever contributes to elevate the taste, and to unmask the deformity of a corrupting literature, confers a great benefit upon his country; and what individual, or what potentate, can effect so much towards the accomplishment of this end as the pure and noble woman who brands whatever is base and degrading with the stamp of her invincible displeasure?

It would be vain to deny that, in the present age, we stand in singular need of such examples, and when these are removed from before our eyes, of such memories. Indeed, we have only to hear what is said by men of letters themselves, at least, on the Continent, to feel assured that we do so. For, in the first place, however disagreeable and even dangerous it may be to keep them company at this moment, they draw a curtain and invite us to behold what is passing behind it, in regard to the character of literary men, their brethren, and then leave us to judge for ourselves whether in following such heroes we are safe. It is not, therefore, that such writers as one of those now at our elbow, will be for judging of others from what is stained within themselves, though such an exercise might, perhaps, help them somewhat, but it is that these others do it for them. Saint-Beuve, for instance, without touching a more acute and delicate and human chord,—which had always best be let alone,—but lightly running over, as it were, certain Satanic strings, declares that even after witnessing political ambition and vanity, one can form no conception of what are in reality, and when seen near, the ambition and vanity of literary men. In this respect, he adds, prose writers are just as bad as poets. Diderot speaks of an editor of Montaigne, so modest and so vain at once, poor man, that he could not avoid blushing when he heard pronounced the name of the author of the Essays; like the sexton, so proud of the fine sermon that he had tolled for. What would be such a man turned original author for the nonce? But Saint-Beuve enables us to see farther into this obscurity behind the scenes; "for," says he, alluding to the whole class of literary men in our age, but still, of course, only his own countrymen, since all others are immaculate and trustworthy, "there are in their common hatreds, a finesse, a quality of acrimony of which political quarrels and animosities, I repeat it, can give no idea. It is passionate, blind, gross, subtile, and irreconcileable." Much chance (by the way, one may parenthetically remark) has poor religious truth when it has to do with such nobility! Our cicerone returns elsewhere to the subject, and says, "for the last thirty years, it is even worse in literature than in any other respect. Cleverness alone gives law there; intrigue, piracy, boundless vanity, venal cupidity. Oh, if among all these people of abundant cleverness, there were only one sound spot in the heart, one ounce, one grain of honesty, one only in each, what a great thing it would be! In these moments of the dissolution of doctrines, and this universal chaos, at any cost we ought to have within us certain invincible and impregnable points, even though isolated and without being in accordance with the rest of ourselves. Yes; sort of rocks of Malta or Gibraltar, where one might retire to in despair of a cause, and keep one's flag floating." Does not a sense of the importance of the lessons, conveyed by a visit to this tomb, increase as we advance, through the recollections that it awakens and the frightful contrasts which it constrains us to think upon?

But let us hear another witness, no gloomy misanthropist, or man behindhand with the age; no ridiculously scrupulous and ultramontane Catholic, or blind disparager of the merit of our light modern literature. I presume it will be yielded, that Jules Janin may come forward modestly, poor man, under no such suspicion. His testimony, then, is thus delivered: "Of all the maladies, which in this age attach themselves to the unhappy carcase of men of letters and artists, the most sad and incurable is pride. Pride escapes through all their pores; they live on it and burst with it. The 'me,' the 'ego' of these people, extends as far as a mortal skin can be stretched. 'I say it, and that's enough. I am here,—make room. I speak,—listen. I sleep,—look at me; at me and no one else. Me yesterday; me to-day; me to-morrow; me always, and after me, still me. I am who am;' and if by chance, while your peacock wheels round, your eyes should wander a single instant, woe betide you! there you are monographied *."

Well, to let the curtain again drop as before. What is less perilous, leaving all talk about the men, at least, as far as such revelations justify, let us cast a glance at their productions, of which, I suppose, we may be permitted to judge without assistance from any such sly traitor to the cause of their authors, as we have been listening to. "La littérature industrielle," says a contemporary, "s'est de plus en plus démasquée." In England, of course, where literary men are solely animated by the pure and heroic love of truth, at any cost to themselves, one may feel at ease in considering the character of their continental brethren, though it must be acknowledged by men of honour, even on the Thames, that there have not been wanting of late among these foreign chiefs,—those imaginative orators, as our journalists call them, emitting only tedious declamation, (for

* Variétés lit.

whatever opposes our view is always tedious,) and that through a factious motive,—that there have not, I say, been wanting some examples that look marvellously like instances of noble independence, and of a fearless devotion to justice and truth. But, nevertheless, let us hear their evidence, though I find, unfortunately, that their judgment of what is produced will still seek to reveal the mind of the producer, and pass sentence upon both together. "The conditions of periodical literature," says Saint-Beuve, "have changed for the worse since the year 1830. It is not to that revolution I impute it, but to the total absence of a moral direction which followed it, and of which the best intentioned have no idea. Whatever be the complex causes, the fact exists. There has risen up, since then, a whole race, without principles, without scruples; which is of no party, of no opinion; skilful and practised at phrases; sharp after gain, with a forehead that has never blushed; a race resolved on every thing to raise itself to live, not modestly, but splendidly; a race of brass that wants gold."

He then proceeds to say, that one distinguishing feature of this contemporary literature in itself is its indication of an extreme personal vanity, which in fact stares one in the face, though one knew nothing whatever otherwise about the men who live by it, — the books themselves displaying a rage for showing one's self from head to foot at all hours. "It was not so," he observed, "formerly. In the time of Racine, there was only one man, or rather a demi-god, Louis XIV., the king, who was on the stage, and remained on it, even from his getting up to his going to bed, in all situations; from the giving him his shirt by his gentleman to his amusements in the bower. The perruque was the only piece which held good against his undress. No one ever saw him without one. But Racine, that is the poet of those times, on the contrary, concealed what related to their own person and privacy to present ideal emotions. In our time Louis XIV. is come down to every grade of society. Each Racine dresses and undresses himself before the public; and the wig even, which the king never abandoned, does not rest on the poet when he tells us (as in the instance cited) about his being asked for a lock of his hair." How often have those who knew Jane Mary heard complaints of a similar kind uttered with that sweet woman's voice which made the force of the objection appear much stronger! We must close this part of our subject with one reflection of no small importance to any of us. With sorrowful surprise used she at times to express her judgment respecting the hostility of a large portion of the literary world at the present day to the Catholic faith. But now, after such lifting of the curtain, after such confessions and revelations, do we not feel that much of the mystery which so afflicted her is explained? for what other result could be expected? "You are a simple creature," writes Mme. de Sévigné to her daughter, "when you say that you are afraid of clever people and men of genius. Ah! si vous saviez qu'ils sont petits de près*!" Besides, to cater like them for the public taste at present is in some respects like what was learning to play the court fool in ancient times:—

> "And to do that well craves a kind of wit;
> He must observe their mood on whom he jests,
> The quality of persons and the time;
> And, like the haggard, check at every feather
> That comes before his eye. This is a practice
> As full of labour as a wise man's heart."

"Literary vices," says Saint-Beuve, "constitute whatever is in this world the lowest and the most vile." How could these dispositions be combined with a willingness to incur personal loss and constant inconvenience, and the impossibility even of having access to the public ear when they wish to address it with views that are opposed to those of its literary journals, for the sake of maintaining a cause that is alike frowned upon by a government, by a trading community that seeks a patron in every house, by religious fanatics, and by a reading public; that only seeks to feed its own caprices, or to be amused, and perhaps to justify its own inclination to ignore every duty but the worship of its own image? Our French academician speaks again to the same purport elsewhere; and these are his words, which some would do well to remark with great attention:—
"One of the most inherent faults in literature at present 'c'est

* Lett. 167.

assurément la fatuité.' Fatuity is only one variety—which it is wrong to think elegant—of pedantry. Fatuity combined with cupidity and industrialism has need of catering for the bad passions of the public. The true is constantly at the mercy of the false, praise is purchased, insults run the street, industry is enthroned as sovereign, and a prudent silence as to what might affect its interests is its last resource." The observation of Saint-Beuve, however, for that matter, is, in regard to its general censure, of all ages. " Literas nescivit," said Cæsar, intending to imply that the want of literature had caused some one to act well, or less basely than his comrades.

In fine, one ought to feel grateful for the exercise of a judgment which anticipated the avowals of one of the greatest friends of literature, when saying, " The bad has now at length taken care to pronounce itself distinctly; and excess has proceeded to its last and most revolting consequences. Industrialism, cupidity, pride, have attained to such extravagant limits, that there is formed necessarily a separate camp, sufficiently large for all persons of moderate views, on their return from seeking adventures, friends to true and beneficent light. It is more than a group that is formed; there is nearly a whole city, by the mere fact of the overflowing of evil, which has rendered the rest of the literary world uninhabitable, causing to draw near to each other the honourable, and those who retain any sense of decorum and dignity."

But to return to consider the lesson that may be drawn from remembering the judgment which was evinced in regard to an appreciation of the beauties and advantages of a sound literature.

We may notice this action in regard to three points; for Jane Mary applied to the best sources; she brought with her a disposition capable of admiration, and above all, as already noticed incidentally, she possessed the thoughts which constitute the source and the rewards of literature.

It is the remark of a contemporary attached to no one political school, that the great literary movement which followed the restoration of the French crown after the first revolution, was effected by means of a Catholic reaction, monarchal and chivalresque. "It has been often observed," he says, "that a striking disaccordance exists between the advanced political principles of certain men and their literary principles obstinately fixed. The Liberals and Republicans have always shown themselves as strictly classic in literary theory, while from their opponents have come the poetical innovations and the brilliant and successful boldness *." One might assert with an assurance of truth, that the noble and pure figure which seems to rise over this grave we stand upon, points to the source from which all true progress in literature must ever proceed. Though she was ever ready to welcome an innovation that did not violate the principles on which literature, and in fact society, depend for their existence, she revered antiquity, and took her stand, meekly but firmly, beneath its banner. There is no denying that, for all her youthfulness of heart, her predilections in this respect were for the old courtier,—

" With an old study fill'd full of learned old books,
With an old reverend chaplain, you might know him by his looks."

And not for the new courtier,—

" With a new study, stuft full of pamphlets and plays,
And a new chaplain, that swears faster than he prays."

" Where are those fine old books you used to read ?" she often said merrily, to one who seemed to waste his time over others of a different class. " Let me see you with them. I like the very look of them; for even their mere outsides present a contrast to all this silly trumpery, a conformity with which would leave you never an understanding friend." " O, you must and will," she added, a few days before her death, " ere this summer wanes, write something that may do good." A month had hardly elapsed after she said this, when the present theme was felt to be thrust upon one, as if to invite one, or rather to constrain one, without reference to it, to endeavour to verify the prophecy. May those who take up the book co-operate, for it is only through their aid that one can succeed.

In order to witness her regard for books that seemed to embody the thoughts of the ancient world of faith and honour, you

* Saint-Beuve.

might have been directed to read those lines of Von Bosch, placed over his library,—

"Hæc nunquam lassat densa venatio sylva;"

and the words of Pope Pius II., that "letters were for plebeians silver, for nobles gold, and for princes jewels." She had even the innocent ambition to take to herself, for consultation, some specimens of the old Christian literature of France, particularly when there was any thing in the titles to strike her attention, as being suitable to what she thought her own wants. Thus she would insist on keeping the "Doctrinal de Sapience," by Guillaume de Roye, and for a long time, also, the "Ménagier de Paris." She had no fellow-feeling for the disparagers of the mediæval period, or for the revivers of a purely pagan way of writing, like that Mehr-Bode, who in the midst of Christians and a contemporary of Sidonius, of St. Loup and of St. Remi, is more pagan than Cicero*. Nor would she ever listen to the sweeping accusations, brought by men of letters, against ages that she knew were Catholic, and, consequently, not without much at least to extenuate their faults. Brucker, in his "History of Philosophy," represents the tenth century, which, by the way, Leibnitz admired, as void of all knowledge of letters, and for proof alters the fact, in the ludicrous anecdote of the Bishop Meinwere, pretending very seriously that he was "in habits of substituting mulis et mulabus, for famulis et famulabus, so little," concludes this author, "did he know Latin;" whereas, the fact was, that on the "fa" having been scratched out from the letters, to comply with the Emperor's frolic, the good Bishop, who for a moment fell into the trap, on the spot recovered himself, and repeated the right words, to the discomfiture of the sly prince and the treacherous chaplain, who had made the alteration in the text to please him. Of instances of this kind she, of course, knew nothing; but her general habits of thinking, formed simply by her faith, guided her, and preserved her from getting entangled in the mistakes or snares of those grave learned men, who prejudged a case through passion.

* Philarete Chasles, Études sur les premiers Temps des Christianisme.

Nor would I exclude from being counted among the sources of the noblest thought those religious orations to which she listened, and directed others to listen, with all the observance of the soul. Though she had never read the treatise of Nicole on the spiritual advantage to which hearing bad sermons may be made subservient, you rarely, if ever, heard her blame or even criticize a discourse of this kind, though it might be delivered by some one whose simplicity would remind you of what is related by a satirist of Maillard, the preacher of the fifteenth century, who pretends that the good man used to mark the word "hem! hem!" at the margin of his pages, in order to assist his rhetorical powers. But her admiration for what was well was unbounded. "What a mind does he possess!" she used to exclaim, with tears still standing in her eyes, returning home after hearing Father Faber preach at the oratory.

This leads me to the second point I just alluded to, namely, to the capacity for praising and for admiration which she brought to the perusal, or to the hearing, of a noble composition; by which she showed herself better entitled to judge of such things, than many who brought forward more formal claims,— "Car pour être critique on n'en est pas moins homme." Recall in her presence a tender or noble idea, and as we observed in regard to painting, again, though it were only suggested in a crude manner, her eyes overflowed; so true is it, as Mme. de Sévigné remarks, that "it is not only grief which makes us cry, but that many kinds of sentiments enter into the composition of tears [*]." Certainly her admiration was not like that of the circumspect and over-cautious critic, who, as some one says, waits ten years to find an object for it—who gravely pulls out his watch to tell you that the day dawns when it is already eleven by the clock. Her praise did not resemble that of those quick intelligences, whose approbation moves like the antique chastisement, "pede pœna claudo." No; but, as we read in the great work of Mdlle. de Scudéry, "fond of praising whatever could be praised justly, and that almost with exaggeration, she is so strongly moved by merit and virtue, that it would be easy to collect, only from this kind of sensibility, what must be

[*] Lett. 664.

her own excellence; while what is extraordinary, too, is to observe that, with a disposition so energetic and serious, her conversation is sweet, agreeable, natural, and even gallant, never wanting to contest a point, but leaving to speak those who desired to do so, and retaining always the power to maintain the justice of her own views." She brought, in fact, to the perusal or hearing of what was noble, that mind which is ascribed by Janin to one of his great literary contemporaries: finding him in the crowd that salutes the passing triumph of a great conqueror, he asks, "What is this young man seeking here?" "He is seeking some one who is neither a soldier nor a senator,—one of Cicero's friends,—or at least a slave with whom he can speak of the man whom he considers great, leaving Cæsar to his fortune, and speaking at their ease of their common master, Cicero." What would she be seeking in such a crowd? some advocate of mind, some tribute of wise men to the eternal King; some trace, some word, some offering, some look, that reminded her of Jesus and Mary. In a word, it was heart and intelligence, it was justice and truth, or to say it more briefly still— it was God that she preferred to all things.

Finally, we derive an instructive lesson affecting literature, while meditating in this chantry, by observing that the unpretending model we are contemplating brought to all mental enjoyment the thoughts which constituted its food and its reward.

With a mind pure in regard to intentions to a degree that one can hardly fancy to one's self, and a heart tender so as to overflow with humanity, while responsive to it, she enjoyed with delight, as some one says of Fauriel, "all that is noble." In her poor innocent way she would any hour have repeated after you with approval as expressing what she too desired, "Innocuas amo delicias doctamque quietem." She gave herself up more and more to sweet affections, to nature, and to faith, and to that intellectual world which sometimes makes one forget this other. One saw her often, during the last years of her short life, seated with her book, which, owing to the shortness of her sight, she was obliged to hold close to her eyes. What is she thinking of? "Of eternity!" might have been her answer, though she would not have made it in such formal terms, so careful was she ever to conceal her merit. There are not wanting any where great readers and greedy listeners; but, as Mme. Cornuel, writing to the Countess de Maure, says of some one, "of the quantity of things which pass in their head, nothing can rest there sufficiently long to descend into their heart. Les frivoles bouchent le passage aux sérieuses." It was not so with her. She remembered ever what she had once read or heard, not to rest in it, but to draw it out into action, and while concealing her emotions through her exquisite tact and sense of what society sometimes required, it was easy to perceive that all true affections, and all serious questions, moved her profoundly. But the delights of literature were not for her an end—she aimed at what was higher. Like Madame the Duchess de Duras, afterwards so celebrated, of whom it used to be said by frivolous people, " Claire est très-bien, c'est dommage qu'elle ait si peu d'esprit!" she never dreamt of showing off; but uniting the cares of her household in domestic simplicity with indulgence in the most elevated thoughts, she could not wholly conceal amidst her career of active virtues the lofty consolations, towards the source of which every day she advanced silently and unostentatiously in the secret of her heart; for it was as if she had heard in her youth a voice of counsel that through her whole subsequent life she sought to practise, saying to her in the words of our eloquent contemporary,

> "Be good, sweet maid, and let who will be clever,
> Do noble deeds, not dream them all day long,
> And so make life, death, and that vast for ever,
> One grand sweet song *."

It followed, then, from all this observation of her intellectual character, that without having ever composed a work of imagination, or a poem, no sign of insufficiency, or of bad taste, perhaps, either, in presence of the sterile fertility of so many authors in these days, she could verify in her own mind the truth of the remark, that poesy itself is a powerful consoler. No doubt, in her its minor rays were lost in the brighter illuminations of her faith; but still these fancies, these remembrances,

* Kingsley.

these aspirations, operated in the same sense as a spiritual beneficent religion; they were, in subordination to the latter, the moderation of happy days contented with raptures of the mind and corresponding actions; they were the courage of times of mourning mingling with what emanated from the sanctuary; they were more than a power—they were strength. Truly, understood in this sense, she was a living example, that all human felicity is uncertain, but that it is still, after all, the Muse, as thus interpreted, which least, or rather, which never deceives.

From these facts, in conclusion, one may derive the important lesson, that what is best in literature consists in the treasury of feelings and thoughts of which it is only the occasional exponent. The power of expression may impart distinction and celebrity to a few; but the secret source of highest inspiration is what every one should covet. When amerced of this, what is all the rest? Alas! how often are seen verified the lines of André Chénier,—

> " Un mortel peut toucher une lyre sublime,
> Et n'avoir qu'un cœur faible, étroit, pusillanime,
> Inhabile aux vertus qu'il sait si bien chanter,
> Ne les imiter point et les faire imiter."

Shakspeare ascribes the same reflection to the Duke, where he makes him exclaim,

> "That we were all, as some would seem to be,
> Free from our faults, as faults from seeming free!"

Oh, how much better and more glorious is it to participate in the truth of this pure and silent poetry which consists in thought and action that corresponds with it! She, at least, whose memory is so vivid within these walls, chose this latter part.

> " Fam'd be her sweetness, and her parts of nature
> Thrice fam'd, beyond all erudition!"

No question, however, in finishing for the day, we must admit that this choice became the more appropriate for her, in consequence of the calamities and sorrows of her last years, when it was natural and so completely characteristic, even of the Muse herself, to say with the poet—

> "À ces vains jeux de l'harmonie
> Disons ensemble un long adieu ;
> Pour sécher les pleurs du génie
> Que peut la lyre ? .... Il faut Dieu !"

CHAPTER VIII.

N returning this time to the Chapel of St. John, let it be understood, from the first, that we are about to hear of homely matters, of which the memory might be thought more impressive at the hearth than in presence of the altar; but in the sequel we shall find that they are in accordance with what is greatest and best.

"Beginning with himself and with his own," says Tacitus, speaking of Agricola, "he first of all kept order in his house, which, in many respects, is a task no less arduous than to govern a province,—a se suisque orsus, primam domum suam coercuit, quod plerisque haud minus arduam est quam provinciam regere."

The memories that are to be awakened on this present visit will not, therefore, for all their homeliness, be found deprived even of dignity, in the sense of the world, since our theme embraces matter that seemed of such importance to the grave historian of the Roman Empire. Nor in this instance does he betray a feeling which our Christian ancestors, who used to say, "Diligence est à noblesse prochaine," would have deemed unworthy or exaggerated, or void of a religious interest; for not to speak of that description of the mistress of a family, which the lesson of the divine office had rendered so familiar to them, in which this attention to household duties forms the most prominent part, we can take up no work of the mediæval period treating on domestic manners, in union with piety, without witnessing, as in the Ménagier de Paris and the Bréviaire des Nobles, proof that they were of the same opinion, to which even the drama gave a faithful echo; for York, with Shakspeare, summing up the qualities which render women admirable, adds, in allusion unquestionably to this very faculty, as well as to self-conduct,

" 'Tis government that makes them seem divine,"

and Salisbury thinks that the same economy can add lustre to the fame of Warwick, saying to him,

" Thy deeds, thy plainness, and thy house-keeping,
Hath won the greatest favour of the commons."

These traditionary notions and manners, practised under the high sanction of the inspired page, were at all events most characteristic of the model which recurs to us in this place. Not insensible to the charms of agreeable conversation, to all who offered it she ever had a willing ear. To poetry, to records of high charitable deeds, and to the tale of youthful heroism, like Desdemona, she too would seriously incline—

" But still the house affairs would draw her thence;
Which ever as she could with haste despatch,
She'd come again."

She of whom we have to speak may be said in general to have been a representative of what is understood by the term—the family, in its general sense. She represented what constitutes the safety, the bond and charm of every home, its wise government, its holy duties, and its sweet affections; in regard to which threefold division we must proceed to speak of her with as much brevity as will be compatible with a true appreciation of her character, which will, in regard to other lessons, appear to be the more exemplary, from our not passing over these in silence as being only a necessary consequence of her faith; but, regardless of the charge of multiplying praises, giving a plain unvarnished statement, to show the fidelity with which she attended to the matters that fall under our observation here.

It is related of Mdlle. de Louvencourt, as of many others, that she united the merits of the active, with the graces of the contemplative and retired life [*]; two kinds of existence which, in the present state of civilization, are not perhaps quite so often found in combination as a cursory announcement of this fact might lead one to suppose. The same remark, however, would be strictly applicable to the character we are recalling. As we read of Virginia Bruni, "she was happy in the church, but she never omitted the duties of her state at home [†]." And it was with a view to the fulfilment of both engagements that, literally speaking, the taper burned ever in her chamber. Her life was laborious, with intervals of repose that were not very easily earned; for nearly every day she had to blend the preoccupations of a kind of temporal government with the solicitudes of a spiritual and charitable existence; a burden, however, which she willingly accepted, as if thinking with the great Condé, "that it is better to perform an hundred useless acts, than to fail in one that is necessary and of obligation." No doubt—

"In summer time, when leaves grow greene,
And blossoms bedecke the tree,"—

she often incurred blame for remaining so many hours in her chamber, when the sun seemed to invite every one to sally forth, and the party was already formed to take her along with them; but even then, and still further back in her career, there seemed to lurk a kind of presentiment in others, which suggested that after all, perhaps, there was not for her such great occasion to pass her time beneath the shade of earthly bowers, since she was so shortly to enjoy the unfading flowers of her native clime. Soon hers would be fair skies, and that perpetual spring which poets have invoked; hers, in glorified perfection, "the soft gales and dews of life's delicious morn;" hers, the long-lost fragrance of the heart; hers, what she always loved, rest and peace for ever. At all events, her part was taken from an early age, and in her apologies for it, there was a mixture of smiling yet thoughtful humanity, which agreed most harmoniously with her

[*] Vie de Mdlle. de L., 1778.
[†] Père Ventura, La Femme Chrétienne, ou Vie de Virg. Bruni.

piety and her faith. Possessing a heart that seemed formed by nature for the perception and enjoyment of all the romantic pleasures of life, she took her stand deliberately and irrevocably on the rugged side of duty and obligation; yet, and the fact seems to reveal her whole heart,—to the advances of the world that solicited her, she would reply less in the Stoic way than in the style of the arch nymph of Sir Walter Raleigh's answer to Kit Marlowe's passionate shepherd, saying—

> "If that the world and love were young,
> And truth in every shepherd's toung,
> These pretty pleasures might me move
> To live with thee, and be thy love;
> But time drives flocks from field to fold,
> When rivers rage and rocks grow cold,
> And Philomel becometh dumb,
> And all complain of cares to come.
> The flowers do fade, and wanton field,
> If wayward winter reckoning yield;
> A honey tongue, a heart of gall,
> In fancies spring, but sorrows fall!
> Thy gowns, thy shoes, thy beds of roses,
> Thy cap, thy kirtle, and thy posies,
> Soon break, soon wither, soon forgotten,
> In folly ripe, in reason rotten.
> Thy belt of straw, and ivie buds,
> Thy coral clasps, and amber studs;
> All these in me no means can move
> To come to thee, and be thy love.
> But could youth last, and love still breed,
> Had joyes no date, nor age no need,
> Then those delights my mind might move
> To live with thee, and be thy love."

But to return from this digression, Jane Mary, as we read of the Marchioness Le Bouteiller, "excelled in the art of conducting a house, that delicate and difficult art, which the Holy Ghost exalts with such force of language. Always distinguished by an admirable spirit of order, of forethought and economy, noble when occasions required it, all was ordained with prudence, and in a Christian manner. She presided with calm and activity, and watched over the domestics, sparing not good advice and encouragement *." This was exactly her method. She administered the interior with order and elegance, which of course included the care of the table, though, as Joinville says of St. Louis, " onques en jour de ma vie ne lui oy deviser ne souhaitier nulles viandes, ne grand appareil de chouses delicieuses en boire ue en manger, comme font maints riches homs; ainsi mengeoit et prenoit paciemment ce que on luy ataignoit et mettoit devant lui." To govern the domestics with firmness and humanity, to take an interest in the thoughts and projects of others, whose province was, without the house, to supply recreation and consolation, to attempt to purify all around her by her own purity—such was the ideal that she sought to realize, and such is the model proposed by philosophers themselves, though she thought but little of their advice, to all who have a family to govern †.

"The wife," says Luis de Leon, generally a very different guide from a philosopher, in his treatise of a perfect spouse, "enriches her family by suffering nothing to be wasted or lost. She buys linen and wool for the dresses of her husband and children and servants; and her savings conduce to the adornment of the house." In our particular instance, remarkable for generosity and bountiful liberality to all who came under any circumstances within her reach, incapable of resisting the fascination of beauty, when it was to be given and applied to a religious object, she might have been said, nevertheless, to have never wasted a shilling. Loving home, in her latter years rarely leaving it, unless for church or for a walk for refreshment, her mornings were always devoted to some useful object; and after her mother's death they were rendered laborious and fatiguing, so as to cause her headaches and extreme exhaustion. Then might sometimes have been heard repeated a scene like that between Virgilia and the other Roman ladies, saying to her, "Come, lay aside your stitching; I must have you play the idle huswife with me this afternoon." "No, good madam; I will not out of doors."—"Not out of doors! She shall,

* Léon Aubineau, notice sur la Marquise Le Bouteiller.
† Paul Janet, La Famille.

she shall. Fy, fy! you confine yourself most unreasonably." "No; at a word, madam, indeed I cannot; I wish you much mirth." In the first page of her account-book, there was found written, by her own hand, a prayer to the blessed Virgin, as if placing herself under her express direction in the discharge of duties which were to herself most irksome.

"I am no fine lady," she used to say when remonstrances were made at her trying, with cruel negligence of herself, to help others. Her doctrinal view of life agreed with that of the Prince de Conty, that we are not meant for self-indulgence and idleness; and therefore, as we read of the Dauphiness Marie-Josephe de Saxe, mother of Louis XVIII., she was always active, and never for a moment idle, ardently desiring to be useful in every way, with a total disregard to her own convenience. Moreover, her assistance was not confined to those within her immediate family; for even in regard to others, while shunning all needless interference, you might have often heard her saying in Shakspearian fashion, "The office becomes a woman best, and I'll take 't upon me." It would be a curious page if I were to relate instances of what in this way she took upon her, and of what her mother took upon her with her enthusiastic approval. But respect for the living imposes on me silence as profound as that of those who reaped the benefit of it. "How many women," says Topffer, "consume their time in a sterile indolence, as inactive in mind as in body!" She was not of the number. Had she an instant to herself? She would take up her chaplet or her prayer-book and nod to you, with smiles, to be off. The clock did not upbraid her with the waste of time. She regulated so well all her hours, that she had leisure to do a thousand things that another could not do; she found time for her prayers, for her meditation, for hearing mass, for regulating the house, for waiting on the poor, for dressing herself with as much elegance as another, for sending money to poor people, for taking a walk, and for receiving her friends—and all that without confusion or embarrassment; though, when morning visits were protracted, she used to say, laughing, when all were gone, that she had lost a whole day, and express her preference for the custom in Paris of paying visits in the evening. When out of season you were disposed to trifle with her, she could have truly said, with poor Isabella, "I have no superfluous leisure; my stay must be stolen out of other affairs." And yet, though always employed, her friends, as Coleridge says of Southey, "found her always at leisure;" but the fact was, she observed method in regard to all such matters; and when that is done, as Fontenelle remarks, "time, well managed, is much longer than those imagine who only know how to lose it." She loved order and regularity. As we read of the home of the Princess d'Epinoy, "every thing was regulated with such precision, that you might have thought it a religious community. The hours of rising and of retiring to rest, the time for mass and for the meals, all was fixed and known to every one *." Nevertheless, neither she nor her mother, from whom she seems to have inherited that love of order, carried it to the excess that has been witnessed in others,—as in the Comte de Fiesque for instance, of whom Mlle. de Scudéry says, "He is so subjected to the force of custom, that it serves him in place of reason and merit. Thus he accustoms himself to the places he inhabits, to the streets through which he passes, to the houses that he goes to, to the porters who open the gates to him, to the common people that he meets on the way †." One chapter of the curious book, which relates the life of the Princess d'Epinoy, treats on the good use which she made of time. This is a topic, therefore, on which there would be much to say with reference to our subject if our space permitted us to remark on it; and surely, view it on what side you may, you cannot think that it is incapable of yielding an important and even an interesting lesson. The illustrious women of the seventeenth century, as those of all preceding Christian ages, were not at least of this opinion. "Nothing," says one of them, "takes up so much time as a protracted idleness, and the making great things out of little things ‡." Such was not Jane Mary's custom. Coleridge might have said of her, "She organizes the hours, and gives them a soul; and that, the very essence of which is to fleet

* Grandet, Vie de Mlle. de Meleun. † Le Grand Cyrus.
‡ Ibid.

away and evermore to have been, she takes up into her own permanence, and communicates to it the imperishableness of a spiritual nature. Of her whose energies, thus directed, are thus methodized, it is less truly affirmed, that she lives in time, than that time lives in her. Her days, months, and years, as the stops and punctual marks in the records of duties performed, will survive the wreck of worlds, and remain extant when time itself shall be no more*." Shakspeare had said nearly all this in the well-known words,

> "——— ——— then to divide the times,
> So many hours must I tend my house;
> So many hours must I take my rest;
> So many hours must I contemplate;
> So many hours must I sport myself:
> So minutes, hours, days, weeks, months, and years,
> Pass'd over to the end they were created.
> Ah, what a life were this! how sweet! how lovely!"

In relation to servants, you might behold what was her character by reading the description of the valiant women of the Bible. She attended to their corporal wants and comforts, and took care that they should be regaled with wine upon great festivals. A certain young Englishman in her service falling sick in Paris, she procured a private room for him in the hospice of St. John of God, where he remained along with students and even noblemen for several months, till his complete recovery, enjoying the advantages, and even pleasures, that persons of the highest class, when placed in the same condition, might envy. As for faults, her rule seemed to be the same as that by which Tacitus tells us that Agricola governed his own household. It might certainly have been described in the words "omnia scire, non omnia exsequi." Though she never wanted firmness and courage when it was a question of regulating her household and suppressing all occasions of vice, of reproving and of advising, still her indulgence and patience were great; and really, towards the young, that of a sister or a mother; for many called those qualities into action by their

* The Friend.

culpable misconduct, while others grievously afflicted by their quarrel her whose kind advice

"Had often still'd their brawling discontent."

Faults against herself she was disposed to ignore altogether, or to turn them to a jest. "I have been well scolded," she used to say, in reference to the complaints of one of rather hasty temper, whose antique honesty she loved. Another time, in allusion to the same person, she used to say, laughing, "The mistress will have it so." Her patience and mildness towards persons who served her, used to excite at times the astonishment of others who happened to observe what passed within her own room. For knowing shrewdly her childlike disposition, there were not wanting some to take advantage of it. On one occasion, her sole reply was to the effect, that really she did not think that any cause had been given for such language; and, sometimes, she would almost beg the woman's pardon if she had said any thing that had hurt her, though nothing but words of good sense, with mild and gentle reproof, ever escaped her lips. In general, her example in these respects might have reminded one of what is read respecting the great and pious ladies of former times; as, for instance, in the life of Mme. de Pollalion, where she is represented regulating her household, taking care of her servants, and sanctifying, by her own example, all who came within the sphere of her influence[*]. Her care for the souls of her servants, not a very common thing perhaps in this age, and, therefore, liable to be misinterpreted, was as assiduous as it was judicious; full of ingenious, almost humorous, devices, it is true, but never without alleviating provisions, never irksome, or imprudent. Like Margaret, Countess of Richmond, "often tymes by herself she wolde so lovyngly courage every of them to do well, and some tyme by other meane persons. Yf any faccyons or bonds were made secretly amongst them, she with grete polycye dyde boulte it oute, and lykewyse yf any stryfe or controversy, she wolde with grete discrecyon study the reformacyon thereof." So you perceive, in what had been just before noticed, she was a mirror of the past. Several persons,

[*] Vie des Dames Françaises dans le xviie Siècle.

both men and women, became converts in her service, either to the Catholic faith, or to a stricter and more pious life. Even after her death, the memory of her example produced these effects, for six months had not elapsed when one of her servants, with his whole family, was, in consequence, received into the Church. No direct influence was ever employed by her. Every one knew that, excepting in the case of absolute wrong, the same kindness and favours were to be expected, whether there was a change or not; but still, as we read of Mme. Acarie, there was her pious example *; and then, too, books were thrown in their way, conversations with others of the same condition induced, means afforded and opportunities of hearing the sermons of impressive preachers; and, finally, when a strong desire was manifested, facilities procured in every form; for there was no condescension too great, and no device too minute, to be employed on such occasions. Both French, Germans, and English owed their conversion to God to the circumstance of having been in her service. Some renounced their former opinions, and embraced the Catholic faith. For years she had despaired of the conversion of her nurse; when, as a last resource, and without expecting any favourable result, but merely in order to leave nothing untried, she induced her to hear a sermon preached in English by the Archbishop of New York at Paris. Great was her joyful surprise, when this excellent person declared on her return, that she could hold out no longer against her own conscience, when that Prelate, with a humility that even in his person seemed astonishing, went upon his knees before her to show the method and usage of performing certain religious acts. There were instances of both men and women, in her service, who either left it for the purpose of entering on a religious life, or, some time after leaving it, became members of a religious community. One took holy orders, with a view to the foreign missions, and, on hearing of her death, wrote in these terms, using the language to which he had become most familiar: "Ma conviction est qu'elle n'a pas besoin de nos prières," (remarkable testimony, by the way, coming from one who had been in her service,) "cependant comme j'ai à son égard une

---

* Vie des Dames Françaises dans le xviie Siècle.

dette immense de reconnoissance et de gratitude dont jamais je ne pourrai m'acquitter entièrement, j'ai fait dire une messe pour elle;" another of her servants in England joined a religious brotherhood; another, and the merriest of the joyful, became a lay sister in an order of charity. This last example deserves particular notice, as showing the twofold influence to which she had been subjected; for, after many years being in France, where it was understood that a suitable match had been proposed for her, her mistress purchased all that was needful to furnish out the wedding, and the setting up in life of the young couple; but the match being broken off, through some cause on the other's part, the girl persisted in her resolution to leave, but it was for the purpose of immediately entering a convent in England, in which she now has passed many, and as she declares with an air of triumph, still laughing as of old, happy years.

It was said in the course of this evening's visit to the chapel, that the subject of our notice might be cited as having represented, also, the sweet affections of the family; and having now to develope this idea, it will be necessary to speak of her relation to others who in different capacities belonged to it.

Her father, a man who was always represented as being remarkable for sweetness of disposition, for high honour and delicacy of mind, having left her almost in her childhood under the sole guardianship of her widowed mother, a woman of rare constancy, and of justice as remarkable, under her wing she passed her early years in the practice of true piety, and the study of all elegant and useful accomplishments. The piety and prudence of her mother,—scilicet sublime et erectum ingenium,—kept Jane Mary less conversant with the world, than with the beauty and grandeur of what is most elevated, which that mother herself, perhaps, as being of a character less compromising, sought with greater vehemence than indulgence. How she loved her mother, it would be less difficult to imagine than to describe. Grandmamma used to say that from her infancy Jane had never caused her a moment's pain; that from that time to the present hour she had ever shown herself, in regard to her, all duty and all love. When there was to be an independent settlement for the daughter, a separation of two such existences seemed to all parties concerned, from first to last, as a measure totally out of the question, and not a thing to be thought of for an instant. The mother, therefore, continued to live with her married daughter, who remained like a girl towards her, always yielding to her the best rooms, and in the minutest details showing herself dutiful, respectful, and affectionate, to the last hour of her life, obeying her, consulting her, and never weary of evincing for her a sort of religious veneration, well merited for that matter, which recalled primitive ages of the world. It is often by mentioning minute circumstances that a biographer conveys the most correct idea of the character he describes. I know not why we should, therefore, now shrink from mentioning that even when they travelled she would always insist on her mother's carriage being driven first, and being attended to before her own ; she would always intimate to others, whether they were her servants, her children, her friends, or strangers, that it was to her mother they were to show attention—not to herself; and on every occasion, whether great or trifling, her first thoughts were for her aged parent, who became an object of that respectful, and one might almost add religious attention, which confers upon those who practise it even a pleasure, a sort of agreeable pride, of which, perhaps, they only discover the delicate intensity when the occasion for manifesting it is gone. In later years, whenever she was going out for a drive or a walk, she would not leave the house without first going to say a few more words to grandmamma, as to a kind of holy recluse, and sometimes when her foot was on the carriage step, she would think of something else, and hasten up stairs again to speak to her. It was the same on her return. Moreover, besides being influenced in this regard by her tenderness of veneration, every day, whatever might be the occasion,

"———— she sought
A nobler counsellor than her poor heart ;"

though one might truly add, a nobler could ne'er be found; but her abilities she thought were all too infant-like for doing much alone. Even in things of indifference she would still consult her mother, who she knew was always in the right. Her will, by a most natural and legitimate deference on the daughter's part, was supreme; and she complied without repugnance, and with a most happy repose of mind which she contrived to communicate to others, who in consequence derived, as already observed, a sort of delicious satisfaction that was felt on losing it as the loss of their own youth. In truth, grandmamma's was a remarkable character, both before and after her life of strict retreat, and well worthy of all the homages she ever received. She was a lady of most confirmed honour, of an unmatchable spirit, and determinate in all virtuous resolutions; yet shrinking from the employment of an influence which attached itself irresistibly to her own merit, she would be just against herself, and fearful of using what another would long to use without deserving to possess it, though with her it was both legitimate and an object of extorted gratitude to those who reaped the benefit. A poet paints to the life this venerable lady when he says,

> "——— Hers was
> A mounting spirit, one that entertained
> Scorn of base action, deed dishonourable,
> Or aught unseemly.
> ——— Wise she was,
> And wondrous skilled in genealogies,
> And could, in apt and voluble terms, discourse
> Of births, of titles, and alliances;
> Of marriages, and inter-marriages;
> Relationship remote, or near of kin;
> But these are not her praises; and I wrong
> Her honour'd memory, recording chiefly
> Things light or trivial. Better 'twere to tell
> How with a nobler zeal, and warmer love,
> She served her heavenly Master."

Just conceive what a heart-wound was there when that grandmamma died! In the moment of that holy soul's departure, the afflicted daughter knelt down before an image of our Lady and begged of her, with clasped hands and streaming eyes, to become to her now more than ever a mother, and as long as she lived afterwards, whenever she went into her mother's room, which used to be the first thing every morning on leaving her own, she used to kneel on the ground, and then say, with a smile on rising, that she felt while she remained in it a sort of religious inspiration. Thus antique and universal was the character belonging even to the form of her affections; for, in this instance, she resembled exactly those afflicted souls, which, for a long time after the death of St. Colomban, used to visit the chamber in the rock on the opposite side of the Trebbia, where, in his last years at Bobbio, that holy man used to pass his days in retreat, and who, as the annals of the monastery attest, used to find themselves on going out consoled, and even in a state of joy, as if in consequence of his sweet protection.

The subject would require us here to make mention of others in regard to her, and though it will devolve on him to speak who should be silent, I see the play so lies that he must bear a part. "His lot is happy," exclaims an ancient author, "who has found in a friend the watchful guardian of his mind. He will not be deluded, having that light to guide; he will not slumber, with that voice to inspire; he will not be desponding or dejected, with that bosom to lean on." It is only like an old and monotonous tale when one hears extorted confessions like those of the Eighth Henry, saying,

> "———— Go thy ways—
> That man i'the world, who shall report he has
> A better wife, let in nought be trusted,
> For speaking false in that; she was alone,
> (If her rare qualities, sweet gentleness,
> Her meekness, saint-like, wife-like government,
> Obeying in commanding,—and her parts
> Sovereign and pious else, could speak her out,)
> The wife of earthly wives;—she was nobly born;
> And like her true nobility she has
> Carried herself."

Nothing assuredly more common than to hear it said,

> "She was a true and humble wife at all times,
> To her partner's will conformable;
> Ever in fear to kindle his dislike,
> Yea, subject to his countenance; glad or sorry,

> As she saw it inclin'd. When was the hour
> She ever contradicted his desire,
> Or made it not hers too? Or which of his friends
> Has she not strove to love, although she knew
> He were her enemy?"

Still, is it not ever an instructive voice which tells of any one who was, or who ought to have been, by such fair influence

> "Foster'd, illumin'd, cherish'd, kept alive?"

Is it not instructive to hear of one loving a stranger to his family, merely for having praised one known to it? of one whose daily prayer might have been expressed in that which sounds in old Castilian poesy, as where we read, "'Lord, King of kings, and Father of all the world, I adore thee, and trust to thy will, and I beseech St. Peter to aid me when I pray that God may guard my Cid Campeador from all evil, since we must part without seeing each other again in this life?' The prayer finished," says the narrator, "and the mass over, they left the church. It is time to part. Then the Cid advanced to embrace Chimène, but she kissed his hand, shedding such a flood of tears that she knew not where she was. All wept; so that one has never seen the like; in fine, they separated from each other as the nail separates from the flesh*." St. Paul has declared that the believing wife would justify the infidel husband, and a contemporary writer has said, when citing the words, "There is a distinction between this living and the formalist Christianity." One cannot wonder at the good man for having such a thought occasionally across his mind, when he might have thought the reins too tightly drawn; for how constantly is the phenomenon, to which the Apostle of the Gentiles alludes, still presented in the interior life of families! With what wonderful sweetness does the woman of faith seek to win to God her partner, when some slight unmeritable man; with what discretion does she avoid every thing that could be a possible ground of legitimate or of needless offence, as if she has read all that has been laid down by abbés, who write on such delicate matters; yet in all this, nothing artful,

---

* Poem of the Cid.

nothing designed in appearance, for there are no tricks in plain and simple faith, but all natural and spontaneous. How often, like the Marchioness Le Bouteiller, does such a woman, by her example, win back the other to the practices of his youth, and from indifference even excite him, at least for a moment, to a generous fervour*. With what tenderness does she speak to the purport of that Shakspearian lesson, saying,

> " Vice repeated, is like the wand'ring wind,
> Blows dust in others' eyes, to spread itself;
> And yet the end of all is bought thus dear,
> The breath is gone, and the sore eyes see clear."

With what a brief and delicate allusion does she sum up, from time to time, that other counsel, which reminds one of mortality, saying, with such gentleness,

> " For death remember'd should be like a mirror,
> Who tells us life's but breath; to trust it, error."

Does she not even tenderly impart the secret that every day of her life she prays for him, and for all his relations who are not Catholics, that God may give them the grace of a happy death? At other times, perhaps, you only hear uttered with a smile, " Poor fellow! don't let us be hard upon him, he merely wants this and that, like many others not over thoughtful!" and all the while what mystic communications between her and Heaven, on account of those she loves on earth! praying, going to communion, giving alms, all with a view to their souls! Is it not the first wish of her deepest heart to see them wholly God's, that is, for ever happy? Is it not her way with sweet smiles to tell them so, and with every act of an ingenuous love to try to accomplish this purpose, to which her life is ceaselessly devoted? Never, O never, should one do her ghost the wrong to hold aught dearer than her memory!

It remains to speak of Jane Mary in relation to those who never merited to hear from her the words of the Roman, "I shall be lov'd when I am lack'd." She was indeed "matrem filiorum lætantem."

* Léon Aubineau, Notice sur, &c.

The memory of these "joyful mothers" imparts a threefold lesson, important for those whom it concerns—lesson of affection, lesson of prudence, lesson of acquiescence in the wisdom of nature.

Who shall describe the love of such a mother for her children, in one respect perhaps corresponding to that want of our nature, the want of living and of reviving in another? "I am proud of my boy," she used to say. Then, after his death, "I see many sweet little fellows wherever I go, but somehow no one now like little John. No, not one." His brother, few taller were so young, came in for his share of love. As was said of the Roman mother, she went adorned with her children for jewels — quand le bord de robe était leur horizon! Then the anxiety of such mothers when danger seems to present itself, though it were only the common risks of the hunting-field; what waiting for the sound of the voice, and of the horses' hoofs returned to the threshold! what prayers during the interval; and what rapturous thanks to God when she hears the horses under her windows, and sees all safe returned! But these things need not detain us; these sweet domestic scenes, these interiors of the family, these children's bowers are common, every one knows all about them. No question, however, but that when recalled as having been witnessed in this form, they impart a lesson which is unnecessary in no age, and which possibly may be sometimes valuable even in our own. Let us proceed, however, to the lessons of prudence, which are yielded by the same memory.

Those who would have been born nearer England, if Paris had been at Calais, are usually clad from infancy until their seventh year in white, to signify under whose invocation their mothers place them; and this devotion is practised afterwards, by the adoption of the same foreign usage in regard to others, who first see light where it is unknown, in order to signify, as it were, that all alike are to be not only loved, but offered, formed, educated. So it was here. They were loved with so strained a purity, that their lessons may be said to have been coeval with their first smiles. Then, what a thing is it to hear these mothers teach the catechism! with such mock anger, so transparently put on when the scholars laugh and trifle, while saying to each, like Hue de Tabarie himself in his Ordène de Chevalerie,—

> " Que vous aijez bien en corage
> De Diu servir tout vostre éage."

In the life of Mme. d'Esturville these points are touched on. But it is later, when the shores of qui, quæ, quod are reached, that this care yields lessons; for then what sacrifices to further the object of instruction! It might be a curious book that would represent in etching the various studies for which teachers are provided, as in that great German volume where we are shown how many things the young wise Kunig was taught; and every boy is a king in his mother's eyes. As, for instance, wie der jung weyss Kunig, die Musica und Saytenspiel lernnet erkennen, &c.* Here the financial prodigality is seen taking a right direction. But to the last there is a field reserved for the exercise of maternal care; for with all their love, such mothers never spoil its objects, though on this point alone they manifest their scruples, expressing fear at times if they ever witness the least impatience, however innocently evinced towards others, lest perchance, through over-petting of their little dears, they may have been accessory to it. Nevertheless such confidence on this head as she ought to have felt, seems not only natural, but consistent with the gravest lessons, as also with the most divine instincts. The mother of René d'Esgrigny, seeing him near death, and fast approaching to his God, desired him on one occasion to pray for a certain friend of theirs, adding, " Et n'oublie pas ses enfants, et surtout son fils, les garçons ont tant besoin de prières." The saintly boy replied, " Oui, je le ferai; mais je ne sais pourquoi, je prie mieux pour les grandes personnes. Il me semble qu'elles en ont plus besoin." However, in the instance more immediately before us, it is to be noted that if any one praised her children in their presence, she was pained and alarmed, and would find another topic for the conversation. But to return. It is related of Mme. d'Esturville, that she inspired her children with an aversion for the worldly

---

* Der weiss Kunig, Wien, 1775.

character. Who can estimate the value of such adorable lessons? I should like to know what there is of good that they do not include. You know what the poet says,—

> "She gave them eyes, she gave them ears,
> And humble cares, and delicate fears;
> A heart, the fountain of sweet tears,
> And love, and thought, and joy."

Is it nothing to hear of such gifts? "Childhood," says a French author, "has natural graces; it has no need of factitious ones. It is a depraved taste which can like to see the forms and manners of the world in childhood. The world rests on conventions which no doubt have their reason, but it is not right to place them on a par with sacred and obligatory laws. A true child will be always just the thing, that is the principle, and that is what is forgotten when children are taught to distinguish themselves by acting and speaking like grown-up people according to conventional shows and rules. It is thus that the world is formed. It has only to compare positions and persons, each one striving to be more than another. This false pleasure and bitter suffering is the life of worldly people. Is it not terrible to instil into childhood these miserable passions? teaching it to compare, to envy, and to despise; whereas left to itself it would know nothing of all that, it being the age of equality and indifference. Nothing more shocking than a child who has the manners, mien, phrases, and dress of a grown-up person. People of taste lament when they see these lovely creatures, whose charm is in simplicity and unconsciousness, stupidly wrapped up in these stiff, swollen, garnished dresses, contending with people of fashion for richness and costliness of dress, and breathing with their elders the withering perfume of vanity. The principle of a wise education is to preserve and prolong childhood in the child as long as possible*." It is hardly needless to add, that in such feelings she cordially participated.

In fine, we are reminded by the voice which lingers under these vaults of the wisdom of conformity with nature in regard

* Paul Janet, La Famille.

to the relation of mother and child. Thanks to that divine maternal tenderness, for the loss of which no lessons and no discipline, however ordained, can ever compensate, such a mother knows the heart of her children better than all the philosophers of the world, and she is loath to part with them.

> "So doth the swan her downy cygnets save,
> Keeping them prisoners underneath her wings."

She cannot bear to hear of children, under any pretext, without a very urgent necessity, being forcibly separated from their mothers. She can never comprehend how the state should be benefited, how religion should be advanced, how minds can gain solid advantages by separating the daughter from the mother, who, besides all that she had already suffered, is so ready to make still any sacrifice for her, counting all her own delights as nothing. She would make no distinction in favour of the higher classes, or to the prejudice of the lowest, when faith existed in a mother. The bond of blood she deems invincible. Like the poor queen in Shakspeare's Richard, she exclaims,

> "Hath he set bounds between their love and me?
> I am their mother; who shall bar me from them?"

Accustomed from an early age to hear the natural and legitimate voice of society in a Catholic country, which perhaps ought never to be wholly ignored, she thought that such things ought not to be without a grave cause for them. She thought that the family should continue to be somewhat,—that the will of parents was not an absolute nullity when it was a question of the destiny of a child. Nor even with regard to these views, when embracing the other sex, do we find that those who entertain them are left without any approval from dispassionate observers. "I fear nothing for a young man," says Janet, "so long as he retains the spirit of the family—l'esprit de famille; but if you deprive him of this altogether, I form no favourable expectations from whatever provision you may choose to make for him. There is no substitute for the love of home, and for the influence at least at short intervals of the maternal example.

The college without the family, is a barbarous and brutal expedient, to which I deem immeasurably preferable the family without the college *." These are the words of one who is himself a Professor of the University, and they occur in a work which has been crowned with academic honours, as useful to the state.

But it is time to close this visit. Let us repeat, as we depart, the lines of the poet, so doubly applicable to the person we have had in view,

> "She was belov'd, she loved; she is, and doth;
> But still, sweet love is food for fortune's tooth."

CHAPTER IX.

OW go with me, and with this holy man, into the chantry by. We are to hear to-day of some singular traits, that may be thought taken from a black-letter chronicle, of justice, humility, and charity, all leading to a great affection for the poor, and even to a familiarity with their fortunes; and here, again, I am to speak what I do know. "Enemies," if there were ever any such, which I disbelieve,

> "———— shall say all this,
> Then in a friend it will be cold modesty."

It appears, therefore, if one may more plainly say it without offence, that our proposed theme will possess the interest which belongs to a description of things, that are placed somewhat beyond the limits of ordinary observation. At least, the poet might be thought disposed to take this view of it; for he considers the pure spirit of justice to be a thing rather rare just at present, saying,

> "———— If the heart
> Could be inspected to its inmost folds,

---

* Paul Janet, La Famille.

By sight undazzled with the glare of praise,
Who shall be named —
Whom the best might of conscience, truth, and hope,
For one day's little compass, has preserved
From painful and discreditable shocks
Of contradiction, from some vague desire
Culpably cherished, or corrupt relapse?

* * * *

Profession mocks performance. Earth is sick,
And Heaven is weary of the better words
Which states and kingdoms utter when they talk
Of truth and justice. Turn to private life
And social neighbourhood; look we to ourselves.
How few who mingle with their fellow-men,
And still remain self-govern'd and apart,
Like this our honour'd friend."

Heinrich, the German traveller of the sixteenth century, seems to have been of an opinion somewhat similar, so far, at least, as Florentine manners, at one particular moment, were concerned; for he says that "all the citizens had two sets of scales, one for their neighbour, the other for themselves." Be that as it may, here we have to speak of one not so

"Dejected, and habitually disposed
To seek in degradation of the kind
Excuse and solace for her own defects;"

but of one ever humble, who yet appeared to stand to every eye, and without the aid of any rhetoric, unless you qualify as such the use of plain English words necessary to express your meaning, distinguished by the greatness of her soul, the nobleness of her inclinations, and the generosity of her heart, making "magnanimity and justice," as Sir Philip Sidney says, "to shine through all misty fearfulness and foggy desires;" just— but not according to advanced notions in this age of morality and progress, but rather as your ancient ballads would distinguish,—according to that

"—— old threed-bare Conscience that dwelt with Saint Peter [*];"

just—but so as to resemble the simplicity of Turenne, having

[*] Percy, ii. 271.

equity for the rule of all her actions, neither friendship nor dislike being able to make it swerve, and ready to refuse to grant a favour to a friend which she would not withhold from an enemy, if she thought it her duty to confer it upon him*; just—but so as even to do violence to her own just inclinations, rather than admit the possibility of her being thought to acquiesce in the least design or action of another that was contrary to what justice required. Certainly, as the old poet says, " to learn thus to do nothing unjustly, is, I think, an elegant apparatus of life." But even this was not all. Her love of justice, embracing every thing that was right in the most minute details, led her to act on many occasions in the spirit of that academician, M. des Billettes, who so greatly respected whatever belonged to the public, and was connected with its interests, that when he used to pass the Pont-neuf on foot, he used to tread on that outward part of the steps which was the least worn, in order that the centre, which was more affected by the feet of the crowd, might not be injured by his own. "Such littleness of attention," adds Fontenelle, who mentions this trait of his character, "was ennobled by his motive; and how greatly might it be wished that the public welfare were always loved with as much superstition †." It was exactly thus that she acted in regard to whatever was exposed to injury; and these points of resemblance, in themselves so singular, between two minds otherwise so differently constituted, while both were equally inspired by the love of justice, cannot be pointed out, I should think, without exciting interest.

In general, it may be said, that her notions and ways of justice were all stamped with the antique mark; whether you referred to the philosopher of old to verify it, or to such mediæval standards as the Exemplary Mirror and Fruitful Instruction of Gilles de Rome, when he treats " de la justice qui est deue à Dieu," and " de la justice que l'on doit avoir en soy mesmes," and, in fine, " de justice retributive qui est payer les loyers et retribuer à chascun selon son merite ‡." Generally,

---

* Mascaron, Oraison fun. de Turenne.
† Tom. vi. 121.
‡ Le Mirouer, &c., du Regime des Roys, &c.

too, it was with her, as with an illustrious French lady, and a contemporary, of whom we are told, that "her influence came from her soul, that what was felt was her goodness, her truthfulness, her forgetfulness of self, her devotion to her affections! Thus she commanded by gentleness, as well as by that rectitude, that intimate sentiment of duty, of which she applied the rigour to herself alone." In this instance, too, that love of justice, which, by the way, one might say her mother gave her, was tempered with a most incomparable sweetness, so as to verify and, as it were, illustrate the remark of Mme. Swetchine, when she said "one must be benevolent in order to be just. When a painter," she adds, in explanation, "desires to represent nature with perfect exactitude, he has to embellish it; for, not being able to impart to his canvas the grace of nature, he has to supply it by another kind of perfection; and so it is only by excess on one side that he gives sufficient. In morality we are also painters of those whom we judge. Not tracing in an exact proportion the measure of the good qualities that we perceive, we at least attenuate the defects; and, perhaps, this is the only secret whereby to make intellectual resemblances exact in the sum total." There was nothing, therefore, in her justice to discourage those who held with Pelisson, that no one takes pleasure in having strict justice rendered to himself in this world, every one wishing to be treated a little better than he deserves. One may speak of it in general as, in this instance, flowing from a pure source, and as producing beneficent, and in the ordinary affairs of life practical results.

The hand that had made her fair had made her good. There was nothing adulterated in any of her virtues; and that is what imparted to each of them a character that one can hardly remember having ever witnessed in the case of any other human being. They were all what they seemed to be, and that as if there could be no help for it; they were the thing itself, neither more nor less; and the principle of every one of them, where any consciousness of it existed, was, we have every reason to believe, true charity. Her purity of intention when seeking to act justly was disclosed every moment in a way that no one could mistake. Her most temporal acts were spiritual acts. She realized, in fact, the type which is laid down by writers on domestic government. "She was," but without any disagreeable scrutiny or officious interference on her part, "the conscience of her family,—not alone in regard to the private duties of its different members, but also with respect to what was required by general interests*." Though she certainly was not accustomed to read your black-letter chivalrous books, she had moreover a high, and exquisite, and quite antique sense of honour; and every one could depend on that delicate and ever powerful spring, where the exercise of mere justice would not have been sufficient to meet the case. Hers was "that exaltation of mind which maintains a heart incorruptible in the midst of corruption." I know that these reiterated touches will offend, but what can I do? I am set down to copy an original picture. Ask those who possessed it whether I exaggerate. This principle kindled a fire in her soul which never became low. Her justice, too, emanated in part from her extraordinary devotion to truth, which made her see every thing dispassionately, and never with eyes that could be swayed by personal considerations. "I cannot help saying," wrote an English physician whom she had befriended when he was a student at Paris, "that I never knew not alone a more kind and gentle, but a more guileless woman." This again presents a theme of which the practical importance is not perhaps at present wholly undiscernible. Probably no one in our actual state of society would dare to profess, as of old, the art of deceiving men according to the categories of Aristotle; but it is to be feared that, when invited to study such a model, we are again called upon ground that is not at any time overmuch frequented. "Ah! qu'il y a peu de personnes *vraies!*" exclaims Mme. de Sévigné, adding, "Think a little of the word, you will love it; I find in it, according to my notions, a force beyond its ordinary signification †." Coquillard, in the sixteenth century, wrote a dialogue "de la Simple et de la Rusée." Jane Mary would have figured admirably in such a conversa-

* Paul Janet, La Famille.
† Lett. 117.

tion, which, even in the nineteenth century, is far from fulfilling the conditions of those that are to be considered as "imaginary." Mme. de Longueville, speaking of a certain society, says on one occasion, "I was simple enough to imagine that these good men acted with sincerity; it is true I only thought so since yesterday evening." Poor Jane Mary—God help her!—would have thought so from her childhood, which in regard to simplicity still lasted. Guileless herself, any one could deceive her who sought, as the poet says, to add "obscurity to his vices and falsehood to his faults,"—

"Noctem peccatis et fraudibus addere nubem;"

but all the while, like St. Louis as described by Joinville, "ama tant verité!" Truth was what she breathed. "Let me have any thing," she used to say, "but falsehood." And I believe, if extreme tenderness had not kept her in check, that she would have wished for a re-enactment of that old municipal decree of the City of London in the reign of Henry III. which enjoined "judgment of pillory for lies, with a whetstone tied round the neck*." She regarded as injustice even the most common instance of exaggeration, and limited her own words to an expression of what she strictly believed. Even to excuse herself from accepting an invitation that she wished to decline, she would avoid alleging a reason that was not founded on exact truth.

It is easy to deduce from all this that she would have but little confidence in the leaders of public opinion, when, like the ancient sophist, they speak to-day in praise of justice, coolly letting us gather from their reserve that to-morrow we shall hear them evincing equal ability in praise of injustice, on the ground of there being what they call a "moral excuse" to justify it; the laying down of which exception is only conferring on every one now-a-days a right to violate justice, and even law, at his own pleasure, since each is permitted to interpret circumstances as it pleases him. In these cases, then, for once she would be armed against deception; and so, when the

* Lib. Albus, 519.

eulogizer of the press speaks of it as "une barrière opposée aux invasions de la force,—une chaine électrique qu'il suffit de frapper pour soulever le monde contre l'injustice," she would be wholly incredulous, and refer the speaker to principles of rather a different order, as better calculated to achieve the result which he fondly contemplated.

We shall not have to dwell upon the second point, which I distinguished as showing the beneficent results which were produced by her sense of justice, yet it might naturally suggest a few reflections. For are we to suppose that this intimate sense of right and equity is a thing imperishable in the world, and consequently that such representations of one who eminently possessed it are supererogatory and uncalled for? It does not seem as if even our times were singularly favourable to such an impression. They rather seem to suggest such thoughts as Coleridge expressed in the "Friend," when saying, "If the power with which wickedness can invest the human being be so tremendous, greatly does it behove us to inquire into its source and causes. So doing, we shall quickly discover that it is not vice, as vice, which is thus mighty; but systematic vice! vice self-consistent and entire; crime corresponding to crime; villainy intrenched and barricaded by villainy! This is the condition and main constituent of its power. The abandonment of all principle of right enables the soul to choose and act upon a principle of wrong, and to subordinate to this one principle all the various vices of human nature. For it is a mournful truth, that as devastation is incomparably an easier work than production, so may all its means and instruments be more easily arranged into a scheme and system." Who does not know that there are occasions when men might repeat Banquo's words, and say, if they retained the power of supplication,

> "Restrain in me the cursed thoughts, that nature
> Gives way to in repose?"

Our ancestors at least were aware of all this danger, when saying, in their homely style, however embellished by such engravings as so quaintly decorate the pages of the Veridicus Christianus by Father David, that he who wants to be rich at the end of the year will come to a bad end before the day of St. John. On which words their municipal enactments, as we find in the Livre des Métiers by Stephen Boileau, in the time of St. Louis, and the Liber Albus of the City of London, which dates from about the same period, formed a fine commentary. The simplicity of their penalties, as when the London baker, who falsifies his measures, is to be drawn upon a hurdle through "the streets that are most dirty, with the faulty loaf hanging from his neck," may seem only amusing now, and semi-barbarous; but the repeated mention in both works of tradesmen's goods forfeited, as for instance furs, because new work was mixed with old work; hides, for being badly tanned; shoes, for being "false," &c. &c., attests what attention was then paid to justice in social relations to "the honour of trade," or as it was expressed, "of the good folks of the mysteries," and to "the common profit of the people." Here I would only infer from such observations, that the memory of one such guileless and truly just soul, imbued with that love of justice from which all such ancient popular sayings and municipal enactments emanated, conveys a lesson that neither individuals, nor collective nations, nor governments, should deem either tedious or unnecessary.

The details which our subject more directly yields, are of course concerned with an humble order of duties, which in themselves will not be deemed to justify any delay, as they belong rather to those who resemble the good preceptors of whom Fontenelle speaks, "who worked hard and assiduously in order to render themselves useless." As we read of a French contemporary, the truthfulness of her character, and at the same time her profound discretion, gave to her presence a security full of charms. Consulted on many occasions, and often on important and delicate questions, her advice was always stamped with moderation as well as dignity. Her action on minds was always soothing, and the part that she constantly fulfilled was that of calming instead of exciting or embittering—moreover, she had instinctively the wisdom of Rome, she loved to wait, and trusted much to time. From her elevated point of view, the most common actions assumed a sort of dignity, and their performance, while often neglected by persons in her condition, to the detriment and misery of the industrious classes, yielded, for the same reason, even pleasure. She could not bear, like Mme. de Sévigné, to see in any one related to her, that certain air of the grand seigneur—of qu'importe? of ignorance and indifference, which, as the sensible marchioness says, "leads quite straight to all kinds of injustice, and even to the hospital *." She would, on the contrary, endeavour to impart a spirit of rule and economy, which agrees admirably with what is often required by principle and honour. It is related of the Princess d'Epinoy, that "she regarded it as a crime to owe the smallest sum to shopkeepers at the end of the year, being so unlike many great persons who take on credit on every side, and live and dress themselves at the expense of those who have to struggle for their existence." Such, too, was the view which Jane Mary took of what justice demanded of her. It was not merely her own debts and the debts of her family that she paid monthly, or even weekly. She used also, on many occasions, to pay the debts of other people; and above all, when within the limits of her means, of the dead who had departed indebted. To her the tradesman's claim was·sacred, and like Margaret, Countess of Richmond, nothing seemed to give her such pain as to find that she had forgotten to pay any one.

One could hardly form a sufficient estimate of the beauty of this character in regard to justice, if one did not at the same time take into account its deep and genuine humility. It was a simple and pure soul, ignorant of its own value, too gay and cheerful to be proud, for pride is near of kin to melancholy, and wholly void of all self-reference. Like her sanctity, it was that quality which is unconscious of itself. At a word escaping from any one that seemed to indicate a high opinion of the merit of her actions, she used to laugh like Isabella, the sister of St. Louis, "Et tournoit tout au neant et tenoit à folie ces choses †." So that with all her piety and justice and solid principles, she never caused any one, however careless, to feel humiliated or oppressed in her presence, as if her merit was a direct reproach, and an importunate criticism to mortify him,

---

* Lett. 822.
† La Vie d'Isabelle, par Agnes de Harcourt.

and put love to flight. In every respect she had a lowly opinion of herself. "Nought is never in danger," she used to reply when interrogated as to the state of her health. She would have repeated the poet's words, and said at any time,

"But the full sum of me is sum of nothing."

She would conceal all advantages that she possessed as she would have slighted her beauty. She would speak to the simplest as the Spaniards say one ought to speak to princes, that is, when giving them good advice, she would speak as if only reminding them of what they might happen to forget, "and not in the least as teaching them that of which they were ignorant." She had not, moreover, the fault of those unfortunate people who take pride in their own abilities, and fancy themselves ten times better than the nine worthies, thinking that the world is attentive to their least words and least actions. She was aware, that as far as any thing relating to herself was concerned, "Le monde," as Janin says, "s'en soucie comme de ça." In fine, if you can pace your wisdom in that good path that she would wish it go, you must be, like her, humble, you must take each man's censure, but reserve thy judgment; and if you would be just, as she was just, you must, as she did ever, temper equity with pity, which latter consideration leads us imperceptibly to what we have to speak of next—namely, the charity which rendered this character so worthy of being studied, and its memory so fraught with instruction for us all.

Notwithstanding what we observed at the beginning of this visit, the words that are read in the church of Notre Dame de Savona—"Misericordia et non justitia," as having been uttered by the blessed Virgin, might seem to have been inscribed within her heart.

"For never saw I mien or face
In which more plainly I could trace
Benignity, and home-bred sense,
Ripening in perfect innocence."

Two classes of men, it seems to one, need the lesson which is yielded here, namely, those who incline to severe justice when discovering some old abusing of God's patience, and those who have yet to learn the blessedness of loving others. To find the former no one has to look long. "Fee me an officer; bespeak him a fortnight before;" very common injunction this. Stephen Pasquier said, "If I had been the master I would have burnt the whole family of Ravaillac, father, mother, brothers, sisters, aunts, and down even to their arrière-petits-cousins." If you think such resolutions fanciful, pray read the Memoirs of John de Troyes, and of Olivier de la Marche. Such men need a turn or two in this chapel; and doubt not, supposing the voice heard in a heart that can be moved, but that the result might be similar to the impression that may have been produced by reading the concluding sentence of a great jurisconsult, which is in these words, "Inscribat hæc Deus, qui solus hoc potest, cordibus eorum, quorum res Christiana in manu est, et iisdem mentem divini humanique juris intelligentem duit, quæque semper cogitet lectam se ministram ad regendos homines, Deo carissimum animal[*]." Of the second class it is harder still to speak, considering at what utter variance they must find themselves with every thing that is remembered and learned over this grave. Hear how one of them is addressed by a poet who had studied well their manners.

> "Franck, une ambition terrible te dévore,
> Ta pauvreté superbe elle-même s'abhorre;
> Tu te hais, vagabond, dans ton orgueil de roi,
> Et tu hais ton voisin d'être semblable à toi;
> Parle, aimes-tu ton père? aimes-tu ta patrie?
> Au souffle du matin sens-tu ton cœur frémir,
> Et t'agenouilles-tu, lorsque tu vas dormir?
> De quel sang es-tu fait, pour marcher dans la vie
> Comme un homme de bronze, et pour que l'amitié,
> L'amour, la confiance, et la douce pitié
> Viennent toujours glisser sur ton être insensible,
> Comme des gouttes d'eau sur un marbre poli?
> Ah! celui-là vit mal qui ne vit que pour lui[†]."

---

[*] Grot. de Jure Belli ac Pacis.
[†] Alfred de Musset.

But let us observe the contrast which is presented by the memories awakened here, recalling compassion on both the spiritual and corporal miseries of all who suffered.

It is the remark of an acute, and assuredly very unprejudiced critic of human actions, "that true Catholics, in many respects, are, of all men, always the most tolerant. Les vrais Catholiques à bien des égards, sont les plus tolérants*." De Thou silenced the opponents of the edict of Nantes by reminding them of that journey of Pope John I., who went to intercede for the heretics, and fell on his knees before Valentinian, to beseech him in the name of the Merciful Being who is all goodness, to spare those unhappy persons. Times that call for such testimonies are only of rare occurrence; but the frailties and sins of our common nature furnish, in every age, and nearly every day, occasion for the exercise of that Catholic spirit, which by its operation in various forms verifies the remark of Sir Thomas Brown, that "there is no man's mind of such discordant and jarring a temper to which a tuneable disposition may not strike a harmony."

Here we must leave others to speak; and there is a most eloquent voice ready to admire and justify what we must feel without venturing to express it. " Our Saviour," observes Lacordaire, " loved Lazarus, Martha, and Mary ; yet in predilection even there are predilections—such a profound thing is love—and of an hierarchy without end. It was Mary, Mary Magdalene, that was loved with this love of preference. The Magdalene had profaned all, and she could present nothing to God but ruins. Accordingly, she enters without uttering a word, and she departs in the same manner. Repentant, she will not accuse herself before Him who already knows every thing; forgiven, she will not express any sentiment of gratitude. All the mystery is in her heart; and her silence, which is an act of faith and of humility, is also the last effort of a soul that overflows and that can do nothing more. He appeared after His resurrection first to Mary Magdalene. That fact on the forehead of this blessed woman is a star that will never grow pale, and which will rejoice, till the end of time, all those who study, in a soul enlightened by God, the mysteries of His

---

* Saint-Beuve, Portrait divers.

commerce with our race. 'Go, find my brethren, and say to them, I ascend to my Father, and to your Father; to my God, and to your God.' These are the last words of the Saviour to Mary Magdalene; these words gave to her, in preference to all others, the revelation of the mystery which is to close the passage of the Son of God amongst us, and to complete the work of our redemption. Magdalene is made the apostle of the Ascension to the Apostles themselves *."

You have the passage. St. Chrysostom no doubt furnishes the explanation of all this when he shows that the foundation of the whole Christian religion is mercy,—" a thing," he reminds us, " that no one sells, but that is given gratuitously, and that too for the sole reason of the want that exists for it,—according to the words ' quod assidue ac diligenter cogitatio hominis ad mala incumbit à juventute sua †.' " These remarkable citations contain the secret of that intimate moral knowledge which, under the austerity of precept or of blame, discloses still the secret tenderness of a loving heart,

> "———————————— throwing another heart
> Against the flint and hardness of its fault;
> Which, being dried with grief, will break to powder
> And finish all foul thoughts."

The world has a contradictory voice here—a different code—opposite examples. Alas! who does not know it? Honour, that rocky and harbourless isle, of which the shores are never seen twice any more than those of death, wills that every stain be indelible, that every wound should retain its scar. The spirit of the world has its code, marked with its incisive stamp of implacability. " The world," continues Mme. Swetchine, "forgets sometimes, but it effaces nothing, and never pardons. Clearly indeed it cannot pardon; for having no true good at its disposal, or real recompense to bestow, the only way it has of self-protection is inexorable chastisement." Here, within this silent chapel so full of a holy memory, so pure, so chaste, reigns a different spirit with regard to the fallen. Here one

---

* Lacordaire, St. M. Madeleine.
† Hom. in Ps. vi.

learns to distinguish "between late and too late;" for, as the admirable woman just cited, who seems to have possessed the same inspiration, says, "between these states there is, by the grace of God, an incommensurable distance. The only irreparable misfortune is final impenitence—death in enmity with God—which only grieves the beholder, the sufferer being ignorant and insensible. But what a sight for others! The impious consummation of revolts, and the Saviour braved at the threshold of eternity! But what precautions does Providence employ to guard us from such a woe! Not being able to obliterate His justice, one might say that God is pleased to veil it in part, to elude it in the other part, so readily does He admit signs of repentance, and appear disposed to be content with them. The Church, consequently, seems willing to accept a word, a look, a sigh, the least seizable flash of lightning, as a ground of confidence. If a hand has allowed the crucifix to approach the lips, if the weakest sign has responded to the sacramental words, the Judge is moved, and ready to revoke the sentence. When all is in vain she surpasses even these limits; and, however dreadful may appear the departure, she forbids us to individualize our fears, and proclaims that there are no proper names in hell*." But let us continue to hear this voice which expresses the exact sentiments of her whose memory is now our guide. "The good that lies hidden in the sinner's soul would reconcile me with the most guilty. The evil that I often meet in one respectable repels and chills me. I understand how actions may be despised, but not how persons can be despised, of which last disposition I see no trace in Holy Scripture. What is a person whom you despise to-day? It is the same whom you may have to admire to-morrow. There are in the infinite resources which God has placed at the bottom of the human soul, a power of reaction, of reparation, and of restoration, which surpasses all the limits of evil."

"The disinheritance of no creature enters into the plan of Providence. God has provided for the duration of all His insensible creatures, and for the consolation of all those that are not such. In this world, where trial is every where, and final

---

* Mme. Swetchine.

punishment no where, equality between the conditions of life is greater than the diversity of appearances would lead us to suppose *." It was expedient to multiply these citations in order to convey an idea of the spirit of charity which animated the admirable woman whose example we are here recalling; for with all her purity and love of justice, with all her delicacy of conscience, her instinctive horror of evil and her inherent dread of the Divine judgment, she seemed ever to be practically convinced that others were never beyond the infinite and boundless reach of mercy. Herself all forgiveness for greatest wrongs, the moment that she could fancy there was a wish for amendment in any one, she seemed confident that all would be forgiven by Him from whom she derived her own wish to pardon. She had compassion on the fallen, even while fallen and prostrate: they left her presence with a ray of hope, feeling that all was not lost, but that all might be repaired. Wherever there was the least indication of a desire to retrace lost steps, or even where she could only fancy that it might exist, she had words of consolation and acts of forgiveness. In her look, in her tone, there was nothing of arrogance, or of irony, or of humiliating compassion, nothing of proud disdain towards our common humanity in its lowest degradation. "These poor creatures," she used to call them, and that, too, with an angel's smile. In great secrecy, by stealth, for she would never speak of it, she used to succour some that had transgressed; for the truth was she had a heart to do any thing that appeared not foul in the truth of her spirit. One hardly dares to refer to the examples that she might have urged, taken from among the illustrious and holy ladies of France in the seventeenth century. I do not mean to imply that in the precise form of their action she followed them, for circumstanced as she was how could she? but her condescension and readiness for any sacrifice to succour others might require, for their justification, some to be put in mind, from time to time, of such things so calculated to shock the pharisaical righteousness of many at the present day. Thus of one we read that she sought to save such persons by supplying them secretly with necessaries, and saying "that it was enough for her if she could be the means of procuring them

* Mme. Swetchine.

merely intervals of good conduct*;" of another, Mme. de Pollalion, that, in order to effect conversions of the same kind, she actually offered herself as a servant, Providence appearing to justify such marvellous conduct by the success that crowned her devotion †.

But let us proceed to recall to mind the more ordinary charity, which had for its object to relieve the sufferings of the poor.

Wordsworth speaks of certain political rights as being able to

"———————— impart
An hour's importance to the poor man's heart;"

but it seems to many as if it were rather the faith of which the memory is living here, that can in a far richer measure achieve this purpose; for what she loved in them, and sought to benefit, was their noble soul. As Agnes de Harcourt says of Isabella, the sister of St. Louis, "Moult avoit grande pitié de ceux qui estoient en affliction, et avoit tres-grande jalousie du salut des ames."

It is not to be denied that she desired also to relieve their physical sufferings in rather an old-fashioned manner. I am afraid that certain political economists would be disposed to arrest some of her friends, as the prefect of the department lately said he would have been in the necessity of doing, in the instance of Joseph Labré, and to censure on ostensibly moral grounds some of her own actions in their regard, if not perhaps even to put her under some restraint, after the manner in which Prometheus was treated, that he might be taught to obey their maxims,—

Φιλανθρώπου δὲ παύεσθαι τρόπου,

being justly obnoxious to their whole governmental scheme in such matters—

Διὰ τὴν λίαν φιλότητα βροτῶν.

But we must take things in this world as we find them, and so for all our displeasure this was rather her manner of proceeding, which, by the way, learned writers assure us was the ancient Christian manner, and what is more, they add, the only manner

* Idée de la véritable Piété en la Vie de Demlle. Pignier Romanet.
† Vie des Dames Françaises dans le xviie Siècle.

that is in accordance with the spirit of the Gospel *, which, they say, requires us to give, after the fashion of Solomon, "to give to the just, but not to withhold our hand from him who is not, for the reason that he who fears God neglects nothing." So she never refused unless when positively told not to give to such a person, and then, I admit, she would strictly obey you; for after all she would have admired those old municipal enactments of London in Catholic times, when the city being full of monasteries, and no distress left unprovided for, it was decreed "that no one who can gain his sustenance by labour shall go about begging;" and that "all those who go about begging, and who can labour, shall leave the city;" and even later, that "all mendicants who can work shall be arrested †." But London in the nineteenth century was not exactly, in regard to the condition of the indigent, what it was in the reign of Henry III.; and for her part she had once heard a sermon by Father Hearn about passing poor creatures by, and even if she had not that in memory she could not see in the faces of man or woman marks of starvation without seeking to relieve it on the spot; being herself decidedly of Elia's opinion, that half of those stories about the prodigious fortunes made by begging, which, by the way, at present form quite a branch of our literature, are miser's calumnies, worthy of that Venetian whom Shakspeare has immortalized under another name—

> "Gernutus, cruel, and a Jew,
> Which never thought to dye,
> Nor even yet did any good
> To them in streets that lie."

She had actually, in her simple ignorance, a purse expressly for the destitute when she walked abroad, and this was filled every week with small change. Sometimes it was difficult to keep this replenished as she would have had it; and when application for change was made at a public-house, the servants used to bring it back with a sly censure, saying, "Here it is; all your own money come back to you after a short absence."

* La Vie des Riches et des Pauvres, ou les Obligations de ceux qui possédent les biens de la terre.
† Liber Albus, p. 509.

We read of a similar censure in the life of the Marchioness Le Bouteiller; for sometimes her domestics used to receive from shopkeepers the charity tickets that had been exchanged by the poor, and these they used to bring back as proof that her compassion had been misapplied *. But they might not have been right for all their perspicuity. The truth was, however, that Jane Mary did not look upon such alms, though it were to "a silly blind beggar of Bednell green," in the light of a charitable assistance. It was merely the act of her natural bountifulness, of her largesse, as Gilles de Rome would qualify it, which was by no means limited to the poor in an ordinary sense, for she was in this way generous to every one. Her mind, to shorten matters, was never mercenary, and she might often have reminded you by her answers of the advice of Menander—

———— μὴ τὸ κέρδος ἐν πᾶσι σκόπει.

She did not, like your new kind of nobility and liberalism, seek gain in every thing. Without having read the Bréviaire des Nobles, by Alain Chartier, she knew that—

"Largesse rend soy et les autres contens,
C'est l'enseigne des vertus en ce monde,
Le prodigue gaste sans nul pourpens,
Et au large le bien soust et habonde."

Of which latter fact she seemed to be as conscious as if she had always before her eyes the example of that generous Philip, Duke of Burgundy, who, as Olivier de la Marche says, had the reputation of being "very liberal, and at the same time always rich." For every one who in any way rendered her the smallest service, she had always her hand feeling for her purse. "Are you sure you gave to them?" she would ask, when the office had to be transferred to another. If overtaken by rain upon a walk, and obliged to return in a cab, she would insist upon the driver having some extra pay, in consideration of the bad weather, as it seemed to her, in this respect again resembling the Marchioness Le Bouteiller, who had a great compassion for the coachmen and drivers of hackney coaches; her biographer telling us that

* Léon Aubineau, Notice, &c.

she always paid them generously, saying that it was a charity to do so; and when people remonstrated, she used to say, "Why calumniate these poor fellows? They have a hard life of it*." Similarly, our English lady of the old rock used to say, "They are the civillest people to women that one can find any where. They are singularly belied." The truth is, that she felt for utter strangers, whatever might be their condition, as if she had always known them; and what moved her most in the news of each day used to be the report of what had befallen any of the populace; so innocently mediæval in that respect was her mind, as may be witnessed in the Liber Albus of the City of London in the fourteenth century, which took pains to chronicle how a certain boy, Adam de Norfolk by name, was drowned while watering two horses in the Thames, being dragged into the water by one of them; and also how, in the twentieth year of King Henry III., a certain boy, Robert Fitz-Payne, fell from a horse in the street of Walbroke through fright, caused by an act of folly in Robert de Donestaple to the horse on which he was riding, by reason whereof within a month he died. The misadventures, and hardships, and calamities of her poor neighbours affected her. As Bishop Fisher says of Margaret, Countess of Richmond, "Mercyfull and pyteous she was unto such as was grevyed and wrongfully troubled, and to them that were in poverty, or sekeness, or any other mysery." Above all, whenever Jane Mary heard of any poor woman near her confinement having need of help, she became anxious to befriend her, sending all necessary clothing and nourishment, and she would make every other employment in her chamber give way to the task of preparing, sometimes even with her own hands, what was required. Moreover, she carried this disposition toward others beyond their natural life, for dead she still remembered them in her prayers. A servant of her nephew being very ill, she went several miles to see him, and then going into his room she knelt down and prayed with him. Then she spoke a few words to entreat him to be resigned to the holy will of God, and reminded him of the divine goodness in having preserved him from death on the field of battle, to enable him

---

* Léon Aubineau, Notice, &c.

to return home and die, with his wife and children round him, and that, too, after embracing the Catholic faith. No one then thought that he was so near his end; but she said she knew he was soon to die, and in fact he departed a few days before herself. Another time, after visiting a poor dying man, some one said to her, "I suppose the poor people felt themselves honoured by your going to see the husband." She was greatly shocked at the foolish suggestion, saying that it was not for them to feel honoured on such an occasion; but in all actions of this kind there was no trace of any pride being fostered by means of it, and still less selfishness, according to the notions in the celebrated treatise that Mme. de Sévigné so greatly admired, "De la ressemblance de l'amour-propre et de la charité," which ends by proving them to be at opposite poles; for she kept the idea of God so constantly before her, that in performing the best and kindest deed in a mere human way, she wholly forgot herself in being only the instrument employed, seeming, by a rare exception, to lose the benefit of that interior satisfaction which is providentially attached to acts of goodness; unless, perhaps, you will say, what possibly would not be inexact, that, as in the case of Mme. Swetchine, "general benevolence had become the romance of the second part of her life, on which she was just entering," though indeed Jane Mary had no acquaintance with abstractions. She knew Jesus and Mary, and that explains all her actions. To whom, then, even amongst the holy women of the sacred Scriptures, might she not be compared? "Suppose not ye," as Bishop Fisher says of the Lady Margaret, "that yf she myghte have gotten our Savyour Jhesu in his owne Persone, but she wolde as desyrously and as fervently have mynystered unto Him, as ever dyde Martha when thus mocbe she dyde unto his servants for his sake?"

Certainly, all her kindness, all her delicate attention, was not reserved for people who carry hawks on their fist, as an old French poet said. There were times, near the very church, in the cloisters of which we are now standing, just out at the postern by the abbey wall, when some young people enjoyed a laugh at her expense, on seeing her walking with a poor woman in deep conversation together, just as if it were really two poor people in company. So far removed was she from worldliness, that one might say she courted the poor. The noble families that were thrown into mourning at her death, to use the phrase of the public journal, were pre-eminently the poor. When the little sisters who tend them came on a wet day, she has been known to insist on their going back in a carriage at her expense, and when their panniers were too heavy, on sending them by some willing servant of her own; for she could infuse her own spirit even into a boy that did her menial service. The poor were her correspondents, her clients, for, as the poet says—

> " Her humble looks no shy restraint impart,
> Around her plays at will the virgin heart.
> Nor was she loth to entér ragged huts,
> Wherein her charity was bless'd ; her voice,
> Heard as the voice of an experienced friend,
> And, sometimes—where the poor man held dispute
> With his own mind, unable to subdue
> Impatience, through inaptness to perceive
> General distress in his particular lot,
> Or cherishing resentment, or in vain
> Struggling against it, with a soul perplex'd,
> And finding in itself no steady power
> To draw the line of comfort that divides
> Calamity, the chastisement of Heaven,
> From the injustice of our brother men ;—
> To her appeal was made, as to a judge ;
> Who, with an understanding heart, allay'd
> The perturbation ; listen'd to the plea;
> Resolved the dubious point ; and sentence gave,
> So grounded, so applied, that it was heard
> With soften'd spirit—even when it condemn'd."

It would have been a curious diary if she had chronicled her charities of each day, her motives and the objects of it, her maxim ever being that no one ever yet was poorer for such expenditure; and it must be observed, too, that every act of this kind was exclusively her own : hers by the thought, hers by the initiative, and hers by the actual trouble and inconvenience of carrying it out. At one period, numbers of labourers and poor being thrown out of employment, notwithstanding the creditable efforts of the town in which she happened to be residing to find some occupation for them, such crowds attended every morning, for some months, at the gate to receive her bounty, in the form of provisions, that the police, without taking umbrage, found it necessary to station there each time an officer, to keep order and see that each one applied in his turn. In general, no small burden would some have felt it if they had only to find the right addresses and direct the envelopes, which she with her own hand used to make out when sending post-office orders to petitioners whom she thought deserving. But of course, it was those who came within the sphere of her immediate observation who might most depend upon her favour. A poor Irish Catholic mendicant, not known to herself, and even a stranger in the place where she was residing, whose husband, an English Protestant, was a wanderer from fair to fair, died during one of his long-protracted absences, and being filled with anxiety respecting the future destiny, with a view above all to the religion of her two little girls only passing from infancy, recommended them on her death-bed, with sighs and tears, as the priest who attended her related, to the care of the blessed Virgin. So she died, and the priest, full of the scene, came to her and mentioned what had occurred. Immediately, with her mother's co-operation, the two orphans, for the father had in fact long deserted them, were placed in a religious house for education; and not till after a space of fifteen or sixteen years, when a suitable position had been found for them, did she cease to pay their pension. They had been so well bred up and instructed that it was natural they should aspire to a respectable condition, and they had the merit to obtain it. The girls, however, having never heard the secret of their origin, which had not been told, partly through fear, lest it might operate to their prejudice while at school with young companions, came at last to the conclusion that there must be some mystery attached to it; but when the priest who attended their mother at her death had been referred to, they learned to smile at their own previous thoughts, which they had to abandon for simple gratitude, as they remarked themselves with great simplicity and delicacy and piety, in a letter that really, for grace and elegance of expression, was almost worthy of Mme. de Sévigné herself.

But it would be endless to cite instances of her religious devotion to the poor. Many lads were placed by her in schools and colleges, especially after the death of her two sons, whom she wished to have represented thus beneath a sanctuary roof. Orphan boys were placed by her and her mother in houses destined for that object, where they might learn trades and other employments; and on days of festival she would have them come to her house to be regaled with cakes and wine. An Irish priest, whose name elsewhere given must not be repeated here, dying in Paris without means,—for her friends were not people to hoard up for themselves,—she purchased for him a grave in perpetuity in the cemetery of Montmartre. Another practice that she encouraged, and which biographers of the old Catholic type would not have disdained to chronicle, was the buying stuff and making frocks for poor children. As we read of Mme. Victorine de Galand Terranbe, "she never felt so well employed as when she was occupied in some way or other about the poor;" but she seldom or never applied to other people to assist them, nor would she ever use her influence with other rich persons to get them to do what she could do herself. She did not even like at Paris to be named a quèteuse for a work of charity, and she only once consented at the Madeleine to sit for that purpose at the church door. Hearing indeed that every one addressed themselves to others when they wanted funds for charity, and being in fact herself applied to often in this way, she thought for once (it really was but once in her whole life) that in a great pinch she would imitate the example. Accordingly, she wrote to one of whom she had an opinion approaching to veneration; but naturally enough, where such a spur was not wanting, no answer was returned to her letter. She who had wound up her courage to play the fine lady for once in her life, was repulsed in that character. So without breathing a word of complaint, after her old fashion, she had to find in her own funds the money necessary, which she lent, or rather gave, for all her loans ended in the same way, to the object of her pity. Returning from Brussels to Paris, the hind-wheel of her mother's carriage, which preceded her own, caused the death of a poor child who had suddenly rushed from a doorway into the middle of the road. No blame was attached to the postilion; but so shocked were both mother and daughter at the accident, that they stopped for some days at Mons, the next town, from which they sent, if I remember rightly, five hundred francs to the poor people of whose direful calamity they thought that they had been in part, though innocently, the cause. In England she never seemed so happy as when she could add a new name of "distinguished merit" to the list of her pensioners. But then still, I repeat it, as we read of Victorine, daughter of the Vicomte de Galand Terranbe, "her alms were always accompanied with good advice*." Even her casual sixpences were never given without some salutary counsel being added; and it is a fact worthy of remark, that these alms were often instrumental to the welfare of the souls of the recipients. She converted from a neglect of their religion several beggars, and even whole families of wandering poor. Some were seen afterwards resuming the trade which for years they had abandoned; but others, it is true, again disappeared, though not till after their rents had been repeatedly paid by her. In latter years, when she had more occasion to meet them, she liked greatly the poor Irish stall-women who regale the London boys, and many of them were recipients of her weekly bounty. She interested herself about their affairs, heard their histories, pleaded their cause with those who seemed hard upon them, and then applied what remedies she thought best to comfort them. As for le dernier des va-nu-pieds belonging to that world of boys of corderoys and hobbedy-hoys "that standeth in midst of their goods," she did not look on them in their troubles harshly; she knew that these creatures can never calculate with precision; she did not treat each after the manner of Poins, exclaiming, "O that this good blossom could be kept from cankers! Well, there is sixpence to preserve thee." She might admire his open countenance, and say that there is a good angel about him, though the devil tries to outbid him too; but for the success of her wishes to preserve him, she looked to a daily breakfast with kind counsels, or to some religious school, and to the care of holy priests, or, if all else failed, even to a distant reformatory, which the grateful parents

* Vie de Victorine de Galand Terranbe.

would then slily designate, when speaking of it to her own children, in order to save blushes, as "a boarding-school." "Yes," said smilingly an aged wanderer, "my daughter is at a boarding-school, and I thank your good lady mother for it from my heart." A charitable office, however, for which she seemed to have an especial predilection, was attending to the spiritual wants of soldiers. Without entering into the speculative views of the Count de Maistre respecting the military profession in regard to providential designs *, she was not far from agreeing with his opinion as to the character of those engaged in it. Like him, she liked the bon sens militaire, and preferred it infinitely to the long circumvolutions of men of business. She thought them more amiable, more humane, less deceitful, than other men; more likely to be intrepid defenders of ancient maxims, more apt to unite honour with religion, and even to practise piety with more fervour; and to evince, as Fenelon also thought, a greater detachment from the world. She had had, in fact, experience of all this to justify her. She could cite you remarkable instances; she was entrusted with the secrets of many of them; collectively also she befriended them. She used to supply whole regiments with books,—not alone prayer-books, but amusing books suitable to their state,—together with piles of rosaries and medals. Some who manifested a solid motive obtained their discharge at her expense; others used to correspond with her from the Ionian Islands, from Gibraltar, and from China. The simplicity and honesty of these letters used to make her cry with laughing, while she extolled the manly spirit and the deep devotion of the writer with so much earnestness, that you might have thought nothing would content her but his being added to the number of les neuf preux, just as the author of that curious book, having completed the number with the three Christians, Arthur, Charlemagne, and Godefroy de Bouillon, "qui estoit moult honneste, simple, et courtois, et couronne d'espines portoit," must needs recommence his labour, and subjoin the name of his contemporary, Bertrand de Guesclin.

In general it would be true to affirm, that more than half of

* Soirées de St. Pétersbourg, tom. ii.

the letters she received were about either the poor or the interests of indigent religious communities of which the sisters of charity and mercy were her especial favourites. But, undoubtedly, still it was the letters of the soldiers that seemed to interest her most. On the very evening after her death, a letter came from a private in Hong Kong begging of her to take charge of his money, and stating to what purpose he wished to apply it. But these details must not detain us longer. In fine, as we read of Mlle. de Louvencourt, you would see her after attending to the interests of poor people generally more joyous, and appearing to feel more flattered, than another would be seen after receiving attention from the highest nobles, or being decked with jewels for an assembly of the great world.

If charnel-houses and our graves must not send those that we bury back, methinks our chantry chapel has at all events a voice not to be suppressed from each of its stones, proclaiming that at least such good as this which has been now recalled to memory must not be interred with her bones.

CHAPTER X.

WE are to dwell to-day for a short time upon the kind and amiable manners that belonged to a life of faith, of which, as witnessed in this pure and noble representative, the memory is like the delicate perfume of a flower on a summer's morning.

"What is sad, bitter, and painful," says Louis Ratisbonne, "is not to be hated, but to hate." It is by no means difficult to find in either sex the person who can ascertain from experience how far this assertion is true,—there are few things commoner than the power to hate. No matter what be the object, one hears continually, this displeases and that is odious; "I don't think so" here, and "I must differ from you" there. What a troublesome companion all this makes, or to use a common phrase in French that is not particularly refined, "Quel mauvais coucheur cela ferait!" On the other hand, to finish the sentence of our author, "what is sweet, noble, and divine, is not to be loved, but to love." Now this latter result constituted the disposition of Jane Mary; and she sought no return beyond what was yielded by the faculty itself. She used to say, indeed, with a kind of inverse nod that was very expressive, "I don't expect gratitude, I never yet met with it;" and this testimony, based upon fact, was itself something assuredly singular. But so it was in her case. Most of those to whom at some period or other she had shown extraordinary kindness, such as is seldom or ever heard of in what is called society where people do not much like disclosing their pecuniary wants, seemed to remember it only to shun her afterwards, or do what in them lay to indicate that they thought no more of it. But she only laughed the while, and said, when you forced her to speak of the circumstance, that such was the world. She had a young heart to the last hour of her life; that is, it was a heart that occasionally showed itself as young as when it animated one of the most beautiful and graceful girls in London, and perhaps, at their own weapons, a match for the best of them.

"You can excite anger and displeasure by seventeen different measures," said gravely the precise Aristotle. Jane Mary was not a proficient in that curious course of instruction; but, on the other hand, I believe it would have puzzled the Stagyrite to say by how many methods she succeeded in conciliating the esteem of those who approached her. Excepting in the cases we have alluded to, where she departed from the ordinary usages of society to help others in their need to an extent bordering on prodigality, it was impossible to know her without becoming her friend. The physicians who came to the house when any one was ill became her friends, though she always spoke to them religiously of God, and nobly of the soul, appearing sometimes to be more concerned about their condition than about what concerned herself. When travelling in France, all the people of the hotels along the road seemed to welcome her as a friend. She hated giving trouble to any one, whether at home or out, and endeavoured to do every thing herself. She would never take any step without first asking whether you would like it, accommodating herself in all things to the desire of others. As for strangers, she used even to incur blame for seeming to take as lively an interest in their welfare as in those of her own family. " Pooh ! is that all ? " some one used to say to her, " why I really thought that it was some rare fortune for ourselves." Whenever she heard of an emergency she had no rest, contriving how to serve the people who were involved in it. As if fearing to incur blame for being so generous to persons of respectable station though of slender fortune, she used to begin or finish her announcements as minister of finance by a certain sly sacrifice to your own prejudices, saying that it was greater charity than giving money to the beggars; she knew that she had you there. On the whole, she might have reminded one of what is said of Angélique Paulet in the Grand Cyrus,—" No one has ever shown a more regular and exact civility. She avoids as much as possible disobliging any one, and seeks with care to oblige all the world." I do not mean to imply that there was any thing of base alloy in her amiability. It is true, as Mlle. de Scudéry would say, this goodness was not a false goodness, capable of causing her to dissemble when it was necessary to unmask a thing; for, as she always spoke and acted under a sense of duty, she never in any serious matter considered whether it would please or displease others, but she sought to serve them by speaking the truth, though still showing herself gentle and polite *. If occasion had ever been presented, there would infallibly have been truth in making the same report of her disposition as we find in the well-known passage of Shakspeare, where it is said to the offender,— " Though she harbours you as her kinsman, she's nothing allied to your disorder. If you can separate yourself and your misdemeanours, you are welcome to the house; if not, and it would please you to take leave of her, she is very willing to bid you farewell." But exempt from the need of such deliverances, the true general tone of her demeanour was complaisance,—as if she had studied in l'Ordène de Chevalerie, and had learned

---

* Le Grand Cyrus.

" D'estre plains de courtoisie
Et fere amer à toutes genz."

She showed a readiness that is not met with every day to oblige; insomuch that she used often to complain jestingly, and say that people in the house were in habits of robbing her right and left. "I can keep nothing from them," she used to say, laughing, "however well I may think to hide things;" and then she would mysteriously let you into some new secret respecting the place in which something you wanted was concealed. But the fact is, she wishes what you wish; she says what you say; you call her, she comes to you; you ask her, she replies; and, above all, whether it be poor or great people that come to her, she has no airs; for, as Cousin remarks in his admirable work entitled "The French Society in the Seventeenth Century,"—"La simplicité est la compagne de la vraie aristocratie *." And she of whom we speak, having our Lord and His blessed mother ever before her eyes, kindness, goodwill, and all the delicate attributes of a pure and affectionate heart (there is really no exaggeration in saying it), did breathe within her lips like man new made. As to the poor, she would have every young nobleman just such as Elia wished, that is to say, the Preux Chevalier of Age—the Sir Calidore or Sir Tristan to those who have no Calidores or Tristans to defend them; and, by the way, that is only what Hue de Tabarie, in his "Ordène de Chevalerie," wished, saying,—

"Car femes doit l'on honourer
Et por lor droit fatigues porter."

Her woman's pride, and her love for the blessed Virgin, would come practically to direct her on all occasions when she saw that sex compromised. She reverenced her sex in the lowest state. She would have her son hand a poor beggar across the kennel, or assist the apple-woman to pick up her wandering fruit, which some unlucky dray had just dissipated. Indeed, in that office, if you would let her, she would take part herself. You might describe her in the very words of Bishop Fisher

* La Société F., tom. ii. p. 288.

speaking of Margaret, Countess of Richmond and mother of King Henry VII., who at her death had thirty kings and queens allied to her within the fourth degree either of blood or affinity, and since her death has been allied in her posterity to thirty more. "She was of syngular easyness to be spoken unto, and full curtoise answere she would make to all that came unto her. Of mervayllous gentyleness she was unto all folks; unkynde she wolde not be unto no creature *." In the society of her equals her kindness evinced an admirable tact in regard to the form which it assumed. Politeness, as we all know, offends where it appears too prominently. There was nothing angular or obtrusive in her civility; it was like the air, —you breathed it and were well. She possessed what the French of the seventeenth century used to term the gallant tone. "L'air galant de conversation consists," says Mlle. de Scudéry, "principally in thinking of things in an easy, natural way; inclining more towards sweetness and cheerfulness than towards the serious and abrupt, and in speaking with facility and in proper terms, without affectation. One ought also," she adds, "to have in the mind a certain I know not what—insinuating and pleasing grace to win over the minds of others; and if I could well express what I feel, I would make you confess that one cannot be altogether amiable without having the gallant air—l'air galant †." There was, however, with all that, a cordial sweetness in her smile, the like to which you seldom saw in any other face. What we read in the memoirs of a French contemporary was literally true of her. "In the most passing relation with strangers she evinced a singular grace and goodness; though it was, above all, in the habits of the internal life of the family that most appeared the charm of her character, the liveliness of her turn of mind, the equanimity of her humour, and her constant desire to please every one. Her politeness was never at fault even with domestics; she was at one and the same time very discreet and perfectly sincere, very indulgent, but very firm; and whenever a senti-

---

* A mornynge remembrance had at the moneth minde of the noble Pryncess Mary, &c. .

† Grand Cyrus.

ment of justice or of duty forced her to depart from her usual gentleness, no one knew better how to give a lesson more clear, more direct, and more impressive." This was precisely her manner. We may add also, that it pained her, when asked a favour in regard to those little things that often interfere most with one's own fancy, to refuse any one; and that only a sense of duty could induce her to deny whatever childish grant might be demanded of her. If she heard that any one who came to the house was in trouble or affliction, she would see them herself, and seek to relieve and comfort them, ever throwing in a word of good advice with a kind, cheerful tone. In general one might apply to her the words of the poet, and say that she was

> " The best condition'd and unwearied spirit
> In doing courtesies."

It seemed to be a want of her own that she satisfied in showing kindness to others; and upon the least occasion her eyes used to tell tales of her heart, for she was to the last hour of her life what she was as a girl, that is to say, as tender as infancy and grace. I fear that this is tedious; but I must observe here in addition, that many of the letters which came in quick succession on her death, sufficiently attested in what manner she had always conducted herself towards every one. Could there be a more striking instance, for example, than the condolence of the venerable and afflicted father of one who had been the first governess in her family, and who had lived several years with her in that capacity before going to Poland, where she died? for after observing how soon Jane Mary had followed her mother, with his own hardly legible hand trembling with age and infirmities, he wrote these words so affecting,—for those who knew that since he lost her he was "always harping on his daughter,"— "Ma fille, ma pauvre fille, retrouve ainsi les personnes qu'elle a tant aimée, qu'elle a tant vénérée, et qu'elle ne quittera plus maintenant." "My acquaintance with her was but of short duration," wrote one to whom she had just begun to look up as a future adviser and valued friend, on becoming her relative by marriage, "but yet long enough to enable me to appreciate her goodness, and to feel towards her an affectionate regard of gratitude." By a singular fate, too, we can produce the testimony of one, the nature of whose profound studies and consequent celebrity through the Latin Church might be thought to have separated at a great distance from her sphere, and who, nevertheless, wrote of her in these terms: "J'avais une vénération et une affection profonde pour cette incomparable femme. La bonté avec laquelle j'avais été reçus d'elle m'avaient donné l'occasion de connoître toutes ses vertues. Dieu, notre maître à tout, a voulu la récompenser."

Then again, to take a particular instance of the way in which this disposition showed itself,—

> "—————— no meed, but she repays
> Sevenfold above itself; no gift to her,
> But breeds the giver a return exceeding
> All use of quittance."

Her spirit, as we remarked before, was munificent; and she could not endure any thing shabby in others. You observed in her all the delights which spring from a desire to return good offices, "kind words, attentions in health and devotion in sickness, conversations, sometimes innocently trivial, and at others profitably serious." "In a word, look you," said a French nobleman, the nephew of a celebrated minister of state under the Bourbons, "she was one of those persons who make you love piety and virtue."

Now, may we be permitted to ask, Is such an example of mere manners, and the lesson resulting from it, of no general interest or possible utility to persons who never heard of her when alive, at the present day? Before answering, I would ask another question,—Is the Chevalier de Mère no prophet in respect to our age, when speaking of the manners which present a contrast to those of the true gentleman, who can't help, as he says, pleasing even his enemies when he meets them; he adds, "There are others who wish to please, but neither honour nor truth, nor the interest of those who hear them, ever influence what they say, if they find their account in it? To do nothing but from interest even in little things, nor to be amiable gratuitously, and even at one's own loss," the Chevalier de Mère calls that "mauvaises mœurs." It is to be hoped, I fear, rather than believed, that there is nothing of that kind in present manners to give a singular or local importance to the instructions we are here gathering.

But let us remark, and in a more special manner, the solid advantage which many persons indirectly experienced from her kindness; for whether they were aware of it or not, she always sought to direct whatever she did or uttered to an elevated and generous end. "Society," says a French writer, speaking of a similar character, "suffers a great loss in the death of such a person, however comparatively removed from public observation. It loses not alone an ornament, but what is felt as a stay even when it lives retired—a character, an example. She was for many an adviser, a model for others. Her good sense, her pure mind, her fidelity in every trial, her boundless generosity, and her indomitable hope were not to be concealed. There was authority often in what she said, and the cleverest men listened to her with the most sympathetic deference. Indeed, what added an additional grace to this authority, was the simplicity of the person, her life apart, her constant application, her profound contempt for all the miserable vanities which arrest the steps of so many. She possessed the power not alone of directly sustaining and raising up, but also that of unconsciously consoling. Hers was the gift of indirect comforting. Wonderful was her power to recall a smile to lips when the heart was torn. With a kind of generous hypocrisy she could cause to reign around her the peace, which, excepting by the pure result of faith, she herself had lost, and carrying in her own breast, during her last years, a wound incurable, she sweetened and cured the wounds of those around her [*]." In a word, she came up to an ideal which had been painted by a stranger, who sought to represent what was the perfection of a woman. As we read, too, of a contemporary, and one known to many of her friends [†], "it is certain, that those who approached her found that for all moral sufferings, for all the sorrows of imagination, which in some minds are felt in such intensity, she was the sister of charity par excellence, possessing as she did, in addition to all the charming gifts with which heaven had graced her, two rare qualities—she knew how to listen and

---

[*] Paul Janet, La Famille.   [†] Mme. Récamier.

how to occupy herself seriously about others." She would turn it all over in her own mind, and then, as Mme. Sévigné says, "she would make friendship for them the president of her council."

But let us for a moment call to memory the action of this disposition when employed in regard to guests, though it certainly never had occasion to be exercised with a view to any such diplomatic end as the good St. Féreol had in view, when " the ferocious king of the Goths," as a contemporary said to him, "feeling the influence of his honied, grave, piercing, and unheard-of words, did what he wished, retired from the gates of Arles; when what the armies of Aetius could not accomplish, he was able to obtain by means of a dinner." Full of delicate attention to all who visited her, she seemed to divine their tastes and habits, providing for them with great alacrity, and conforming herself to them. She seemed to think, too, that each of her guests was a person who was always of the sweetest and most equable temper; because, naturally enough, during these intervals people evinced no other. At all events, it was her way, as soon as strangers' backs were turned, to hold them up for examples of whatever is good and amiable, no such grave fault perhaps, even after imagining that we see through the error which may have led to it. The most attentive and assiduous of persons as mistress of a house, she used to have each morning a certain number of plans to propose to her guests, to suit their respective tastes. There would be for some a carriage, for another a boat, for a third a horse, seldom making any provision for her own amusement; while all the material details required for an expedition by others were present to her, and she took the pains to combine as far as possible whatever might serve to the interest and pleasure of every one, her foresight not disdaining to provide for the most vulgar wants to which rowers and riders might be subject, who could always reckon upon hearing from her lips on the return of the party, though some of them perhaps were strangers to herself, such words as those of Capulet, in old Verona,—

> "Nay, gentlemen, prepare not to be gone,
> We have a trifling, foolish banquet."

Above all, when in the country, she preferred thus the ancient way of having a project for each of her guests, who wished to be guided, and she would furnish means for their seeing whatever was worth visiting within twenty miles round. In the circle formed round her, her simple and unpretending conversation was always intended to draw others out, in order to fulfil what she considered the duties of politeness and hospitality, always paying more attention in this respect to persons of diffidence and obscurity, than to others of more pretensions. She would, however, treat all with affectionate respect; and the very last evening of her life she said playfully to some of her own, whose style she sometimes used to imitate, as if paying them with their own coin, "What a shame of you to leave me to talk and find conversation like that, when you knew that I should be at a dead loss for it." For she had a horror of allowing long pauses and silence to appear like a cold welcome. When circumstances were difficult, she would rack her brains to find out some topic, in order to break such intervals by speaking kindly to every one, however hard it might be to discern what would interest him; and even then she had last words, as if she could let no one, however insipid he might be, leave the room with a consciousness of his own deficiency. There was always something still left in her heart that she sought to communicate. However, the fact was, that, even when she was trying to convert them to views that were congenial with her own faith, people would listen to her with so marked a pleasure, that it seemed as if her very voice, independent of what she said, had been delightful to them. I would not intimate it as having been a common occurrence, that any one on coming to her house, and in her presence, had real cause for saying, like young Viola acting the page's part, "Some mollification for your giant, sweet lady!" for when she could anticipate any thing unpleasant, she had already provided, by entreaties, against the danger of a surly reception. Whenever there was the least reason to apprehend any neglect towards a guest on the part of others, she used to say, with endearing earnestness, "Won't you be kind to them? they mean well; they never intended to displease you," adding perhaps, like another Capulet confronted with a Tybalt looking displeased,—

"I would not for the wealth of all this town,
Here in our house, do him disparagement;
Therefore be patient—
Show a fair presence, and put off these frowns,
And ill-beseeming semblance for a feast."

But now, leaving the memory of her kindness under the hospitable form, let us remark how totally unselfish was this character in general, and with what gentleness it sought to fall in with the views of others. She hated selfishness: she never thought of herself. There was no preoccupation of the *me*, or a robust sentiment of her own merits, and of what they ought to receive. She used secretly, and under other pretences, to abandon the use of many things, in order to economize for the sake of others, and of the poor. In fact, if she could have had her own way in all respects, she would have denied herself the most ordinary things belonging to her station; she was always thinking about what others wished, to obtain which she would admit of great expense, and not what she might want herself, however trifling might be the cost that it would involve. Two days before her death the secret escaped her lips for an instant, when she said, "I really fear that I am not strong enough to do this to-day," without something which she named, that would involve a trifling expense, but relieve herself, though one had been silly enough to fancy that it was for her own pleasure she had so often refused to accept it. Indeed, at no time had she any care of her health, which in one deplorable instance suffered in consequence irreparable injury. But all thought of personal ease or enjoyment was excluded by those delicate and simple habits of life, which betrayed every day a sort of childlike generosity, that, if suffered full play, would have known no bounds.

Mme. Swetchine used to say, that it is by entering into the views of others that one can reconcile them to one's own. Without any such intention this was generally her manner of proceeding; simply, I believe, through the overflowing of her extreme good nature. Others might direct all her movements. She gave up her own wishes in every thing. She loved Paris, but to comply with the inclination of others she ceased to reside

in it. She loved the place where she had built this chapel, of
which she so admired the beauty, from which she hoped that
some spiritual good might flow to others, that it seemed as if
her eyes could not be satiated with beholding it. " How graceful
it is," she used to say, " and cheerful." And yet, after all her
pains and sacrifices to leave it as you see, and all her desires
to hear mass again over the remains of those she so dearly
loved, she consented for the last summer, as it proved, that she
was to pass in this world, not to visit it, but to remove elsewhere for the sea-bathing; and this, in opposition to all her
combined feelings of preference, and merely to comply with the
desire of those who thought that if she had come hither, she
would have passed the whole of each day in the church, praying at
her mother's grave. She liked the sea-side when it was prescribed
for the health of others; but she grieved for " the poor fellow "
who might not relish the idea of repairing to it. She would
always try to engage others to do what she thought might
please some one else; and she would turn off the conversation
from any topic that she thought uncongenial with that taste, or
rather that manner of regarding things, which sometimes perhaps did not involve any thing genuine or just. All this is
common; and yet to speak generally, what a tender mystery to
think upon, when a wise and holy woman loves thus to accommodate herself, as far as the widest conscience that respects
duty can permit, to the inclinations and habits of some one who
is perhaps "audessous de la définition," though the destiny of
life has given him a certain title to her indulgence! In brief,
nothing seemed to give her greater pleasure than when she
could minister, not alone to the comfort, but to the most childlike and wanton gratification of others. I am not prepared to
say, to use a professional phrase, that in conversation she might
not have occasionally resembled, without being in the least a
purist, that Mdlle. Vandy, one of the precieuses, who, through
affected modesty, could not endure to hear of certain common
words, and who in consequence interrupted a story about court-
ship, by saying to the narrator, " Hé bien! l'autre qu'a-t-il
fait?" So that ever afterwards the word lover was never heard,
but only *l'autre*. With her it was a delicacy not of language
that was travestied, but of conscience that was tried to be

R

appeased and dilated. But when this conscience felt secure, there was a most indulgent compliance with the quirks and fancies of others, as when, for example, in order to please her sons, as if she would learn the humour of the age, she used to try to repeat out-of-the-way terms that they had picked up for the nonce, and talk laughingly of "swells," and other things of that peculiar world to which such young aspirants belong, which sounded on her tongue the more delightfully, from every one feeling how little right she had to pass herself off for knowing any thing about that region, to say nothing of what was so notorious, namely, her instinctive aversion to vulgarity, in whatever rank, and under whatever form, it might chance to betray its existence, which of course made the ambition on her part, in this instance, only the more curious and meritorious; the general fact, however, being that

> "——— nothing she does or seems,
> But smacks of something greater than herself."

Having briefly made allusion to her tastes and inclinations in regard to locality, and of her readiness to sacrifice them at any time to please others, there seems to be an occasion presented which ought not to be neglected, of recalling her disposition with respect to residence in a country, according as its religion agreed, or was at variance with her own, and of speaking also generally, and at greater length, of what most pleased her in regard to the conditions of the place she lived in.

She greatly liked, for different reasons, the French and the English—as for those of Ireland they had her heart, for their faith, and their affectionate and chivalrous character, identified them with what she esteemed most divine and most noble.

Your "tawny ground," as Henry V. so tauntingly called France, associated with the last years of her father's life, and with her mother's presence, she loved almost as if it were her native soil; and in fact, thanks to the intolerance and persecution of former times, she found her paternal name inscribed on the triumphal arch of the Etoile. Spiritual even in her affections, she could not but feel drawn towards loving a country that contained towns like Amiens, in which you see bronze statues in the public squares, of such men as Ducange, of whom she had so often heard others talk in praise; and Peter the Hermit, with whose words, "Dieu le veut," inscribed upon the pedestal, she had been herself familiar. She would have liked Jean de Troye only for speaking of France as " tant jolie que Dieu sauve et garde." Enamoured of light to an extent that was almost mystical, she loved that sky so bright and clear— of a joyous temper, those towns so gay and cheerful, formed to grace society—those conversations so intellectual and charming—of exquisite sensibility, that language so full of delicacy and subtle artifices to Christianize all things of life and manners. Coleridge hated the French with such intensity that he says in the Friend, "a nation, the very phrases of whose language are so composed, that they can scarcely speak without lying." This was a kind of national spirit that she, being no great philosopher or metaphysician to aid any one's reflections, could hardly conceive; but she could perfectly comprehend, for the reasons just alleged, Brunetto Latini, the preceptor of Dante, calling French "un moult délitauble langage." As for the circumstance of its being spoken in a foreign land, why, though no one could love her country more than she did, her catholicity of mind and feeling went far to neutralize that inconvenience. "Minimum refert," writes a bishop of the fifth century to a colleague, " quod nobis est in habitatione divisa provincia, quando, in religione, causa conjungitur." Such were her sentiments when in France. There are some who for their poor parts cannot blame her; for they do like to feel themselves on friendly footing with your French juveniles, generally so sharp-witted and urbane. Having rowed a skiff from Asnières, you might have thought it in the hottest day that prognostication had proclaimed, they were cooling themselves under the trees on the island below Neuilly Bridge, when presently two French boys with "improvised" fishing-rods of willow came down in a sort of punt and landed where they were sitting. "Will you sell me your fish?" said one of the former party in a jeering way. "Ah! we had plenty for all your jesting," one of them replied. "Come," asked the first speaker, "are you from our country Asnièrs?" "Tiens," after a pause and some searching investigation from head to foot, "you are not of Asnièrs, but from England," was the answer.

Then, as great friends of long standing, they united company, exchanged presents, and had a hearty laugh at one of them resembling "un petit nègre," as his comrade called him. Adventures of this kind were not of course exactly in her line; but then great used to be her innocent joy to talk with simple Catholics in that country, though it were only with common peasants, or the servant-maids of the hotel which for a night received her. On these occasions she might have put you in mind of Mme. de Sévigné talking of her Pilois, the gardener at her seat in Brittany, and saying that she preferred his conversation to that of many who have preserved the title of chevalier in the parliament of Rennes*; and giving an instance elsewhere of his coming up to her with his spade on his shoulder to congratulate her on the birth of her grandson, or, to use his words, "un petit gars," which makes her say, "Cela vaut mieux que toutes les phrases du monde †." Speaking generally, Jane Mary was not insensible to the charm of that legendary world which has still left so many traces in the manners, sayings, and songs of the simple population of many of the provinces; as when she heard the aphorism of the Breton mariners handed down from St. Hervé, that he who does not answer the helm will have to answer the rocks; and as among the fisherwomen of Brittany, who, as at Croisie, may be heard singing,—

> "Saint Goustan,
> Notre ami,
> Ramenez nos maris;
> Saint Goustan,
> Notre amant,
> Ramenez nos parents."

But what she liked above all things in France was severally its incomparable priesthood, its solemn churches, its beautiful offices, its inspiring sermons, the patriarchal character of many of its families, their indissoluble connexion and attachments—all the members continuing to live under one roof—and philosophic demarcations between generations, after the

---

* Lett. 111.   † 155.

manner of governmental statistics when applied to the breaking up of domestic union, not being so much thought of as elsewhere. She was attracted to that country also in general by its sweet and easy social manners; for, as Gibbon remarks, while you have in London to make your own way into houses, which only open with great difficulty, and where people think to confer a favour and do you a pleasure by receiving you, in Paris they think that it is done to themselves, which is the reason he assigns for his knowing more people in the latter than in the former city, however improbable, as he adds, the fact might appear*. She liked, moreover, the pure decorum of its social tact, still formed by Christianity; the lofty standard of its ultimate hopes; the almost certain return of its frailty to make a happy end; and though last not least, the extraordinary fidelity of its friendships, which there, when once that their adoption has been made, are grappled to the soul with hooks of steel that neither time nor absence, however for years protracted, can dissolve, so as to obliterate, or even cool or weaken in the least, that consonancy of former fellowship, or the obligation of an ever-preserved love. She found the people of that polite country very much behind the English world in regard to the theory and practice of friendship. The art of losing sight of people had not been learned there. Each was such as one of them in the seventeenth century was described in the Grand Cyrus. It was the result of her experience to know, that when any one there becomes once accustomed to another, like the Count de Fiesque in that once celebrated romance, no length of absence will be able to disaccustom him towards the person. Though he were to be ten years without seeing one of his friends, if fortune should cause them to meet again, he speaks to them with the same familiarity as if he had seen them every day, and he is as much pleased to speak to them about past things as if he could not live without them. So much for her estimate of France, and of its polished and amiable people.

View her again returned to England, and admire the resources which were yielded to her in rich abundance by her

---

* Memoirs, i. 163.

tact of right, by her good sense, and by her faith. In England, it is true, she could not but know, that, without incurring the disgrace of an anachronism, the language of society is often still that of Lord Bolingbroke's sixth letter, as audacious as it is false, while discrediting what it is pleased to regard as "gross ignorance and credulous superstition;" since in general she found that there much, if not all that she esteemed, was officially ignored and systematically scorned, and much that she abhorred and dreaded secretly adored. She could not shut her eyes to the local verification of the general prophecy which said, "In vobis erunt magistri mendaces, qui introducent sectas perditionis." True she had not to observe what Tacitus describes as being the state of Britain when the Roman could say in a sense of his own, "nec aliud pro nobis utilius quam quod in commune non consulunt." What she could not avoid witnessing was concord whenever it was a question of attacking the faith of Rome—there being no disunion on that ground in any of their files, but rather the spectacle of men, and what is far worse and more unseemly, of women too, sometimes, like the bulls in Burrowdale, running, as it would seem, mad with the echo of their own bellowing. Therefore, for all these reasons, as the poet says,—

"In the throng of the town like a stranger is she,
Like one whose own country's far over the sea;
And falsehood, while through the great city she hies,
Full ten times a day takes her heart by surprise."

Wordsworth even would not confine such observations to the town, when portraying the rustic boy abandoned to the same influences, and bidding you

"——————————— mark his brow!
Under whose shaggy canopy are set
Two eyes, not dim, but of a healthy stare,
Wide, sluggish, blank, and ignorant, and strange,
Proclaiming loudly that they never drew
A look or motion of intelligence."

"For," he adds,

"——————————— no town
Nor crowded city may be tax'd with aught

> Of sottish vice or desperate breach of law
> To which in after-years he may be roused.
> This boy the field produces; his spade and hoe,
> The carter's whip which on his shoulder rests
> In air high towering with a boorish pomp,
> The sceptre of his sway; his country's name,
> Her equal rights, her churches and her schools,
> What have they done for him? And, let me ask,
> For tens of thousands uniform'd as he?
> In brief, what liberty of mind is here?"

Nevertheless she has left us an instructive lesson under such circumstances, which after all no one living has brought about, to foster our patriotism, to temper our zeal, and to moderate our discouragement.

In the first place, not alone was she in a general way susceptible of affection for all her fellow-creatures, according to the precept of the Pope St. Leo, " quia in omnibus hominibus naturæ est diligenda communio*"—but, independently of that disposition, as is usual with religious Catholics all over the world, she recognized and cordially loved the great natural virtues of the English character, when not tampered with, but left to themselves and developed in a common way. One can never forget her satisfaction after the revolution of '48, and her return home, on finding herself in the midst of a people that was subject to law and order, and that retained a sense of respect for the principles that keep society from dissolution,—a people that, excepting in the way of some petty local persecutions even against the spirit of the government, left religion free, and meddled not with the personal freedom of the subject, —a society less brilliant no doubt, less ingenious, less susceptible of permanent friendships, less affectionate, and less delicate than what of late she had been used to, but resolved and able to defend some of its ancient institutions, and above all its freedom, while respecting moreover even things of the supernatural order in regard to God, wishing to sanctify the Sunday, to preserve the spirit of the family, and showing itself ever powerful by the energy of its social faith.

* Serm. 31 de Quadrages.

> "She loved that character of peace,
> Sobriety, and order, and chaste love,
> And honest dealing, and untainted speech,
> And pure good-will, and hospitable cheer,
> That made the very thought of English life
> A thought of refuge for a mind.
> Where now the beauty of a Sunday kept
> With conscious reverence; as a day
> By the Almighty Lawgiver pronounced
> Holy and blest."
>
> "———————————— she praised
> The ancient popular character, composed
> Of simple manners, feelings unsuppress'd
> And undisguised, and strong and serious thought."

She would say with Droz, that "when we see men whose errors deprive them of powerful means surpass Catholics in manners, we should blush for ourselves, and pray to God to make us less unworthy of the favours that we enjoy[*]." Of course she had looked on the reverse of the medal; there was no mistaking that; but it did not cause her to abate in her esteem and admiration for so much that is good on the other side. Her words still, even when reminded of the former, resembled those of the poet,—

> "Be not afeard; the isle is full of noises,
> Sounds, and sweet airs, that give delight and hurt not."

As for those dull, cold, formal maligners, who rail against the whole race of its juvenile plebeians, though they singled out the archest and most remorseless whistler of the crew, she would only laugh to hear the boy's answers, and treasure them up, as when told of such a dialogue as this. "Well, my lad, can amuse yourself, I see?" "Oh! pretty well for that," when snatching up a stump of cigar, the lad thus accosted, rejoined triumphantly, that "this was better than whistling." Your Sunday citizen might exclaim against the fustian rascal and his poor lack-linen mate; but the gentle lady would only praise his cheerfulness, and contrast him perhaps with all those "that

---

[*] Pensées sur le Christianisme.

were of the new tryck," as our old ballads call them, and speak of him somewhat in the style of Mme. de Sévigné, as when she mentions some one having the look of a very honest boy, as proper a subject for the galleys as you are to seize the moon with your teeth, "propre au galères comme à prendre la lune avec les dents."

Such was her manner of viewing things that presented the least plausible claim to Pharisaic favour. Upon the whole, therefore, there was nothing in her example to influence in a depreciatory way the sense of patriotism, in which we all take an honest pride and pleasure.

But I said also that it supplied a lesson, teaching the necessity of tempering our zeal, when it threatens to grow rather bitter and immoderate. Let us not be misinterpreted here. We have long since observed enough to feel assured that she never dissembled her sense of the infinite superiority in value of what related to the soul, and to the eternal interests of mankind, over all that was limited to this life; so that at present we have plenty of solid ground to stand upon. Indeed, for that matter, her opinion, or rather her faith, was never hidden or even disguised. Of course she had praises for many and for much; but the praise, as Saint-Beuve says of his own eulogies, "the praise (take care to observe) used to be often only superficial; the deep conviction, with the just criticism, being below it—a judgment à fleur d'eau. Examine ever so little downwards and you always touch it [*]." In point of fact, she used often to say that the only danger in such a country, in her estimation, was the succumbing to a temptation of pride from feeling there, more than any where else, the immense privileges that her religion conferred; and she used to boast, while laughing, that no drop of blood flowed in her veins but what had been from time immemorial Catholic. Well acquainted with their manner of wrenching the true cause the false way, as when Lord Bolingbroke calls the hangman the chief abettor of Christian unity, and feeling that their heads at the best had not much intellectual armour suitable to spiritual combats, she was never in the least intimidated by the vaunts of those who were personally

[*] Portraits Contemp.

hostile to her faith. She would only quietly say, like a true Shakspearian woman as she was—

> "We grant thou canst outscold us; fare thee well;
> We hold our time too precious to be spent
> With such a brabbler."

She might have added too with some one else, "and see the advantage of the religion that you insult; for what does it teach us to reply? It is this: That you are the most well-meaning and good-natured of men—a little tiresome, but good and humane; morose, but not envious, man of study and gravity, but of somewhat ill-humour, which diminishes the effect of your style, imparting to it more shade than colouring. That is what we say, and what we think; and we think also, though we don't say it, that some one must have sadly fooled you in your younger days, to see you already so forgetful of all bright and happy inspirations." But perhaps we need not have insisted here so much on recalling the purity, the constancy, and the power of her faith. All this was sufficiently known to us before; but what we must remember here, is the manner in which these precious and inestimable qualities were combined with sincere respect for the persons of those who were not in communion with the Church—how they were united with intellectual tolerance in regard to such persons, and besides, always and every where, for all the world, with a great patience. I do not mean that she felt indifferent when her servants told her of an errand-boy losing his place the moment that his master fearing customers heard that he was a Catholic; but I do intend to state the fact that she used to respect religious Protestants; and whenever any one in her presence seemed disposed to look on the ridiculous side of some of their practices, that she used to check them on the spot, saying that we ought never to laugh at things of that order, however twisted and got wrong; but, on the contrary, to feel a great respect and esteem for them. As we read of the Lady Anne, Countess of Arundel and Surrey, "she would by no means permit that any publick sport should be made on Sundayes at the times of the Protestants' service, not to give them offence *." Of course

---

* The Life of the Countesse of Arundelle, 238.

she would always say, when there was an occasion presented,

> "That he wants wit, who wants resolved will
> To learn his wit to change the bad for better."

But her zeal for conversion, which was unwearied, never led her to exceed the limits of truth and charity. Her mild winning manner of expressing the tolerance and sanctity of her heart was certainly the more remarkable, from the fact that she could not have checked herself, had she departed from such usage, by following up the self-reproach of Cicero, when pleading for Ligarius, and saying,—" Nimis urgeo: ad me revertar, iisdem in armis fui!" Innocent moreover, and with a pure conscience, her general rigour, and the severity of her judgments against persons in a state of separation from the Church, were not augmenting gradually in direct ratio with her scruples and remorse. She had no penance to do at the expense of others. On the contrary, each year of her life which seemed drawing her nearer to God, witnessed the increase, if possible, of her charity, in regard not to expressions, which are of small value, Heaven knows! but to the real sentiments of her heart and the judgment of her understanding. "These persons whom you are disposed to look upon with such condemnatory eyes," she would say, "are very probably

> ' Pious beyond the intention of their thought,
> Devout above the meaning of their will.' "

"It is not," she would continue with Mlle. de Scudéry, when speaking of people in the same position, "that I think he does not believe what we others are bound to believe, but that he confounds in his poor head superstition with religion, and that he has contracted a habit of offensive and foolish raillery which our ladies will have great difficulty in correcting *." She applied to the English generally such observations as Droz had made during his residence with the Moravians on the Rhine. "It is neither," says our clear-sighted Academician, "by strange institutions, nor by extraordinary customs that these

---

* Le Grand Cyrus.

men realized their views. What is then the source of their
union and peace, which shine even on their countenances, so
gay and sweet is their physiognomy? The source of all this is
the religious sentiment which animates them. Christians, unfortunately separated from the Catholic Church, they have great
errors, and are deprived of great succours; but in the wreck
which remains to them of Christianity there exists still a living
principle, a belief in Christ, and the practice of His maxims.
Now," he adds, "my observations among the Moravians have
enabled me to see clearer than ever the immense superiority of
the Catholic religion over all separated sects; for the principle
of life which is involved in the débris that come down to them,
belongs only to the truths which the pretended reformers
derived from Catholicity. Having met a Moravian pastor,
to whom I lamented the decay of the religious principle
amongst men, in spite of faith in Jesus Christ, and the
observance of His precepts, he replied, ' With these two means
brought by Christ all is easy, but nothing can supply their
place.' True profound wisdom, he says, is in these words; but
please to remark that they are Catholic, and that the pastor has
retained them from our fathers."

It only remains to add, that these views respecting religious
differences in England were not confined to the limits of her
thoughts and conversation, but were made to influence her
daily actions. From the Protestant servants whom, like Mme.
de Montmorency*, she had no objection to employ, even
without any view to what they might later become,—as many
of them in both instances did in fact become,—from the
poorest person with whom she might be brought into casual
relation to the young prince of whom she used always to say,
after hearing of his public conduct, "That is my boy," she
evinced the respect and affection of one who was accustomed
intellectually and religiously to pierce below the surface of
things, and to be guided in subordination to faith by natural
good sense and womanly affection, both in her judgments and
in her deeds.

In fine, it was said that we might expect to find in this

---

* Vie de la Duchesse de Montmorency.

Chapel of St. John a lesson that will teach us, in regard to the same circumstances, to moderate our discouragement. This indeed is a natural consequence from what we have been just observing. But besides, she had been too well instructed in her youth, and she was too familiar with the traditional charity of religious Catholics, not to feel herself always inclining to the side of hope respecting others. "Nec de Platone," says a learned father, "Seneca, Epicteto, aliisque, si parem cum doctrina vitam secuti sint, est desperandum *." Another learned and holy writer † would lead us to conclude that there is still more grounds for hope respecting the masses of the ancient world whose names were never celebrated. How much less then are these poor ignorant people in our own times to be despaired of, who are simply obedient to the discipline which the circumstances of life have exclusively pressed upon them, and whom, as St. Augustin said of others, error and the world persecute from their cradles? One does not mean to imply that she defended her views in this respect by citing words from the learned, or even evincing what they term, as in one instance just observed, a useful curiosity respecting the felicity of human life; but that she had, as it were, of herself, and from personal observation, those hopes for England which extended beyond its temporal greatness. And have we not always reason for cherishing such views, at least as respects individuals generally, even when they are defaulters in regard to the moral law? Very approved and cautious writers seem to think that we have. " Congregaverunt omnes—malos et bonos," and yet there was only one man seen by Omniscience who had not on the wedding-garment. What does that mean? Is it not that many whom we should perhaps condemn wore it? or, in other words, that they too had accepted the robe given them gratis at the door, according to the usage to which the parable refers, which was to denote that they accepted salvation through faith in the merits and death of Christ, according to the doctrine of the Catholic Church, pronouncing with St. Paul that "for such there is now no condemnation?" But

---

* Utilis curiositas de humanæ vitæ felicitate.
† Collius de Animabus Paganorum.

this is trespassing on ground on which she would not follow any one, though he were only seeking a loophole for himself. She esteemed it safer to be content with fostering hopes in silence, or with hearing read and applied some old prediction, such as some think that they can find with Shakspeare, as in the words,—"When as a lion's whelp shall to himself unknown, without seeking find, and be embraced by a piece of tender air; and when from a stately cedar shall be lopped branches, which, being dead many years, shall after revive, be jointed to the old stock, and freshly grow; then shall Britain be fortunate and flourish *."

Though the present visit has been already long protracted, I would not depart without recalling another feature in this life of faith, which is in connexion with what we have been just observing, and for the consideration of which, perhaps, we might not find later so favourable an opportunity; for after reflecting on these habits with regard to taste, and the preferences evinced for certain circumstances of a local kind, while always sacrificing her own pleasure to that of others, one is naturally drawn on to speak briefly of that intense love for nature, and for the charms of rural associations, whether of scenery or works, which she always nourished in her secret heart. Her love for the country, and her notions respecting the influence of country life on men, which, by the way, were similar to those of the author of " Modern Painters †," though opposed to those of Crabbe, were certainly remarkable in a person of faith in England, who was so devoted to the churches, so fond of their music, and ceremonies, and instructions, and so susceptible of nervous fears; for she used to say that she liked the noise of the street in the night-time, as a guarantee of security. This ardent love for the country she sacrificed, like many other inclinations, to please others who preferred the "town;" but it seemed to increase rather than diminish by her absence from it, so that a consideration of it enters naturally enough into the delineation of her kindness. "To refresh my spirits," says Mme. Swetchine, "I need the reunion of those good things which are implied in a clear sky, a poetic

---

* Cymbeline. † Vol. v. p. 5.

nature, leisure and friendship." A clear sky and brightsome beams seemed elements necessary for Jane Mary. It was not merely that she was alive to nocturnal terrors. The night-time and the dark seemed to depress her spirits; she used to hail the lengthening of the days in early spring with pious gratitude, and loudly to exult when tapers might be disused and curtains drawn back, seeming to dislike what is called comfort by those who, without Hamlet's passion, "shut up their windows, lock fair daylight out, and make themselves an artificial night," if she could exchange it all for another half-hour's enjoyment of the all-cheering sun. "The first condition," says Mme. Swetchine, "for my being at my ease is, that I should find myself in a beautiful spot which does not belong to me; for the right of possession would draw after it so many troubles, that repose would be impossible." With similar feelings we find the Doctor Récamier writing to his celebrated relation, and saying to her, "Profit by your stay in the country to be in the open air. It is there that the body recovers its force, which had been impaired by residence in cities; it is there that the contemplation of nature recalls to the mind that sweet and satisfying philosophy which makes one love and admire its author." In simple natural expressions of this kind we seem to hear speak Jane Mary. It is, as it were, her familiar voice in domestic privacy that comes to us; and the subject is so attractive, that one must ask leave to pause a moment over a few details, with which a great French writer condescends to furnish us. The promenade, we are told by Cousin, constituted, after conversation, one of the passions of the society of the seventeenth century, in so many of which our Jane seemed to participate. Mme. de Rambouillet, for instance, was known to love greatly making courses with her friends in the neighbourhood of Paris, in order to enjoy the spectacle of those beautiful points of view, which people go now in search of to so great a distance, and at such great expense, out of France, while they can be found at the very gates of the capital. Even within the city pleasant walks were not wanting. There were gardens for the inhabitants of the Place Royale, as well as for those of other central positions; but the favourite promenade was on the banks of the Seine,

between the Tuileries and Chaillot*. A bathing-place, too, in
rivers seems always to have been part of the picture of what
was then considered as agreeable scenery, and which the subject
of our notice, too, could enjoy with lively pleasure when residing at St. Germain, where was a watery bower provided for
the Naiads of that locality, "with their sedg'd crowns and ever
harmless looks." In the Grand Cyrus, which represents the
manners of that age, in many respects so like her own, in those
parties of pleasure on the water described, each boat containing
seven or eight persons, besides those who conducted it, the
absence also of domestic affairs was regarded as one of the
items essential to the pleasures of an agreeable hour †. From
these passages, which possess a certain interest in their way, it
appears that there was nothing singular or novel in the circumstance of finding a person, who seemed well qualified to figure
in the circles of a brilliant society, and who was at the same
time susceptible of the simple enjoyments of a rural scene, and
ever disposed to regard it with a love of preference. Jane
Mary was unconsciously, in this respect, a disciple of that old
philosophy which spoke through the lips of Menander, saying,
"I count him most blessed who, without sorrow, contemplates
beautiful things, such as the sun, the stars, clouds, water, and
fire. Such a man will always see what he admires, whether he
live an hundred or only a few years; and than these spectacles
no one will ever see any thing more beautiful!"

> "——————— what good is given to men,
> More solid than the gilded clouds of heaven?
> What joy more lasting than a vernal flower?"

As we read of Mme. Swetchine, the subject of our story "loved
nature. She saw the work of God in each blossom, and she
was often filled with wonder and admiration as she looked on
it. Nature, with its different aspects, like art, has a voice
which spoke to her intelligence." As the author of the Souvenirs
remarks, "every thing in the visible world expresses or answers her own heart; for it was another tongue, but the same

---

* Tom. ii. 367.   † Le Grand Cyrus.

history; and nature also she could discern, without having read the Soirées de St. Petersbourg, is what the fall of man has made it." Like the person described by Mlle. de Scudéry, Jane Mary used to be moved greatly by the beauties of the universe; and it constituted one of her chief pleasures as she sat alone to admire the grandeur of God in the wonders of His works. She beheld Him every where present in what she too would qualify as "this goodly frame the earth; this most excellent canopy the air; this brave o'erhanging firmament; this majestical roof fretted with golden fire." Without even being in the state of mind that Hamlet owned to be his own, it is not every one who can enjoy as she did the rising and the setting of the sun; or a tranquil night sowed with stars; or the ripple of a fountain; or the vast expanse of ocean, which last spectacle always filled her soul with a sort of awe in contemplating the power of the Almighty; though in the circumstance that her conversation was ever joyous, she resembled De Scudéry's friend, by being gay and amusing.

This allusion to the sea, so near to which she wished to be entombed, suggests a thought which we shall do well to hear developed by others; for one was often tempted to ask, how came she and her mother to feel such an inclination at certain seasons to revisit it, that their fondness for it might remind one of what is related in an amusing way of a certain Portuguese fisherman, who being received with great kindness by the king Don Sebastian in his palace, and being seized with languor and fainting fits, caused by the sweet perfumes of the royal palace, the king's physician, Thomas de Vega, being sent for, and investigating the case, and hearing that he was a fisherman, ordered him to be carried to the sea-shore and covered with sea-weed; when, no sooner did this odour encompass him, than he began to breathe again freely and recovered [*]. This is ludicrous; though, in order to suit some enthusiasts, perhaps the anecdote is worth repeating; but certainly, in the instance before us, it was not alone that there seemed to be something in the air from the sea which revived and invigorated a frame that had never been accustomed to long confinement to the atmosphere

[*] Masenius, S. J., de Humanæ Vitæ Felicitate, 47.

of cities. There was more than a physical effect which she experienced from it; and this impression in one so tender, so affectionate, and so human, is what might at first occasion surprise; for after all that can be advanced in praise of the ocean and of its sublimity, there is much truth in what Mme. Swetchine remarks; saying, "The sea is solemn, admirable, majestic. It elevates me; but it is to overwhelm me under a boundless greatness, without return or without pity for my nothingness. What is there between it and me? The immensity of space and depth. What does it yield me? The sentiment of the infinite and the gulph which separates me from it. The ocean in its force, its moving immutability, and its proportions which surpass the boldness of my thought, is God, but God without His Christ." Our poor Jules Janin, at all events, seems rather to recoil from the spectacle, saying, " The agitations of the ocean leave us cold if we do not discover at least a boat of fishermen in the distance. In the tempest of the Odyssey, the winds and the sea, it is true, are described; but the great poet relates, above every thing else, what passed in the mind of Ulysses; for, in fine, all the waves of the ocean are not worth one swelling of the human heart." St. Basil had expressed the same opinion in one of his most eloquent passages, where after exhausting, as one might suppose, all that could possibly be advanced in praise of the beauty of the sea, he concludes by saying, "But if before God and man the sea is thus glorious to behold, how much more beautiful is that multitude, that human sea, which has its sounds and murmurs made up of the voices of men and women and children, which resound continually, ascending to the throne of their Creator." It may be believed, however, that the secret of her predilection in this respect, which would reveal that also of her mother, consisted in the extreme innocence of all her final intentions, which caused her, notwithstanding her dread of the supreme perfections of the Almighty, to regard every manifestation of His power as a guarantee for herself.

But let us to the fields, amidst which all through the year she would have been so content to live, even when winter came, according to " an inconvenience in all almanacks," and much more, when you were only entering into the sign of the Scorpion, of the Twins, and of the Balance. "It is not every man," says Coleridge, "that is likely to be improved by a country life or by country labours. Where original sensibility does not preexist, the mind contracts and hardens by want of stimulants; and the man becomes selfish, sensual, gross, and hard-hearted." It would not have been so with her, though she had lived like that Olivier de Serres, Seigneur de Pradel, whose habits of life are described in his own Théâtre d'Agriculture, in which one sees the patriarch of agriculture, the good parent surrounded by his servants—a book which Henry IV., who was no reader, used to have read to him every day after dinner. She loved the corn-fields, as if she hoped to glean in them, the woods, like Mme. de Sévigné, the meadow, as if she thought no perfume equal to its new-mown hay; she loved a rustic bench and a fine day, and with cheerful spirits to breathe, as when a girl, the common air.

> "Rich are her walks, with supernatural cheer;
> The region of her inner spirit teems
> With vital sounds and monitory gleams,
> Of high astonishment and pleasing fear."

In her last years she could not even catch the first glimpse of any thing like rural scenery, as when emerging, after passing through a long suburb and the sombre atmosphere of smoky roofs, upon Barnes Common, which she had to cross on her way to Roehampton, without seeming to breathe new life with that purer air and more extended horizon, and exclaiming how beautiful the furze and the grass patches, and saying, what no one doubted, how in general she loved the country and all that appertained to it.

> "Oft was occasion given us to perceive
> How the calm pleasures of the pasturing herd,
> To happy contemplation soothed her walk
> Along the field, and in the shady grove;
> How the poor brute's condition, forced to run
> Its course of suffering in the public road,
> Sad contrast! all too often smote her heart
> With unavailing pity."

Unused to the fabrication system, as Topffer styles it, which he

remarks has disfigured nature, the fields and the woods above
all, where she had influence, were safe. Like Mme. de Sévigné,
she would almost have wept to see the face of a country spoiled
to maintain the spendthrift proprietor living in the capital.
"Here were old woods," writes the marchioness, "and my son
on his late journey ordered the last of them to be felled. This
is pitiable—he has gained some 400 pistoles, of which he had
not a sou left a month after. All these afflicted dryads, all
these old sylvans, who knew not whither to retire; all these
ancient rooks, established for two hundred years in the horror
of these woods; these owls that in the obscurity announce by
their sinister cries the misfortunes of all men—all that con-
spired to raise a lamentation which sensibly affected my heart *."
It was just thus that she would have felt. She had the thoughts
of a true poet in the woods and fields and gardens, so intense her
sensibility and so lively her admiration for the workmanship of
God. Others might exclaim, like Mme. de Stael, when the
beauties of the country were extolled, "Oh! le ruisseau de la
rue du Bac!" She possessed that artistic mind, without which,
as the same Topffer says, nature can spread out its beauties,
and shine in sunlight while it is neither felt nor expressed.
Without being a painter, she possessed that mind, and she
received from natural objects an impression of the peaceful,
the sweet, the amiable. Only two days before her death, being
shown a new painting full of light, which represented the
Thames at Halliford, with its willow and its groves, its tall
reeds and its swans, it caught her fancy as if she had known
the spot, and she said, "Oh, how lovely! Won't you keep
that picture for me? I love the bright quiet of that peaceful
scene." No question, particularly in her latter years, what she
delighted in was the quiet which that spot seemed to involve.
Her "salon" would be the corner of the field, or the bench in the
garden, where, during the last fortnight of her life, opening
her heart to some confidential friend, she wept. Still, of course,
she would look with rapture at the graceful beauty of the
common flowers. A true daughter of the fields, she would
inhale with transport the fragrant air that came from them;

* Lett. 031.

but what she prized above all then was silence, quiet, and, though but little advanced in years, even at times solitude. There was a field about half an hour's saunter from this church —there was a seat in the desert part of her grounds at Kensington, where one can never pass now without fancying that one sees her with her book or her chaplet.

> "Thither would she tend
> Remembering thee, O green and silent dell,
> And grateful, that by nature's quietness
> And solitary musings, all her heart
> Is softened, and made worthy to indulge
> Love, and the thoughts that yearn for human kind."

She was from the same mould as that Mdlle. Angélique Paulet, of whom Mdlle. Scudéry said, " She likes company, but she is never discontented in solitude, and she can amuse herself as well in the country on the banks of a rivulet, and hearing the nightingale, as if the whole court were present*." Unflinching in the discharge of all her active duties, her cry was no less ever, " Vive le repos de chaque jour! vivent les ombrages de chaque été!" "Sereiner" was a charming French word in the sixteenth century, that seemed made for her lips. "Philosophy," says Montaigne, "doit sereiner les tempêtes de l'ame." She had no tempests in that pure region to appease, and if she had, it was not to philosophy she would have been obliged to have recourse for soothing them. It was not either to indulge in a romantic reverie that she sought this retirement, after the manner of those who wrote shortly before the great French revolution, inviting each other, as in the Soirées Provençales, to separate themselves from the world, to penetrate into what they called, in their unpleasant jargon, " the mysterious asylum of Vaucluse, and there, alone with their memory, to direct for a moment their refreshed imagination, to linger over the charming illusions which compose the fugitive felicity of mortals †." As we have said once before, there was no such stuff in her thoughts. But the repose and peace of nature affected her heart. It was, I repeat it, that she used to feel then, as it were,

---

* Grand Cyrus. † Soirées Provençales, tom. i. 19.

more in the company of God. "Why," asks Topffer, "does the aspect of inanimate nature exercise such a charm over minds? Why do they feel when alone with it as if in a crowd? Is it the limpid tint of the air, the brilliancy of colours, the disposition of lines, the glory of light and shade, which cause these transports? Doubtless these have an attraction for the senses, reflecting on thought itself calm and cheerfulness; but it is not by this way that they communicate themselves to the heart. It is that man cannot separate in his thoughts the work from the workman; the created object from the Creator. With great difficulty can that separation be effected, even in the heart of cities, when he stifles his faculties and restrains one by the other. But such is not the condition of the majority. From nature they mount invincibly to its Author. The more they are alone with it, the more they feel Him near them. The greater the silence, the better heard is His voice. No where, then, is this sentiment more powerful than in the rural solitude. No where else is it embellished with such smiling colours, with so much grace, and impregnated with such a calm and charm and happiness!" This quiet of late became also needful to her on another account; for the world in her regard, and since her mother's death, seemed to be following the policy of Agricola in Britain, "et nihil interim quietam pati." Yet it failed; for still she might in this respect have been thought to have sat for her picture to the poet Marvell, where he says—

> "Meanwhile, the mind from pleasure less
> Withdraws into its happiness,
> Annihilating all that's made
> To a green thought in a green shade.
> Here, at the fountain's sliding foot,
> Or at some fruit-tree's mossy root,
> Casting the body's vest aside,
> Her soul into the boughs does glide;
> There, like a bird, it sits and sings,
> Then whets and claps its silver wings,
> And, till prepared for longer flight,
> Waves in its plumes the various light."

Of course, as before noticed, she used to be rallied a little for all this; perhaps even at times reproached for such a love of seclusion. Yet there had never been wanting, at any period, a voice, albeit to most inaudible, that could only find utterance for the secret love and veneration which inspired it, by repeating the lines of the poet which were once to her so applicable,—

> " Dear child of nature, let them rail!
> There is a nest in a green dale,
> A harbour and a hold,
> Where thou, a wife and friend, shalt see
> Thy own delightful days, and be
> A light to young and old.
> There healthy as a shepherd-boy,
> As if thy heritage were joy,
> And pleasures were thy trade,
> Thou, while thy babes around thee cling,
> Shalt show us how divine a thing
> A woman may be made."

But it is late to remain here. Let us withdraw in silence.

CHAPTER XI.

NOW the morning light changes the aspect of this chapel, and the stony entrance of this sepulchre, from that which it wore on our last leaving it! What brightness! What cheerful illumination in this place of peace! 'Tis an image of the mind that we are about to speak of in regard to its joyful temperament.

It would avail, perhaps, but little towards accomplishing any general purpose of recommending with effect a life of faith in any century, to show that it was accompanied with all kind of grace and virtue, if we were to be left under the impression, that after all it was a sad and gloomy life, amerced of that spirit of "joy and sunny gladness" to which the Psalmist looked forward as actually a consequence of conversion, saying, in the well-known words of the Miserere, "auditui meo dabis gaudium et lætitiam;" for, if men would speak their conscience, there is nothing that can obtain with more facility the secret consent of their will to engage or to persevere in any mode of life than a belief that it will make them cheerful; that instead of proving wearisome, so that a mere narrative of its details would be enough to put them to sleep standing, turning out to be things, as Mme. de Sévigné says, "à dormir débout," it will produce just the contrary effect, and tend to impart that kind of pleasant spirited character which attracts every one who beholds its outward manifestations, while in an humble way, in due subordination to other things, it constitutes, as far as this life is concerned, the most enviable condition to which any one perhaps can aspire. This fact so forcibly presented itself to the mind of a recent apologist and defender of the Christian religion, that he undertakes to disprove the common notion of melancholy being a consequence of embracing it. "The first ages of the Christian era," he says, "were marked, it is true, by great calamities. Idolatry rose against Christ, error combated truth, and the blood of martyrs flowed in circuses and on the scaffold. The barbarians invaded Europe; many men fled into the deserts. The sadness which enveloped the world was not produced by religion; this, on the contrary, diffused serenity on the countenance of the martyrs; this sweetened the manners of the barbarians, and vanquished the conquerors; this enabled the anchorites to find peace in privations and exile. Now that these calamities are only memories, and that religion remains to the people whom it has civilized, how ought it not to embellish the existence which in those ages it had rendered supportable! Opening the Gospel, I light on this passage: 'Come to me, all ye who suffer, and ye will be comforted!' Upon the whole, then, the cause of sadness comes from us, and is in ourselves; and when people say that religion is sad, they impute to it what we should attribute to ourselves, and to ourselves alone [*]."

[*] Droz, Pensées sur le Christianisme.

"Our sorrows," Mme. Swetchine used to say, "are often among our faults." She speaks precisely to the same effect as Droz, for she adds, "Christianity, which seems to disdain happiness, and to be an enemy of the body, honours the one and protects the other more than any religion or any system has ever done. What a divine character does it impart to happiness on earth! What a caressing sanction does it give to all the legitimate tendernesses of the heart! How many invitations to love ever more and more! Of the three great means of human happiness, faith, hope, and charity,"—all which, by the way, Mme. de Sévigné calls medicine to cure the sick,—" Christianity makes duties, so that no one can escape from being happy unless through his own fault; and then what a delicious calm does it induce in the possession of ourselves, in the sense of the harmonious equilibrium between all the powers of our being! What freedom within us, and how wise and beautiful is the world seen with a free and serene eye!" And here I cannot refrain from citing the words of a most eloquent author, when showing the difference which necessarily exists between the Christian and the Greek artists; "for the latter, while endeavouring to escape from the idea of evil, remembered it only as a painful dream, yet with a secret dread that the dream might return and continue for ever; whereas the former were taught that its contemplation and endurance entered into the duties of men. The Christian had been taught a faith which put an end to restless questioning and discouragement. All was at last to be well; and their best genius might be peaceably given to imagining the glories of heaven and the happiness of its redeemed. But, on the other hand, suffering was to be endured and honoured upon earth. The Christian was, therefore, in his inner mind less serious than the Greek; in his superficial temper sadder. In his heart there was none of the deep horror which vexed the soul of Æschylus or Homer; his Pallas-shield was the shield of Faith, not the shield of the Gorgon. All was at last to issue happily, in sweetest harpings and sevenfold circles of light; though for the present he had to dwell with the maimed and the blind, and to revere Lazarus more than Achilles*." Still,

* Ruskin.

come what will, though one's self had to be changed into Lazarus, where there is such a foundation of hope, the temper, even in its external manifestations, cannot but prove comparatively lightsome and happy.

These observations are necessary while recalling the joyous and yet thoughtful disposition which characterized this life of faith in the nineteenth century. One might have misunderstood it else; for in fact there are men who need having their attention called to the fact, that even in itself mirth cannot be a thing of human invention or contrivance, but that it must have entered into the divine ideal respecting human nature; that the music of a common dance can bring tears into the eyes; that joy in itself is more religious than sadness; that joy will be in heaven, but that sadness finds no entrance there. Many also need being informed that, as old and profound thinkers show, to the happiness and even cheerfulness of this life the worship of the true religion is necessary, in opposition to the persuasions of novelty. Masenius, one of those authors, does not indeed develope his theme—" vera religio ad felicitatem necessaria "—but he concludes that nothing ought to be dearer to those who seek happiness than the true religion, since all human felicity is from God [*]. One needs being reminded that there is a close relationship between joy and all that conduces to the health of the spiritual part of our nature. One needs being presented with an example that verified to the letter the well-known words, " Providebam Dominum in conspectu meo semper, propter hoc lætatum est cor meum et exultavit lingua mea [†]." It is well, therefore, to visit what one may term the school of the Chapel of St. John, in order to have this object most strikingly fulfilled.

As with regard to principles, and the turn of mind inwardly resulting from them, so also in relation to persons, and to what is external in their ways, it is not uncommon to identify faith with the absence of those sprightly and gracious manners, that in reality constitute so large a part of our social happiness. Of course one can understand how such a mistake should arise,

---

[*] Utilis Curiositas de Humanæ Vitæ Felicitate, cap. xx.
[†] Ps. vi.

since religion does undoubtedly sometimes present itself rather in a way that savours of a malicious caricature, and in connexion with the person whose character might be summed up in the words—"vive et triste, et qui ne s'amusait que de ce qui la faisait pleurer." There is the man of gravity wanting to get farther than paradise, as Mme. de Sévigné says, that is, to surpass St. Francis de Sales, and St. Jean de Chantal, counting his body for nothing, and perhaps, as she says, counting also for nothing the inconvenience inflicted on his neighbour, who, after being told of what is now about to be recalled to memory, may be expected to mutter some such words as " Laughed ! ce n'est pas ce qu'elle a fait de mieux." But, no question, these are only exceptions to a rule that may be qualified as general; and in regard to these cases, which often admit too of a melancholy construction that no one cares to dwell upon, we may begin by stating that, during the whole course of her life, the subject of our notice struck one as presenting a most instructive contrast to this character. Jane Mary, with all her piety, could never have been mistaken for one whom the French would designate as "dévote;" for, as the old poet says of some one,

" She did not wish to seem, but to be good *."

She never affected the gloom of poetic exaltations, intending to represent what is common and natural as something divine, which has to be treated with the seriousness of theology. She could not but treat things indifferent with gaiety, and consequently there was no appeal to the human heart and conscience from the justice of her religious decisions. But the truth is, her piety was too genuine a thing, her faith too living for any other result to have been possible. One must be careful, however, for one's own sake, when speaking of such a person, lest one should be accessory to misrepresentation on grave topics. It must be acknowledged, therefore, that having been accustomed in France to hear the theatre spoken of as a formal school of impiety, which in that country of late it has too often proved, and having had no opportunity to form an opinion

* Æsch. Sept.

respecting the present character of the English stage, it would have been a natural conclusion to draw from her occasional conversation, that, in regard to the subject in general, she participated in the feelings and opinions of Mme. de Louvencourt, and of many others, who certainly could never have been mistaken for patronesses of the theatre. But yet a truly pious and most charitable French lady, a worthy representative of whatever is holy and Catholic in manners, said lately of her, "When I saw her on her last visit to Paris, she left an impression on me that I shall never forget. Observing her joy one evening at taking her children to the opera, knowing how little she cared for such amusement herself, her heart being ever in the churches, I said wonderingly to some of my friends, 'Lo! what an admirable mother! what an example for those who love religion!'" Such was the very trait that she fixed upon to account for the noble idea she had formed of her character; but then it must be admitted all the while, that this estimate so spontaneously formed, came from one whose notions of a devout life savoured less of Port Royal than of the spirit of St. Francis de Sales; it was not the sanction of one like the Jansenist lady, in allusion to whom Saint-Beuve says, "St. François Sales, qui a l'air de permettre quelques *affiquets* aux filles en vue d'un honnête mariage, lui paraît trop indulgent." To relieve one's conscience it is necessary, however, to acknowledge, in concluding such allusions, that, in this solitary instance, one is rather playing the part of a special pleader, desirous of making out a case in presence of rather awkward facts ready for production. I fear the truth was, that she disliked what we have been speaking of. Innocent fun she would have loved; noble tragedy would have melted her to tears; but the Porte St. Martin or the Rue Richelieu were not precisely where she would direct herself to be driven to of an evening. So we had better say no more on that subject.

It is true, again, daughter of a mother charged in late years with cares, and perhaps disappointments gently borne, who seemed disposed to raise up her head no more after she had bowed it down at the foot of the altar, where she would remain absorbed for hours—herself, in the last years of her life, tried and afflicted as we shall subsequently observe, seeming impressed at times with such feelings as dictated the affecting lines of the French poet, where he exclaims,

> "——— O monde ! O vie ! O temps ! fantômes, ombres vains,
> Qui lassez à la fin mes pas irrésolus,
> Quand reviendront les jours où vos mains étaient pleines,
> Vos regards caressants, vos promesses certaines ?
>   Jamais, ô jamais plus !"

It is true, I say, that seen under circumstances which might appear so hostile to the development of a cheerful disposition, one might not be prepared for hearing that she was born with a taste for enjoyment, and to shine in any light and airy pastimes, to sing or play on the guitar. Yet such was her natural capacity and turn of mind. It was her part in girlhood, as poetry says,

> "To range the grassy lawn in vacancy,
> To breathe and to be happy, run and shout ;
> Idle, but no delay, no harm, no loss."

To the last she was of a remarkably cheerful turn of mind ; and a very small thing would amuse her, though it were only some one saying that he regarded it as a compliment to his appearance to be invited by a poor stall-woman to buy her unripe fruit. One cannot be indifferent to any details respecting her. "Try to get rid of this hatred for details," says Mme. de Sévigné, " in the case of those whom we love ? they ought to be as dear as they are tiresome when concerning persons whom we dislike or despise." Il y a du ragoût, she would add, in being able to remember them. Pleasant-spirited, the retirement in which her later years were spent did not render her sad, or unable to take pleasure in the mirth of others. Indeed, at all times what she seemed most to desire was to hear of those about her enjoying themselves and being happy. "Why not?" she would reply; "what is there to prevent you from going to amuse yourself? If you are happy, that is sufficient for me." Another might naturally think, that, in his own case, was not enough; but such was the confidence she felt in herself, that any thing like envy or jealousy was out of the question, so that when absent her letters would be still to the same purport. Like Imogen, she would demand,—

"Is he disposed to mirth? I hope he is."

Even amidst the shades of life's premature evening that natural gaiety of her disposition remained with her, accompanied with a fund of goodness which savoured of the innocence of primitive ages. The charm of her smile was felt by every one, as well as the delicacy of her mind and the elegance of her manners. A man like M. Colin would say of her what he predicated of Epicharmes, "that she found philosophy in the comic, and the comic in philosophy." She might have put one sometimes in mind of the touching words in Lear, "Since my young lady's going, sir, the fool hath much pined away." The witty humorist used to enjoy her aptitude and facility for paying him off with his own coin. For your repartee there was not a better girl in England; and even the poor people whom she used to relieve in France, many years afterwards, on hearing of her death, remarked to one who spoke of her, how singularly cheerful and joyous she had always seemed to them. She liked to watch a dance of young people, following it with her glass, or to see any innocent diversion, in any rank; though of course, naturally enough, she had never known what it is to be elbowed by the people, finding one's self, as Topffer says, "under the trellice on a holiday, and observing the charming play of light and shade, the animated picturesque groups, and that human face on which are painted so many thousand traits of joy and peace, and infantine gaiety and modest reserve." Upon the whole, one could find no words perhaps more exact to complete her portrait in regard to this feature, than those which Mdlle. de Scudéry employs, when saying, "With a mind so elevated she had the sweetness and docility of a child; she had neither presumption nor vanity, and she so pleased those who knew her well that it was impossible not to love her. There was a modest joy in her soul which communicated itself to those who conversed with her. It is not that she had not a passionate inclination, but it is that what she loved with passion was her duty and her friends."

It will be well now to institute an inquiry, with a view to ascertain the causes to which this extraordinary cheerfulness of her character may be traced, and we shall be led to conclusions that are of general interest, and replete with even curious instruction for ourselves.

It was clear, then, that besides a certain natural disposition, which I would not pass over in silence, though it entered but little into the composition of her gaiety, there should be noticed, in the first place, a singular youthfulness of heart, which was retained all through her life. There was a great contrast, therefore, between this living representative of the valiant woman of the Bible, and the character opposed to it, though known under the somewhat similar title of the strong-minded woman in the world! The one, in all respects, where it is not a question of the fulfilment of a duty that belongs to maturer age, like a child.

> "What joy is joy
> Unless it be to think that she is by,
> And feed upon the shadow of perfection?"

The other in every relation like—but it is better immediately to look another way, lest some one should startle the company, crying out, "Darkness and devils! Saddle my horses!"

I will not say that Jane Mary would ever join the circle of the culpably foolish; but, without intending it, she would play the girl admirably well, and I promise you she could laugh like one; to be sure, she could cry like one too, and that in part explains it—helping, by the way, to verify the mirthful lines of the poet,—

> "Auld Nature swears, the lovely dears
> Her noblest works she classes O;
> Her 'prentice hand she try'd on man,
> An' then she made the lasses O."

But why should we not be impressed, after witnessing her example, with a sense of the value of mirth, and of its compatibility at least with usefulness? The spirit of joy is a thing that comes to our aid from time to time in a most effectual manner; and while it seems to trifle, it is ever ready to help us. Being on such a topic, I see no reason why one should not as lief have the foppery of freedom as the stateliness of restraint, and so relate a pleasant anecdote. A certain stranger, then, with Arcadian propensities, sitting, with a book in his hand, in the gardens of the Tuileries, a pigeon that must have been rather ailing, as we say, sent down upon him a shower of sticks, which were not left without an accompaniment in their descent. An aged veteran on the same bench seemed to take the matter very quietly; but a young scholar, who happened to be passing, was seized with so many successive fits of laughter, that one was really growing alarmed lest he should expire in the convulsions. Nevertheless, though both age and youthful jollity came to his assistance, the latter proved most effectual. Age, indeed, supplied him with a toothpick to scrape his coat; but youth, after the fit was over, yielded him a piece of advice that led to better results; for the young scholar gave him his decided opinion that he ought to wash immediately the unfortunate garment in the adjacent basin. Though he made use of both, it was, I repeat it, the mirthful aid which led to the satisfactory restoration of his original appearance. The moral I mean to draw is, that your gay merry teacher is often the wisest one.

Then again, how differently are children, like Jane Mary, and older people of only half her age, moved by the same things, and with what greater advantage are the former impressed by them! Describe, for instance, before both a scene from the Trovatore, where there is the song from the tower while the bell is tolling for the execution of the poor minstrel; and one of the latter will reply, perhaps, "How ridiculous!" while the child cries out, with an emotion that comes from the heart, "Oh, how dreadful for him!" Genius, I believe, prefers the character that is disposed to draw the latter conclusion; and it is to such persons that one can apply the lines,—

> "Thou liv'st with less ambitious aim,
> Yet hast not gone without thy fame;
> Thou art, indeed, by many a claim,
> The poet's darling."

When she laughed, which in later years, was not of course so often, she laughed like a child or a girl of seventeen. That sound seems still to ring in one's ears! She laughed so from her heart! She understood a laugh so well! with so much grace! while, pray observe, loving so dearly noble poems, noble prose, plaintive music, and high tragic art. So you see no two characters could be more opposed than hers and that of the mere laugher, who parodies and scoffs at the serious. But she could no less completely enter into the joys of the sunny world, and that with expansive gaiety and intimate contentment; evincing that inwardly with her it was like a May morning! Hers in truth, in almost every respect, was the life of a child, and the conversation of a child,—recoiling, as she always did, from such talk as revolves around

> "Feuds, factions, enmities, relationships,
> Loves, hatreds, sympathies, antipathies,
> And all the intricate stuff quarrels are made of."

This, in fact, explains her cheerfulness; for, as Saint-Beuve observes, "what injures gaiety in our kind of existence at present is the complication which is in every thing. It is the fatigue, the excitement, the disquietude, which reign in material life, as well as in that of the imagination and intelligence*;" and therefore Desaugiers, in his song "Les inconvénients de la Fortune," says,—

> "Depuis que j'ai touché le faîte
> Et du luxe et de la grandeur,
> J'ai perdu ma joyeuse humeur;
> Adieu, bonheur! (bis.)
>
> Je bâille comme un grand seigneur—
> Adieu, bonheur!
> Ma fortune est faite."

Again, in another,—

> "Tout va bien, (bis)
> Grâce au ciel. Je n'ai plus rien,
> Je n'ai plus rien, je n'ai plus rien."

---

* Portraits divers.

And, in fine,—

> " Peuple Français, la politique
> T'a jusqu'ici trop attristé ;
> Rappelle ta légéreté,
> Ton antique
> Joyeuseté !"

She realized these lines in their different allusions. Her heart was still young, and without the preoccupations of the world. Alas! perhaps, for some resembling her in this respect, we touch here a chord that might reveal also a source of their sorrow; for what a sad thing, look you, is it when there exists the disaccordance and the contradiction of a fresh heart and of a dried-up one; of a heart amorous of exquisite emotions, and of a heart frozen by abuse; of an inexperience full of charms, and of the experience of one discontented and wearied with his own perversity!

But to return. One could see at the bottom of this happy soul, that it was not a factitious gaiety which illuminated it, like that ascribed to Arnauld de Corbeville, of whom Mlle. de Scudéry said, that what was striking in him "was the contrast of his melancholy humour with an inexhaustible fund of gaiety, which qualified him for diversions of all kind;" but that it was the pure joyfulness of the innocent child that in this instance was to last for ever.

Another cause to which no question this cheerfulness of mind must be traced, consisted in the moral goodness of her character. Masenius, in his book entitled " Useful Curiosity about Human Happiness," inquires whether the demon can conduce to the increase of human happiness. The experience of modern times, I should think,—for after reading all your essays and reviews I really believe in the existence of that elderly gentleman,—must have pretty well settled this question. Indeed, for that matter, the ancients might have been able to answer it. "The demon of sadness," says St. Chrysostom to Stagyrus, " when you were living in frivolous pleasures, will be cured when you marry and have children." And our poet seems to point an instance where he describes one so returned, saying of him,—

> "Then could he meditate on follies past,
> And, like a weary voyager escaped
> From risk and hardship, inwardly retrace
> A course of vain delights and thoughtless guilt,
> And self-indulgence—without shame pursued;
> Then, undisturb'd, could think of and could thank
> Her whose submissive spirit was to him
> Rule and restraint—his guardian."

Desaugiers, in his Hymn to Gaiety, says—

> "Il n'est donné qu' à la vertu
> D'épreuver ton heureux délire."

She whose memory we are recalling, was an example in point,

> "——— with thoughts
> Pleasant as roses in the thickets blown,
> And pure as dew bathing their crimson leaves."

And it may have been in allusion to such a grace that Fauriel said to a friend, "Oh, take great care of that rare plant which is called happiness; it is so difficult to obtain it, and so impossible when lost to recover it!" for her mirth was very innocent. If any jests were uttered after the manner of Voiture, she would have said, like Mdlle. Scudéry, "Qu'y a-t il donc là de beau? Trouvez-vous cela si gai*?" When some one else perhaps would laugh, she would turn away as if to shun what she detected

> "——— ——— in an eye,
> Base and unlustrous as the smoky light
> That's fed with stinking tallow."

Her mirth was more Homeric than that of manners in a waning age, when greatness and virtue are too often separated; for, as some one remarks, "there is not a grain of Rabelais in Homer: frankness, but no indecency, all is grave, serious. There is a moral grandeur in Homeric manners, which you find not in later times even of paganism." There was this truly classic element therefore in her mirth. But, indeed, whichever way you look, with many persons gaiety has not that innocence which it pos-

---

* Cousin, La Société Française, au xviie Siècle, tom. ii.

sessed with her; pleasant tongues are not without malice, and at the bottom of all their pleasantry there is a little grain of satire as of scepticism. Well, with her nothing of the sort—gay, she does not cease to be kind. She resembled one of Mdlle. de Scudéry's characters: "susceptible of amusement of all kinds, whether exquisite or simple, rural and common; for she has no greater pleasure than seeing shepherds dance to the sound of hautboys, under the shade of poplars in a meadow. She can play with a child, and is capable of being directed by little things when great are wanting *." Topffer says that lounging or enjoying, as we once said, "serene hours," which he qualifies as flânerie, forms part of education. "The man," saith he, "who does not know what it is to idle so, is an automaton who passes from life to death, like a steam-engine from Liverpool to Manchester. A whole summer even passed in this kind of idleness would not seem to me," he adds pleasantly, "to be too much for a finished education. Indeed, I do not think that one such summer would be enough to form a great man. Socrates idled so for years, La Fontaine all his life—and what a charming way of working is it to lose one's time so †!" One could not expect so good a housewife to say all this in precisely such terms; but she evidently had great indulgence for you who practised what this thoughtful artist recommends, even while you seemed disposed to trifle, as Shakspeare says, "till you had measured how long a fool you were upon the ground." There were moments therefore of her well-occupied time, when you might induce her to enjoy a short interval in the style of Lamb; at all events, seeing you

> "Thus outstretched in very idleness,
> Nought doing, saying little, thinking less,
> To view the leaves, those dancers upon air,
> Go eddying round; and small birds, how they fare,
> To mark the structure of a plant or tree,
> And all fair things of earth how fair they be."

She would soon start up, it is true, from her seat, as it were from such a dreamy mood, to pursue some task that was self-allotted;

---

* Grand Cyrus. † Réflexions et Menus Propos.

but a mind so free from all distraction could not but be gay whether it laboured or reposed.

> "No sad vacuities her heart annoy,
> Blows not a zephyr but it whispers joy;
> Moves there a cloud o'er mid-day's flowing eye?
> Upward she looks—and calls it luxury.
> Whilst chast'ning thoughts of sweetest use, bestow'd
> By Wisdom, moralize her pensive road."

The fact, meanwhile, might have been expressed in fewer words; for the law of God constituted, without doubt, a main source even of her delight. "David," as a great author remarks, "cannot contain himself for joy in thinking of it. 'How love I thy law! it is my meditation all the day. Thy testimonies are my delight and my counsellors; sweeter also than honey and the honeycomb*.'" No question she felt and realized all this within herself.

In fine, her cheerfulness was in a great measure the result of her faith, and of the Catholicity of her understanding informed, guided, and inspired from above. Indeed, there was no mistake possible on this point; for even her cheerfulness was, in a profound sense, religious, and had she wished, like the Venetian painter that Ruskin speaks of, to represent those whom she loved as happy and honoured like him, she could have imagined no greater happiness or higher honour than that they should be presented to our blessed Lady, to whom she would accordingly have supposed them brought by the three virtues—faith, hope, and charity. Now, if ever the lesson yielded by such a portrait was of practical importance, methinks it must be at the present day, and in the very scenes of our unbridled dissipation; for you have only to look around you to see how uniform are the facts every where. "In spite of our avidity for happiness," says Mme. Swetchine, "and of our repugnance for necessary trials, satiety is at the end of all our pleasures; but how could it be otherwise when there is not a single elevated, profound, and pure sentiment, which has not a holy sadness for its enjoyment? This secret attraction towards an unutterable

---

* Ap. Modern Painters, v. 150.

disquietude is mixed with the affections even of every elect mind. The elements of joy and melancholy exist in the same heart, and often near each other; they are confused together, and present themselves in a contradiction which denotes the happy inconsistency that arises from our double nature. What must it then be with others, when to the incitements of pride are added, as in our age, a vague disquietude, a want, as in the sick, of not being better, but otherwise? All that is absent becomes an object of worship, the will leading us in a contrary direction to the destiny which God has given us. Yet," she concludes, turning to look as it were on such a portrait as that of our Jane Mary, "there is in the world a silent apostleship, a living symbol, an incessant and impressive mission—it consists in the natural radiance from a profound and true contentment; for the joy which such persons taste in religion is of all homages the least suspected, while the contrast between our known troubles and the tranquillity of this peace which rises from the heart to the countenance, can effect great impressions on those who observe it." As Jules Janin says, "People of good humour render service to suffering humanity. How many tears do they dry up, how many fears allay, how many hearts encourage! Such persons, without pretension, do more real good to some nations than ten great philosophers like Descartes and Malebranche *." Afflicted as were her later years, there was nothing in the mind of this woman of faith to trouble her. Seek her when you would, and never were her eyes fixed to the sullen earth. M. de Montmorency, writing to Mme. Récamier, whom he desired to see more responding to the voice of faith, speaks of the profound sadness which he remarked in her last letter to himself. There was no trace of this spirit to be detected in Jane Mary's correspondence. As Mdlle. de Scudéry says of Angélique Paulet, "No one had ever the art in greater perfection of mixing gaiety and enjoyment with wisdom and modesty. There is ever in her disposition I know not what source of joy, which rejoices a whole company, though she is one of the most serious persons in the world, and she knows so well what to say to all those who visit her, to amuse, and please, and oblige

---

* Portraits et Caractères Contemporaires.

them, that they are all delighted." In her therefore you saw realized the poet's line,—

"Hilarisque (tamen cum pondere) virtus."

Catholic, that is to say, having graduated not alone in a school of respect, but in one which keeps the mind from fastening upon any detached fragment, there was in consequence, as we already suggested, no tendency in her mirth to that satire which is suggested by taking a party view of things, without a consideration of the whole. You saw the exterior and scorned. She saw the motive and admired. The Comte de la Feuillade, eldest brother of the maréchal, said of Mme. Cornuel, the witty lady of the Marais, that "if she liked it she could turn to ridicule the battle of Rocroy, the most beautiful thing that has been achieved since the Romans." Be that as it might, there is a sort of gaiety in which she never indulged. There is the man, not uncommon in the times we live in, who is incapacitated for joy by his very gaiety, which is evidently a mere thing put on. Nothing that is great, nothing that is amiable exists for him. He fears, he envies, he suspects, but he never loves. The sublime and beautiful in nature, the excellent and becoming in morals are things placed beyond the capacity of his sensations. A sneer is perpetually upon his face, and malice gnawing at his heart. She had in horror the mirth of old infidels. She would have approved of any one saying, even with the more aged truant, "'Tis not for gravity to play at cherry-pit with Satan." There was one she knew whose loud forced laugh of ceaseless irony used to fill her with a kind of terror. No trace did you ever detect in her of that ironical philosophic merriment of the old age of nations, symptom of their decay and forerunner of their ruin. Pulci laughs at his own soul, saying to it, "How did you get in? How did you get out? How can one be so silly as to occupy one's self about a being that has neither head nor tail, and which one cannot even say what it is? I wish you good evening, and if my down bed, my well-roasted ortolans, and my sweet wines in my cellar are to your taste, I am content." She did not like that sort of raillery, which characterizes the epoch when society, satiated with enjoyment, and time, and thought, grows old. It was in her laugh alone that you did not read the middle ages at their close, with their indelicate buffoonery, nor the sixteenth century with its sarcasm; but you could trace in it the joys of paradise before the fall, the ecstasy of angels, the mirth of heaven.

> "She was a woman of a steady mind,
> Tender and deep in her excess of love;
> Not speaking much, pleased rather with the joy
> Of her own thoughts. By some especial care
> Her temper had been framed as if to make
> A being, who, by adding love to peace,
> Might live on earth a life of happiness."

For she possessed

> "Health, quiet, meekness, ardour, hope secure,
> And industry of body and of mind;
> And elegant enjoyments, that are pure
> As nature is,—too pure to be refined."

Catholic duties, Catholic hopes, almost of necessity in a character like hers, produced a constant sunshine. She might have reminded one of what Mme. de Sévigné says to her friend M. d'Orves: "Ah! que vous êtes gai! que vous êtes gaillard! que vous vous portez bien dans ce Boulay!" "What a punishment is it," some one says, "to have to amuse a man who is no longer amuseable!" "See that poor Anacrise," says Mlle. de Scudéry, "there are so few things which satisfy her, so few persons who please her, such a small number of pleasures which suit her inclination, that it is hardly possible for things to be so well adjusted as to enable her to pass a single happy day in a whole year,—so delicate is her imagination, so exquisite and peculiar her taste, and her humour so difficult to content." While as for Julie d'Angennes, "she does not know what ennui means. She takes from all places in which she happens to be what is agreeable without being troubled by what is not, and she carries with her wherever she goes a spirit of accommodation which makes her content with any place[*]." So also was it here. The Catholicity of her mind taught Jane Mary to

---

[*] Le Grand Cyrus.

love life as a passing thing; to love it as a medium of utility; to love it with its labours, its fatigues (and she knew what these things were), its numberless pains; to love it with courage, as one ready and resolved to accomplish all its duties. As for this dreaming, doubting, mourning gentleman, who has not time to amuse any one, much less to make any one fall in love with him—who is dogmatic in his doubts and sceptical in regard to all ordinary duties, besides that she was extraordinary at a repartee, as we have just said, she used to maintain that the way not to succumb to such humours is not to love them; not to take pleasure in chimerical miseries, in childish chagrins at the cloud which passes, at the wind which blows, at the owl which cries, at the dog howling before the gate of the manor. She treated with legitimate irony all these little maladies of diseased minds; and in general, as a palliative against all these vapours of self-love, she recommended the labours of real life, with faith, and hope, and charity.

I deny not, that in her last years, confronted with calamity in its bitterest form, you could detect a pensive element even in her gaiety. As we read of Mme. de Courton, she had at times a certain I know not what, witty and melancholy smile, which moved people much; but still there was the bright example of a mind ever cheerful and at rest, such as so moved the poet when he cried,—

> "I praise thee, Lady! and thy due
> Is praise—heroic praise, and true!
> With admiration I behold
> Thy gladness, unsubdued and bold:
> Thy looks, thy gestures, all present
> The picture of a life well spent."

The bell of the Angelus tolls,—let us kneel, as she would have asked us with a look to do, and depart.

CHAPTER XII.

"IT is beautiful," says one of our contemporaries whom a noble friend has lately cited as having had a deep insight into the secrets of holiness and charity, " to find human weakness in strong minds. The antique heroism is of marble or bronze; but Christianity has placed the souls of heroes in hearts of flesh, in which it destroys none of the endearing frailties of nature, but finds in them, on the contrary, its strength. We were not made for being hard*." In this sense, then, at least, we are permitted, as Mme. de Sévigné wished, "to love our weaknesses, and to love them far more than the sentiments of Seneca and Epictetus †."

The Marquis de Saluces wrote a description—and its mere announcement strikes one, by the way, as rather long—of "the twelve virtues that a nobleman ought to have in his heart." In these visits to a tomb we have been seeking no ideal picture of humanity in any form. Strict fidelity to an original portrait has been our rule, and a lesson of instruction in regard to life and manners, spontaneously, necessarily arising from having beheld it, our final object. Let the subject of our consideration for this day be the heart of Jane Mary. Strictly speaking, indeed, as Mascaron says in his funeral eulogium on Turenne, "it is only in his heart that each man is found whole and entire, and such as he really is. In every other part he can be either divided or disguised, misrepresented or deceived;" and St. Augustin was so convinced of this fact, that he says it is only in his heart that man is truly what he is: " Cor meum ubi ego sum quicumque sum ;" and David, after inviting an examination of himself, stops at his heart, as at the only subject to which this whole inquiry should be directed, saying, " Proba me, Deus, et scito cor meum."

---

* Ozanam ap. Montalem., Les Moines d'Occident.
† Lett. 77.

It is a charming subject, then, which is proposed for our consideration here; since we shall have to speak of the affectionate disposition which characterized this life of faith in one whose soul now seems as yet but a little way above our heads, as if staying for ours to keep her company—for she hoped ever.

Let me for preamble call attention to a passage from Lacordaire, begging you, however, to remark at the same time, that neither now nor on any occasion do we begin our visit by unfurling a richly emblazoned standard, robbed, as it were, from some eminent treasury to which we have had access, and then resolving to colour and accommodate the facts that are to be brought forward, whatever they may be, to suit it; but that as a natural way of introducing the subject, we indulge at first each time in certain reflections which arise of themselves from that anticipation of the character we are about to paint, which is unavoidably produced by a previous acquaintance with the mass of evidence that exists to direct us, and to establish the correctness of our copy.

"Jesus Christ, then, has loved souls," says this eloquent author, taking no doubt very elevated ground, and drawing conclusions that will seem exaggerated to many in our age, "He has loved souls, and He has transmitted to us this love, which is the foundation even of Christianity. No true Christian, no Christian living, can be without a particle of this love, which circulates in our veins as the blood of Christ. As soon as we love, whether it be in youth or in mature years, as a father or as a husband, as a son or as a friend, we wish to save the soul that we love; that is, we wish to impart to it, at the price of our own life, truth in faith, virtue in grace, peace in redemption; in fine, God,—God known, God loved, God served. This is that love of the soul which surmounts all other loves; and which, so far from destroying them, exalts them and transforms them, so as to make of them, however natural in themselves, something divine *." You have the passage; and there spoke Jane Mary. There our loved one's grave did utter forth a voice!

It was said that this view would be thought exaggerated;

---

* St. M. Madeleine.

and yet there are some at present, who, without being Christians, might be appealed to in order to justify it. What a sense also of the dignity of this theme is evinced by men who are not even identified with the cause of Christianity! Here the form of expression will of course be different. We shall perhaps be invited to take as it were the romantic point of view; but' the extorted concessions coming from men who all the while pretend, and even propose to themselves to take pagan views of virtue, will be sufficiently remarkable. M. de Senancour, for instance, cannot be suspected of partiality in regard to her banner; and yet, borrowing much unconsciously from what he did not sufficiently appreciate, he says, "Love (and what was her heart but the seat of love?) ought to govern the earth, which is wearied by ambition. Love is that peaceable and fruitful fife, that warmth of the heaven which animates and renews, causes to bud and flourish, gives colour, grace, hope, and life. All other sentiments are lost in this sentiment; all thoughts lead back to it; all hope reposes in it; all is sorrow, vacancy, bereavement, if love departs; if it approaches, all is joy, hope, felicity. A distant voice, a sound in the air, the movement of branches overhead, the murmur of waters, all announce and express it. The grace of nature is in the motion of an arm; the harmony of the world is in the expression of a look . . . I will not condemn him who has never loved, but only him who cannot love. Circumstances determine our affections, but expansive sentiments are natural to the man whose moral organization is what it ought to be. He who is incapable of loving is necessarily incapable of a magnanimous sentiment, of a sublime affection. He may be honest, good, industrious, prudent; he may have gentle qualities, and even virtues by reflection, but he is not man; he has neither his soul nor genius. I might wish to know him; he may have my confidence and even my esteem, but he will not be my friend." We may be permitted, I hope, to add, that the gravest doctors of the Church, all devoted as they were sometimes to philosophic abstractions, cannot be alleged as giving any sanction to the opinions or habits of expression that have become of late so familiar to us, which seem at least indirectly to disparage the value of the natural affections, if not to dispense with them altogether. "Far be from us," said Bossuet, "heroes and worthies without the common affections of humanity! They may be able to force respect and extort admiration, like all extraordinary objects, but they will never command hearts. When God formed the heart and bowels of man, He placed first goodness as the proper character of the divine nature, and to be, as it were, the mark of that beneficent hand from which we issued. Goodness ought then to be the foundation of our heart, and at the same time the first attraction which we should possess in ourselves to gain other men. Hearts can only be won at this price;" and, adds Saint-Beuve, when citing the words, "true glory."

But when it is a question of seeing all this verified, beholding is better than hearing what we love extolled; and therefore I would say,

"—————————— Hither come,
And let this gravestone be your oracle."

"I would hazard any impeachment," said Coleridge, "rather than abandon my belief that there is a sex in our souls as well as in their perishable garments; and he who does not feel it, never truly loved a sister,—nay, is not capable even of loving a wife as she deserves to be loved." Does the distinction that we find in the language of Bishop Fisher, where he uses the two words "saints" and "saintesses," in allusion to the next life, in the same way as Jean de Troye speaks of "les Saincts et Sainctes de Paradis*," yield any doctrinal countenance to this delightful opinion? I am not competent to reply; but, be that regarded as an open question or not, it is difficult not to be of opinion, when standing within this chapel, that the noblest and most divine part of our nature is that which belongs to the affections of the heart. Think upon those gone! Let them direct thee! I do not see how you can escape from coming to the conclusion of Mme. de Sévigné, when she says, "I always place in the first rank, whether it be good or evil, whatever comes from the soul; the rest seems to me supportable and sometimes excusable. Sentiments of the heart alone appear to

* Chronique.

me worthy of consideration. It is in their favour that one pardons every thing—they constitute a fund which consoles us, and which repays us sufficiently*." Let us add, that God seems always to bless and reward those who possess them. With that treasure, on which faith itself depends, one cannot say you will be without suffering, for life is full of things that wound such a heart; but you will, for all that, be happy in this life; you will have hope at your death, and, judging from what is recorded in the sacred Scriptures, heaven for your everlasting destiny. In times when philosophy is seen running mad, and madness philosophizing, when reason and the heart are so often at variance, any one who is content to be an Idiota, or common person, might be caught acknowledging with the Swiss artist, that he prefers following his heart to his reason. Each of course will account for his choice in a different way, according as his general habits may require. Topffer naturally appeals to the interests only of art, and exclaims, "What is one to do thus divided? Reason is my master, I must believe him; but the heart is my comrade, and it is with him I saunter and range over past ages, and fix myself where I like; but far from manufactories, and tall chimneys, and modern ideas of comfort, and the objects that a purely masculine ambition now covets. Then we two laugh at the master, and nourish rancour against his new and stern things." It is Coleridge again who says that "the wisest maxims of prudence are like arms without hearts, disjoined from those feelings which flow forth from principle as from a fountain." Even mysticism of heart, as Mme. Swetchine observes, "is much more safe, and of better alloy than mysticism of mind." Of course—I repeat it—the affectionate disposition involves a greater liability to suffering than any other. To-morrow, and thenceforward to the last of our visits here, we shall witness proof; but what great goodness is exempt from this contingency? And after all, the sorrows of the affectionate are better than the triumphs of those whom Carlyle calls "the Dry-as-dusts." "I would sooner believe," says a French author, "in a happiness sprung from tears, than in a happiness compatible with dryness of soul. The obstacles

* Lett. 429.

to the felicity of a loving heart are outside of it; the dry heart contains them imbedded in itself. Some plants raise their humid heads above the plain inundated, but the sands of the beach are for ever sterile." At all events, " with a woman who is truly a woman," as Louis Ratisbonne remarks, "the heart will always be supreme. It is from the heart that a woman derives ever her happiness and her truest glory."

But to the goal. Let us converse with shadows that tell of the sun. The living are grown stern and cold, "fricaseed in snow," as some one once said of another. Few there are who are not false; I think many are without natural affection. There is the young man with grey deliberation, as Charles Lamb says, systematic in all his plans, and all his plans are evil—his very vice systematic. At times one fears almost that the poet may be in the right when saying,

> "——————— The date of love
> Is out, expired, its stories all grown stale,
> O'erpast, forgotten, like an antique tale *."

From her childhood Jane Mary was distinguished by the warmth and purity of her affections. One fears to touch with an unskilful hand those fibres of the human heart, where resounds in a thousand harmonies the music of her early years; yet, as Lamb says, "these promises of character, hints, and first indications of a sweet nature, are to many dear." Accordingly, she was her father's pet, her mother's darling, her sister's plaything, her brother's pride, her husband's soul. To no one would she ever say, " I love you;" but, you simpleton ! it was because she loved you that she would not say it. By nature warm, impassioned, susceptible, ardent, womanly; by grace checked, curbed, refined, and hallowed.

All through life devoted to what Rodolphe Topffer calls "the obscure charm of solid affections," her heart, which no moment found unsanctified, was her monitor on every occasion, whether little or great. In one respect she might have repeated, in reference to herself, the words of Mme. de Longueville: " She was dead as death to every thing that was not in her head,"

* Lamb.

where her heart occupied the throne, "and all alive to the least particle of the things that moved her affections." She united

> "A self-forgetting tenderness of heart,
> And earth-despising dignity of soul."

She felt for others in calamity as for her own. "I shall never forget her conduct on the death of my boy," said a father whose gallant son had been killed in the Crimea. Devoted to her own to a degree that was calculated to shorten the number of her years, for, as Mme. de Sévigné says, "such affection can have no rest—la grande amitié n'est jamais tranquille*;" by her whole life, nevertheless, she disproved the opinion that for a sentiment "to be powerful it must be exclusive; as if, so far from that, lively affection, if successful, did not always call into play all our loving faculties, adding to them activity beyond the circle of the first interest." Accustomed, as we remarked elsewhere, to the warm-hearted and delicate courtesy of the ancient French society, she seemed to have occasionally experienced a painful impression, which she disguised by laughing at it, from observing the apparent obduracy, selfishness, and neglect of social forms that belong at times to manners elsewhere.

> "She sang of love with quiet blending,
> Quick to begin and never ending;
> Of stedfast faith and inward glee;
> That was the song—the song for me!"

Mdlle. de Scudéry being at Marseilles, and receiving a letter from Mdlle. Paulet, replied to her, saying, "My joy on getting your letter was so great, that those persons who saw me receive it, and read it, thought that it contained an announcement of some one having given me at least 100,000 écus; for, as the inhabitants of this place are ever looking to their interest, they are sensible to no pleasures but to such as bring them profit." It is of persons of this kind that Jasmin speaks, saying you observe in them no caresses, there is no affectionate gladness in their eyes; to see them so indifferent and so frigid one might

---

* Lett. 134.

have taken them for people of very singular greatness. If it be not open indifference from the first, it will be a result that can remind one of what Mme. de Sévigné relates of Mme. de Ludre. "She accosted me," says the marchioness, "with a superabundance of affection that surprised me; she spoke of you too, my daughter, in the same tone; and then, all of a sudden, as I was about answering, I found that she was not going to listen to me, and that her beautiful eyes were trotting about the room. I saw it in an instant, and those who saw it with me could not help laughing*."

Then, again, with many there is a fear, or an affected fear, of being duped, there is mistrust—that ugly child of misanthropy. Oh, how unlike to all this is that sweet sanctity of love which animated Jane Mary! Here is no perpetual struggle between the heart which says, Believe, love, hope, and the mind which says, Doubt, despise, and distrust. There were periods of her later life when, among the public around her, every thing in the way of friendship, I rather think, was very hollow. It is never indeed rare to find the man

"———— to whose smooth-rubb'd soul can cling
Nor form, nor feeling, great nor small;
A reasoning, self-sufficing thing,
An intellectual all in all."

The Chevalier de Mère wrote to Mme. de Maintenon, saying, "Your ancient friends don't seem to hold a very secure place in your memory." He then speaks of the singular address which she employs in order to get rid of them, and rallies her on the enchantment which causes them notwithstanding it all to adhere to her. It is after considering contrasts of this kind, that one learns to appreciate best the affectionate qualities of this kind and unselfish friend, whose words are bonds, loves sincere, thoughts immaculate, tears, pure messengers sent from the heart, whose heart is as far from fraud as heaven from earth. It must be admitted, on the other hand, that she liked to be loved in return, and even perhaps at times to receive some little tribute of affection, such as in other countries friends are apt

* Lett. 83.

to present to each other. Loving and affectionate, it pained her when she did not witness love and affection in others. She detested baseness and ingratitude, but evidently tried to forget instances when they were manifested. She might have desired to meet with people more demonstrative in this way than some from whom she had the greatest right to expect even a show of affection, though the reality did exist without it. She would have been happier; but of such persons thus sweetly and richly furnished by the hand of nature, disappointments seem to form a necessary part of the destiny. Neither did she by any means approve of the facility with which people in the modern society forget their deceased friends, as well as those separated from them for any time, and dispense with all real mourning for them. For in this respect again she was quite left behind the age, with St. Louis and Joinville, and the rest of that world. "The king," says the young seneschal, "grieved much for the death of his brother, the Comte d'Artois. One day, during his voyage, he inquired what his other brother, the Comte d'Anjou, was about, that being in the same ship he did not come to him; and on being told that he was playing at dice with Messire Gaultier de Nemours, he rose, and went staggering, through the weakness caused by his sickness, and when he came to them he took the board and the dice and threw them into the sea, exclaiming against the count for his having so soon played at dice after the death of their brother, the Comte d'Artois. But Messire Gaultier de Nemours got served out better still; for the king threw all his money into the sea, to keep company with the dice and table."

Moreover, as one of the eminently affectionate, Jane Mary could not but dote on frankness in social intercourse; and she would have felt rather hurt if she had received very reserved answers, after the fashion of Talleyrand or Machiavelli, where there was no necessity for such being given. She did not like diplomatic cleverness and address in private life. She would have rather disliked one who could have prompted an observer to tell her of the old Spanish saying, that "when a fox sleeps nothing falls into his mouth." Content as she was with much retirement, there were in her last years evenings when, like the young prince, disliking the idea of repairing to the Tower, she wanted more faces here to welcome her. After her mother's death she would leave her place vacant, both at the fireside and at table. No one with her express permission, or even without wounding her feelings, could have taken that chair. Her general notions too of the claims of relationship were all derived from her heart, and perfectly natural, though, as a German author complains, they seem to have become obsolete in the class immediately below her own. "In this intermediate rank, at present," he says, "it is no longer the fashion to regard as relations those who are not inscribed on the first branches of the genealogical tree; whereas, for the aristocracy and the peasantry, in this respect the two powerful columns of the social edifice, the idea of the family and of relationship has a much wider extension. With the peasants a distant cousin is a near relation, having a right to all the privileges and favours that relationship can confer. Cousins are sought after down to the most distant degrees. Who would not envy," he continues, "the genealogical trees of the aristocracy, not from a sentiment of pride, and to derive personal honour from an antiquity which after all is the same for every one, but through a true filial piety, indifferent to the grandeur of a name, but profoundly attached to the honour of a family?" This, at all events, was the view she took of her obligations; and her affection for those related to her showed itself in regard to the future as well as to the present life; for while they lived she never allowed a month to pass without having masses said for her intention with regard to them, and on their decease she took care to have them remembered at many altars.

In general, one must say of her that, like the mother of King Henry VII., "she was good in remembrance and of holding memory." She possessed a singular faculty for recollecting dates, anniversaries, births, first communions, fêtes, wedding-days, and every epoch that was associated with affection, especially when any thing pensive was involved in it. She would not talk long beforehand of the day dear to a private memory, or even intimate her knowledge of its approach or presence till perhaps the eve or very morning, and the last minute before mass; but then with a whisper or a look, that went right through to your heart, she used to remind you of it. She remembered every thing relative to those who are gone. Retentive to a surprising degree, all the past seemed ever present to her; and this is a trait which we find ascribed to many holy persons, as, for instance, the Lady Anne, Countess of Arundel and Surrey, of whom the writer of her life says, as if speaking of Jane Mary, "Verily, myself have marvell'd many times to hear her recite things so perfectly, which she had learned many years before; and in discourse she would mention so many particularities and petty circumstances of things she had either seen or heard from her very infancy."

Full, again, of kind and delicate attention to others, she was herself most grateful for the least favour. As Bishop Fisher said of Margaret, the Countess of Richmond, "she wolde never be forgetfull of ony kyndness or servyce done to her before, which is no lytel part of veray nobleness." So it was with Jane Mary. The smallest act indicative of attention or of kindness, drew from her in return the most cordial thanks, and caused her no rest till she could return it, or at least make known her feelings. Eminently generous, as well as grateful, it used to be her care then to determine what would be a suitable present. Like Desdemona herself, she was "of so free, so kind, so apt, so blessed a disposition, that she held it a vice, in her goodness, not to do more than she is requested." She resembled Angélique Paulet, as described by Mdlle. de Scudéry, "her heart was full of generous and heroic sentiments. She was lofty-minded, but it was an elevation which did not prevent her from being gentle; and if there was height in her soul, there was very lowly tenderness in her heart *."

If we wanted proofs, indeed, of her affectionate nature, perhaps we could not select an instance more in point than that curious consequence of her disposition to cultivate the remembrance of others, which consisted in her keeping as a great treasure whatever could minister to it. She presented a singular example in this respect, to verify what Gilles de Rome says in his Mirror, "Comment par sapience nous debrons recorder les choses passes—les benefices de dieu;" and also all that he lays down when, treating "de la memoire du faict des parens," he says,

* Grand Cyrus.

"Et pense comment ils ont vescus parceque pourras veoir aprendre maintes belles exemples *." For this purpose, then, she used to keep tokens of all kinds with a deep religious respect—in memoriam! She had a perfect treasury of them, such as they were. Midst all her trumpery, not a counterfeit stone, not a ribbon, glass, boy's sash, pomander, brooch, table-book, ballad, knife, tape, glove, shoe-tie, bracelet, but that it told of ancient love. Even her prayer-books were swelled almost to burst their clasps with holding tokens of the by-gone; here it was a prayer in manuscript, given her by some holy friend, there a rose-leaf, one of those that had been scattered before the blessed sacrament, in some procession in which she had walked with her children when they were very little; there again a print that some valued hand had placed in it. In her drawers were found the broken toys of her dead child, and the poorest, homeliest articles of dress that he had worn. How ghastly they looked when she who had treasured them was gone too! Mais ne parlons pas de cela!

She had, therefore, what the French call the religion des souvenirs. Any little object associated with some trait of kindness, though it might have been only a token of regret for having vexed her for an instant in earlier life, seemed to possess a great value in her eyes. Thus for years she used to treasure up a little work-basket, of which the silk lining, originally pink, had become blanched with age; and the reason of all this regard for it was simply, that some one had given it to her one fine day, after making up a sort of child's quarrel. "O ye know not what ye lose," she would have said, "in despising these petty topics of endeared remembrance, associated circumstances of past times." From the same principle she cherished a great affection for the dogs that had been fond of her departed sons; always speaking to them as if they could understand her, which for that matter, in fact, they seemed to do pretty well, being both of them (that I may insinuate here a little fragment of curious antiquity) the kind of "genteel dog," gentilx, like one of Burns's twa dogs,—

* Le mirouer exemplaire du regime &c. des roys, &c.

> "Whose locked, letter'd, braw brass collar
> Show'd him the gentleman and scholar,"

which in old times had the exclusive privilege of being free of the city of London, through which such alone had permission to circulate both by day and night, while all others were fined forty pence for appearing within the franchise [*]. In like manner, there was a black hunter, which she ever afterwards seemed to regard as one of the remaining members of the family, for whose death she would no doubt have grieved after the manner of St. Fructuosus, who, when his deer was killed, prostrated himself on the pavement of the church, testifying intense sorrow, which elicits from a recent author the remark, that "one is pleased at seeing this gracious and innocent tenderness in such strong minds [†]." She had even, I repeat it, that kind of attachment to old familiar inanimate objects, which Topffer ascribes to himself, and which he says belongs more to the working classes than to idle people, and is more general in young societies than to ages that have attained the last stage of refinement in civilization. Saint-Beuve cites as an instance of this disposition some lines from an English poet, which he thus translates—

> "Je n'ai jamais jeté la fleur
>   Que l'amitié m'avait donnée,
>   —Petite fleur, même fanée—
> Sans que ce fût à contre-cœur.
>
> "Je n'ai jamais contre un meilleur
>   Changé le meuble de l'année,
>   L'objet usé de la journée,
> Sans en avoir presque douleur.
>
> "Je n'ai jamais qu'à faible haleine
>   Et d'un accent serré de peine
>   Laissé tomber le mot *adieu;*
> Malade du mal de la terre
>
> "Tout bas soupirant après l'ère
>   Où ce mot doit mourir en Dieu."

---

[*] Liber Albus, 389.
[†] Montalembert, Les Moines d'Occident.

To an affectionate disposition like hers belongs, as a natural consequence, a susceptibility for all deep impressions, whether of admiration or of displeasure. One must accept, without cavilling, the offerings of nature as they are presented to us, or rather we should trace the law of harmony and proportion in all that is of God's workmanship. You cannot have the heart of a St. Peter with the frozen kiss of a Judas, or combine the cool politeness of one who is far in the devil's books for obduracy and persistency with woman's love.

The character of Jane Mary presents, no doubt, here an instance in point. She failed in many things which are deemed by some to be very desirable and indispensable to philosophy and all that. Notwithstanding her remarkable prudence and perseverance, she was impulsive, and liable, as people say, to be led away by first impressions and sudden thoughts; but in this respect many eminent men have resembled her. Did not St. Gregory the Great, for instance, show himself as one liable to be led away thus, when he received such an impression from seeing the countenance of the English lads, that he must needs run immediately to the pope, obtain his consent to start off immediately for England, in order to convert the natives, and actually set out and got as far as three days' journey from Rome before they could overtake him? Her ardour, and, without a word, burning resolution in an emergency, could best be described after the manner of the old ballads, which represent the thing as done before one can speak of it; as when, having to relate how May Margaret was to repair to the king to save the life of young Logie, it only says,—

> "May Margaret has kilted her green cleiding,
> And she has curl'd back her yellow hair;
> If I canna get young Logie's life,
> Farewell to Scotland for evermair*."

It was the same when any thing occurred to excite her admiration. "Admiration is the label on ignorance," says Balthasar Gracian; "a fine mind is always sparing of admiration; custom deadens admiration." There is a whole choir of such

* Minstrelsy of the S. Border, i. 246.

voices, amongst which Mme. de Lambert may be heard. Be it so. Jane Mary thought differently though; let me tell you, she was in that way very ignorant, and had a deplorably unrefined mind. Utterly void of mistimed doubt and of egotism, she had a passion for what is good. Her wish to praise was boundless. Hers was a nature very capable of admiration, as are all elevated and truly poetic natures. To love and to admire has been the joy of her existence. Do you say she could be angry? I would not dispute about words; I believe as you mean it, that you are in great error. But, undoubtedly, there was not in her society a wearisome uniformity of manner. What you saw was not a statue, of which the beauty, however regular and gentle, will in the end prove monotonous; there were traits of innocent caprice if you will, perhaps instants of humorous impatience; a tinge of playful girlhood, with "a military air," imparting that variety which is so essential to every figure that is to inspire love, and which could displease no one with a grain of manhood,—all these "angry" fits, or whatever else you might call them, finishing in a way so contrary to hatred! It is true, also, she did possess "that faculty of honest indignation, that palpitating and involuntary sense of energy, which nothing can cool down to indifference," and which, as Saint-Beuve says, "is a distinctive mark of certain valiant souls, constituting a great portion of their morality." I admit, then, that to her character belonged these spontaneous acts or words of disinterested honour, and those bursts of generous indignation which do the heart good amidst all this prudent egotism and this habit of indifference with which society in our age seems as it were frost-bound. One must admit also—I repeat it—that there were occasions when her language was not conformable to that cool tone of Satanic politeness which can be remarked in all the mediæval representations of the character of the evil one. "It had been often observed," says Coleridge, "and all my experience tended to confirm the observation, that prospects of pain and evil to others, and in general all deep feelings of revenge, are commonly expressed in a few words, ironically tame and mild. The mind, under so direful and fiendlike an influence, seems to take a morbid pleasure in contrasting the intensity of its wishes and feelings with the slightness or levity of the expressions by which they are hinted; whereas those who express themselves warmly, may be seen the next hour cordially shaking hands with the very man whom they had been denouncing, and even perhaps risking their lives for him." The good-natured Gratiano with Shakspeare,

" ———— too wild, too rude and bold of voice,"

exclaims,—

" ———— O be thou damn'd, inexorable dog,
And for thy life let justice be accused ;"

while Shylock only says tranquilly,—

" I stand here for law."

There were times, therefore, when she would speak after the fashion of the Roman diplomacy, and hold up treachery and sacrilege not as merely " throwing alarm into scrupulous minds," but as worthy of the execration of mankind. But—I repeat it—even psychologically considered, how could it have been otherwise? All this only proves how well, how intensely she could love. As the Count de Maistre says on an occasion somewhat similar no doubt, " the girl who might find fault with her superstition in this, as in every other respect, would be perfectly right as to her expressions ; and what she might say to expose its weakness would be quite true ;" but one is tempted to add with him, " Tell me, grave philosophers, if you had to marry the one or the other of these two, would you choose the logician, or the superstitious and impulsive creature?" You have already seen what was the warmth, and sanctity, and heroism of her affections. Give her an occasion, and she would exclaim, like Isabella,—

" O, were it but my life,
I'd throw it down for your deliverance
As frankly as a pin."

It is true, with all this she was prudent. She has been often heard to speak like the mother of St. Louis, proving that her prudence extended beyond the limits of this life; and yet, on the other hand, as Mlle. de Scudéry says of some one else, "there was something in her temperament which does not commonly belong to those who are thus mystically prudent; for she was ardent as a girl, and if her wisdom and docility had not accustomed her to keep a command over her passions, she would have been at times deeply and visibly moved, in a way perhaps to amaze you. But this fire, which she kept under invariably, produced in her a thousand good effects; for it only showed itself in her intense anxiety practically to serve others, and in her resolution always, without disguise or duplicity, to keep the straight road, and accomplish her object by open and direct means." Upon the whole, therefore, I really do not see how the most cautious observer can avoid assenting to the justice of our words, if we were to finish for to-day with our Arabian bird, by exclaiming, after hearing of the defects which injuriously blended with the very graces of others,

"——————— But you, O you,
So perfect and so peerless, were created
Of every creature's best."

CHAPTER XIII.

TIME, that pleases some, tries all.

"Jamais nous ne goûtons de parfaite allégresse.
Nos plus heureux succès sont mêlés de tristesse *."

"In hoc mundo non dolere, non timere, non periclitari impossibile est," saith St. Austin. It is impossible to live in this world and not to sorrow, not to dread, not to be in peril. Mme. de Sévigné was a cheerful

* Corneille, Le Cid.

creature, and disposed to look always on the bright side of things; and yet I should fear to transcribe the passage in that letter to her daughter, when speaking of life, on which she found herself embarked "without her consent," she describes the fears and thorns with which it is beset; and yet confesses that she would return through them all rather than face that terminus the thought alone of which is enough to make her hate existence*. " Life and sorrow are near relations," says Menander; and one likes to hear cited together, as forming one immense chorus, those voices that come down to us from all generations. "With the poor, men and sorrow grow up together, and come to old age in company;" but the bond exists also in the midst of opulence, and in the instance as well of a public and illustrious life. Take the rich and prosperous, whom calamity, it would appear, never visits; they only verify, if you could see their hearts, the truth of what the same old poet said,—"There are who externally seem happy, but within they are on a par with every body else,"—

τὰ δ' ἔνδον εἰσὶ πᾶσιν ἀνθρώποις ἴσοι.

"Such is the life of man and woman," says Philemon; "we rejoice less often than we grieve,"—

Εὐφραινόμεσθ' ἔλαττον ἢ λυπούμεθα.

Such is the natural view of things, which in this respect revelation does not seem to have changed; for, as Philip de Comines says, "aucune creature n'est exempte de passion. Tous mangent leur pain en peine et douleur. Nôtre seigneur le promit, dès qu'il fit l'homme, et loyaument l'a tenu à toutes gens." But there remains what the Comte de Maistre passes over in silence †, another perspective seen, in which there will seem to be at first more cause to wonder at the phenomena of human life; for it will seem as if there was a distinction that he did not recognize amongst mortals, and that, too, not in favour of the good. The Christian dispensation, however much we may read

---

* 188.
† Soirées de St. Petersbourg, l.

the Bible, is not to be in every regard identified with that of the Old Testament; for its promises are different, or otherwise expressed, though they are kept with the same "loyalty." Who, pray, are those that are now under the former most commonly afflicted? No one should complain; for a constant and visible reward for goodness in this world would overthrow the whole order of human life as a probationary state; but it certainly does not look as if those who have to suffer most were the kind of people who are least liked even in the world, which, after all, whatever it may say, is in its secret judgment more often right than wrong. Who are those whose days now are often the shortest in the land? It is they who honoured, one might almost say while standing in the Chapel of St. John, who have venerated their parents. Sister Anne, sister Anne, do you see any thing coming? It is not exactly persons of the worst dispositions that are most likely to be disappointed, if they are waiting, like our nursery friend, for the arrival of a deliverance from sorrow. Strange to say, it is those who grow up in the favour of God and man, whose eyes seem often destined to be full of tears, their hearts of grief. To be sure, there is one very natural way of accounting for much that strikes attention in this respect; since it is generally on innocent, childlike creatures that consummate villains are most likely to fasten, as wasps infect the fairest and most delicate fruit; but this will not explain all. Bishop Fisher, in his discourse at the month mind of the noble Princess Margaret, glances for a moment at other facts which remain in all their mystery, exclaiming, "These mercyful and lyberall hands to endure the most painful cramps, so grevously compellyng her to crye, O blessed Jhesu helpe me, O blessyd lady socoure me! It was a mater of grete pyte!" But may not facts of this kind lead us to a consideration of the applicability of the pains of innocence to enter into the scheme which is the great mystery of the universe,—into the sacrifice which was the end of ancient prophecy, and which is the basis of the new revelation, of which the doctrine appeared constantly as a luminous point amidst the darkness of paganism, and in accordance with which dogma the Christian Church has ever been disposed to recognize in human suffering combined with a state of grace, something, to use the words of Origen, that was "differently similar" to what was offered on the altar of the cross, and which, like that supreme expiation, "by virtue of a certain force that cannot be named, procures inexplicable succour for men," in the same manner partly as the father of a family pardons one of his children for the sake of another whose prayers prove irresistible? But, without following the Count de Maistre on this mystic ground *, let us observe what, in this respect, are the phenomenal facts of human life. See how all the great, holy, charitable ladies of France, in the seventeenth century, were women, in one sense, who presented "a mater of grete pyte:" Mme. de Chantal, the patron saintess of our Jane, left a widow at the age of twenty-nine, and losing her sons; Mme. Acarie, whose repeated accidents caused her such long and painful maladies; the Marchioness de Belleisle, who so mourned for the death of her husband; the Marchioness de Magnelais, a widow after three years of marriage, then losing her only son, then having to mourn for the marriage of her daughter to the barbarous son of the Duc d'Epernon, who treated her so cruelly, then the death of that daughter,—at each of these blows nature feeling such poignant sorrow while grace triumphed; then becoming suddenly stone-blind before her death, when she invited her servants to sing with her a Te Deum,—the end of her life being accelerated by several fits of apoplexy; in fine, by the last of them losing even her speech and the power of moving her limbs,—continuing to the last instant her charity to the poor, yielding thus "a mater of grete pyte." See again a Mme. Helyot losing her child with such bitter grief, having her legs swollen with such long and intense pain; Mme. de Miramion, a widow at the age of sixteen, losing her beauty with the small-pox (and I won't omit that circumstance for all your stately looks), insulted in consequence, latterly afflicted with an incurable cancer; Mme. du Houx, whose life was written by the Chevalier d'Espoy, who calls her the spouse of the cross, from her life having been a chain of reverses and sorrows, which all contributed to her sanctification; the family of the Princess of Epinoy, the celebrated Mlle. de Meleun, overwhelmed with misfortune; her own

* Éclaircissement sur les sacrifices.

grief on losing her brother, the last hope of her illustrious house [*],—for St. Jerome even would not pass that over in silence. But coming down to modern times, see how the amiable, and kind, and good, and affectionate, have been visited with calamities beyond the common run. See that Alexis Monteil, for example, after losing his wife Annette and his only son Alexis, who had already given such promise, assisting his father in collecting materials for that great work which has immortalized him. See him without means of purchasing a grave for this child; repulsed with stately formality by the prefect of the Seine, when he wrote to implore him not to allow his son to be cast into the common pit,—into which, however, it was reserved for him to see disappear this companion of his life, this young associate of his labours, this last and only remnant of his Annette; but the story should be read in the pages of Janin [†].

Of course, it would not be right for any one to argue, that because persons were singularly afflicted and unhappy, therefore they must have been eminently good,—that would be a fine and flattering unction for the soul of some one else. But no one can altogether be blind to the fact, that human life in this respect presents phenomena of a very remarkable uniformity, though interrupted, no question, by exceptional differences.

On the other hand, however obstinately men may close their eyes to realities of this order, it is difficult not to have been impressed, at some period or other of one's life, with a sense of the advantages that belong to human suffering, which tend, in a great measure, to clear up the mystery in which otherwise the whole subject would be inextricably involved. Without recurring to the source of these mystic reasons alleged by our Christian forefathers, as, for instance, where Alain Chartier accounts for the fact by reminding us of what takes place in the family, where, within his own hotel, a father corrects a son that has committed a fault, but merely sends away out of it altogether, without any punishment, a grown-up man who has committed the same offence,—there are not wanting analogous

---

[*] Vie, par Grandet.
[†] Jules Janin, Portraits et Caractères contemporains, 178.

reasons to serve the same purpose, as where the Greek poet says,—

> Εἴπερ κακὸν φέροι τις αἰσχύνης ἄτερ,
> Ἔστω· μόνον γὰρ κέρδος ἐν τεθνηκόσι *.

It is true, we live in an age when speculations of this order, or even the results of observations of real life, are not received with as much favour from "the reading public" as they would have been in the days when Benvenuto Cellini, being in prison, composed a book on the happiness of being a prisoner. In confirmation, by the way, of which extravagance, as we should call it, he might have cited the lines of Æschylus, affirming that chains constitute an excellent medicine for diseases of the mind †. The obscurity of a dungeon, as our literary guides might perhaps tell us, while extolling what they substitute for it, a military execution, suited the dark ages. It would not be very easy to find in any of our modern works of art, as exponents of the thoughts which pervade the later generations, any trace of the notion or sentiment which we can see expressed in the Hôtel Cluny for instance, where there is a figure in ivory of a woman with the legend " Souffrir ou mourir." Nevertheless, as Ballanche says, " we should be less astonished at suffering, if we knew how much better grief is adapted to our nature than pleasure. The man to whom every thing succeeds according to his wishes forgets how to live. Grief counts in life, and one might sometimes be almost tempted to conclude that there is nothing real but tears. Show me," he continues, " one who, after thirty years of life, has never been deceived. Show me the privileged mortal, and that a woman. Her imagination has kept all its promises; love has led her by the hand—happy spouse, happy parent; she has purchased by no torment the charm of the heart—affections; she has known the pleasures of society without being ignorant of the delights of solitude; she has met on her way with only the good and generous; she has enjoyed her memories as she enjoyed her hopes; she has found in the past the pledge of the future.

* Æsch. Sept.   † Agamem.

Show her to me. You smile and sigh. You know not where to find her. In effect such a creature does not exist."

> "The fineness of men's constancy is not found
> In fortune's love; for then, the bold and coward,
> The wise and fool, the artist and unread,
> The hard and soft, seem all affin'd and kin;
> But in the wind and tempest of her frown,
> Distinction, with a broad and powerful fan,
> Puffing at all, winnows the light away;
> And what hath mass, or matter, by itself
> Lies, rich in virtue, and unmingled."

There are other reasons, of course, within the limits of more mystic ground to explain why the combination of goodness and sorrow should now be as frequent as we behold it. But even without taking them into account, methinks, when turning to the example of her whose calamities are seen recorded upon marble within this chapel, one can understand sufficiently why her latter years should have proved so full of sorrows; and the fact is, that during the last three years of her life, hardly a day passed without some one catching a glimpse at pearly drops within her large eyes. Oh, she could weep the spirit from them! for, as old Philemon said, "Grief is like the tree, and has for its blossom tears." Her happy days, in a natural sense, had died before her death. What mere humanity would deem

> "The crown and comfort of her life
> She did give lost; for she did feel it gone,
> But knew not how it went.
> Woes on woes assailed her,
> ———— But now I see
> The mystery of her loneliness, and find
> Her salt tear's head."

She was told to drink of the torrent by the way, in order that, like Him whom she loved and followed with a Mary's love, she might rise up and be exalted for ever.

> "But soft! I think she comes; and I'll prepare
> My tear-stain'd eyes to see her miseries."

Nothing at first perhaps, you will think, uncommon or remarkable in what she suffers. Early in life she has lost her father, of whom, as before noticed, she was "the pet;" then later her only sister and her sole brother; then four children were taken from her, three of them within six months of each other, and two of them by death; then a few months before her own decease her mother leaves her, from whom she had never been separated. Nothing singular in such an enumeration, which could make fools smile in the ale-house, where "keeping vile company," as Prince Henry says, "will in reason take from us all ostentation of sorrow." It is pretty well though already, others will say, for a heart like hers, overflowing with affection. How could she, so formed and constituted, as we observed on our last visit here, be expected to moderate such grief?

> "If she could temporize with her affection,
> Or brew it to a weak and colder palate,
> The like allayment could she give her grief;
> Her love admits no qualifying dross;
> No more her grief, in such a precious loss."

Another poet, even from that cheerful disposition alone which belonged, as we have seen on a former occasion, to Jane Mary, would deduce a similar consequence, saying,

> "If there is one who need bemoan
> His children laid in earth,
> The household hearts that were his own,
> It is the man of mirth."

To speak of what she went through generally, will engage us necessarily in details, which if viewed in disconnexion with the mystery of her life, would seem very ordinary matters. Her physical sufferings at different periods had been great. When a physician in Paris, who loved her as his own child, the celebrated Beaudelocque, told her that, in consequence of catching cold under certain circumstances, she would have to suffer a long and "very painful illness," the tears were in his eyes, as he said it in a half-suppressed voice, but not in her own. The event justified his prediction; but she accepted all this with a gay and incomparable patience. In the successive accidents

x

and maladies of different kinds which she had to undergo, her heart each year seemed to grow younger and more loving. She had, like her mother, a manly turn of mind; while her understanding, as Lamb might say, was not more masculine than her manners and whole disposition were delicately and truly feminine. During each illness that she suffered, it was she who with pleasant looks, and mirthful words, and unaffected smiles, encouraged every one that approached her. The sick chamber was the most cheerful room in the house by reason of her who so enlivened it.

> "But truly strongest minds
> Are often those of whom the noisy world
> Hears least."

In her last years, in consequence of never attending to what the most ordinary care for herself required, and avoiding as much as possible asking others to do what she thought she could achieve by her own efforts, afflicted in a manner to impair her facility for active exercise, she bore up with wondrous courage, and if you had been in the secret, you might have thought that she esteemed all she had to support a privilege. As we read of Mme. Helyot, she was never heard to complain of what she suffered. Neither was she ever known to find fault with the weather or the season, and, unless it was with the poor that she spoke, she used to rally those who did so. The only thing that she used to lament, and that was while laughing at her own consequent mistakes, was the shortness of her sight, which debarred her many enjoyments. She doted, as we before remarked, on light and on the long days of summer; and whenever she regarded any one or any object through glasses, which she seldom allowed herself to do, she used to speak with the rapture of a child on getting a new plaything.

In her care of the sick, a task which often devolved upon her, there was something that one might truly qualify as wonderful. While others were melancholizing in woods, and sighing in gardens, and groaning on their soft beds, she was busy, hopeful, animated, and devoted to the minutest details; never discouraged, never cast down, never relying much on physicians, but looking for help to God, and resolved to abide the manifestations of His holy will, as if all the while repeating, almost mirthfully,

> "Hope is a lover's staff; walk forth with that,
> And manage it against despairing thoughts."

She might have reminded one of a pleasant anecdote of the Dauphiness Marie-Josephe de Saxe, mother of Louis XVIII., when attending her husband in the small-pox with such assiduous care, that M. Poupe, the celebrated physician, called in for consultation, and a stranger at court, said, pointing her out to some one, "Voilà une petite femme. There is a poor woman quite invaluable for the care she takes of M. le Dauphin." He mistook her for a garde-malade*. Oh, common as such things may be thought, one ought not to forget all the sorrows and sufferings she underwent during the sickness of others! What voluntary imprisonments, what risings before the lark, or what nights passed in wakeful solicitude! Diana leaves Hippolytus at his death, saying, "Receive my last farewell, for it is not permitted me to see the dead, or to defile my eyes by mortal exhalations, and lo! I perceive you are approaching the fatal moment," and she disappears. To the goddess tears are interdicted, and she flies away from the odour of departing breath. Alas! in her latter years Jane had to present a great contrast to this example from the heathen mythology and that natural condition of humanity to which we are tauntingly referred as so superior in elegance and nobleness to the Christian.

Again, no question, she greatly needed the antidote which she possessed in her faith and piety for the res angusta domi, interpreted in the sense of domestic troubles generally, which, as Charles Lamb remarks, "always presses most heavily upon the most ingenuous natures." Common life is for such spirits like a continual battle. She was not like one of those who expect every thing and is prepared for nothing. She looked before her, not alone to to-morrow, but to next month, and to next year, and ever forward. After her mother's death these cares pressed upon her, in the absence of any one who could share

* L'Abbé Sicard, Vie de Mme. la Dauphine.

their burden with her, to an extent that no doubt proved injurious to her remaining strength. There were moments when, through groundless anticipations, she seemed to fear that a time might come when she would feel like the poor Sire de Joinville at Cyprus, on being presented with the accounts of his knights, and had only 240 livres tournois to pay them, when he says of himself, " Lors fu quelque peu estably en mon courage ; mais tousjours avoye fiance en Dieu." By constitution nervous, so as not even to feel at ease driving in the streets of London, her first words when in the least alarmed out of doors being always Jesus and Mary, she naturally suffered from the troubles and annoyances to which every family is more or less exposed; for, as Alain Chartier says, "On frappe souvent à la porte d'un riche homme. Es hauts palais y a tousiours noises et murmures *." And being often frightened by some needless cause, she might have said in her own defence, like poor Queen Constance,

> "That she was sick and capable of fears,
> Oppress'd with griefs, and therefore full of fears.
> Bereaved of relations—subject to fears ;
> And though perhaps just now thou didst but jest
> With her vex'd spirits, she cannot take a truce
> But they will quake and tremble, all this day."

And yet when occasions presented themselves, she met danger with the courage of a young hero. After effecting her escape from the fire which consumed her house, and which, in the dead of night, did not leave her a minute to save any thing but her children, she seemed even cheerful under the calamity, retracing with much laughter all the circumstances of her flight, perfectly resigned to the loss which she sustained of things that to her were inestimable, unique portraits of her dead friends, tokens of old affection, and memorials of religious veneration; but still acting after her accustomed way, which, like that of the Lady Anne, Countess of Arundel and Surrey, was " to take all worldly losses as sent and ordained by the paternal providence of God for her greater good, or as things happening by chance, according to His general laws."

* Le Curial.

"If you look close," says Mme. Swetchine, " you will find that it is passion rather than self-interest which influences men." This she said in allusion to the manner in which they meet the collisions of the world in general. There would unquestionably be much to learn from observing the way in which a life of faith meets them, and how it differs in that respect from all other lives. Differences of place, of temper, of treatment, affected Jane Mary but very little. As for the first she was always contented and happy wherever she found herself. If in Kensington, she liked the oratory with its sermons and grand offices, and the privacy of her own gardens, in which she could think over in her heart what she had heard there; if in the country, as before observed, she doted on the fields and the aspect of nature. She regretted leaving any place in which she was accustomed to reside, and that even as if she took leave of it for the last time. With respect to the treatment she experienced from others, their slights or neglect, for in some states of society no one can escape these, made little or no impression on her. In fact, as Mme. Swetchine observes, " we may suffer from the faults of others, and yet the greatest part of this suffering comes from ourselves. It is our own faults which make the cup overflow; without them the provocation would be harmless. After all, our only efficacious action is on ourselves, and it is less troublesome to reform one's self than others." These were evidently her thoughts also. In this respect she kept a watchful guard over her lips; and if ever there had been manifested towards her any trace of personal slight, no word on the matter ever escaped them; perhaps not even a thought had been harboured. She seemed not only content, but actually and unfeignedly pleased, even to laughing, that so it should be; so little did she wear the mind of the world, of which more perhaps have even died than that poor Langlade, whose death was caused by grief that the minister Louvois, on passing through Poitou, did not stop to pay him a visit. When overlooked, where politeness had not attained to any remarkable perfection, in a manner that was characteristic of the coldness, or hurry, or ignorance of either local manners or of persons who had never taken trouble to inquire, she never would let any one perceive that she was even conscious of the circumstance.

> "She made her wrongs
> Her outsides; wore them, like her raiment, carelessly;
> And ne'er preferr'd her injuries to her heart
> To bring it into danger."

Instead of taking fire herself, as so many others would have done, all her care was to put the fire out in others, loving her who remarked it. She did not hide the fact with affectation, or put on airs of mental superiority, as if she thought all the better of herself in consequence, but with an air that was truly wonderful, since it was constituted by the purest simplicity, she often succeeded in making it appear as the mere result of chance, or of some oversight such as she was guilty of, or merely thoughtlessness that was most innocent; as if a conduct as strange as it was uncivil "was something of their negligence, nothing of their purpose;" and certainly by the elevation of her mind, to say nothing of any thing else, though perhaps her truly noble habits of life, if the whole truth were known, were quite as much the cause, she felt herself unaffected by such little miseries, and perfectly calm when confronted with them. It would, however—I repeat it—be more exact perhaps to say, that on these occasions she seemed rather pleased than hurt at being overlooked, and that she thought only of banishing from the mind of others what would prevent their being pleased. Who knows? Perhaps she really was pleased at such neglect, otherwise she could not have carried herself as she did. At all events, such treatment had the interest of novelty for her; as her life in former times had been in that way without the benefit of such experience; and she might have felt it even naturally pleasant to see more and more verified what she had always thought and told others of certain circles which for her had never any enchantment; indeed, so far otherwise, that, judging from her evident resolution to keep clear of them, you might have thought that she held them for the haunts of the most dangerous of all the dangerous classes of society, though not known to the police; in which opinion Mme. de Sévigné would probably have coincided with her, for she says that a lady from the country who wants to be thought of the court is always a very dangerous person.

But passing from the domains of ideal difficulties and misfortunes which never detained her for the space that we have just employed in discussing them, let us proceed to study this life of faith when confronted with true calamity in its most stern and distressing forms. " Now was the hour," says an ancient poet, " when every traveller and guardian at the gates of cities begins to desire sleep; when drowsiness comes over even the mothers whose children are dead *." Our Shakspeare has the same sense of the supreme intensity of this sorrow, saying,—

> " As looks the mother on her lowly babe
> When death doth close his tender dying eyes."

"One knows," says Léon Aubineau, "or rather one does not know, what is the heart of a mother; fathers only can see something of it. The death of a child is not only a sorrow, but like an overthrow of nature. Yet in souls united to God, that sorrow, however lively and cruel, is associated with an intimate sentiment of the divine goodness. Through the ruins of the thoughts of earth, the best and the most authorized, the wonderful goodness, the unutterable goodness of God is felt; the soul suffers, but it is happy with the idea of that suffering being in fulfilment of the divine will; nature would resist and revolt, but nature is vanquished and the cross adored †." All this representation is true generally. How hopeless then would it be for me to attempt to describe her grief, when, for the first time, she felt what it was to lose a child in her Frances Mary Venetia, whom, at the age of eighteen months, she had already taught to say, " God bless Fanny ;" and then later, when, within three months of each other, she lost her eldest and her youngest son, and in the same year found herself without the daughter to whom she had ever been in habits of looking as one capable of advising her, if not of supplying her own place as guardian of others. Recur to what was said on a former visit respecting the joyful

---

* Apollonius Rhodius.
† Notice sur la Marquise le Bouteiller.

character of this mother when repairing to the church upon a
Sunday morning. Look at the delightful picture; and behold
her now,—

> "When bells were rung and mass was sung,
> And every lady went home,
> Then each lady had her own young son,
> But Lady Mary had none."

Well, I said from the beginning that you could read pages of
old history in her young heart, and here is an instance; for on
these occasions she acted precisely, literally as did St. Louis
under less trying circumstances. Many remember the words
of Joinville, describing him, "quant le bon roy veoit celle
pitié, il joignoit les mains, la face levée au ciel, en benissant
nostre Seigneur de tout ce qu'il lui donnoit."

Of course every one is aware of the way in which people
of the world, or even persons externally consecrated to religion,
speak of such lessons generally; and yet with their fine phrases
still ringing in one's ears, I know not how we can proceed without
expressing an opinion that these events furnished an occasion
for regarding Jane Mary with somewhat of astonishment
as well as reverence, so great was her victory over nature, and
her intrepidity arising from resignation to the will of God.
Extraordinary in itself, it was moreover left without any extraordinary
support visible, such as the combined action of religion,
and of long previous admiration for the singular qualities
of its particular representative in the hour of trial has frequently
in the case of others yielded. She was not, for example,
in that respect privileged like the Maréchal de Grammont,
when it was no less a person than the Père Bourdaloue
who came to announce to him the death of his son, the Comte
de Guiche, and who remained with him for six hours, when, as
Mme. de Sévigné wrote to her daughter, "il luy parla de Dieu
comme vous savez qu'il en parle;" admirable expression, which
conveys an idea of the singular advantages which were extended
to the maréchal. And yet this brave soldier of France,
who was also a pious Christian, seemed overwhelmed in a sense
totally unlike her. He lay upon his bed without a tear, but
saying, what she felt in silence, that it was a blow equivalent to
his own death; that the object of his heart's love, and of all his

natural inclinations, was taken from him; and then, when the Père would insist upon leading him to the church of the Capucines, he entered it staggering and trembling, rather borne along and pushed than on his own limbs, his countenance not being recognizable, and returning afterwards to solitude, "comme un homme condamné*." Nothing like this in the conduct of Jane Mary. The tender mother left to her own thoughts, with only the ordinary aid that is yielded to the commonest and most obscure Christian, under her successive visitations, equally cruel, and following each other at short intervals, is calm, firm, active, fulfilling all her accustomed duties almost as if nothing had happened, though no one for an instant can mistake the extent of her desolation. But there are contrasts still more striking. We expressed fear on our first and second visit to this tomb lest we should be taxed with exaggeration in suggesting that we could behold in her a certain shadow of the character of the Roman ladies immortalized by St. Jerome; but in this instance we cannot shut our eyes to the fact, that she presented a courage in her intense sorrow which formed more than an adumbration of the piety of those patrician races; for at the funeral of Blesilla, her eldest daughter, Paula, not being able to restrain her grief, fainted, and it required all the authority of St. Jerome, expressed in an eloquent letter, to bring her back to resignation to the divine will, by showing her that the excess of her grief was a scandal in the eyes of the Pagans, and a dishonour for the Church. No woman amongst the Gentiles, said they, ever lamented her children like that: this comes of her miserable religion! and twenty years later, when Paula died at Bethlehem, Eustachia besought God that she might herself die and be buried with her in the same grave, when it was again necessary at the funeral for St. Jerome to interpose, with a view of leading back the orphan to sentiments more Christian. I repeat it, no heart was ever more inundated with maternal and filial tenderness than that of this mother and daughter living a life of faith in the nineteenth century; and yet the courage, the intrepidity when face to face with death, in the persons of her sons and of

* Lett. 270.

her mother, the calm confidence, the pious, simple resignation, requiring no eloquence, no authority to inspire them, unaided visibly, unsustained by any venerable human presence, surpassed—it would be a falsehood to deny it—what is commemorated in the pages of St. Jerome!

Nevertheless in this nature, capable as we have seen of such profound affections, religion in the presence of death could not weaken the vivacity of her maternal and filial love. These taken from her tenderness became matters for her thought in worship. I must ask leave to give the brief narrative in the poet's words,—

> "——————————— our angel boy,
> Caught in the gripe of death, with such brief time
> To struggle in as scarcely would allow
> His cheek to change its colour, was convey'd
> From us to regions inaccessible.
> With even as brief a warning,—and how soon,
> With what short interval of time between,
> I tremble yet to think of,—our eldest son
> His brother follow'd, and was seen no more;
> The mother still remain'd, as if
> This second visitation had no power
> To shake, but only to bind up and seal,
> And to establish thankfulness of heart
> To heaven's determinations—ever just."

When the daughter of Daniel Manin died at early dawn, some one knocked at the door of the broken-hearted father,—it was the painter, Ary Scheffer, who happened to live in the neighbourhood, and who hardly knew Manin. He spoke not. He seated himself at the bedside and painted for the poor overwhelmed father the portrait of the departed one. An incident somewhat similar occurred on the evening after little John's funeral. A Protestant lady, and an utter stranger, called at the door, and begged permission to send up a paper containing some verses on the death of a child. May God reward that kind act of tender sympathy which could never have been shown to greater woe! After the lapse of three years this paper was found in her pocket when she died. She had never laid it aside, but kept it there with her rosary, as if to verify the lines of Brizeux in his poem of Marie,—

> " Lire des vers touchants, les lire d'un cœur pur,
> C'est prier, c'est pleurer, et le mal est moins dur."

How can I resist the desire of giving the lines thus entombed, and if one may so say, by her cordial acceptance and pure usage sanctified? for her heart, sweet boy, had been thy sepulchre, and from her heart thine image had never gone.

> " My lovely little lily, thou wert gather'd very soon,
> In the fresh and dewy morning, not in the glare of noon;
> The Saviour sent His angels to bear thee hence, my own,
> And they'll plant thee in that garden where decay is never known;
> How peacefully, how sweetly, ebb'd thy little life away,
> Oh! blest for ever be the God who heard thy mother pray!
> He did not wish to keep thee in this world of sin and strife,
> So she pray'd that thou without a pang mightst yield thy little life.
> She watch'd thee, how she watch'd thee! thro' that anxious night and day,
> And only turned her eyes from thee, to look to heaven and pray!
> ' Deal gently with my darling!' was still her fervent cry—
> And ' Trust me with thy little one,' seem'd still our Lord's reply.
> My lily! oh, my lily! I saw thee hour by hour,
> Still drooping nearer to the earth, my pale and precious flower,
> And as I mark'd the glaring eye, and felt the cheek grow cold—
> The mingled thoughts that fill'd my heart, they never can be told!
> 'Twas in thy mother's arms, my own, thou didst resign thy breath,
> And she will bless her God for that, till she too sinks in death!
> Oh! tenderly indeed, my boy, the Saviour dealt with us
> When He in pitying love disarm'd the king of terrors thus.
> And often, often, ere it came, that last, sad, solemn day,
> Beside thy little coffin she would sit, and gaze, and pray;
> And never, never from her heart, can thy sweet image fade,
> So pure, so white, so still, so cold, as if of marble made.
> And years have pass'd away since then, and many a joy and care
> Have fill'd by turns thy mother's heart, in which thou hadst no share;
> But still within that heart she keeps one sacred spot for thee,
> And there, my lily, thine alone, that spot shall ever be!"

And then were added these lines—

"I fondly hoped my child to rear, a servant for his God,
A labourer in that blessed sphere which sainted ones have trod;
But who am I, that I should be
The chosen of His destiny!"

These lines acquired, at all events, a value, from the fact of her having read them, and brooded over them till her death, having always kept them, as we have just noticed, in her pocket with her beads. Now hear another little trait of her faith in sorrow. She used to say that since he was to die, she was glad that little John was taken away just as he was about to begin his Latin studies, and before he knew any thing about the Pagans. She knew that children take all things seriously, seeking truth in fiction, as when Mdlle. Bertin represents her little Chloé interrupting Homer when he sung, and asking—

"Connoissais-tu Priam, Pâris, son frère Hector?
Et le fils de Laërte et le sage Nestor?
D'Achille au pied léger habitais-tu la tente?
Quand on a rapporté la dépouille sanglante
De son ami Patrocle, Homère, étais-tu là?
Oh! mon père, réponds, as-tu vu tout cela?"

So without having ever read the Ver Rongeur, or dabbled with such questions as are there discussed, not quite dispassionately perhaps, the exquisite purity of her mind caused her to see a certain advantage in the circumstance that her boy, since he was to die so young, and before he could turn it to any profit, was never to have heard of the perversity of the Pagans, or of any thing, however capable of being well used by Christians of maturer age, that savoured of their crimes.

On this occasion, as when her Thomas followed his little brother, one sees, therefore, what some boast of in a way to put one out of humour with religion, namely, the life of faith confronted with sorrows, divinely, but not ostentatiously, sustained. She greatly liked the affectionate disposition of the French when death enters their dwellings; but in one point she would not follow their fashion; for with energy, with sorrow, and calm and holy austerity, she would persist in wearing mourning for her own sons, though indeed without that form, the intensity of her grief could not have been mistaken. Whenever, for instance, she heard sung the Prairie Flower, her eyes overflowed with tears; and by her looks you knew the reason why. It was that she was thinking of little John. She would try to conceal the greatest sorrow rather than sadden a passing guest.

> "Un esprit mâle et vraiment sage,
> Dans le plus invincible ennui,
> Dédaigne le triste avantage
> De se faire plaindre d'autrui *."

But for all that, as Moschus says, she "who always hitherto had been so joyous to behold, with such glad and smiling looks, now sheds tears." But Faith forbids them not, and let us hear Lacordaire explaining this fact by reference to the death of Lazarus. "As a scene of friendship," says the eloquent Dominican, "nothing comparable to this narrative exists in any age or in any language. Tenderness overflows in it; and yet one might say that tenderness is not expressed. It is all within; and while feeling it, one only hears it by these few words:—'And Jesus wept.' Jesus was not to weep during His passion; He did not weep when an apostle gave Him the kiss of treason, nor when Peter denied Him through fear of a servant-maid, nor when He saw at the foot of His cross His dearest friends and His mother. That was the supernatural hour of our redemption; and the divinity of the Just One who was ransoming us with His sorrow was not to make itself visible excepting by force and majesty. But on the eve of this moment when the Christ, still free, was living with us of our own life, He could not refuse to the tomb of a friend the weakness of compassion; He groaned and was troubled, and in fine, as one of us, He wept. Holy struggles, happy trouble, precious tears, which prove to us that our God was even like one of us, pitiful and just in our own poor way, and which permit us also to weep in our friendships and in our sorrows."

Her resources, on these occasions, were characteristic of her faith. She now undertook to educate two young men for the

* Gresset, La Chartreuse.

priesthood, one for each of her sons—then she changed this disposition into an endowment, with the obligation to educate one young man for the priesthood for ever. Like the valiant woman of the Bible, she also "considered a field, and bought it;" and like Henry V., without his motive, so far as remorse was part of it, she will build a chantry where the sad and solemn priests shall sing for her poor son's soul. It is under its vault that we are now standing. In these foundations she had in view, as usual with her, the general good; for she said that these cloisters, and the serener beauty of that sepulchral chapel, might awaken religious sentiments in those who saw them, and become instrumental towards leading them on the road of final happiness. Still her old thought, you see, the salvation of others! Then, when completed, she sends to Hales Place and removes the coffin of her youngest to find its last deposit in that dim monument where Thomas lies. Then, like Leontes, in the Winter's Tale, not anticipating another sacrifice in submission to the well-meant wish of others,

"———— Once a day she'll visit
The chapel where they lie; and tears, shed there,
Shall be her recreation; so long as
Nature will bear up with the exercise,
So long she daily vows to use it."

An ancient resource this, for that matter, since St. Ambrose said, "Ille tumulus vobis habitatio sit, ille sit aula palatii in quo vobis cara membra requiescunt."

But come, let's leave her for a while to these sorrows; she can extract from them much that is precious.

In what next follows we must proceed with caution, though we profess to speak only of her power of sympathizing with others, which kind of trial at least was eminently hers.

"I was Pia. Sienna gave me life; Maremma took it from me. He knows it well—he who adorned my finger with the ring, and made to shine on it the wedding gem." Do you know, reader, the exact meaning of these Dantesque words? It is that her death was caused by her husband confining her to the pestilential air of the marshes. So, without excusing or blaming the author of her death, she only speaks of him in alluding to the first pledges of his faith—the ring and wedding gem! What pathetic simplicity in this laconic statement! Alas! it is but of little advantage to have studied in the book of the countenance, which, when we have read it long, and thought that we understood its contents, has to be completed by a countless list at the end of heart-breaking errata! The woes of others were in her mind's eye; and she might have exclaimed, in the words of Silvia to Proteus, "Thou counterfeit to thy true friend!" The private wound is deepest, and she knew that many have this within their heart to change all to wormwood. Abused beyond the mark of thought,

"Have they with all their full affections
Still met the men? lov'd them next heaven? obey'd them?
Been, out of fondness, superstitious to them?
Almost conceal'd their prayers to content them?
And were they thus rewarded?"

Oh! what a thing it is to think upon, when a woman full of holy love, and who has done nothing to bring such a calamity on herself, is beheld ever watching for a return of affection, and saying each day it will be to-morrow, regarding meanwhile her earthly happiness as absent! "While the other," to use the words of a great observer, "either triumphs in deceiving like a cunning person, or as one of less vulgar nature is humiliated by his success." We have seen elsewhere how she felt for others as if for herself, and it must not seem therefore wholly irrelevant if one enumerates, among the trials which she was called to endure, a fellow-feeling for those who had reason to complain thus. "Where there is no honour there is no sorrow," say the Spaniards. Great assuredly must have been her sympathies, possessing so keen a sense of honour and of justice, of equity and right; for how often, when under the impulses of these solemn hours, in which she has felt with clearer insight sacred truths, does the woman of this type labour to win to her own practical belief those whom she loves! Was she checked by their cool indifference, or by their horrible affected levity? Was she confronted on these occasions with one

> " So ungently temper'd,
> To stop his ears against admonishment ?"

Thou dead elm! The more angel she!

Though comparatively ignorant of the world and its ways, she could not but be conscious of what the best of her sex are often liable to endure. But to such persons her example, without their experience, presented a noble model for imitation, for it was clear how she would have acted. "Exposed to deception, as those who know least of human corruption not unfrequently are, she would never have renounced the hope of maintaining order and happiness around her. Easily cast down, her lively nature would have risen up again with the same facility, and her first thought always would have been to struggle with courage. If she were unsuccessful, she would not have given in for that, nor till every thing had been tried. Patience, tenderness, liveliness, diversion, tears, or silence — all would have been arms in her hands. Nor could she have wholly failed; though if she had failed after all, it was not success that she most thought of, but what she ever accomplished, maugre the world, her duty. Strange it would have been to observe how she could then have reconciled affection with the horror which she felt for disorder. But she knew that God is all-powerful to make sorrows and their causes cease*."

Similarly, without the least stretch of imagination, one might have conceived her yielding an example of patience and sweetness under the ordinary provocations arising from caprice, bad humour, and mutability, which are enough sometimes to bring over strangers, who observe their effects, to the opinion of Mrs. Page, who would exhibit a bill in the parliament for the putting down of men. Truly, if men have learned to bear themselves with any honour, or any regard to what it demands of them, one might often say with truth, that their wives' gentleness was guilty of it. It is a lesson in itself to think how she would certainly have conducted herself, if she had had to live, for instance, with one acting the part at times, without any cause for it, of Le banny du royaume de Liesse; or resem-

---

* Paul Janet, La Famille.

bling that Comte de Fiesque whom Mdlle. de Scudéry describes, being not only different from himself on certain days, but having in his heart so many contradictory things, and opposite inclinations,—being gay one moment, sad the next; now ardent, presently indolent; capable too of reversing the whole order of life,—sleeping when he ought to wake, and waking when he ought to sleep,—and all according to the humour in which he happens to find himself. "Changeable he is too," she continues, "in his tastes; for at one time painting is his dominant passion, and he only speaks of pictures and schools of art; then at another music will have its turn, when, without thinking of his first passion, he is wholly given up to harmony. At another time his imagination is only filled with balls and assemblies; and then, after a little, nothing pleases him but books and verses*." One might equally learn from her, anticipating as one might have done how she would have acted under all circumstances, in what manner it was best to meet such humours as those ascribed by the same subtle observer to Arnauld de Corbeville,—"light and constant at the same time, having, it is true, at the bottom of his heart a dominant passion which nothing can ever efface—one object, and that herself—to which the affections of his heart's core are irrevocably, though secretly and almost unconsciously attached; but for all that, passing suddenly from one extreme to another: some days seeming lost in such a reverie, that you would think him meditating some great design; and then, after this long silence, beginning to talk of trifles and diversion as if he had never thought; showing himself this way towards the most serious person in the world as well as with the most gay; ready to play, too, with a child as if he were one himself, and with as much application as if he had nothing else to do; and being equally inconstant in the presence of all alike, old and young, wise and foolish †." Leontes, in a position to which many others in all ages might lay claim, says,—

"———————— whilst I remember

---

* Le Grand Cyrus. † Ibid.

> Her and her virtues, I cannot forget
> My blemishes in them."

No doubt even Jane Mary could understand, from observing others, what Charles d'Orleans meant when saying of himself,—

> " Quand mélancolie mauvaise
> Le vient maintes fois assaillir;"

when there would be "a partridge's wing saved, the fool that night being resolved to eat no supper." But in all ages, on occasions of this kind, such is the general provision of nature, or rather ordinance of grace, that " the other," whatever might be the provocations that he offered, is in strict truth

> "——— ——— yoked with a lamb
> That carries anger as the flint bears fire;
> Who, much enforced, shows a hasty spark,
> And straight is cold again."

The truth was, that, in this particular instance, the affections of the woman we are seeking to portray, like all her other attributes, had a certain range in one way or another beyond this life; and so here she only verified what ancient ballads say, that

> "——— true love is a lasting fire,
> Which viewless angels tend,
> That burnes for ever in the soule
> And knowes nor change, nor end." .

But we draw near the close of her sorrows—'Ὦ πόνοι δόμων υἱοι. The death of her mother, which occurred six months before her own, left an indelible impression* on that daughter's heart, though it is true her courage and resignation on this occasion again astonished every one who knew the phenomenal attraction that glued those two souls together. It was she who knew that the time was come for the last rites; it was she who calmly told her so; and then, kneeling at her death-bed, she repeated with a loud clear voice, her heart seeming ready to burst while she pressed it in, all the prayers and responses for the parting soul. Now was she indeed absorbed in the thoughts of heaven; but previously to the last moment her calm serenity had not forsaken her. As we before noticed, it had always been marvellous to observe her freedom of mind and her unruffled constancy, and on occasions of danger even that tranquillity of countenance which inspired hope if not joy in all who surrounded her; and now you again saw in her face the same firmness and the same high mystic resolution to be composed, when the danger of the worst misfortune became imminent—" Exterminabitur de populo anima ejus qui non fecerit Deo sacrificium in tempore suo *,"—that malediction, at all events, could not approach her. Many a time had she suffered

> " Dire overthrow, and yet how high
> The re-ascent in sanctity !
> From fair to fairer ; day by day
> A more divine and loftier way !
> Even such this blessed pilgrim trod,
> By sorrow lifted tow'rds her God ;
> Uplifted to the purest sky
> Of undisturb'd mortality."

Little remained to complete her sacrifices; nevertheless, even that little was reserved for her.

" O king of the Pelasgians," exclaims the chorus in Æschylus,—

$$\text{———— } αἰόλ' ἀνθρώπων κακά.$$
$$\text{Πόνου δ' ἴδοις ἂν οὐδαμοῦ ταὐτὸν πτερόν †.}$$

Certainly there came a strange wing over her path, of which few before had felt, precisely as she did, the fanning.

> " The robb'd that smiles, steals something from the thief;
> He robs himself that spends a bootless grief."

It is not, however, every one that has courage to practise the maxim.

* Levit.   † Supp.

> "Tell me what sad talk was that
> Wherewith one held you in the garden."

Her heart was exceeding heavy; there was woe above woe, grief more than common grief. Some had thought her conscience too maternal. I will not say,

> "They hid a thousand daggers in her thoughts
> Which they had whetted on their stony hearts,"

for of a cruel intention she acquitted all; but it was that she feared "the other" might be grieved, provoked, overwhelmed. "Orpah kissed her mother, but Ruth clave unto her." There were still left ties to home; but these were threatened. Therefore,

> "Quand j'y cherchois le baume
> Et le nectar de son âme,
> Une larme j'y trouvai,
> Voilà donc ce que m'envoie,
> Ce que nous promet de joie,
> Le meilleur jour achevé!"

The common sorrows of humanity in which she had been steeped, her faith could teach her to endure with calm courage. Antique in that respect, as we have before often remarked, her mind was impressed with the sense of this necessity as if she had said with the old poet,—

> Τὰ κοινὰ κοινῶς δεῖ φέρειν συμπτώματα.

But sorrows not sent by her God, as far as seemed to many probable, to spring out of the very element of her supernatural joy!—but faith itself to be inordinately enlisted against her maternal heart! circumstances combining without perhaps the direct fault of any one, so as to yield what looked like all the coarse accompaniments of ruthless vulgarity! circumstances made to appear requiring a violation of what she thought she owed to others! This was a trial. For herself, she was resigned to every thing in advance; but then, as we just observed, she feared to behold shocked the feeble understanding of another whom she loved only too well; for, as we have repeatedly noticed, her piety did not prevent her from being affectionate in all her domestic relations. And now all this danger of an unlooked-for contingency was suddenly brought before her, couched in solemn terms fitting the ear of impious parents, such as it had not entered into her dreams to conceive applicable to herself! judge if she had not occasion for her whole panoply, and for all her high religious courage—

>'Αλγεινὰ μέν μοι καὶ λέγειν ἐστὶν τάδε,
>"Αλγος δὲ σιγᾷν.

In fine, public and political fear came in, to add, as it were, the last drop to the chalice that was held to her pure lips.

She would fill no eye with a prophetic tear—" La vraie foi ne se trouble jamais."

>Τί γὰρ πέπρωται Ζηνί, πλὴν ἀεὶ κρατεῖν *;

" Yet, my God," exclaims a poet, " it is a melancholy thing

> " For such a one, who would full fain preserve
> Her soul in calmness, yet perforce must feel
> For all her human brethren. O my God!
> It is indeed a melancholy thing,
> And weighs upon the heart, that she must think
> What uproar and what strife may now be stirring
> This way or that way o'er these silent hills;
> Invasion, and the thunder and the shout,
> And all the crash of onset! "

Her last weeks beheld the whole nation in suspense, and London certainly more uneasy than in those ancient times when it seems to have been thought sufficient security to make a municipal decree, that "no boatman, after sunset, shall have his boat on the other side of the water, but on this side;" and that "no boat shall at night remain anchored upon the bankside of Southwark under pain of loss of vessel and imprisonment of body †." She saw and heard the preparations for war, according to the

---

* Prometh.
† Liber Albus, 499.

new portentous fashion, on all sides. Dover heights and Castle, beneath which the last week of her life was spent, sent forth each morning the thunders of experimental artillery, and there was some reason to apprehend that England was again to see the days when each tuft of trees contained an ambuscade, and one had to exclaim,

> "O pity, God, this miserable age!
> What stratagems, how fell, how butcherly,
> Erroneous, mutinous, and unnatural,
> This deadly quarrel daily doth beget!"

To some, it is true, all this might have seemed like the mending of high ways in summer, when the ways are fair enough; but she at all events armed herself to welcome the condition of the time,

> "Which could not look more hideously upon her,
> Than she had drawn it in her phantasy."

She would say, though not conscious that she was all but citing Shakspeare,

> "It is most apt we arm us 'gainst the foe;
> For peace itself should not so dull a kingdom,
> Though war, nor no known quarrel were in question,
> But that defences, musters, preparations,
> Should be maintain'd, assembled, and collected,
> As were a war in expectation *."

The state of uncertainty around her in these last days was, no question, painful. She could only offer to God the confused sentiment of her regrets and of her fears. So among her latest prayers was one resembling that tender supplication ὡς πόλις εὐτυχῇ! for she loved England, and she would have said with the ancient chorus—

> Δέδοικα δὲ σὺν βασιλεῦσι
> Μὴ πόλις δαμασθῇ †.

And then remember in what state all this found her; think of the profound wounds already in her heart; how she suffers,

---

* Henry V. † Sept.

physically and morally; how she has trials, so withering, so disenchanting, so calculated to throw one into bitterness, that you might think, when all was moved together, the soul of an angel would give in. Yes, to her the time seemed coming, thus did she follow it, that foul sin, gathering head, shall break into corruption.

> "The blood wept from her heart when she did shape,
> In forms imaginary, the miserable days
> And rotten times, that some should look upon
> When she was sleeping with her ancestors."

So her daily aspirations more and more resembled those of Chateaubriand on the death of the Duc Mathieu de Montmorency, when he repeated those solemn words, "Eternal Being, object that never ends, and before whom all disappears, sole permanent and stable reality, Thou alone meritest that one should be attached to Thee; Thou alone fillest the insatiable desires of man. In loving Thee, no more disquietude, no more fear of losing what one has chosen. Thy love combines ardour, strength, sweetness, and infinite hope." Ever, as we formerly remarked, animated with a Davidic spirit, her hope, her consolation being in God, she was seen to be one

> "That fortune's buffets and rewards
> Has ta'en with equal thanks; and bless'd are those
> Whose blood and judgment are so well commingled,
> That they are not a pipe for fortune's finger
> To sound what stop she please."

It is true, with the spirit of a martyr, she would have marched to the block any day for her faith or for her honour, using to her enemies the very words of St. Louis, for there is a monotony even in the expressions of such characters, "qu'ils en povoient faire à leurs voulenter, et qu'il aymoit trop mieulx mourir bon chrestien, que de vivre au courroux de Dieu, de sa Mère, et de ses saints." It is true she would have proved herself in this respect "as fierce a Christian" as you had ever known. But, nevertheless, already, as we have observed, she had been ordained to suffer afflictions which no courage or constancy of faith could render sweet; she had been called to verify the lines,

> "Years to a mother bring distress,
> But do not make her love the less."

So that we have only to say in conclusion, how like an awaking from an ill dream must have been, a few days afterwards, her sudden passage to the other world, when all that had been lost was found again, and all the jarring confusion of this life of contradictions changed into the peace of God and the felicity of Heaven! This world is a scene of warfare, a constant combat. "All those," as the Count de Maistre says, "who have fought bravely in a battle without doubt deserve praise; but, no question also," he adds, "the greatest glory belongs to those who come back from it wounded." That lot was eminently hers. As we leave the portal, methinks that one might think audible a voice addressed to her in the words of the poet,

> "———————— All thy vexations
> Were but my trials of thy love, and thou
> Hast strangely stood the test."

CHAPTER XIV.

A CELEBRATED writer has said that a Christian like Alexander reserves to himself only hope. One might be reminded of this saying when contemplating the spirit, not alone of courage to face calamities, but of resignation when they were victorious, in which Jane Mary's last years were spent; showing the force of that conviction which lay at the root of all our ancient Christian literature, namely, "que en ce mortel monde ne faut y prendre ses aises ny constituer sa fin *."

* Alain Chartier, L'Espérance.

A great modern author, generalizing certain observations, says, "that an accurate analysis of the schools of art of all times, might show us that when the immortality of the soul was practically and completely believed, the elements of decay, danger, and grief, in visible things, were always disregarded." "However this may be, it is assuredly so," he says, "in the early Christian schools. The ideas of decay seem not merely repugnant, but inconceivable to them; the expression of immortality and perpetuity is alone possible." Then, as if he had known personally the character we are delineating, he adds, "A similar condition of mind seems to have been attained, not unfrequently in modern times, by persons whom either narrowness of circumstance, or education, or vigorous moral efforts, have guarded from the troubling of the world, so as to give them firm and childlike trust in the power and presence of God, together with peace of conscience and a belief in the passing of evil into some form of good. It is impossible that a person thus disciplined should feel, in any of its more acute phases, the sorrow, I should rather say the precise kind of sorrow, for any of the phenomena of nature which would occur to another*."

Mme. Swetchine has left some striking pages on this topic, which sooner or later proves of such immediate interest to every human being; and as expressing the thoughts of a woman, I shall the more willingly avail myself of them before proceeding to give any strictly personal details.

"Resignation then," she says, "signifies nothing else but a will to make use of all the remedies offered to humanity by God. Fiat voluntas tua; this is the tenderest word, the most devoted that love has ever uttered, by which we accept and bless a will that is yet unknown to us. His will is our peace. ' Et fons de domo Domini egredietur et irrigabit torrentem spinarum.' Resignation is a generous profession of our faith in the charity of the designs of God on us. The more complete are the trials, the more we should arm our courage, perceiving the providential thought. It is against chance that one has no courage. But the moment when one perceives a

---

* Ruskin, M. P. V. 209.

divine intention, one is ready to bow down to the wisdom and mercy of the enigma that is not yet solved. The most difficult trial for resignation," she continues, "consists of course in misfortunes that are said to be without remedy. Irrevocability is a degree added to grief—the last which completes all. It is the nature of all irreparable woes to stop movement, to paralyze every action; it renders a contest useless. The mere natural life has nothing to offer for this in the way of consolation. Of all events which wear the formidable character of irremediability, the death of those who are dear to us is, without doubt, the greatest. To see taken away a part of one's self, to survive by grief the affections which constituted our glory, our strength, our joy, our security, and perhaps all that together, is to feel one's self broken, impoverished, and transpierced. These sorrows so legitimate are more than permitted. It is of our dignity not to lose them, and it is only against their excess that Christianity would arm us; it only changes our point of view, and causes us to penetrate into the reality of our affliction, in order to render it conformable to its divine spirit, and disengage it from what embitters and envenoms. Christianity is ready to admit the full extent of our sorrows; it is always ready to acknowledge how a void in joys once experienced may become an abyss; how the disappearance of one creature may make the world to us like a desert; but after all these concessions, it demands whether it be just that an immortal being should stop at a doleful point of space to spread its shadow over its whole career, whether this irrevocability of death incontestable on this side of the tomb keeps its name beyond it; whether faith has ever spoken to us of an eternal separation, and of friends being lost rather than merely absent for a time."

But now there is a difficulty suggested which it behoves us to consider; for, remembering the natural and undisguised anxiety of Jane Mary to be delivered from the common dangers and calamities of life,—to escape from which along with those who were dear to her, (believing, be it said by the way, in the efficacy of prayer, just as she would have believed in that of water to extinguish fire,) she daily besought God, ever desiring others to join with her in supplication to the same purport,—a question occurs which has been agitated in all ages, though at no epoch perhaps with less wisdom, as even the ancient schools of philosophy would have thought, than at the present day. Are such prayers, it will be asked, compatible with the very state of mind that we are about to describe, and with a right belief in that order of Providence which requires it? or are they based not alone on ignorance and superstition, but on a spirit of impatience and disobedience? Christian antiquity, which knew something about universal laws, by the voice of St. Augustin, conditionally in many of his works, but still more expressly and absolutely by that of St. Bernard * and by that of St. Thomas †, pronounced such invocations to be strictly compatible with resignation, as well as logically and philosophically wise. As far as regards our immediate subject, the spirit of resignation, the same question presented itself to the thoughtful and inquiring mind of this illustrious Russian lady, and she states and answers it as follows:—" Is resignation compatible with the prayers addressed to God to deliver us from the evils which afflict or threaten us? Oh!" replies our author, "assuredly yes. Our Lord prayed not to be abandoned. The Church prayed for the deliverance of St. Peter. It would be a false spirituality that would consider as an imperfection the recourse to prayer in the order of preoccupations which belong to the material world. We may intercede for the objects of our pure and lively affections, not only in their spiritual interest, but also in their human interest; not only for them to obtain immortal life, but also to protect and prolong their days upon the earth. In the greatest fervour, the Christian admits that the interests which are nearest us are the most esteemed in our eyes; that a certain value is attached to inferior good when legitimately possessed; he does not invent a gratuitous incompatibility between our salvation and what God has given us for our present happiness. Life, health, and fortune, may be even all instrumental to the highest good, therefore their preservation may be the object of prayer. God wishes that we speak to Him of every thing. He not only permits, He orders us to lay before Him our wants, our desires, our repugnances, our sad-

---

* Serm. 5, in Quadr.   † ii. 2, Q. 83, art. 6.

ness, our thoughts, even the most fugitive and careless." Our poor chivalrous friend, Alain Chartier, would reply to the question in fewer terms, but not less satisfactory. He says in his book of Hope, " Dieu veult et souffre estre prié d'omme selon l'affection temporelle et humaine. Mais il veult l'exaulcer selon sa raison eternelle et divine." Jane Mary, no doubt, was accustomed thus to pray, according to the temporal and human affection; she could only pray as she felt; and God replied to her as He ought to have done. Fragility and want were the motives of her prayer, and power and perfection were the source of His gifts. Thus did she act through life, and thus may she be excused.

From the different allusions to events and characters associated with her early and maturer years, the reader, I think, must feel by this time as if in some way he had lived on terms of intimacy with the subject of this notice. We have seen her in her happiest years.

> " Mais, dis-moi, rien n'a-t-il changé dans ses beaux traits ?
> Son œil a-t-il toujours ce tendre et chaud rayon,
> Dont nos fronts ressentaient la tiède impression ?
> Sur sa lèvre attendrie et pâle, a-t-elle encore
> Ce sourire toujours mouvant ou près d'éclore ?
> Son front a-t-il gardé ce petit pli rêveur
> Que nous baissions tous deux pour l'effacer—
> Quand son âme, le soir, au jardin recueillie,
> Nous regardait jouer avec mélancolie ? "

Alas! the different circumstances which we passed in review upon our last visit, will have sufficiently explained the causes and extent of the alteration now visible; for methinks, when viewing her under their immediate influence, 'twas but the shadow of her that you saw—the name and not the thing. She has felt so many quirks of joy and grief, that the first of neither, on the start, can woman her unto it; still sacred and sweet is all you see in her; and this itself is worthy of being remarked.

The last picture that Ary Scheffer ever painted was to represent the sorrows of the earth,—those experiencing them being drawn upwards by their means till they are lost in the rays of eternal victory which emanate from Christ,—a fine idea, but one, we are told, that is not always realized. St. Jane de Chantal asked Mme. de Montmorency how she came to be disposed by her sorrows to religion; "for," she continued, "experience has taught me that sorrows of this kind make as many sinners as saints; and I have seen many, who, instead of going to God for consolation, have had recourse to whatever is most opposed to Him." The duchesse replied, that in her case misfortunes had contributed to her union with God. So it was experienced here. This other Jane, who so venerated her holy patroness, had been a quiet sufferer. From the beginning of her calamities it was given to her not to see the operation of a mere general law, still less the hand of man in them. She perceived a mighty arm, which none but herself could behold with the same clearness, extended over her; she gave her heart to the Purifier and her will to the Sovereign Will of the universe; and this was another instance in which, with all her youthfulness of heart, she evinced that antique form of mind which we before alluded to, expressed in reference to this point in the line—

'Αλλ' ούτε κλάειν, ούτ' όδύρεσθαι πρέπει *.

But to see that gentle figure so often in the retired shade of her gardens silent and motionless, like what the French call a songe-fête, might furnish a fine commentary on that passage in the work of Droz where he says, "I used in my youth to like solitary walks. I used to seek out smiling spots; they pleased my eyes, my imagination, and my heart; they were in harmony with my serene and gentle ideas. In those times, if I perceived a cross on the summit of a hill, or on the side of the path that I was following, I used to look away. Why, I used to say, sadden, by the sight of an instrument of punishment, these places which the Creator has made so beautiful? I used to feel a sentiment of repulsion. The sign of redemption raised near a lighthouse, produced in me, on the contrary, quite a different impression. Oh! said I, surely here this sign of hope is well placed! Sailors struggling against the winds and waves

* Æsch. Sept.

can see it from afar and invoke it, while their wives surround it, making the shore resound with their prayers. When I came back to my charming inland sites, this remembrance of the tempest recurred to my thoughts. These particular spots, I said, are smiling; but those who inhabit them, have they no sorrows to endure or to dread? What earthly residence is exempt from storms? Cross of the Redeemer! blessed be the hand that raised thee wherever could pass a wanderer who mourned *!"

This book doth draw my spirits from me with new lamenting ancient oversights; for in truth one did not at the time sufficiently understand the sweetness and depth of that heart with which, no question, the invisible world itself hath sympathized. Niobe, in that immense grief of a mother who loses all her children, preserves still her cold beauty, "vivebam, sum facta silex." "Rather than disfigure a woman who weeps, you should imitate," says a French author, "the poet, and change her into a fountain or a willow." Such is the world's view of the matter, when it is pleased to be poetical; but the Christian's thoughts are of a different order. The Count de Maistre was of opinion that there might have been in the heart of Louis XVI., and in that of the heavenly Elizabeth, "a certain movement and acceptation, capable of saving France †." It certainly struck an eminent Parisian priest, impressed with a sense of what his countrymen call the "solidarité" which exists between men, and who knew what were the virtues and sorrows of Jane Mary, that she might have been one of that long procession of secret mourners in an uninterrupted state of grace, in whom Christ ever sacramentally dwelt, who in consequent union with His Passion in the depth of providential counsels, have been preparing, unknown to the world, happy days for England, suffering for her if she wishes that it should be for herself they suffer. It was a thought at least in harmony with that doctrine, before glanced at, of the applicability of the sorrows of innocence to the profit of the guilty, which, with the sanction of the Christian teachers, beginning with St. Paul, has been handed

---

* Droz, Pensées sur le Christianisme.
† Considérations sur la France.

down to us from the most remote antiquity. Be that however as it may, she keeps her sorrows to herself, and rarely speaks of them.

'Ἐντὸς δὲ καρδία στένει.

Like Mme. de Sévigné, suffering in her heart, being in consequence obliged to have ever in her hand the sole remedy—that holy book of the Christian's Day, just as you would hold aromatic vinegar, to smell it every moment through fear of fainting, she is a living proof of what that other devoted mother said, "qu'on est à plaindre quand on aime beaucoup!" But there also, kept close to her bosom, was, as she remarks, the reviving essence. So now, seated in front of the fountain in that garden, whose seclusion deep had been so friendly to her thoughtful hours, John and Thomas and her mother, and perhaps others too, for a different reason, are in her mind, and she prays; for prayer, says St. Jerome, is a sigh. And, as St. Chrysostom remarks, she who was pardoned "was found weeping and asking nothing*;" for our sighs are prayers. The grief is in itself an involuntary appeal to that invisible power of which our soul invokes the aid. So one might say, in the language of the poet, that she never told her grief, but pined in thought, and sat smiling at sorrow. For still there is, strange to say, the smile as of old.

> "——— Nature, ever just, to her imparts
> Joys only given to uncorrupted hearts.
> Mild dawn of promise! that excludes
> All profitless dejection;
> Though not unwilling here t' admit
> A pensive recollection."

It is only another portrait taken from old traditionary manners, those ages of faith. "When the body of Messire Jaques de Lalain, the young knight, whose soul by the mercy of God, and by the appearance of the life he led, gives us hope that it has taken the road to paradise, was brought to Lalain in Haynaut, it was received very piteously, says Olivier de la Marche, by Messire

* Hom. in Ps. vi.

Guillaume de Lalain, his father, knight of honour to the Duchess of Burgundy, and by Mme. Jehannette de Crequi, his mother, who mourned, as you may suppose; mais toutesfois se monstrerent sages et constans, en portant leur deuil patiemment, cognoissant que du plaisir de Dieu chacun se doit contenter." Precisely so was it in the instance before us; and hence the twofold aspect of this heart's wound. The equability of what some would call her humour, continued to be always the same, and constituted, to her last day, one of the charms of her society that never failed.

> "—— She is one by whom
> All effort seems forgotten; one to whom
> Long patience now doth seem a thing of which
> She hath no need."

Alive still, as in her happiest years, to the loveliness of art, to the charms of poesy, to the inspirations of nature, all bright and immortal things pass

> " Undisturb'd and undistress'd,
> Into a soul which now is blest
> With a soft spring day of holy,
> Mild, delicious melancholy;
> Not sunless gloom, or unenlighten'd,
> But by tender fancies brighten'd."

In other words, we behold in her one whose sorrows and moral courage, exercised from the first to meet them face to face, had subsided into a deep and sweet, and even mysterious resignation; for I doubt not in her heart floated mysteries ineffable, while to the eye of the world she only presented one who seemed to verify what is described with such beauty in the line of Young,

> " Soft, modest, melancholy, female, fair."

CHAPTER XV.

LIFE so innocent, so holy, so useful, and still so full of promises, (for how many were depending on her, and what a noble part remained for her to play!) ought to have been long. So also says the author who relates the life of Mdlle. de Louvencourt. " The interests of the glory of God," continues that writer, " the comfort of the poor, the good of souls, demanded the prolongation of days so precious to humanity and religion. But," he adds, " the designs of God are different from those of men." A trite observation this; and here was another occasion in which it naturally presents itself, furnishing an instance too of the truth of the saying, that on this earth there are only beginnings. " Il n'y a sur cette terre que des commencements." But what great things are these beginnings! what results already! Assuredly, here also was a most remarkable instance of a good tree yielding good fruit—of a tree consequently that one little thought to have seen so soon and unseasonably, as it would seem to human eyes, cut down. " The best of mothers has been taken away," wrote an English priest, remarkable for the penetration of his glances, " a mother who, through the whole of her innocent life, was a model of perfection." One of the first scholars of England, presenting the rare union of the highest erudition with the graces of a most amiable nature, who had been for some years preceptor to her sons, and who had had daily occasion to observe her own character—one the most reserved, the most cautious, the most exact in his expressions, so deep and practical was the reverence which he always entertained for truth, did not think it an exaggeration to render to her a similar testimony, saying, in a letter written long after he had left her family, on hearing of her death, " She was a person to whom, in all truth, it would be nearly impossible to find an equal. She had attained a degree of perfection, I really do think, almost beyond an ideal standard. I regard so very

sudden a departure as a signal mercy vouchsafed to one who required not the trial of suffering, which most of us must undergo."

Moreover, notwithstanding what we have recalled on our two last visits, one cannot but be still struck with the fact that the innocent, and one might add, divine ties which bound Jane Mary to this life, were still manifold and strong. Much, I grant, had been effected providentially to diminish their number and weaken their hold upon her mind; but there was still sufficient to attach her to this present existence with a love as intense as it was pure. One might add, though no doubt in regard to one instance that is a small matter, that she was every day more and more connected with the life of others, bound up with it, identified with it. "The honeymoon is short," says an author who treats on the family. "Yes; but what sentiment loses in freshness it gains in maturity. The flower fades, but the roots strike deeper—and under this cold and monotonous intimacy there are knots secretly entwined with so much force, that their rupture tears to pieces, often in an irreparable manner, the heart of the survivor *." Let it be permitted to speak with the boldness of Lacordaire, and to use his words. "Friendship is free—an act of supreme liberty, seeking no law, human or divine, to consecrate its resolutions. It lives by itself. Time even confirms it. I used to think for a long time that youth was the season for friendship, and that friendship itself was as a gracious preamble of all our affections. It was an error. Youth is too frivolous for friendship; it is neither in its thoughts nor in its will. On the other hand, maturity is too cold for this great sentiment; it has too many interests which preoccupy it and enchain it.—It wants the generous liberty of one who belongs not yet to the world, and also that simplicity which believes, that impulse which gives itself up, that independence which fears nothing in life. Youth brings more promptitude in sympathy, maturity more constancy, but old age more detachment and depth. Friendship is a divine thing, and the sure sign of a great soul. It is the crown of the marriage state; for beauty fades, but the mind does not grow old.

* Paul Janet, La Famille.

Confidence, esteem, respect, the habit of an intimate and reciprocal penetration, maintain in hearts the focus of an affection which gains strength with purity; tenderness survives under a new form. Friendship is, in Christianity, the term and the supreme recompense of the conjugal love*." In fine, to mention what is apparently a legitimate ground for surprise at what ensued, there was in this instance a great natural fear of death, and no doubt a reluctance to the thought of meeting it ere half the natural course of life was run. Perhaps, even with the holy, this is not uncommon. We certainly read that Mdlle. de Lamoignon had for a long time experienced the same impressions. One can hardly understand, indeed, how with a mother it could be otherwise. Besides, with reference to any one it is easy to say,—

"Why, he that cuts off twenty years of life,
Cuts off so many years of fearing death."

It is easy in the way of an hypothesis to accumulate disappointments and bereavements in life, and so conclude that it is well to be quit of them.

"———— And yet death we fear
That makes these odds all even."

The saint after all, one must reflect, in general has human feeling, perhaps with quite as much intensity as that young and brilliant Marquis de Laval, who, at the siege of Dunkerque, we are told, " in spite of his bravery regretted life somewhat." Nevertheless, there seems to exist, even independently of Christianity, a kind of traditional wisdom, a certain science founded on observation of facts, and developed by the reflections of the thoughtful, which comes to the aid of humanity on such occasions as we are about to speak of. The voices which convey it come to us, not to speak of what is heard every day in lowly circles, through the Oriental monuments, as well as the Greek and Roman classics; but it is perhaps in the fragments of the ancient Greek poetry that they are most audible.

* Lacordaire, Sainte M. Madeleine.

Menander, for instance, tells us with solemn brevity that he dies not a happy death who lives to be old,—

$$\text{Οὐκ εὐθανάτως ἀπῆλθεν ἐλθὼν εἰς χρόνον.}$$

"There is a judgment hereafter," says Philemon, "which God, the Lord of all, hath instituted, whose name is terrible, not to be uttered, who grants long life to sinners,"—

$$\text{Ὅς τοῖς ἁμαρτάνουσι πρὸς μῆκος βίου}$$
$$\text{Δίδωσι.}$$

Coming down to ages of the Christian faith, the tenor and consent of these voices, even when expressed in popular or dramatic language, become only more remarkable. Witness what the dear friar says in Romeo and Juliet, uttering no doubt what Shakspeare had heard others in common life say before him,—

> "She's not well married that lives married long;
> But she's best married that dies married young."

The voice is heard in the very office of the Church at All Saints; for in the lesson read on that day, and taken from the venerable Bede, we are told that "the immense and ineffable goodness of God hath provided this, that the time of labour and anxiety should not be extended to any great length, but that it should be short, and, as I may say, momentaneous; that in this brief and rapid life there should be labours and struggles, but in that which is eternal crowns and recompenses; that the labours should finish quickly, but that the rewards should last for ever; that after the dark shades of this life they should see that most brilliant light, and receive that beatitude which is so much greater than all the bitterness of their passion." The poets, inspired by the Christian muse, refer us even to an observation of the law of all visible nature to explain why it must be so, saying,—

> "Sweet day, so cool, so calm, so bright,
>   The bridal of the earth and sky!
> The dew shall weep thy fall to-night,
>   For thou must dye!

"Sweet rose, whose hue angry and brave
  Bids the rash gazer wipe his eye;
Thy root is ever in its grave,
  And thou must dye!

"Sweet spring, full of sweet days and roses,
  A nest, where sweets compacted lie;
My music shows ye have your closes,
  And all must dye!"

The summer had come. It was thought necessary for the health of some belonging to her that there should be a removal to the sea-coast, and she never opposed sage counsels through humours of her own. "For myself," said Jane Mary, "I should be well content with this sweet quiet garden were we to remain here the whole season; but one must think, you know, of what their interest requires."

The Prometheus of Æschylus makes it his boast, that in order to benefit men he contrived means of hindering them from foreseeing their fate, which he effected, he says, "by inspiring them with blind hope." In this instance he failed. It is true, the wise mistress of a family makes provision for what the comfort of those whom she loves, and even the decorous beauty of her house in accordance with usage, may require, in view to the exigencies of the ensuing year; but no delusive expectations as to herself entered into her motive in making these parting arrangements, the mere sight of which, when fulfilled, added a fresh poignancy to grief on a return that was too sad for tears. "If I should not be with you again in Kensington," she said to a confidential servant, "you will remember where I place these things, and recognize my handwriting." She had, in fact, a presentiment of her death, just as her son had foreseen his own three years before, which she concealed from those who would be most affected by it, but expressed to others repeatedly, saying that she knew she was not to live long, and that she even thought her summons hence might be sudden. She used to say in a careless way, "I have suffered so many afflictions of late, that I often think I shall die suddenly." A few days before leaving town she talked of testamentary dispositions in the event of others' deaths, but she assented to the impetuous remonstrance made against such looking forwards, and added, to account for her compliance, that she did not think that God would bring all her earthly hopes, which naturally extended far beyond the natural term of her own life, to so abrupt and improbable an end. For she would have wept, like St. Benedict, if she could have foreseen any impending and complete destruction of the family that was in her heart. During the last six months that preceded this journey, she used to say to some who rallied her for melancholy anticipations, though they did not make her melancholy, "I am not what I was. I feel my nerves shattered, my heart somehow affected; I shall never recover my former health; but what of that?" The fact is, the hour for payment was come for having been all through her past life so intensely affectionate, or, as Mme. de Sévigné would say, for having loved "with attention." She had been greatly devoted to that kind of study, and she must now discharge her obligation; for as that tender French mother exclaims, "Que de chagrins on a quand on aime avec attention!" and you know that life in general is full of things which wound the heart. The last blows, in fact, had gone through and through poor Jane Mary's heart. She would not say it, but you read at times in her countenance words like those of Mme. Tastu,—

> "L'éclat du jour s'éteint aux pleurs où je me noie,
> Les charmes de la nuit passent inaperçus;
> Nuit, jour, printemps, hiver, est-il rien que je voie?
> Mon cœur peut battre encore de peine, mais de joie
>   Jamais! ô jamais plus *."

"Most kind this saintly lady ever was to me since I first had the edification of forming her acquaintance," wrote a mitred father abbot, for whom she had a great veneration, "and I greatly revered her. But the departure of her mother and sons made her more and more sigh after her own nest. She has entered into it, and we are called on to rejoice." Upon the whole, take them all together from the death of her sons, and

* Mme. Tastu.

look you, clearly, Time, that wears out all other sorrows, could never have modified or softened hers.

> "Bootless were plaints and cureless were her wounds."

Her tender spirit could no longer bear these harms;

> "Sorrow and grief have vanquish'd all her power;
> And, vanquish'd as she was, she must perforce yield to death."

"The broken heart! the broken heart! What a noble thing is the heart!" exclaims Charles Lamb, "in its strengths and in its weaknesses!"

> "No, no, she cannot long hold out these pangs;
> The incessant care and labour of her mind
> Had wrought the mure that should confine it in
> So thin, that life look'd through and will break out."

Instances of sudden death in the case of persons eminently good and religious are not uncommon. The holy and charitable Marchioness le Bouteiller, to whom we have so often alluded, in 1856 died suddenly, being seized with certain spasms, and expiring without agony at the end of five minutes. The virtuous and holy Duc Mathieu de Montmorency died in a similar manner; it was on Good Friday, the 24th March, 1826. He had been in the enjoyment of perfect health till the beginning of the holy week, when he felt some slight indisposition, to which he attached no importance, as having no distinct character. On Good Friday, being present at the crowded office in his parish church of St. Thomas d'Aquin, while he was prostrated at the feet of the tomb of his divine Saviour, or rather, as I heard from eye-witnesses, while in the act of kissing the cross at the communion rails, he was observed to stoop down profoundly, as if through redoubled fervour. He was dead. Every one admired such an end. The Duchesse de Broglie, writing to Mme. Récamier, said, "Mais quelle belle mort! Ainsi lui-même l'aurait choisie, le lieu, le jour, l'heure. La main de Dieu est là! Il est à présent avec lui!" The death of the pious Count de Saint-Géran, some of whose descendants were known to Jane Mary, presented a striking similarity to that which we are about to relate. It was, however, in the church itself, and not, as in her instance, a few paces from it, that he suddenly fell, without any previous pain or illness, when, for the sake of medical aid, he was carried into an apothecary's shop opposite the doors of St. Paul's, where his friends, on hastening to the spot, having heard of what had happened, found him dead *. Mary Jane's own dearest friend, Count Peter Yermoloff, of holy and beloved memory, preceding her about a year, departed in like manner, quite suddenly. He had been to communion in the morning; and sitting down about eight o'clock to dinner, at his own table, without any previous illness, further than his known malady of the heart, expired. Father Dominick, the celebrated Italian Passionist, he whose life in the odour of sanctity was devoted to the spiritual welfare of England, another too of her friends, died suddenly on a journey, and was left lying upon straw by the side of the railroad, as if a poor beggar abandoned by all the world. It is curious to hear how the austere Abbot de Rancé explains such instances. De Rancé, speaking of the death of M. de Nocé, who was a man of quality, and about whom Mme. de Guise inquired, replied to her in these terms: "There are no brilliant circumstances to be described. His passage was without agony; one only perceived that he had departed from his not breathing any longer. God did not wish that he should say any thing remarkable, because that shortens descriptions when it is a question of relating how he left the world." Singular identity of views! for really this would have been just Jane Mary's thought. She used always to say that she disliked the idea of dying like great people, with many persons round her, "making a fuss" (to use her very expression), and that she would prefer dying like any of the common poor, left alone, in quietness. At all events, there were many indications of her being in a state of readiness for the great change. We others, whatever general care we take for making the road before us tolerably smooth, have in most cases perhaps some little secret disguised burden or another, which may prove heavy and troublesome at the end. She had nothing of the kind; she

---

* Mme. de Sévigné, Lett. 1073.

had given up all to God: affections, hopes, half-wishes even, all were as God ordained them; and in the deepest recesses of her hallowed heart His presence already reigned, without any pretence of opposition. Accordingly, for such a state could not be hidden, what was once said by a celebrated observer of human events might be repeated here, "It has never entered into the head of any one, however scrupulous, to imagine that it could have been otherwise than well with her at the last. But it is a thing to remark more than once, that no pious creature has ever breathed a doubt but that God received her with open arms—such a general confidence in her salvation seeming to be almost a kind of miracle reserved for herself." Then looking only on the human side, why was she to stop any longer in such a world as this, even supposing it had been in its best condition, and not dismantled, profaned, and embittered as we see it now? She had nothing on her hands unfinished which interested her very much; unlike in that respect to the virtuous Lavoisier, who, when called to the scaffold, asked in vain for one half-hour to finish the last problem that he had imposed on himself. Still less, I need not tell you, was she in the position of those whom millions of chains keep bound to the earth, when, suddenly on finding them snapped by death, they vainly would invoke a respite such as Mme. de Sévigné supposes would have been desired by De Louvois, exclaiming, "Oh, heavens! grant me a little time; I want to stop the Duke of Savoie, to checkmate the Prince of Orange, and hearing for answer, No, no, not a single moment[*]." Could she have divested herself of those merely natural fears to which, seeing things from a distance, she was liable, there was nothing to prevent her from meeting death after the manner of that amiable Marquis de Champcenetz, who, so late as in 1792, wore lace, going to his death with a smile, as if he was still in the gardens of the Petit-Trianon, being after all one of those noble spirits of an age of faith, chivalrous and Christian, who thought it well to smile even on the scaffold; who felt themselves superior to their judges and to the spectators; their good humour, a consequence most unquestionably of their faith and

[*] Lett. 997.

hope as Christians, not failing them for a single moment. At all events, Jane Mary was now about to be

> "Deliver'd from the galling yoke of time,
> And these frail elements—gather flowers
> Of blissful quiet 'mid unfading bowers."

The ancients called the dead οἱ καμόντες, the wearied. She was, as we have noticed at some length, one of the wearied. She had besides immortal longings in her; she was the dew-drop of the poet,

> "Not framed to undergo unkindly shocks,
> Or to be trail'd along the soiling earth ;
> A gem that glitters while it lives,
> And no forewarning gives;
> But, at the touch of wrong, without a strife
> Slips in a moment out of life."

It was at Dover, a place once, as you may remember, associated in her mind with different anticipations, on Wednesday, the 18th of July, 1860, about the hour of six in the afternoon, that this gentle and noble creature, scarcely arrived half-way in her career, and as a friend said later, like an angel who had accomplished some prescribed mission, finished her mortal act and departed to the regions of real and immutable life, as if unwilling to remain longer in the life of illusions and of changes. The sun that day had been eclipsed three hours before her departure, while from an unusual accumulation of affairs, and through a neglect of the natural phenomenon that seemed strange in her at the time, though really it now suggests a different and very sublime interpretation, she was still, after her accustomed manner, busily occupied with finishing some affairs of the family, involving wearisome household details. Impute it not a crime to the narrator, on his swift passage through the scene that now commences, if wishing to keep this record lively in his soul, he speak minutely of a great moment, during which he was not judged worthy to bear a part in what it witnessed, telling of a sequel tearful to many, though

Καλόν τ' ἀκοῦσαι καὶ λέγειν μεθυστέροις.

It was about three o'clock in the afternoon, just as he was

going out to roam over the hills with two of her children, the eclipse being now over, when she called him from her room, where she was bringing her occupation to a close with a confidential servant, and accompanied by one who was very dear to her. The stairs were high, and the others were already outside the door. For the first time in his life—(he tasks his memory and repeats it)—for the first and only time in his life he did not hasten to her when she called him. 'Tis true a sweet girl's voice, echoing her mother's, replied from the top of the stairs that it did not matter. He ran out after the others, and from that hour never again did he see alive Jane Mary.

The others having then left the house, with an agreement that all were to meet later at the chapel, about half-past three, she left the house with the tender girl that was her ever faithful companion, both in a lively mood, as in fact throughout the morning she had evinced more than ever her accustomed cheerfulness; but then, as Shakspeare says,

"How oft, when men are at the point of death,
Have they been merry!"

They proceeded and walked to a lonely pier that stands out to the east of the harbour. On the way, meeting a poor man, she gave her alms after her accustomed fashion, and then sitting down to enjoy the breeze from the sea, with the returned warmth of the sun, no longer shorn of his beams, she opened her prayer-book, her custom always in the afternoon. One object of her prayers that morning at mass had been suggested no doubt by the festival, which was that of St. Camillus de Lellis, patron of those in their agony, of which the Collect was as follows:—"Deus, qui sanctum Camillum ad animarum in extremo agone luctantium subsidium singulari charitatis prærogativa decorasti, ejus quæsumus meritis spiritum nobis tuæ dilectionis infunde ut in hora exitus nostri hostem vincere, et ad cœlestem mereamur coronam pervenire per Dominum nostrum Jesum Christum,"—the same thought being repeated at the communion, in the words "sit in extremo agone solatium et tutela per eumdem Dominum Jesum Christum." The epistle of the day might, in other regards, have been supposed written expressly for her; but her thoughts had evidently been turned in an especial manner to the subject of the prayers, which was that of our mortality. So after some silence, raising her head from the book, she abruptly asked her companion if she had at mass that morning remembered the soul of her nephew's servant, lately deceased, whom she had visited before leaving London on his death-bed, saying that an old soldier like him must not be forgotten in their prayers.

Before leaving town, in fact, she had been in habits of preparing for him, with her own hands, a sort of jelly that had been found useful in the sickness of her daughter, recovered from a dangerous fever the preceding summer, which she had passed in consequence in great anxiety, and which she would again persist in making for this stranger as for her own child, over a fire in her own room kept lighted on both occasions, during weather of extreme sultriness, expressly for the purpose. Then suddenly apostrophizing her with an altered tone, she said, "Poor dear, ever since thy birth thou hast had sufferings and sorrows!" The other stared at such a sudden and unusual expression; but turning off the conversation—for girls even have a wonderful secret for dealing with the heart—they both rose, resuming sprightly ways, and proceeded to the chapel, rallying each other in a playful manner as to their mutual fears of being run over in a street, and as to which of them was best acquainted with the shortest way to their destination; and one of them saying, looking on her watch, "It's time for us to be in the chapel." It was as if she had said to her, "Mamma, let us hasten, for it is there that you are to pay your last farewell visit to the blessed sacrament." Arrived at the chapel, her companion, now rejoined by a maid, went up to the tribune to examine the harmonium, which she had consented to play on the following evening at the Benediction, as on week-days there was no one who could attend for that purpose. The mother stayed below, with her rosary and her book, praying devoutly before the blessed sacrament. After half an hour she rose and left the chapel unperceived, excepting by a poor woman who had been also at her devotions there, and who now followed her, till after a few paces, seeing her about to fall, she flew to her support, and begged her to be seated on a stone that marked the spot. Her first act was to

feel for her purse, from which she pulled a shilling and gave it
to her,—the poor one being long known to her in former sum-
mers, when, during her residence there, she used to relieve her
wants. The steward of a French packet passing at the moment,
heard her say that it was the gown which had tripped her;
and thinking she was not hurt, after saluting her with his cap,
passed on, to his great affliction afterwards, as he related; for
he had often attended her on her voyages to France, and, as
before noticed, she was liked by every one who had ever observed
her, though but for an hour. By this time her companion and
the maid, missing her in the chapel, hastened after her, and
found her thus seated and somewhat recovered, but complaining of violent palpitations about the heart. They then all
three proceeded to walk on; but the palpitations not ceasing,
a carriage that was passing was stopped, and without assistance
she entered it, giving directions to be driven home. She was
heard praying as they moved on; but the palpitations becoming
worse, she said she must alight. The shop of an apothecary
was opposite; she alighted from the carriage unaided, and
entering the shop accosted the good man, whom she had long
known and long respected as a truly religious Protestant. Asking for a glass of water, which she drank and seemed relieved,
she begged permission, however, to remain for a few minutes.
Shown into the back shop, she leaned upon her daughter, re-
clined her head upon that fond breast, and then said, "Is it
possible that this can be dying?" She was heard, as when in
the carriage, praying,—uttering "Jesus and Mary," and repeating the Memorare. She was praying to the last instant; and
then, almost like St. Benedict, still standing, for she sunk on
the sofa but at the final moment, with eyes fixed stedfastly for
an instant, as if seeing some object in front of her, she bowed
her head gradually lower and lower, and quite down. She was
gone! As we read of the patriarch, to one of whose sanctuaries she had confided the bodies of her sons and mother—" ulti-
mum spiritum inter verba orationis efflavit *." And, as Bishop
Fisher demanded in the case of Lady Margaret, " who may not
now take evydent lykelyhode that the soule was borne up into

* St. Greg.

the country above with the blessed aungells deputed and ordeyned to that holy mystery?" "Quelle différence," exclaimed Renau, the great geometrician and metaphysician, alluding to his own approaching departure, "d'un moment au moment suivant! passer tout-à-coup des plus profondes ténèbres, à une lumière parfaite[*]." In about a quarter of an hour after her first attack the other arrived. There she lay, with eyes that now are dimmed with death's black veil, though still her old accustomed smile lingered upon her face; the loved one, she who "clave to her," standing motionless at her feet; the poor woman kneeling at her head, kissing the scapular which had been round her neck, but had now fallen from within her dress, and with expanded arms praying, and proclaiming with a sort of ecstasy that she was in heaven. Besides these two no one present. In death quiet, gentle as she lived,—a picture which is as noble as history can pattern, though devised and played to take spectators,—such a strange antique departure! In a profoundly Christian sense, a death so after the high Roman fashion! Truly a celestial blazon never yet conceived in heraldry. Supporters of a novel kind, and very appropriate, Weakness, with tender devotion in the person of her child, and Holy Poverty in that of the grateful beggar! In life she loved the poor,—well, at her death she saw them thus. It is not every rich person who has at her death one of the poor of Christ calling out that the soul departed must be in Abraham's bosom. It was all in all a kind of departure to which we dare not give the name that might be first suggested,—none of the pains or horrors of death, the time being, as we said already, the Feast of St. Camillus de Lellis, the patron of those in their agony; Wednesday, the day of St. Joseph, who is also the patron of the dying; the solemnity being closed by a Dominican friar, who happened to be passing at the moment, and who, entering with the rector of the town, said to him, "Trouble not yourself; it's all over now, and I promise you it is well with her; I knew her from a child." Such was the funeral panegyric—simple and natural, singularly appropriate—which proclaimed her praise, methinks,

---

[*] Fontenelle, tom. vi. 105.

quite as magnificently as could have been effected by "the Fléchiers and the Mascarons."

All, of course, spake not so.

> "————— Out, alas! she's cold;
> Her blood is settled, and her joints are stiff;
> Life and those lips have just been separated:
> Death lies on her, like an untimely frost
> Upon the sweetest flower of all the fields."

But this instant an honoured lady—now thus! "Yet did you remark what a sweet placid smile was on her face as she lay there?" asked a physician who had rushed in, and who called the next day. True, it was strange—stark as you see, yet smiling as if some fly had tickled slumber, not as death's dart being laughed at.

> "That face, which cannot lose the gleams—
> Lose utterly—the tender gleams
> Of gentleness and meek delight,
> And loving-kindness ever bright.
> Such was still her mien."

It was, they said, a spasmodic affection of the heart which ended thus. Her heart was broken after the days when she lost her children and her mother. She had been told by a physician that it was attacked, and that violent emotions were to be avoided. She concealed it all from those she loved—this knot intrinsicate of life became thus at once untied. But death, which in life she feared, treated her thus with rare clemency, veiling, as we have just seen, all its terrors, and gently transferring her, as if by angels wafted to her eternal spouse.

> "Passant qu'à son exemple un beau feu te transporte,
> Croy qu'on ne meurt jamais quand on meurt de la sorte *."

' Of course to the ears of the world such a death sounds, when at all noticed, as a thing worthy of compassion alone—it is only what it was reported to be at the time in the public journals—"a melancholy instance of sudden death, the poor lady dying within a quarter of an hour of her attack." The

* Epitaph on Mma. d'Esturville.

idea of such a woman falling under the world's notice as worthy of compassion seems at first rather strange, startling, and even paradoxical; but when you come to think of it you feel that, however the contingency may prove for you unpalatable and revolting, even so it must be. She at all events would not have quarrelled at the epithet employed by well-meant sympathy, for humility in any form was welcome to her. But such is human life, that the greatest and most known to fame have been at one moment only thus qualified. Mlle. de Vertus, for instance, writing to Mme. de Sablé of the celebrated princess, Mme. de Longueville, says "cette pauvre femme;" and Saint-Beuve adds in a note, Mme. de Sévigné, speaking of the death of Turenne, said "ce pauvre homme," which gives him occasion to say that, however great we may be or fancy ourselves, there are circumstances, and a day will come sooner or later, when people will say of us too, "ce pauvre homme! cette pauvre femme!"

But how Faith, emanating, as it were, in consequence of hearing of such an example from the Chapel of sweet St. John, in which we now are standing, changes all thoughts, appreciations, language, style, every thing, almost the very character of facts themselves; for the thing that was melancholy becomes glorious, and what was poor perdurably rich and blessed. Yes! reflect and consider with as much scope as you can desire, turn the narrative to all lights as you will, and the Christian beauty of such an end will remain unchanged and unchangeable.

But to die without the sacraments! Say rather to die after having thrice received them in those administered to her sons and to her mother; for those who heard her respond to the prayers at their deaths, with such an intensity of faith, amidst the agony of her maternal and filial sorrow, must have felt that she had received them more than to her own soul. True, from a sudden death also to be delivered had been long her daily prayer; but "we ask in folly, and we are answered in wisdom." Clearly she was one of those few mortals who, as a Christian, might have repeated the prayer of the chorus with Æschylus,

$$\phi\epsilon\tilde{\upsilon},\ \tau\acute{\iota}\varsigma\ \grave{\alpha}\nu\ \grave{\epsilon}\nu\ \tau\acute{\alpha}\chi\epsilon\iota,\ \mu\grave{\eta}\ \pi\epsilon\rho\iota\acute{\omega}\delta\upsilon\nu o\varsigma,$$
$$\mu\eta\delta\grave{\epsilon}\ \delta\epsilon\mu\nu\iota o\tau\acute{\eta}\rho\eta\varsigma,$$

μόλοι τὸν ἀεὶ φέρουσ' ἐν ἡμῖν
μοῖρ' ἀτέλευτον ὕπνον *.

A quick and easy removal hence, for her was best; and from an unprovided death, by God's mercy, she was effectually delivered, if it were not more correct to say that, through His grace, she delivered herself, seeing that her whole life had been spent in preparation for it. From her childhood, and in her happiest years, she had never gone to bed without repeating, with all the emotion of her heart, the simple lines—

"Should I die before I wake,
Jesus and Mary my soul may take."

On the Friday before her death she had been to confession, and on the Saturday, Sunday, and Monday, to communion—the last of those days having been the festival of our Lady of Mount Carmel, in the habit of which order she was entombed, having always, on her journeys, carried it about with her for that purpose, from the days that she had clothed in it the bodies of her son and mother, who dying had put on those weeds.

And then only to think of the tender affection of the God whom she had loved, so visibly manifested in the manner of His ordaining all things for this child of His own heart, so as to make her transit short and just as she wished it, without parade, without disquietude, and what He knew was best for her, almost imperceptible—showing Himself indulgent thus even to her old inclination never to cause trouble to others more than the stern exigencies of nature required, as if He would preserve her from the sorrow she would have felt for involving any one in the care of herself during a long illness. "I feel deeply impressed with the details concerning the end of this departed saint," wrote an illustrious foreign general on hearing of them; "she has taken her flight to heaven as would have done an angel, its mission on earth fulfilled, without suffering, without agony, without the unavoidable regret of leaving behind those she loved. This was certainly a grace from above." His nephew, a nobleman whose father had been her intimate friend, took a similar view

* Agam. 1423.

of the event; for after remarking in his letter from the Pyrenees, that her death resembled in many particulars that of his own lamented father only two years before, he went on to say, " Si affreuse que soit une catastrophe aussi inattendue pour ceux qui demeurent dans cette vallée de larmes, n'est-il pas permis de croire qu'il y a là un effet de la bonté de Dieu qui a voulu épargner à des âmes mûres pour lui les angoisses d'une fin lente et douloureuse? cette dernière aumone offerte à notre Seigneur dans la personne du pauvre n'est-elle point comme le sceau de la miséricorde, et le dernier fleuron de la couronne que Dieu n'a point faire attendre à celle qu'il aimait d'un si tendre amour?" The same were the impressions of an English priest who wrote, saying, "In what holy dispositions did she close that sainted life." "To those who have lived like her," said a Protestant and a man of letters, who knew well the world and society both abroad and at home, "death is but the messenger of heaven." "How full of consoling thoughts," wrote a gentleman of an ancient Catholic race, "is the departure of one whose whole life was directed towards heaven!" "Quelle noble fin et digne d'une telle vie!" wrote a French nobleman long intimate with her. " Entre la prière et la charité—sur l'épaule de son enfant et le sourire au bord des lèvres!"

True, if Heaven had pleased to have given her longer life, and a different pass by which to leave the world, we had not parted thus. True, her beloved one was present at the moment, and there was the representative of those poor of Christ to whom her life had been devoted; true, she did not want tears shed over her, and yet " novissima in luce desideravere aliquid oculi tui"—for her youngest was not present, nor her boy, though this too was a fiat of mercy, both being tempered as they were. True, again, there was an occasion lost for hearing beautiful admonishments—

"——————— Her grace in speech,
 Her words y-clad with wisdom's majesty."

" O mort trop soudaine!" to use the words of a great orator, speaking of a similar event. " O death too sudden, though by the mercy of God long foreseen! Of what edifying words, of what an example hast thou robbed us! what a spectacle would it have been to see die slowly and humbly such a Christian! Her lively faith and her fervent charity would, without doubt, have touched many, and there would have been left to us the memory of a trust without presumption, of a fear without weakness, of a constancy without affectation, and of a death precious before God and before men *." But then, not to recur to De Rancé's explanation, so accordant with her own way of viewing things, remember that she was a mother, who would have felt for others more than for herself, more than her body's parting with her soul. Think what a last farewell would have been to her. How could she have relinquished hold without poignant anguish of the hand that she would have wished to press for ever on her heart! The thought of such an adieu seems almost intolerable to the affectionate; and here I am reminded of a remarkable example. Renè d'Esgrigny, the son of her dear friend, had to endure this lingering act of separation, and in the diary which his mother kept there is an instance most affecting, which can show you what he thought of it, and what Jane Mary too would have thought of it; for after his long and painful malady of three years, which involved at the end a terrible agony of fifteen days' duration, after for months invoking death and beseeching God to grant him a deliverance from his pain, saying, "Je voudrais mourir, Seigneur Jésus, mourir à présent, tout de suite, et que la Sainte Vierge vint m'emporter dans ses bras;" yet when the thought of parting with those he loved came across his mind his language totally changed, insomuch that on the 7th of September, three days before his death, he said, "Je sens que je meurs, c'est trop tôt, c'est triste de vous quitter—and you, my mother and my father, and you, my little sister Jane—elle est si gentille Jeanne!" The ways of Heaven are inscrutable; but you see by merely citing this one recent touching instance, what an exemption and what a provision was made for Jane Mary; for still, in fine, all the cords that attached her to the earth had not been dissolved. As a woman and a mother she knew, even after all that had happened, how to be satisfied with the present; she knew the art and joy of humble life—" proposing to itself," as a great

* Fléchier, Oraison fun. de Turenne.

author says, "no future aggrandizement, but only a sweet continuance—the life of domestic affection and domestic peace, full of sensitiveness to all elements of costless and kind pleasure, including the loveliness of the natural world *." We repeat it, to such a heart what would have been a long-protracted malady, involving her in all the agony of this severance and of this unutterable adieu? "Surely," as Sir Thomas Brown says, "there is no torture to the rack of a disease, nor any poniards in death itself like those in the way or prologue to it." There was to be no prologue for her. The painful part was to be left out.

What has been already observed is much; and yet there are still other considerations which bespeak the indulgence which was extended to her by Heaven in determining the time, as well as the precise manner of delivering the summons which called her hence; for in the first place, speaking generally, as Bishop Fisher said of the Lady Margaret, " yf she had contynued in this world, she sholde dayly have herde and sene mater and cause for sorrow, as well in herself as in her frendes peraventure." And then, secondly, in this particular instance she escaped witnessing what was manifested so shortly after, in the way of an expansion or new development of the "matter and cause of sorrow," that the good bishop himself lived to have a glimpse of at its birth, when, I mean, the Revolution of which, in one sense, he saw the commencement, operating, not at intervals, and in disguise, leaving space for breathing to the world, but continuously and openly at work, avowing its design of revolutionizing thoughts, seemed ready to proclaim the accession of a new reign, and principles that would be subversive of the whole fabric of the ancient supernatural civilization of Christendom,—in allusion to which events (for the language of states may be an event), knowing above all how she would have suffered from them, one might so appropriately address her in the words of the chorus in Æschylus, exclaiming—

Νῦν τί σε ζηλῶ θανόντα πρὶν κακῶν ἰδεῖν βάθος †.

For in fact, although governmental instruction has no doubt of late been very widely diffused, one could hardly expect a

---

* Ruskin. † Persæ.

woman who had never received it to be prepared for welcoming as the progress of humanity towards a happy era designs and acts (for the latter were not wanting either) precisely similar to those which we are told in all our history-books resulted formerly from the progress of the Danes, and Huns, and Mahometans. There is therefore no use in adding rhetorically that she did not see revealed the policy which was to realize the vows of those leagued together in the great antichristian crusade. She did not see the facts accomplished; she had not heard of things which, in whatever light they may be viewed, cannot but strike honour sad,—base and execrable means, employed for an end professing to be good, with the betrayal and driving out of kings, after the manner of the heathen wars, which the Count de Maistre, bad as his own times were, thought could only be found in books, or with nations seated in the shadow of death; and all acts being deemed right that could conduce to the formation of what seemed to be a preparation for only another "great camp," as an English statesman called it, to be an additional pest to future ages by threatening the peace and happiness of the world. Above all, who can doubt for an instant what she would have suffered through her veneration for the holy see? Already, as it was, the horizon in that direction growing dark, it was clear that she felt what words could not express. With a mind so constituted, with that charity for all mankind which naturally made her wish to have prolonged till the world's end, and for the sake of the world's interests, that homage to the Saviour which consisted in the temporal dominion attached to the chair of Peter, how could you expect that she could endure without a pang the operation of a mighty change in that respect effected by men of earthly views armed with their appropriate weapons, even if they were accomplishing a providential design, and if the events which were about to happen should prove to be bringing about a transition state intended for a future good? She said little, as in such times perhaps the wisest are observed to do; all her conclusion being that the gates of hell would not prevail; but, happily for herself, she saw not what actually did ensue shortly after—the provinces of the Church invaded in defiance of all law and justice, the character and person of the Holy Father vilified and exposed to danger. She heard not revived among the faithful the cry of the early Christians, "Quid salvum si Roma perit?" or that voice of St. Jerome, "Totius orbis mortuo plango, Romanus orbis ruit!" The fall of Ancona, the defeat of Lamoricière, not to be considered in the light of a reverse in ordinary French warfare, though he would have it so vulgarized,—the dispersion of his brave French and Irish brigades were facts not yet accomplished, and consequently unknown to her; neither, as already suggested, did she live to hear of the persecution of the religious merely for being such; of the suppression of convents and monasteries, on the ground of prayer being useless and obsolete; of Perugia and Assisi, the sanctuaries of St. Francis, and of her own beloved Subiaco, the cradle of St. Benedict, to which she had so lately sent her devout offerings, being at least in the hands of the new Italians. She did not live to hear the language of the English press, seeming at times to verify the accuracy of Gibbon's sly distinction when he spoke of his being left at Oxford without "a single lecture, either Christian or Protestant *"—the echoes of those triumphing in the supposed downfall, not alone of the work of Constantine the Great and of Charlemagne, for ever dear to the memory of civilized Europe, but of the very faith which constituted her existence,—for in God she lived, and moved, and had her being. She beheld not the hideous aspect of that advanced system of Protestation which identified its own religious interests with the triumph at least of the principle—view the particular instance to which it was applied in whatever light you will—that nations should be exempt from all law of moral obligation. She did not therefore, one may add, live to see again, and in times still more portentous than in 1830, "the heathen come," or to hear rise in consequence from all Catholic hearts throughout the universe, the cry of conscience and of honour equally outraged. Thou wert happy, therefore, noble woman, "non vitæ tantum claritate sed etiam opportunitate mortis."

But let us yield now to the influence of what was granted her—a quiet consummation—and conclude with the forest

* Miscel. Works, vol. i. p. 60.

youths lamenting Imogen, and saying, with the fervour of their artless nature, "ever renowned be her grave!"

What remains but to speak of the grief of others with

"Thoughts too deep to be express'd,
And too strong to be suppress'd?"

while following her poor remains along the very road for more than twenty miles (so full of tender poetry are the sternest events of life's drama), which on the day of her marriage had once beheld her pass a bride. Ah! what an unkind hour is guilty of this lamentable chance! All things once for festival ordained, turned from their office to black funeral; our cheerful songs to sullen dirges, our wedding flowers serve for a solemn bier, and all things change them to the contrary. Buried under this chapel as she would have willed it, and on the day of St. Anne, when the Church reads of the valiant woman,—her own portrait,—entombed upon the very hem of the sea,—upon her grave was placed this inscription :—

"Hic superimposito requiescit pondere terræ
 Cara suis mater, cara marita viro,
Cara Deo, servisque Dei, quos illa fovebat,
 Pauperibus; luctum pauperis urna tulit.
Non illi fatum diro languescere morbo,
 Nec longa vires imminuisse die;
Occidit, ut medium vix jam transegerat ævum,
 Rapta licet propera morte, parata mori.
Pauperis optarat mortem; Deus aure benigna
 Audiit ancillæ tam pia vota suæ;
Dives in obscuram periit delata tabernam,
 Languentesque oculos clausit egena manus."

One might speak of the mourning of friends and of the poor; one might describe those old priests in Paris who wept like children when they heard of her death, saying, "O my God, what a world is this! another name to add to my list in the memento of the dead. O my God, what a loss, and what sadness in this life!" Just as if they had been repeating,—

> "O Lord, what is thys worldy's blysse
> That changeth as the mone!
> A somer's day in lusty May
> Is darked before the none."

One might tell of what was spoken in the salons, in the gardens, on the steps of churches,—verifying again, after so many years, what Mme. de Sévigné said to her daughter: "Ah! my dear child, for what a length of time have I been of your opinion! rien n'est bon que d'avoir une belle et bonne âme; one sees it in every thing as through a heart of crystal; it cannot be hidden. There are no dupes in its regard; the shadow is never long mistaken for the body; there is no appearing without being, the world's injustice is not lasting." Accordingly, in conversation and by letters it was now but one voice of spontaneous lamentation. "Que cette vie est une triste vie," wrote the translator of St. Augustin's Confessions on hearing of her death; "je ne puis jeter un regard autour de moi sans trouver un voide, un deuil, une irréparable absence, mais l'on a le fruit de sa souffrance; quelque consolation dans le temps et pour l'avenir une espérance infinie." "For myself too," wrote a revered Russian friend, "allow me to say, it is a most cruel loss, as I had, from the bottom of my heart, attached myself to that angelic person." "Je suis ému jusqu'au fond de l'âme," wrote a French nobleman of deep Catholic impressions. "J'ai un mortel regret de n'avoir pas revu cette chère sainte que j'ai toujours et depuis tant d'années aimée tendrement; M— n'a pu retenir ses larmes." "It is as if I had lost an old and esteemed friend," wrote the Protestant physician who had last attended her, "for during my short acquaintance with her I had learned to know and value her for her admirable qualities of heart and head." In fine, an English priest related to her family made use of this expression: "I would have gladly died to have had her spared." "I feel I have said nothing," wrote his illustrious superior. "But then it is such a sorrow! No one but God can reach to the depths of such a grief!" A priest from the west of England concluded his letter by saying that the poor woman, his servant, burst out a crying when he announced the news to her; and another vicar, resident in London, related that on communicating the event to a new-married couple in humble life, neither of whom, he supposed, knew her, the young bride seemed so overwhelmed, that he felt regret at having been the first to announce to her such intelligence. So that, in fine, this event of yesterday presented somewhat of the same old scene so often acted, and described with such fidelity by St. Ambrose, saying, "plorat ecclesia in sapientibus suis, plorat in sacerdotibus suis, plorat in virginibus suis, plorat in pauperibus suis." As a benefactress, churches prayed for her, and by the desire of distant friends many an altar in foreign countries heard whispered the name of Jane Mary. A solemn dirge for her soul was sung in the two monasteries at Subiaco, of St. Scholastica and St. Benedict, also in the monasteries of Praglia, Genoa, and Pierre-qui-vive; besides, by order of the abbot, a daily mass, for a long while, at Ramsgate.

One must draw a veil over the solitude of the domestic hearth and the leavings of the fell intruder. What's thy interest reader in this sad wreck? One must be silent as to holy and poetic usages, Homeric and Sophoclean, and eminently Christian, disappearing from one's eyes; rooms becoming deserted one after the other; observances hallowed and dear to memory rendered impossible for want of instigators and admirers, of agents and players. Time rolls on. What a silence still! There is the chair vacant. "There's a change here," solemnly whispered a stranger, grave though another Yorick, raising his shoulders and piercing you through and through with a look and a brow that spake more than his words! One must draw the curtain over the dismemberments, "all broken implements of a ruined house," and think it enough to hear the dull faint accents of "Undone! undone! and now forgotten are all former woes!" But one should attend an instant to the fact to which these last words refer. It was even so. There was the same astonishment as before. There had been no sense of the value of what had been left, and that only was prized which had already been taken away. "He who does not know how to welcome Fortune when she comes," and who—one may ask it in her presence—sufficiently glad and grateful, and aware of what he possesses?—"has no right to complain when she departs." Poor consolation, but most just reproof yielded by the familiar proverb. So now you have the interior empty, the house like a body from which the soul had departed: "Un seul être vous manque, et tout est dépeuplé." No longer seen or heard the faithful one,—the personification of prayer and faith, of constancy,—the inseparable handmaiden of the blessed Virgin, on whom one could always reckon in gladness and in sorrow, in health and in one's last moments. But no more! Others too have mourned thus; though there is a voice at all times to check, when unbridled, such lamentations; for, as the Friar says in Romeo and Juliet,—

> "The most you sought was—her promotion;
> For 'twas your heaven, she should be advanc'd:
> And weep ye now, seeing she is advanc'd
> Above the clouds, as high as heaven itself?"

And if we cannot read any longer in the heart of the creature which received from its God so many marks of an ineffable predilection, at least as the eloquent Dominican, so often cited, says, "we can follow the Gospel with the modesty of a tender admiration, and seek there, in the shadow of our weaknesses, the imperfect joy which is permitted to us here below." No more lamentation for her. "Woman, why weepest thou? He did not say that to her when on the day of her conversion she wept at His feet. Now the hour of tears is past. Penitence, the cross, the tomb, all have disappeared in the triumphant splendours of the Resurrection! Woman, why weepest thou*?" "Now, therefore, wolde I ask you this one question," says Bishop Fisher, speaking of the death of Lady Margaret. "Were it, suppose ye, a metely thyng for us to desyre to have her here amongst us agayn? To fọrgo the joyous lyfe above; to want the presence of the glorious Trynyte, whom she so longe hath soughte and honoured; to leve that moost noble kyngdome, to be absente from the moost blessyd company of saintes and saintesses, and hither to come agayn to be wrapped and endangered with the myseres of this wretched worlde, with

---

* Lacordaire.

dyseases and with the other encomberaunces that dayly happeth in this myserable lyfe. Were thys a reasonable request of our partye? were thys a kynde desyre? were thys a gentle wyshe? after she hath bene so kynde and lovynge unto us?"

"Oh! blest are they who live and die like her,
Loved with such love, and with such sorrow mourn'd."

CHAPTER XVI.

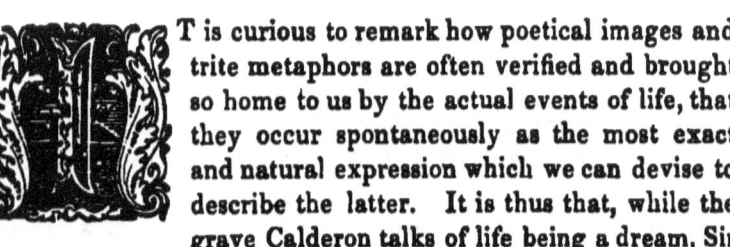T is curious to remark how poetical images and trite metaphors are often verified and brought so home to us by the actual events of life, that they occur spontaneously as the most exact and natural expression which we can devise to describe the latter. It is thus that, while the grave Calderon talks of life being a dream, Sir Thomas Brown even adding, that "surely, it is not a melancholy conceit to think we are all asleep in this world, and that the conceits of this life are as mere dreams to those of the next;" while the philosopher compares life to a phantom of the night, and another poet to a drama, the man who is least addicted to the muses or the schools, finds that in point of fact his own experience in the relations belonging to it could not be qualified by any terms that would express with more popular exactness, in common-life language, the impression which it has left upon his mind. Not to pretend to any anticipations of what may be the waking up of our soul, we are all of us in fact assisting here below at a certain show, which bears a close resemblance to what we call a dramatic representation; and when, as Ballanche said to Mme. Récamier, we do not survive ourselves, as in these times men often do, we behold at least the exit of others off the stage, so quickly are we all overtaken and passed by events, when after this short eventful scene in which they played their respective parts, the dark curtain as it were falls, and we see

them no more. It has been remarked by a recent historian that among the last poems of St. Colomban, in which he playfully endeavours to amuse the mind of a friend, one perceives that his thoughts all of a sudden were somewhat darkened by a glance at the rapidity with which his own part had been played; "for I am already," he says, "in the eighteenth olympiad of my life. All passes and irreparable days roll on. Live, be strong, be happy, but remember what awaits you!" It reminds one of the lines placed on a scroll in a picture that represents mortality, which ends with—

> "Ut leve folium quod vento rapitur,
> Sic vita hominum, hæc vita tollitur,
> Nil tuum dixeris quod potes perdere,
> Quod mundus tribuit intendit rapere,
> Superna cogita, cor sit in æthere,
> Felix qui potuit mundum contemnere."

Standing within this sepulchral chapel at least, it is but natural to think that such impressions must come with a force that cannot be resisted. For how quickly has this beautiful life that we have been considering passed away! The first meeting and the quick wooing; the simple espousals and the romantic journeys; the brilliant assemblies of friends, and the juvenile circle with its ever fresh and enlivening incidents; the presence of what itself taught respect, the grandmother and her prudence; the sight of what, like Shakspeare's holiest page, showed religion in its noblest form—the mother and her faith; the magnificent moments of the churches and the processions; the startling scenery of accidents and hair-breadth escapes from fire; the moving episodes of joys and sorrows; the plot undeviatingly carried out in infinite variety of the well-directed and nobly sustained life, with the unsparing accompaniments of generous actions—all are but a memory. The play is over. The spectator has only to retire.

> "La terre est un séjour d'épreuve,
>   L'homme n'est qu'un hôte en ces lieux,
>   Nous descendons le cours d'un fleuve
>   Où mille objects frappent nos yeux :

> L'endroit plaît, la rive est fleurie,
> On ne s'éloigne qu'à regret,
> Mais une voix d'en haut nous crie,
> Marche ! marche ! et tout disparaît."

It is not, however, merely to such considerations that we should have our attention directed at the commencement of our last visit to the Chapel of St. John. It enters into the design of presenting a life of faith as a study worthy of imitation, to speak, not alone of the grief and lamentation with which its departure was witnessed, as we remarked yesterday, but of the void which it leaves in the world long after it has passed, and of the regrets, fraught themselves with instruction, which are ever associated with its memory. Every one is interested in the question, whether on the whole it is a life of faith that is most loveable, that is regretted most, that of which the loss is felt to be the greatest, whether it be the kind of existence that obtains this last tribute from mortality in testimony of its supreme excellence. We need not therefore fear to incur a charge of needlessly introducing details which concern but a few, when we speak briefly of the feelings with which it was remembered by those who were best acquainted with its real character. Take the case, for example, of those who visited any of the former haunts with which it was associated, and who contrasted the vacancy occasioned by its absence with what they remembered as having been the consequence of its presence. What did they think of a life of faith then? Would they like to dwell thus upon the superior attractions of a life of dissipation, of a life of worldliness, or of a life devoted to profane philosophy? The absence of each of the latter is sometimes felt perhaps as a relief, as yielding a short interval of peace, of quiet pure enjoyment. But what is it to feel that the former is gone? There, look you, is one notable difference, quite enough to set you a thinking about its merits. We can picture to ourselves some one into whose mind such contrasts must have thronged but recently in Paris, and above all when left to himself alone, wandering disconsolate in the forest of St. Germain. How he must have found the capital and its churches, St. Roch and the Madeleine, for instance, successively her parishes, and Notre

Dame des Victoires, the sanctuary of her heart, where one might seem still to see her kneeling with eyes bedewed, you knew not whether with joy or pure devotion, and when you expected almost every moment to distinguish in the holy melody the sound of her sweet voice—how must he have found, I say, all these places embalmed, and in a human way, one might dare to add, sanctified by her gentle memory! Her very smile would seem to meet one before each altar. But above all, it would be in the deep and silent shade of the wood, in the green lanes of that sublime forest, and on the cheerful terrace where she used so often to sit and gaze upon her children, that you can imagine the past, with all its incomparable attractions, returned to such a person with a sense of ghostly reality.

>'Ιὼ βρότεια πράγματ' εὐτυχοῦντα μὲν
>Σκιά τις ἀντρίψειεν· εἰ δὲ δυστυχῇ,
>Βολαῖς ὑγρώσσων σπόγγος ὤλεσι γραφήν.

Wordsworth speaks of seeing some one seated on a public road weeping, and he qualifies it as a strange and to him unprecedented thing to witness. Others, however, have seen it, and thought it not remarkable. We can represent to ourselves one who might of late have found himself in that condition; for when he would look upon that prospect from the public walk, so often in the afternoon her favourite haunt, to see her eldest boy frisking on his pony, and the rest admiring him, when he would pass through that street of Lorraine, where in happy days she lived with all she loved about her—the house now shut up, the very number changed—for places now change as quickly as men—but still the little window by the door as of old, where used to sit the old porter, who plied his cobbler's trade, and taught the boy to sew leather for his harness, faithful honest creature, whom she persuaded to resume his religious duties, after for years omitting them, and who on the first Sunday of his going to church astonished every one by his reburnished and respectable appearance; when, I say, such a person would pass along that street, still grass-grown, through which she used to be seen every morning walking with her mother to and from the church, often with her children all about her, and her baby in the nurse's arms, herself smiling and so purely happy; when he would revisit that parish church of the Stuarts in which she used to kneel, without weeping then! and when turning into the green forest so pleasant and fair, he would find himself in the silence of that chequered shade, by those verdant patches straying through those tall grey-spotted trunks, and now alone! " to see the harts skipping and dainty does tripping, all a long summer's day," with no companion at least visible; can we not easily imagine that one so circumstanced should unconsciously present the spectacle which our poet deemed so singular of a wayfarer whose tears made hollows in that soft sand? Was it wonderful that such a person should then wish to accost every one that met him, who seemed a native of the place, regarding each with a sort of religious respect and most human affection, for the reason that, for aught he knew, it might be some one who had once seen her, perhaps had sat on the same bench with her, prayed with her before the same altar! Alas! alone still, and no way now left to find her, unless in the sense perhaps of the ancient minstrel, singing—

> " Over the mountains
> And over the waves;
> Under the fountains
> And under the graves;
> Under floods that are deepest,
> Which Neptune obey;
> Over rocks that are steepest
> Love will find out the way."

And then to think to how little purpose, when over-mastered by such thoughts, is all this reverie and dimpling of the sand to her now? But let us not say it. Who knows? Perhaps even where such spirits dwell, beings like her accept a gratitude, poor inky tributes of this kind, though yielded by constrained feelings too late expressed,—accept the offering of a love more demonstrative than what they received on earth in latter years, more turned perhaps for a moment to the faint hope of a personal amendment, and to the desire of a union not more instinctive or more habitual, (that would be impossible,) but more reflective, with a consciousness of its being for ever. You mark the conclusion, however, to which these merely personal retrospects alone must lead, as affecting the general purpose we have had in view; for what, we asked, is the life most loveable, most regretted when it passes away, that leaves the greatest vacancy behind it? That, we wished you to conclude, must be the life for all to study, with a view of becoming conformable to it. Then, assuredly, we can now with confidence affirm that it is a life of faith which should be held up to the imitation of every human being; for need we again glance at every thing opposed to it? Ah, such a life does not lead to the disappointment of those who trusted in it; its pleasures do not end in weariness, in disgust; its affections in dislikes, in recriminations, in hatred; its memories in remorse, and possibly, which God avert from every one, in despair.

Such then, in general, from first to last, was a life of faith in our own times. As the audience rises, what upon the whole are we to think of it? how is it to be appreciated? Are all traces of it to be obliterated? In the torrent that carries off pride and grandeur into dull oblivion is this memory to pass away with the rest? Not so. God is often pleased in one way or another, and by means too sometimes, as we should think, the least efficacious, to honour, under some form, even already, even in this life, the lowliest of those who honour Him, who yield as it were the testimony of their whole existence to the truth and excellence of what He has ordained for the happiness of the human race, and it will therefore not pass away. No; but by means of a simple record of the facts involved in it, (for moral phenomena, revealing what passed within one such heart, constituted facts, and the noblest of facts,) it will be handed down; and we may give utterance to a conviction which is purely based upon a belief in their power to act upon the minds of those who hear of them, that, to speak in a human, and even profane way after the manner of the world, it is consecrated to immortality.

Some, who never saw the original from which this imperfect copy has been made, will say perhaps that the whole statement throughout, as conveyed in the preceding pages, has been merely a panegyric and not a true representation, a bolt of nothing shot at nothing, which the brain makes of fumes; or but a custom in our tongue without a graver purpose. An opinion of this kind is to be expected; I am aware that if there is no confidence in the good faith of the writer, it is even a judgment which seems founded on justice or probability; but, though I know how almost inevitably offence is generated by such protracted admiration, still, with all fine writers' leave, it was not for any one so to invent faults and blemishes, or what would no doubt be almost as easy, to represent as being so many faults and blemishes the virtues that were in direct opposition to one's own vices, in order to render this character more dramatically interesting, as many would now say, and in greater accordance with the spirit and manners of any century. On the other hand, it is not unlikely that some will tell us, as on a late occasion, when an eulogium was pronounced by a Prince of the Church upon an illustrious duke, who exhibited a life which, under another form, bore a certain resemblance to her own—that there was something in this whole representation which was to them unintelligible; but as others replied, their difficulty in the way of understanding it admits of a very prompt explanation. And I will add that many of us can find it in ourselves; for, while deprecating all "strong opinions," invoking men of "moderate views," which often mean no views at all, we are daily tempted to judge of what is above us in this respect precisely as those critics, the only difference between us consisting in this, that we distrust our judgment, and prefer to it the solution given by St. Paul; for, when all is said and done, these lives, like Christianity itself, are supernatural; that is, they are such as could not have existed in a state of nature, supposing that there was no divine faith, that there was no such thing as the Eucharist, that prayer was not a positive influence emanating from God. Consequently, some men, believing in nothing but what is subjected to their senses, and therefore standing as it were aloof from the circle of what governed and attracted them, cannot apply to their actions or to their principles any but a natural rule and measure. Their attempts to comprehend such persons are as vain as the labour of a blind man to comprehend light and colour, the simple fact being that these critics see the natural qualities, while the supernatural are as much beyond their perception as the tints of nature beyond those of a man born blind.

Nevertheless, there is much, assuredly, to awaken attention

and even to excite the astonishment of those persons who are in this respect the least capacitated to form a correct judgment of a life like this; for to every mortal that witnesseth such an example, one might say, "Quod obierit fragilitatis est, quod talis fuit admirationis." Only let them reflect an instant, and consider the contrast which it presents to all that the world regards as so essential for the acquirement of its favour—how, as we read of Mdlle. de Louvencourt, "what she did was not to acquire celebrity, to make for herself a name," though Gilles de Rome will tell you that such might be the motive of a king. Let them consider how different was her final intention, as he calls it, which had in it in fact nothing of this earth. Let them consider, on the other hand, how she did not act through fanaticism any more than through cupidity; how that she was not influenced by spiritual pride or attachment to her own fancies, or the spirit of bad humour with mankind, or through disgust at any circumstance of her own position, that it was not to conceal in retirement faults of which she would have to blush in the society of the world, seeing that, as we have so often shown, her manners were noble, exquisitely gracious, and most charming; but how she did all from believing, in the due and harmonious exercise of all her faculties, that it was what God required of her; and in fine, that the object and intention of her whole life, so active, so rational, and so stamped with the character of the soundest good sense, and the tenderest humanity, was Heaven. All this passed in our time, to add to the grounds which should logically excite their curiosity. Subsequently, then, to the Reformation, after which, a great author thinks, though still following its banner, that " it was no longer possible to attain entire peace of mind, to live calmly and die hopefully [*]." It all passed under our eyes, in the midst of us, while we conversed, while we went about our affairs, while we sat at table. We have neither exaggerated nor embellished the details; we have not even attempted to glaze them down by any transparent colour, to bring them into more harmonious and prominent relief than they were seen in the original.

[*] Ruskin.

Surely, then, such objective realities ought to produce on all who are presented with them a very strong, and, in fact, come what may of it, irresistible impression. The uninterrupted consciousness of a pure, of a divine intention! To glance back at nothing else,—is that no phenomenon in the moral world to make philosophers muse a little? Coleridge speaks of facts contributing to make it probable that all thoughts are in themselves imperishable; and that, if the intelligent faculty should be rendered more comprehensive, it would require only a different and apportioned organization, the body celestial instead of the body terrestrial, to bring before every human soul the collective thoughts of its whole past existence! Let them think, then, what a blessed book will prove to this woman that in whose eternal pages all her past thoughts in time are written! Let them say, in fine, through consideration for him who has presented these facts to their notice, and in his excuse of which he profoundly feels the need, whether it does not seem to them as the most natural and least meritorious of all impressions, for one conscious of his own demerits to wish and to attempt to put some kind of order, or to insert something that may lead to order later in his own heavy and miserably confused accounts with Heaven, by seeking at least to honour, and though at the risk of incurring every obloquy that scorn can suggest to a worldly mind, to induce others to honour one who, in this nineteenth century of ours, so honoured God.

Now take another view of this life of faith, and observe how immortal are its beauties. "Certainement," says old Alain Chartier, "vertu qui vient du ciel, où habitent les choses perdurables, retient la trace et la semblance du lieu de sa nativité*." It is not inconsistent with what has just been observed respecting the difficulty that some experience in the way of comprehending what is supernatural, to insist here upon the invariable and imperishable character of the moral loveliness comprised in such an existence. These are in themselves, and not conventionally and mutably, admirable in the eyes of all who are capable of any degree of moral discernment. Contrast them with what takes place in regard to art. Excepting

---

* Les Trois Vertus.

for the circle of connoisseurs, amongst whom the traditions of highest painting and music are preserved, the greatest masters, Michael Angelo and Pergolesi, are every day, they tell us, less and less understood. They strike and astonish, but they appear strange, out of nature. The crowd being unable to interpret what was conventional in their expression, thè beautiful of one epoch in this regard is but imperfectly, or not at all, the same as the beautiful of another epoch. It is so in architecture also. Gothic or Grecian—object of rapture for a few of the learned by means of a reaction, but not of an admiration both intelligent and popular; there again, the beautiful of former times has become a dead letter for the multitude. All these beauties vary perpetually with epochs, with nations, with schools, with individuals. This is what a great authority has of late pronounced. But look at a faint sketch of these moral beauties, such as are seen in the portrait of Jane Mary; they are of old origin, lost in the night of time, but they are eternally young, and ever adorable by the wise and the ignorant, by the learned and the simple.

> Διάφοροι δὲ φύσεις βροτῶν,
> Διάφοροι δὲ τρόποις· ὁ δ' ὀρθὸς
> 'Εσθλὸν σαφὲς αἰεί *.

In what times do we cite this passage of the old tragedian! The world is now full of hideous scenes, to surprise those who are most versed in its past history, indicating an opposition of a new character, opinions subversive of all that is vital, and deeds corresponding; the Church even is said, in some countries, to have to mourn for internal scandals. How one rests, as if by a fountain of living water, in the quiet contemplation of such a figure as this! One of the faithful, born and bred within the bosom of the Catholic communion, growing out of the old root of faith, and bearing such fruits, to refresh and cheer our parched lips, that find in every thing else that is offered to ·them only bitterness, if not death!

Then view the subject in fine on still another side. Here was a woman! Now let us say, to use the language of the

* Eurip. Iphig. in Aul. 559.

Père Ventura, speaking of Virginia Bruni*, whether life, in the solitude of sacred cloisters, and amidst the holy exercises of silence, would authorize us to hold in cheap estimation such an existence as that which we have been observing here. Just think once more of that delicacy, without any morbid scrupulosity of conscience; of that innocence of disposition in regard to all human things; of that mysterious inclination to prayer; of that profound conviction of its efficacy; and of that ardour, in accordance with all that the clearest reason could require to promote in the precise manner most consonant to the dictate of philosophy itself, the glory of the Creator, and the eternal salvation of His creatures; ardour, impassioned if you will, but no less wisely directed, which even still seems to encompass us, and to emit an audible voice, like that of conscience itself, saying, in words similar to those of Mme. de Sévigné to the Count de Bussi, "La vie est bientôt passée; si nous étions bien sages, nous n'aurions qu'une seule affaire en ce monde, qui seroit celle de notre salut †." Reflect, I say again, once more on these collective graces, so simple, and yet so marvellously adapted to the different and multiplied exigencies of human life whether you regard its natural or its supernatural interests; and consider how all were acquired and exercised amidst the cares of a family, social duties, and in presence of a dissipated and profane world.

These last reflections invite us to generalize; let me have indulgence for complying,—it is but to pay a debt of gratitude, which is an act that can never be ungracious or untimed.

"Women," says Don Fernando de Ladena, "are the best part of the world; they constitute its force and its joy; they know how to make themselves loved, and yet they know how to suffer; they know how to make themselves honoured and served, and yet they know how to serve and to honour; they can inspire content, though at times little content. Take those of the highest rank and those of the lowest rank, it is the same goodness and the same intelligence of their duties."

Πείθου γυναιξὶ, καίπερ οὐ στέργων ὅμως ‡.

---

* Lett. 983.   † La Femme Chrétienne.   ‡ Prometh. Sept.

You could not perhaps expect the Greek tragedian to use stronger expressions than these; while, no question, there is more true heart as well as wisdom in the sentiments of our knightly forefathers, when each would say, in the words of Alain Chartier,

> " Je suis aux dames ligement.
> Car ce peu qu'oncques j'euz de bien,
> D'onneur, et de bon sentement,
> Vient d'elles, et d'elles le tien."

Indeed, for that matter, the acknowledgment is only conformable to what is more or less the universal experience of mankind in all ages, as can be witnessed in that sentence of an old Indian book which says, " whenever women are honoured, the divinity is satisfied."

Recurring, then, from what is so general to our particular instance, let us comply with these invitations from so many voices, ancient as well as modern, and feel assured, that when we love and honour this one memory, when, scorning the maxims of a false and worldly sentiment affecting delicacy, we name for eternal honour Jane Mary, God Himself is pleased.

But to the goal. We are leaving, for the last time, the Chapel of St. John; and it is to be wished that, one may add, leaving it with a resolution, or at least a desire, to preserve that general impression respecting the certainty of what faith involves, and the reality of what is comprised in the supernatural view of human life which these visits to a tomb have from the commencement fostered. That is the main point to be aimed at; that would be a worthy termination to all these retrospects.

We are met, however, on leaving the portal by men who would dissolve the charm, and counteract the impressions with which we were departing, by intimating that these are dissipated by their own superior knowledge, esteeming themselves philosophers, for the sole reason that they confine their views to what they call the natural side of all visible phenomena. We meet then men who speak always about eternal and invariable laws, which exist only in their own imagination, as if, to repeat the remark of the Count de Maistre, the real thing they had at heart was to sap all the foundations of faith, and prevent men from that custom of praying, which is its strength, to obtain which object their process no doubt presents an infallible way; men so blind as to seek causes in nature, as if nature were not itself an effect, and as if the very expression 'physical causes' did not involve a contradiction in terms*. We are met by others, speaking, less sophistically no doubt, but with equal hostility to the views which have been involved in this memory from the beginning, of the "omnipotence of fortune," with the heathen poet; of the universal reign of fortune, with Sallust; of its supreme power, with Livy and with Cæsar; of its undeniable force with Cicero and the tragedians, and content with Aristotle's definition, who calls it the accidental cause of things †, as if it were not more philosophic to hold with our theologians, that it is nothing else but the assent of the divine will, either permitting or ordaining things to occur, and so disposing all events to the accomplishment of a good end, though it may be beyond our capacity to embrace it at one view. But to such persons let us say, in the language of one whom they cannot but regard as a very competent judge of things within the very domain to which they so foolishly lay an exclusive claim, "Look round you, and you behold every where an adaptation of means to ends. Meditate on the nature of a Being whose ideas are creative, and consequently more real, more substantial than the things that, at the height of their creaturely state, are but their dim reflexes; and the intuitive conviction will arise that in such a Being there could exist no motive to the creation of a machine for its own sake, which is what men seem to suppose when they limit their views to what they conceive to be the natural side of life; that therefore this material world must have been made for a spiritual object, and for the sake of man, who alone presents intelligence in the midst of it. If then in all inferior things, from the grass on the house-top to the giant tree of the forest, to the eagle which builds in its summit, and the elephant which browses on its branches, we behold—first, a subjection to universal laws by which each thing belongs to the whole, as

---

* Soirées de St. Pétersbourg, 1.   † ii. Metaphys.

interpenetrated by the powers of the whole; and, secondly, the intervention of particular laws, by which the universal laws are suspended or tempered for the weal and sustenance of each particular class, and by which each species, and each individual of every species, becomes a system in and for itself, a world of its own : if we behold this economy every where in the irrational creation, shall we not hold it probable that a similar temperament of universal and general laws by an adequate intervention of appropriate agency, will have been effected for the permanent interest of the creature destined to move progressively towards that divine idea which we have learned to contemplate as the final cause of all creation, and the centre in which all its lines converge*?" No doubt during these visits much has been taken for granted respecting the action of that providence, and the influence of that prayer which determines events, as we believe, for the personal good of his creatures. Without entering into a review of his proofs, though merely echoing the common voice, it might be thought that we had taken our stand with Malebranche in his Recherche de la Vérité, which, as Fontenelle remarks, is full of God—God being supposed the sole agent, and that, in the strictest sense, all action appertaining to Him, secondary causes, as they are termed, being considered, not causes, but the occasions which determine the divine action. The very manner of Jane Mary's death we have ventured to ascribe, as she herself and Mme. de Sévigné would have done, to a merciful interposition of Him who, according to the ancient belief of the human race, without entering into the metaphysical question, is the cause of all things, the effecter of all things.

Τί γάρ βροτοῖς ἄνευ Διὸς τελεῖται;
Τί τῶνδ' οὐ θεόκραντόν ἐστιν †.

We have viewed the last scene under the impression that, as Sir Thomas Brown says, "there is some other hand that twines the thread of life than that of Nature." But are philosophers justified in telling us to reject such views? "All religious sects, of course," they say, "look on these things one way, but we look at them from a different platform. No question," they

* Coleridge, The Friend. † Æsch. Agam.

continue, "the kind of good easy people that belong to the different sections of the religious world (they must include amongst them Æschylus and Homer, Aristotle and Plato, but that is no difficulty to stop them) are all found to talk in this strain; but we—we who are philosophers," &c. &c. However, trying to imitate their coolness, as I suppose for once may be excusable, is it quite reasonable for these clever men, as no doubt many of them are, to separate those who do not agree with them on this point from the school of philosophers? Perhaps some of those who entertain very different views from theirs may have graduated there longer than themselves; and as for the peculiar platform that they claim for their own, why, one had always thought that it was the part of a philosopher to have no particular platform, as they call it, but to perambulate the regions of the universality of thought, and to see things from all points of view, including, with their leave, even those taken by such men as the poets and sages of antiquity, who may be thought worth listening to, though certainly they never practised writing in the cool, polite, and as 'we' of the nineteenth century have at last found out, mendacious style of Bolingbroke. What we have taken for granted from the first, namely, the more particular and obscure method of divine providence directing the operations of individuals, and determining their end, which some call the action of exceptionless laws, and others fortune, is that more unknown and secret way which Sir Thomas Brown says he has ever admired—observing that there are in every man's life certain rubs, doublings, and wrenches, which pass awhile under effects of chance, but at the last, well examined, prove the mere hand of God[*]. But, to use again the language of Coleridge, in application to this particular point on which we are at issue, and with a view at parting to speak more after the manner of the philosophers who meet us, seeking to obliterate our impressions, and to overthrow our hopes, "Do we see throughout all nature the occasional intervention of particular agencies in counter-check of universal laws? If to this question our answer must be affirmative, then we too will acquiesce in the traditions of humanity, and yield-

---

[*] Religio Medici.

ing as to a high interest of our own being, will discipline ourselves to the reverential and kindly faith" that is fostered and kept alive by all these recollections. If it be objected, that, in nature, as distinguished from man, this intervention of particular laws is, or with the increase of science will be, resolvable into the universal laws which they had appeared to counterbalance, we will reply, with this philosopher, "Even so it may be in these cases; but wisdom forbids her children to antedate their knowledge, or to act and feel otherwise, or further than they know. But should that time arrive, the sole difference that could result from such an enlargement of our view, would be this: that what we now consider a departure from the laws of nature in opposition to ordinary experience, we should then reverence with a yet higher devotion, as harmonious parts of one great complex whole."

In fine, the supernatural view of life involves also, of course, a conviction of its immortality. Those entombed within this Chapel of St. John, as elsewhere, may be said to repose indeed

"Secure from worldly chances and mishaps;
Here lurks no treason, here no envy swells,
Here grow no damned grudges; here are no storms,
No noise, but silence and eternal rest."

But this, we believe, is not all. Great God doth not leave his gifts imperfect. She who in life walked with the Creator of the flowers and trees, and of this beautiful world, ever present to her, we believe in death to be His for ever, in a manner transcending all form of expression or human thought, since even in the divine records we are presented only with inadequate, imperfect images; as when, for example, we read that to them will be given the morning star,—as if to convey to us, by a word fraught with brightness, a faint idea of the felicity which is enjoyed amidst the effulgence of that celestial light which on this dim earth she whom we commemorate had always loved to think upon. Yet, on this point too, we have need of being armed against certain doubts which elsewhere lie in wait for us, and which we ought not to depart without seeing dissipated. "In the cruel losses which we experience here below, we have need," says Droz, "of thinking that one day we shall see again the beings whom we regret, and that the pure bonds formed on this earth will be riveted for ever in heaven. But is not this an illusion? Shall we find again the objects of our tenderness? Is reason in accordance with our wish,

> 'O think'st thou we shall ever meet again?'

When we try to form an idea of the happiness of the just in the eternal abode, we suppose to exist there all that our heart and our imagination can conceive of enchantment, and we say with confidence, 'Such are the delights reserved for the blessed.' This reasoning, of which the justice rests on solid ground, ought to satisfy us; but it addresses itself more to our mind than to our heart. It does not solve the question, and it leaves subsisting an afflicting doubt. This doubt increases when we examine the possibility of prolonging in heaven the affections of earth. Our first reflection tends to destroy our hopes. What delights can approach the happiness which will arise from the contemplation of God? This happiness will absorb all our faculties, all our power of knowing and of loving. No philosopher, we think, at first, no logician, will admit the contrary; therefore we must renounce terrestrial illusions. We must regard the relationships of husband, son, father, and friend as essentially passing, fugitive, and destined to be effaced without return! The heart is troubled. Be ye born again," he continues, "cherished hopes! At the voice of Christianity and of our human soul, to which it imparts a mysterious light that is itself miraculous,—all that is pure in our sentiments can be allied with what is most elevated in our intelligence. My error resulted from this—that the soul, being subject to the senses, attaches the idea of truth to what is simple; but in another life there will be nothing any longer complex for her." It is owing to the limited conditions of our present capacities that we cannot conceive the simultaneous enjoyment of what we loved on earth, and of what will be imparted in the eternal felicity of the redeemed. Our belief rests therefore upon solid ground, even though we did not urge what Droz proceeds to remark, and which by some might be thought depending upon theologic views, namely, "that Christianity proves the contemplation of God to be not subversive of the relationships which we hold so dear, and without which we can hardly conceive an immortal felicity; for the angels and saints enjoy this contemplation, and yet they hear our vows, and present them to the feet of the Eternal. The blessed pray for me in heaven. The guardian angel upon earth is not an exile,—he tastes celestial joy, and yet in this life sustains the sinner. The contemplation of the eternal wonders, therefore," he concludes, "will only sweeten our sweetest affections, purify our purest sentiments, and will not destroy the relationships which God Himself has rendered holy upon earth *."

Then, again, let us take another view respecting what exists in confirmation of the sweet and exalted impressions with which we leave the Chapel of St. John.

One is not surprised to behold philosophy ranging itself, as we have seen, with Christianity; that is an ancient phenomenon, which can surprise only the ignorantly vain. But one likes to see also pure literature coming to our side, on occasions when we instinctively prefer to all the pomps of the former listening to the harmonies of the fresh common heart of which the latter is the echo. M. Xavier de Maistre then, the man of letters, under the influence of these sounds, has an affecting chapter † on the death of a friend, and the certainty of a life to come; and Saint-Beuve, himself a representative of the same world, says that Mme. Guizot, following in the like path, and summing up the different opinions which are afloat in the poetic and literary, as well as in the purely intellectual world, concludes with certainty for the persistence of the individual soul in the bosom of God. "A belief in the eternal reunion of souls that loved on earth is," says Mme. Swetchine, "another of those exponents, the doctrine of the heart. Religion allows it, and the universal presentiment, the strongest of all proofs of sentiment, confirms it. Where would be our personality if all memory were banished from it? Of course I know," she adds, "that we must not judge of things of heaven from things of earth, but are not these latter a shadow, an echo

---

* Pensées sur le Christianisme.
† Voyage, xxi.

of the former? and what is a shadow, an echo, but an image or a sound weakened, indeed indistinct perhaps, but always, as far as it is visible or audible, true?" A strong argument in proof, drawn by the combined action of the head and heart, occurs, almost naturally and irresistibly, to every one who has any tincture of intellectual cultivation in any form, and who thinks at all; for we are convinced of the existence of Infinite Power. Now we cannot be insensible to the fact of there being also goodness imparted to creatures, as in this very instance brought to our memory in this chapel. It seems impossible then to suppose the annihilation of such gifts in the person of such an agent, where there is omnipotence to perpetuate in some way or other that we cannot perfectly understand, their being. Moreover, the head and heart—and we speak not to men who have no heart, and who consequently do not represent humanity—alike proclaim that all power and all goodness are united in God. Now it is in the nature of a powerful and good Being to call as many other beings as possible to the enjoyment of His happiness. St. Augustin, indeed, concludes from these premises that it is through the plenitude of His goodness He has made His creatures. Logically, then, we cannot but believe that the same goodness will never disappoint the hopes which these favoured creatures had always cherished of enjoying it for ever. These last considerations are more potent than all purely metaphysical deductions; for assuredly there is much sense in what an eminent French author affirms of the superiority on such questions of moral over scientific proof. "The heart alone," he says, "can perfectly solve the enigma of immortality. How much time and fine spinning of words lost in discussing in the world this question of the future life! Would you have a solid proof that death is only a passage, and that life is eternal? or do you wish to have what is better than a demonstration, an intimate conviction of our immortality? Let us not live, as we cannot do without opposing even nature, by the body only, but by the heart and soul. Loving with love, loving passionately the good and the true,—thinking, acting, developing all our intellectual and moral energies, then we shall no longer ask of philosophy to solve, by convincing and demonstrative proofs, the question which torments us. We shall no more repeat without ceasing, like Hamlet, 'To be, or not to be?' We shall have the consciousness of our duration; we shall feel ourselves made for eternity. But in truth I admit," he adds, "one is often tempted to say to some who complain of their uncertainty respecting this problem of immortality, 'I can readily believe that you doubt it.' For," he continues, harshly perhaps, but in a way that is calculated to excite the conscience of those whom he addresses, "why should you wish to be immortal? What is there in you," he adds, still speaking rather "as a man" to those whom he would awaken, "which is worthy of lasting? What is it," he concludes, without heeding the fact proclaimed by philosophy, "that you would rescue from annihilation? Is it your love—you who perhaps have never loved any thing but yourself; you who have been never devoted either to a duty, or to a man, or to a woman, or to a child? Is it your free activity, which you have always sacrificed to your whims, to your appetites and passions, or employed in the service only of mean and perishable interests, often perhaps in that of force and injustice? Activity, wholly material and earthly, what could you do with it now that you lose earth? Is it your thoughts that you would save? thoughts perhaps like those of the rebel angels—while thoughts of obedience you never valued. You think of them as little as you can; and, as a philosopher asked, 'Must Heaven and eternal beatitude be yours for designing mischief, or indulging in thoughts of questioning the right of God, or perhaps for not having been a villain, for not having assassinated your mother*?'" No, no! let us turn from such proficients, and study the grand whole, implied in our own impressions during all these visits to a tomb—that whole of which each part is cemented into the other and indissolubly conjoined. "The religion of the cross," as a French academician says, which is what this grave proclaims to be true, "is the most astonishing phenomenon which was ever offered to the observation of men; and," he adds, "I can hardly conceive how any human creature can exist without having ex-

---

* Louis Ratisbonne, Nouvelles Impressions Littéraires.

perienced at least once in its life the desire of examining it with all the seriousness and capacity of its mind and heart*."

But let us finish—finish as Jane Mary would have wished us to do—that is religiously, waiving the aid of philosophy, of literature, of the heart even, and appealing simply and solely to that voice which had led her so safely through all the darkness and perils of the world's mutability. It is well, of course, to have heard what philosophy and literature have to say on such grave and vital questions; and it is no doubt better still to have attended to the voice of conscience and of the heart; but what surpasses them all, in regard to the determination of the understanding, as well as of the whole conduct of a life, beyond all doubt is a simple hearing in obedience to what this noble woman would have enjoined, of what the Catholic Church announces, and of the echoes in consequence which resound under such vaults as these that now enclose us. Truly, as the Prince de Conty says in instructing the great, "this is what is to be believed, though all the rest should seem at any moment to be combined against our hopes." This is what yields the true solution of our difficulties, the sum and end of all our aspirations; and then, to arrive at the conclusion which interests one even more than any general considerations, as Bishop Fisher says, speaking of the Lady Margaret, "this confirms all our fondest hopes in regard to her whose life we have been studying, for this assures us that every person that putteth their full trust in Cryst Jhesu, albeit they be deed in thyr bodyes, yet shall they nevertheless have lyfe in their soules, and lyfe that never shall have end." Applying then his words to the instance which has led us hither, she whom we have been remembering "put her full truste in Cryste Jhesu, verayly beleyvyng that He was the Son of God, and came into thys world for the redempcyon of sinners; wherefor it must necessarily follow that, albeit her body be deed, her soule is in the joyous lyfe that never shall cease. Credis hæc? said our Saviour to Martha. What is that thys gentlewoman wolde not byleve? she whose whole lyfe was spent in the worship of Cryst Jhesu? Ego credidi, she would have truly answered. Therefore put we

---

* Droz, Pensées sur le Christianisme.

asyde all weepyng and teers, and be not sad ne hevy, as withouten hope, but rather be we gladde and joyous, alwaye praysynge and magnyfyenge the name of our Lord, to whom be laude and honoure endlessly. Amen."

It looks as if we could never finish, for there is yet one word more; but then we separate.

After leaving here, why should we any longer suffer ourselves to be imposed upon by the pretensions of that kind of wisdom which is now so prevalent whithersoever we direct our steps, claiming for its disciples, without deigning to show them on what ground, broader views, clearer insight into the intentions of nature, and conceptions of the universe, more worthy of what is called adult humanity than are imparted by such studies as we have been proposing in the Chapel of St. John? As the author of the Imitation, a book of which the philosophy has not as yet been disproved, says, "Nisi homo sit in spiritu elevatus, et ab omnibus creaturis liberatus, ac Deo totus unitus; quidquit scit, quidquit etiam habet, non est magni ponderis*." One does not observe that such are precisely the effects resulting from proficiency in these new studies. We may feel assured in consequence, that these mutual congratulations which now resound on all sides of us, and never more loudly than when decrying what we have been learning here, are, in point of fact, significative of nothing that weighs much. Let us depart then from the Chapel of St. John with a great indifference as regarding them, but with this conviction, which every memory that lives within it confirms as if with a blaze of heavenly light, that what holy women, uninstructed in their schools, have taught us, that what Jane Mary taught by her life, and what she still teaches by the memory of her example—that alone is of weight, that alone concerns us, that alone is necessary.

> "As every present time doth boast itself
> Above a better gone, so may this grave
> Give way to what's seen later."

We know it; and what may not some be called upon yet to witness? But though the fashion of the world should change,

---

* iii.

and manners with it, the airy tongue within this cave where echo lies, this voice that still lingers in it will not change. We should ever listen to it; we should make a recordation to our souls of every syllable that she ever spoke. Each word of hers remembered will guide to Heaven, and not alone that, though what else should we covet? Each will conduce to make us happy here; for, as Saint-Beuve says, when concluding one of his inimitable portraits, " the remembrance of such a friendship is enough to fill and illuminate a whole life." It was so with the Beatrice of Dante, the companion of his early years, and the object of the passion of his whole life, ever present in his inmost heart, to moderate his resentments, and to sweeten the sentiment of his regrets. It was so with the ideal that haunted that other Italian of an age of faith, whose finest sonnets are those which he composed after the death of her whom he loved, as if presenting an instance of that friendship which St. Anselm expressed when saying, " Qui nos scidit ab invicem, ille me docuit quantum te diligerem!" What should be prescribed to those who knew Jane Mary might be expressed in ancient and well-known words,—it would be so to venerate her memory,— " Ut omnia facta dictaque ejus secum revolvant, formamque ac figuram animi magis quam corporis complectantur;" not that they should take away what the poetry and the painting which are here before our eyes could preserve on marble walls; but as the countenance of men, so the images of their countenance, whether expressed in words or colours, "imbecilla ac mortalia sunt." The form of the mind is eternal, which to hold and express, not by any other matter or art but by your own manners, you have the power. Heaven and those she loved had part in this fair creature; now heaven hath all, and all the better is it for the creature:

> " Their part in her they could not keep from death;
> But heaven keeps his part in eternal life."

Whatever in her we loved, whatever we admired, remains, and will remain, in the minds of all who hear of her, and, what is better than that which presented itself to the mind of the Roman—yea, rather, what is paramount and Alone according to the peerless perfection of the divine fiat, in the unchanging felicity of the eternal years!

Is this the last we have to speak? O hasten us not. We are come indeed to the whole depth of our tale, and ought to occupy the argument no longer. Perhaps the impatience of others tells us we should be gone; but yet methinks we have still somewhat to communicate; the moment is not come for the last adieu; we can yet stand here, forgetting any other home but this, parting is such sweet sorrow. Let us, then, I would continue, remember her to whom we have been debtors for that which will be ever to pay while we pay still. Let us keep fresh within our mind that recollection, which, by a consequence that ought to be inevitable, would fit us for a readmission to her society hereafter. She now walks the paths of upper air,—

"Sed longe sequere, et vestigia semper adora!"

Statius is thought to have won by this one line the heart of Dante. Applied as we propose it, let us cherish it as a panoply for our own. We should follow thus, and even imitate her fond example, elsewhere noticed, of never leaving one we love without seeming to linger still and multiply last words.

"I hear, I hear, with pleasing dread,
The plaintive music of the dead;
They leave the amber fields of day;
Soft as the cadence of the wave,
That murmurs round Jane Mary's grave,
They mingle in the mystic lay."

Sweet saint! Oh, ever breathe the powerful strain, and thy faith will live within the book and volume of the brain unmixed with baser matter. Yet stay; even such love has danger. Hamlet, after converse with the ghost, dismisses his companions without more circumstance at all,—holding it fit that they shake hands and part; and adding, for his own poor part, "Look you, he will go pray." There's the deep-toned music of our Shakspeare's soul; but his Paulina,—mark this,—thinking of her "that's never to be found again in this life, would wing her to some withered bough, and there lament till she was lost." Fearful and impotent conclusion! leading us to distinguish between strong impressions, when closing all, and to perceive that there is one direction fraught with peril, in which men's mournful steps can move—path sinistrous, "eiry," as old minstrels say, and full of gloom, to which Prospero too alludes when saying,

> "———— ———— Now I want
> Spirits to enforce, art to enchant;
> And my ending is despair,
> Unless I be reliev'd by prayer;
> Which pierces so, that it assaults
> Mercy itself, and frees all faults."

Let Love hear therefore the right voice, and fear, lest, by neglecting just distinctions, the stone we stand on should rebuke us for being more stone than it. Hears not Religion herself its grave accordant voice, attesting yet another witness? Another who sealed her testimony, to be added to the long list of those inscribed on adamantine rolls,—

> " Hears not also mortal life?
> Hear not we, unthinking creatures!
> Slaves of folly, fear, or strife,
> Voices of two different natures?
> Have not we too?—Yes, we have
> Answers, and we know not whence,
> Echoes from beyond the grave,
> Recognized intelligence!
> Such within ourselves we hear
> Ofttimes, ours though sent from far;
> Listen, ponder, hold them dear;
> For of God—of God they are!"

THE END.

www.ingramcontent.com/pod-product-compliance
Lightning Source LLC
Chambersburg PA
CBHW032026220426
43664CB00006B/379